SEATTLE
ACCESS

D1306061

Orientation	**2**
Pioneer Square/International District	**14**
Business District	**30**
Pike Place Market/Waterfront	**48**
Belltown/Seattle Center	**68**
Capitol Hill to Seward Park	**86**
West Seattle	**108**
Queen Anne/Magnolia	**118**
Ballard	**132**
Fremont/Wallingford	**142**
Green Lake/Greenwood/North Seattle	**152**
University District/Ravenna	**162**
Eastside	**174**
Day Trips	**192**
History	**206**
Index	**210**

Orientation

In November 1851, when city founder Arthur Denny and his party of 23 anchored their ship in a rainstorm off what is now **West Seattle**, they dubbed their new home *New York-Alki,* Chinook for "New York By-and-By." This bit of wishful thinking came to seem prophetic more than a century later when, in 1989, the city's skyline had grown so tall and dense that height-restrictive building codes had to be instituted. Fueled by both the tourism industry and the national media, who "discovered" the city during the 1980s, the area's population grew by 18 percent (twice the national average) during that decade. Attracted by low unemployment and exponential growth in the high-tech industries, its reputation for cleanliness and safety, and an innovative and enthusiastic arts community, people from as far away as Vietnam and as nearby as Los Angeles flocked to Seattle. The newcomers couldn't shut the entry gates behind them fast enough to safeguard what they'd found, but the influx could not be stemmed. Housing prices shot up, and residents started to fret that air pollution, not just fog or rain clouds, was obscuring the city's noble vistas.

And the panoramas are noble indeed, filled with breathtaking beauty. There are the sharp peaks of the **Cascade** and **Olympic Mountains** embracing the city from the east and west, neighboring **Puget Sound** aswim with giant octopuses and sea lions, and sparkling modern downtown towers of glass and steel alongside the gleaming white terra-cotta structures of earlier days, all seen through the drizzle of winter ... and spring ... and fall ... and sometimes summer. In *Another Roadside Attraction,* Washingtonian Tom Robbins describes the Puget Sound basin as having "a blurry beauty (as if the Creator started to erase it but had second thoughts)." And though Seattle hates to be called mellow, life among its 533,000 or so residents remains relatively calm; after all, it's mostly ferries—rather than more expeditious bridges—that carry commuters across the water to the city.

Visitors, too, should take their time enjoying the city. Not the mythological Seattle of rain-washed skies and leaping salmon, but the real city, which is

Seattle Skyline

much more interesting. Without doubt, the city's most popular attraction is the lively 90-year-old **Pike Place Market,** where there's far more color than just that of the carrots, crabmeat, and chrysanthemums for sale by the more than 600 merchants. **Pioneer Square,** with cobblestone streets and 19th-century brick buildings built after the Great Fire of 1889, was the city's original downtown; today it's home to many art galleries and boutiques. North and west, through the **Business District'**s high-rise office buildings, is the recently renovated **Seattle Center,** a futuristic remnant of the 1962 World's Fair, complete with the **Space Needle** and **Monorail.** Architecture buffs might want to wander the streets of **Capitol Hill** or **Queen Anne,** and bibliophiles may head for the **University District'**s many bookstores and cafes. Hikers and cyclists can meander the city's many areas of green—there are 6,189 acres of parks spread from one end of Seattle to the other. The watersports enthusiast can also find lots of pleasant activities—from windsurfing on **Green Lake** to sailing from **Shilshole Marina** in **Ballard.** And, finally, back to West Seattle, where it all began, where the **High Point,** literally the highest point in the city, affords skyline views of the self-proclaimed "Emerald City" in its splendid setting of mountains and sea.

How To Read This Guide

SEATTLE ACCESS® is arranged by neighborhood so you can see at a glance where you are and what is around you. The numbers next to the entries in the following chapters correspond to the numbers on the maps. The text is color-coded according to the kind of place described:

Restaurants/Clubs: Red   Hotels: Blue

Shops/ Outdoors: Green   **Sights/Culture:** Black

& Wheelchair accessible

Wheelchair Accessibility

An establishment (except a restaurant) is considered wheelchair accessible when a person in a wheelchair can easily enter a building (i.e., no steps, a ramp, a wide-enough door) without assistance. Restaurants are deemed wheelchair accessible *only* if the above applies *and* if the rest rooms are on the same floor as the dining area and their entrances and stalls are wide enough to accommodate a wheelchair.

Rating the Restaurants and Hotels

The restaurant star ratings take into account the quality, service, atmosphere, and uniqueness of the restaurant. An expensive restaurant doesn't necessarily ensure an enjoyable evening; however, a small, relatively unknown spot could have good food, professional service, and a lovely atmosphere. Therefore, on a purely subjective basis, stars are used to judge the overall dining value (see the star ratings at right). Keep in mind that chefs and owners often change, which affects the quality of a restaurant. The ratings in this guidebook are based on information available at press time.

The price ratings, as categorized at right, apply to restaurants and hotels. These figures describe general price-range relationships among other restaurants and hotels in the area. The restaurant price ratings are based on the average cost of an entrée for one person, excluding tax and tip. Hotel price ratings reflect the base price of a standard room for two people for one night during the peak season.

Restaurants

★	Good
★★	Very Good
★★★	Excellent
★★★★	An Extraordinary Experience
$	The Price Is Right (less than $10)
$$	Reasonable ($10-$20)
$$$	Expensive ($20-$30)
$$$$	Big Bucks ($30 and up)

Hotels

$	The Price Is Right (less than $100)
$$	Reasonable ($100-$140)
$$$	Expensive ($140-$200)
$$$$	Big Bucks ($200 and up)

Map Key

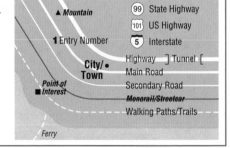

▲ *Mountain*	(99) State Highway
	(101) US Highway
1 Entry Number	(5) Interstate
City/	Highway] Tunnel [
Town	Main Road
Point of	Secondary Road
■ *Interest*	*Monorail/Streetcar*
	Walking Paths/Trails
Ferry	

Area code 206 unless otherwise noted.

Getting to Seattle

Seattle-Tacoma International Airport (SEA)

This sprawling airport—also known as "Sea-Tac"—sits 13 miles south of Seattle. The layout is simple: a main terminal with four concourses, and two satellite terminals. An efficient subway connects the main terminal with the satellites; be sure to allow an extra 15 minutes to reach the outlying gates.

Airport Services

Airport Emergencies	911
Business Service Center	242.6977
Currency Exchange	248.0401
Customs	553.7979
Ground Transportation	360/431.5906
Immigration	553.5956
Information	431.4444, 800/544.1965
Interpreters	433.5367
Lost and Found	433.5312
Parking	431.4444, 800/544.1965
Police	433.5400
Traveler's Aid	433.5288

Airlines

Aeroflot Russian Airlines	800/995.5555
AirBC	800/663.8868
Alaska Airlines	800/426.0333
America West Airlines	800/235.9292
American Airlines	800/433.7300
Asiana Airlines	800/2.ASIANA
British Airways	800/247.9297
Canadian Regional	800/426.7000
China Eastern	343.5583
Continental Airlines	800/525.0280
Delta Air Lines	800/221.1212
EVA Air	242.8888
Harbor Airlines	800/359.3220
Hawaiian Airlines	800/367.5320
Horizon Air	800/547.9308
Martinair	800/366.4655
Northwest Airlines	800/225.2525
Reno Air	800/RENO.AIR
SAS	800/221.2350
Shuttle by United	800/SHUTTLE
Southwest Airlines	800/435.9792
TWA	800/221.2000
United Airlines	800/241.6522
USAir	800/428.4322
Western Pacific Airlines	800/930.3030

SEATTLE-TACOMA INTERNATIONAL AIRPORT (SEA)

Concourse Locations for Major Airlines

A TWA
USAir
Western Pacific

B AirBC
America West
Continental
Delta
Harbor
Reno Air

C American
Canadian Regional
Horizon

D Alaska

North Satellite
United

South Satellite
Aeroflot
Asiana
British Airways
China Eastern
EVA
Hawaiian
Martinair
Northwest
SAS

Concourse B
Concourse C
Main Terminal
South Satellite Terminal
South Satellite Transit Loop
Ticketing
North Satellite Terminal
North Satellite Transit Loop
Baggage Claim
Concourse A
Parking
Concourse D

▬ ▬ ▬ Transit System

Getting to and from SEA

By Bus and Shuttle

The trip between the airport and downtown Seattle takes from 30 to 50 minutes by bus, depending on traffic conditions. **Gray Line Airport Express** (626.6088) buses leave every 15 minutes from 5AM to midnight and drop off passengers at seven downtown hotels. Return trips to the airport run daily from 5AM to 11:05PM; departure times depend on the stop. The trip takes about about 50 minutes. One-way adult fare is $7.50; round-trip is $13. Reservations are not necessary.

Metro Transit (553.3000) has three separate airport buses: Nos. *174*, *184*, and *194*. All three run every 30 minutes during the day, but only the *184* runs after midnight. Schedules are posted outside baggage areas at the airport, and they are available at Metro stands and buses around the city.

Shuttle Express (622.1424, 800/487.7433) operates 24-hour, door-to-door service for $18 (one way) to Seattle and $23 to the east side of **Lake Washington.** Note: Two people traveling together cost only a few dollars more than one. Reservations are essential when traveling to the airport, but are not required on the way into town. One warning: the company's policy is to get you to the airport *at least* an hour in advance of your flight.

By Car

The airport is about a half-hour drive from downtown, except during peak traffic periods (between 3 and 6PM on most days) when the trip can take up to an hour.

To get to downtown Seattle from **SEA,** take **Freeway 518** east and then take **Interstate 5 (I-5)** north; to get to the **Eastside,** stay on Freeway 518 east, which becomes **Interstate 405 (I-405).** There are well-marked exits all along the way.

To get to the airport from downtown, head south on I-5, or take I-405 south (becoming Freeway 518) if you are coming from the Eastside. Long- and short-term parking lots are within easy walking distance of the main terminal.

Rental Cars

Most national and local car-rental agencies are located at and around **SEA,** and most major hotels have car-rental counters. Weekly (a minimum of five days) or three-day weekend rates are usually the best deals, but you should always shop around. Contact the following major companies for their current rates:

Advantage 824.0161, 800/777.5500

Alamo..............................433.0182, 800/327.9633

Avis 433.5231, 800/331.1212

Budget/Sears/Save More...243.2400, 800/527.0700

Century 246.5039, 888/288.6768

Dollar 433.5825, 800/800.4000

Enterprise.........................246.1953, 800/325.8007

Hertz 433.5262, 800/654.3131

National............................433.5501, 800/227.7368

Rent-A-Wreck 246.8486, 800/535.1391

Thrifty 242.7275, 800/367.2277

U Save...............................242.9778, 800/272.USAV

By Limousine

Those who prefer private car service can make arrangements with **Washington Limousine** (523.8000) or **Ashton Limousine** (628.6461). The trip between the airport and downtown costs $45 to $85, depending on the size of the limo.

By Taxi

There are usually taxis waiting at the airport for passengers; if not, pick up one of the "hot line" phones outside the baggage claim area. The fare to downtown Seattle is about $25, excluding tip.

Getting Around Seattle

Bicycles

Most of Seattle and the suburbs are laced with bicycle routes, clearly marked with the universal two-wheel bike trail symbol. Cyclists have several scenic recreational options; chief among them are **Myrtle Edwards Park** (see page 82) and the **Burke-Gilman Trail** (see page 169). Bikes can be rented from **Gregg's Greenlake Cycle** (7007 Woodlawn Ave NE, at Ravenna Blvd NE and NE 70th St, 523.1822), which also offers information and maps of bicycle routes.

Buses

Negotiating the streets of Seattle aboard **Metro Transit** buses is easy. Be sure to request a transfer while paying the fare to the driver. If you are traveling beyond downtown, you will need to show it as you leave the bus. Transfers are stamped with the current time, and they are good for approximately two hours on any bus in the same zone.

Service is free in the commercial core (bounded by the **Waterfront** on the west, I-5 on the east, **Jackson Street** to the south, and **Battery Street** to the north) from 6AM to 7PM daily. But beyond that, a two-zone system charges 85¢ within the city ($1.10 at peak times, Monday through Friday from 6 to 9AM and 3 to 6PM) and $1.10 if you travel beyond the city limits ($1.60 at peak times). Heading out of downtown, pay when you get off; going in, pay when you board. Drivers don't carry change, so have the correct amount in hand or overpay in dollar bills. On weekends and holidays only, an All-Day Pass (costing $1.70) permits an unlimited number of rides for one day.

Bus stops (identifiable by their yellow-and-white signs) are usually posted with current timetables, but schedules are also available aboard the buses and at most public locations around town, including libraries and shopping malls. The buses are generally clean, comfortable, and on time. Most are wheelchair accessible, and some even sport exterior bicycle mounts (you'll see them on the fronts of buses).

Drivers can be quite garrulous, launching into tour monologues as they pilot through the city.

An L-shaped bus tunnel, designed to shave a whopping five minutes off the time needed to travel through the congested downtown traffic, runs beneath the commercial core; there are five entrances between the **Washington State Convention & Trade Center** and the **International District.** Call **Metro Transit**'s help line (553.3000) for trip-planning information 24 hours a day.

Greyhound (628.5526, 800/231.2222) handles long-distance bus service from Seattle; the terminal is at 811 Stewart Street, between Ninth and Eighth Avenues.

Driving

Residents of Seattle voted back in the late 1960s to pump money into more freeways, rather than into mass transit—a big mistake. Today, even the most placid and reserved Seattleites have begun to honk their car horns downtown, as the cumulative swell of bicycle couriers, buses, cabs, and pedestrians forces motorists to run an obstacle course between red lights. Beware especially of the human crush at **Pike Place Market,** where pedestrians always enjoy the right-of-way. Even some outlying routes, such as **45th Street** between **Wallingford** and the University District, **Broadway** on Capitol Hill, and **Lake City Way** and **Bothell Way** rounding Lake Washington's upper reaches, crawl on weekday afternoons. And it's a wonder there haven't been riots in front of the **Fremont Bridge,** which opens to allow boats passage through the **Lake Washington Ship Canal** while overheating cars are forced to wait.

Freeway traffic snarls here don't yet rival LA, but they're close: the average commuter takes about 30 minutes to drive into downtown, and even that sounds zippy to some folks living east of Lake Washington. The average speed during rush hours is 22 mph, and peak-period delays are only expected to worsen. The two floating bridges that cross Lake Washington are particularly congested. Express lanes relieve some of the pressure north of downtown along I-5; and there are High-Occupancy Vehicle lanes (for cars carrying two or more people) on both I-5 and westbound on the **520 Freeway. Highway 99,** or **Aurora Avenue,** remains a decent alternative to I-5. In general, however, you're better off avoiding freeways and highways altogether Mondays through Fridays from 6 to 9AM and 3 to 6PM.

Ferries

The **Washington State Ferry System** is the nation's largest. The busiest run on weekdays is between **Bainbridge Island** and downtown, a 25-minute commuter chug. On weekends, and especially during the summer, the **Edmonds-Kingston Ferry** is shoehorned full of tourists, and it's not uncommon to wait three hours for car space on ferries at **Anacortes** (about 90 minutes north of Seattle) bound for **Victoria, British Columbia.**

Walk-ons stand a better chance than drivers of catching their boat of choice. Most passengers pay a round-trip fare up front, and costs vary according to distance. Food and beverages on the boats are mediocre at best, so you may want to pack something to snack on. Credit cards are not accepted, and travelers headed for Canada must have a passport or another official form of identification (such as a driver's license, birth certificate, or voter registration card). Schedules change from winter to summer; call 464.6400 or 800/843.3779 for current departure times and rates.

Monorail

Built for the 1962 World's Fair, the **Monorail** runs only a 90-second, 1.2-mile route from downtown's **Westlake Center** to the old World's Fair grounds, now the **Seattle Center.** It's great for children, who love the train's smooth and uninterrupted ride. Adults pay 90¢ one way, kids ages 5 to 12 go for 70¢, and children under 5 ride free, while seniors and disabled riders pay 35¢. Trains depart every 15 minutes from 9AM to midnight during the summer; in winter they run until 9PM on weeknights and until midnight on Friday and Saturday. Call 441.6038 for more information.

Taxis

There are about 2,300 cabs in King County, and they're a fairly cheap means of transport, but they're controlled by dispatchers and almost impossible to hail from the street. They usually can be picked up at the bigger downtown hotels (especially the **Four Seasons Olympic Hotel** and the **Westin**), as well as at the **King Street** train station. Otherwise, call; one will arrive in anywhere from 10 to 30 minutes. Companies include: **Checker Deluxe Cab** (622.1234), **Farwest Taxi** (329.7700), **Graytop Cab** (622.4800), and **Yellow Cab** (622.6500). **STITA** (246.9999) is a cooperative cab enterprise offering transportation between downtown and the airport.

Trains

Long-distance train service is provided by **Amtrak** (382.4120, 800/872.7245); there are daily arrivals and departures from **King Street Station** (Third Ave S and S Jackson St).

Trolleys

Seattle's real trolleys were stripped from service decades ago, but **Metro Transit** (553.3000) has imported vintage machines from Australia to make the 15-minute trip along the Waterfront from **Pier 70** through Pioneer Square to the International District. The fare is $1.10 Monday through Friday from 6 to 9AM and 3 to 6PM; 85¢ all other times; children under five ride free.

Walking

Long city blocks, some daunting hills, and the polar separation of Seattle's two principal tourist meccas, Pioneer Square and **Pike Place Market,** make downtown an area best taken in small doses—take a bus from one point of interest to another, and then walk around in that immediate area. There's an impressive diversity of architecture and street life in the city, but green spaces are mostly relegated to the neighborhoods, with little open space downtown; it's basically concrete canyons between **Cherry** and **Pike Streets.**

Neighborhoods offer better strolling opportunities, particularly along Broadway on Capitol Hill, along **Market Street** in Ballard, and down **University Way** in the University District. On the suburban Eastside, only downtown **Kirkland** boasts enough sites within a small area to be walkable.

FYI

Accommodations

In addition to the individual hotel and bed-and-breakfast listings in each chapter, there are general reservations services available that help match visitors' needs to available properties. The **Seattle Supersaver** (800/535.7071) offers one-stop shopping for price and location of downtown hotels. **A Pacific Reservation Service** (784.0539) lists over 200 bed-and-breakfasts, cottages, condos, and guest houses in Seattle and throughout the Pacific Northwest. Both services are free and operate from 9AM to 5PM Monday through Friday.

Climate

The predictions of local meteorologists are often studies in equivocation, along the lines of "partial sunshine, followed by partial low-cloudiness, and maybe turning to showers in the afternoon." Look out your window for an accurate assessment, but remember that the weather you see may be quite different from what's going on only two miles away. Warm offshore currents, mountains, and cold fronts from the north conspire to give Seattle a changeable but fairly moderate climate. July and August are the warmest months of the year, with relative humidity of 50 percent, and usually no more than an inch or so of rain. Winter is wetter, with an average of five inches of rain each month, but the temperature is warm enough to make snow and ice infrequent; when they do hit, however, the city turns into a huge frozen sculpture and traffic stops dead in its tracks.

Months	Average Temperature (°F)
December-January	46
March-May	58
June-August	73
September-November	53

Drinking

Washington's legal drinking age is 21. Bars usually stay open until 2AM, and wine and beer are available at most supermarkets and groceries. Hard liquor must be purchased at one of the many state-regulated liquor stores.

Hours

Opening and closing times for shops, attractions, coffeehouses, etc. are listed only by day(s) if normal hours apply (opening between 8 and 11AM and closing between 4 and 7PM). In unusual cases, specific hours are given.

Money

Banks are generally open Monday through Friday from 9:30AM to 5PM, and some also open on Saturday mornings. Most of the larger downtown institutions will exchange foreign currency and traveler's checks. Better rates, however, may be available Monday through Friday at **American Express** (600 Stewart St at Sixth Ave, 441.8622) or at **Thomas Cook Currency Exchange** (906 Third Ave between Marion and Madison Sts, 623.6203). In a pinch on weekends, **Check Mart** (1206 First Ave at Seneca St, 622.2274) exchanges money on Saturday from 9AM to 9PM, and Sunday 11AM to 7PM.

Parking

There are numerous covered garages and open-air lots throughout the city. Facilities like the **Kingdome** and **Husky Stadium** have their own lots, as do most downtown hotels. Centrally located garages charge up to $8 per day; less expensive ones are located on the fringes of downtown—along **Alaskan Way** on the Waterfront, in the **International District,** and near **First Avenue** and **Bell Street.** Free parking options in the city are relegated to the rim areas—at the southern end of the Waterfront near Jackson Street, for instance, or on **Elliott Avenue W** bordering **Myrtle Edwards Park.** Closer to downtown, most meters offer only a half-hour's time, and many others (marked in yellow) are off-limits except to delivery vehicles. Beware of parking infractions: An overtime parking ticket costs about $20; for parking in a truck-loading zone the fine is a little higher; and parking illegally in a handicapped-only spot results in a $50 ticket.

Personal Safety

The Seattle police force patrols the streets by motorcycle, car, mountain bike, horse, and on foot, which is reassuring to everyone but jaywalkers (more than 3,500 jaywalking tickets are issued here annually). Pickpockets are rare, but they do turn up in such crowded areas as **Pike Place Market,** along Broadway on Capitol Hill, and in shopping malls. Panhandlers can be a problem, too, although they are essentially harmless. Seattle isn't known for its violent crime (theft is the principal threat here), but as in any large city, be more careful at night, especially in the downtown area.

Publications

The city's two daily newspapers—the *Seattle Post-Intelligencer* (also called the *"P-I"*) and the *Seattle Times*—have been in the velvet grip of a Joint Operating Agreement since 1983, ending an often vituperative rivalry. Both publish separate papers Monday through Saturday, but only one Sunday edition. The Hearst-owned morning *P-I* is strong on news and sports, but unimaginative in feature sections. The more successful afternoon *Times* is owned primarily by the local Blethen family (with a minority share held by Knight-Ridder), and is better known for its feature writing. The Eastside's principal paper is the daily *Journal American,* which is loaded with upscale-neighborhood stories.

The free *Seattle Weekly,* published on Tuesday, has shed its scrappy "alternative" image over the years, becoming successful and mainstream, but the tabloid continues to attract readers with its arts coverage, essays, and opinionated calendar of events. A sister publication, *Eastsideweek* (available on Wednesday), covers communities east of Lake Washington with a slightly more irreverent eye. Slick bimonthly *Seattle* magazine covers a scattershot of topics, from politics to gardening and history, while *Pacific Northwest* offers a nine-times-a-year editorial menu of travel, food, and pictures. *The Rocket* (biweekly) concentrates on the local pop-music scene, as does *The Stranger* (available on Thursday), an often outrageous weekly tabloid.

Puget Sound Business Journal (weekly) and the *Daily Journal of Commerce* both keep track of local financial transactions, but the *PSBJ* is usually more readable. *Seattle Skanner, The Medium,* and *The Facts* all serve the African-American community on a weekly basis. The monthly *Seattle's Child* features a wealth of activities and health materials directed at families. Every Friday *Seattle Gay News* reports on subjects of interest to the local gay and lesbian population. *Seattle Chinese Post,* a Chinese weekly newspaper, publishes an English-language edition, *Northwest Asian Weekly.* The *North American Post* (published three times a week) is the Northwest's only Japanese-language paper, and *Hispanic News* is a weekly published in Spanish and English.

Up-to-date calendars of events can be found in *Seattle Weekly,* the *Seattle Times'* Thursday "Tempo" section, the *Seattle Post-Intelligencer's* Friday "What's Happening" section, and *Eastsideweek.*

Radio Stations

KBSG	Oldies 97.3 FM
KING	Classical 98.1 FM
KING	News 1090 AM
KIRO	News 710 AM
KMPS	Country 94.1 FM
KOMO	Adult contemporary 1000 AM
KUOW	Public Radio 94.9 FM
KVI	Talk Radio 570 AM
KZOK	Rock 102.5 FM

Restaurants

Reservations are necessary for most popular restaurants, and it's best to book far in advance for the hottest dining spots such as **Flying Fish** and **Cafe Flora.** In general, jackets and ties are not required (except at the poshest of places), and most establishments accept credit cards.

Shopping

Galleries and antiques stores abound in the Pioneer Square area. Downtown, **Rainier Tower** and the **US Bank Centre** offer several upscale shops; **Fifth** and **Sixth Avenues** are also lined with specialty stores. There's **Pike Place Market** for fresh produce, seafood, flowers, and souvenirs. Bargain hunters will want to head for **Fremont**'s resale shops; shopaholics for the **Bellevue Square Mall.**

Smoking

Health-conscious Seattle has a low threshold of tolerance for smokers. Restaurants that don't outright ban lighting up usually have separate smoking sections; many hotels have separate floors for smokers. Bars and taverns tend to be more lenient, but it's the rare place that permits cigars or pipes. Smoking is prohibited in all city-owned buildings.

Street Plan

You can generally tell the location of a place by the directional reference tacked on to the street name: For example, a place in Ballard will have an "NW" somewhere in its address, while an address in the **Seward Park** area will have an "S." Most north-south roads in Seattle are "Avenues" and their compass directions are listed *after* their name or number. East-west thoroughfares are "Streets," and their compass directions appear *before* their name or number. Aberrations are the occasional "Ways," which usually run diagonally to the city grid, and the I-5 highway, which slices right through the city.

If you're lost, remember that Seattle is shaped like an hourglass, with downtown smack in the middle. Puget Sound is always west of the city, and Mount Rainier rises up to the southeast.

Taxes

Washington state sales tax is a hefty 8.2 percent on all purchases except groceries. The hotel tax is 14.2 percent.

Telephones

The area code for Seattle, Everett, and Tacoma is currently 206, but at press time, the phone company planned to add two new area codes: 425 for regions east and north of Seattle (such as Bellevue, Kirkland, Bothell, Redmond, and Everett), and 253 for communities to the south (including Tacoma). The new codes are being phased in during 1997. In addition, the 360 area code has been assigned to the rest of coastal Washington. Phone numbers in this book have the 206 area code unless otherwise specified. If you have trouble reaching attractions listed here, contact either directory assistance or the **Washington State Convention & Trade Center** (800 Convention Pl at Eighth Ave and Pike St, 461.5840).

Local pay-phone calls (including those from Seattle to Bainbridge Island and the Eastside) cost 25¢. Note: Hotels generally impose a hefty charge for outgoing calls, so it may be worthwhile to dial from a public phone booth.

Tickets

Two clearinghouses offer tickets to a variety of performing arts and venues. **Ticket/Ticket** sells half-price, cash-only, day-of-show tickets from two locations: **Broadway Market** on Capitol Hill and **Pike Place Market** (they're both open Tuesday through Sunday; call 324.2744 for more information). **TicketMaster** (628.0888) is a computerized charge service for concerts and sports that sometimes offers discounted tickets; there are several cash-only centers around town. Some theaters (including the **Bathhouse Theatre,** the **Empty Space Theater,** and the **New City Theater**) schedule special "pay-as-you-can" performances, and many offer reduced-price preview tickets.

Time Zone
Seattle is in the Pacific Time Zone, three hours earlier than New York City.

Tipping
A 15- to 20-percent tip is standard in restaurants and taxis, and $1 per bag is expected by hotel porters. Concierges anticipate tips based on the quality of their service and a guest's individual largess: $20 for a week's worth of consistently good advice would be a healthy thanks, although some guests prefer to give $1 per service.

Tours
The city's most popular tour is **Underground Seattle** (682.4646), an hour-long excursion literally beneath the streets of Pioneer Square. When this district was rebuilt after the Great Fire of 1889, the decision was made to raise the land higher above water level to improve drainage and expand buildable acreage. To allow for this regrading, structures adopted double sets of entrances—one at the original ground level and another one story up, where sidewalks eventually would be laid. Engineers finally made the roads and the sidewalks even, but they did so without destroying the lower-level pedestrian ways. The remaining "underground city" is what you'll see on this entertaining and unusual expedition. Tours leave from **Doc Maynard's Public House** (610 First Ave between James and Cherry Sts) and last about 1.5 hours; they're available from late morning until mid-afternoon most days of the year; reservations are recommended. In July and August, tours run daily from 10AM to 8PM; the schedule varies the rest of the year, so call ahead.

Chinatown Discovery Tours (236.0657) is a company that escorts visitors through Seattle's International District, taking in such attractions as a fortune-cookie factory and an herb dispensary, and breaking for a dim sum lunch. **Show Me Seattle** (633.2489) takes visitors on three-hour tours of downtown, the waterfront, Pioneer Square, residential neighborhoods, the **Hiram M. Chittenden Locks,** and possibly (depending on the weather and the mood of the group) the giant **Fremont Troll,** the "floating home" on Lake Union seen in the movie *Sleepless in Seattle,* and other offbeat sights. **Seattle's Best Walking Tours** (226.7641) trek through the **Pike Place Market,** along the waterfront, and through Pioneer Square and **Chinatown,** taking in the architecture, hidden gardens, and waterfalls along the way. Half- and full-day tours are offered daily year-round, rain or shine. A firm called **Viewpoints** (667.9186) presents architectural walking tours with various themes (such as Art Deco, The Olmsted Legacy, and Terra Cotta) Monday through Friday and two weekends a month late April through October. **Gray Line** (626.5208) offers a

variety of sight-seeing excursions, including runs along Seattle's waterways and, in the summer, out to **Mount Rainier, Snoqualmie Falls,** and the tiny town of **North Bend. Argosy** (623.1445) schedules cruises through the **Hiram M. Chittenden Locks** and around Lake Washington and historic **Elliott Bay.**

Brochures for most tour companies can be found at the tourist information booth on the galleria level of the **Washington State Convention & Trade Center** (800 Convention Pl at Eighth Ave and Pike St), and at **Sea-Tac International Airport** (lower concourse, baggage claim area).

Visitors' Information
There are two main visitors' information centers: on the galleria level of the **Washington State Convention & Trade Center** (800 Convention Pl at Eighth Ave and Pike St, 461.5840), and at **Sea-Tac International Airport** (lower concourse, baggage claim area, 443.5217). Both are open Monday through Friday from 8:30AM to 4PM, and Saturday from 10AM to 5PM.

Phone Book

Emergencies

Ambulance/Fire/Police 911
AAA of Washington 448.5353
AIDS Hotline..296.4999
Auto Impound 684.5444
Auto Theft 684.8940
Bartell's Pharmacy (open 24 hours) 284.1354
Dental..362.3644
Hospital (Harborview Emergency)..............731.3074
Hospital (University of Washington)..........548.3300
Locksmith (AAA 24-hour) 325.1515
Medical 726.2000
Poison Control Center 526.2121
Rape Crisis...632.7273

Visitors' Information

American Youth Hostels...........................622.5443
Amtrak 382.4120, 800/872.7245
Better Business Bureau 448.8888
Washington State Convention &
  Trade Center 461.5840
Convention and Visitors Bureau 461.5800
Greyhound Bus 628.5526, 800/231.2222
Handicapped Visitors' Information 362.2273
Metro Transit 553.3000
Time..464.6400
US Customs 553.4676
US Passport Office 220.7788
Washington State Ferries 464.6400
Weather 526.6087

The Main Events

Seattle residents, ever the aspiring extroverts, love to party. Inspiration may come from occasions as noble and mystical as the return of salmon to Northwest spawning grounds or as ignominious as the approach of fall and winter rain showers. Calendars in this area weigh heavily with annual fests, sporting events, and artsy convocations. Some of the most popular year-round celebrations include:

January

Chinese New Year The **International District** comes alive with fairs, dragon-dense parades, and cultural displays. Festivities celebrating the symbolic expulsion of demons used to last a month, but West Coast Chinese have whittled their events down to about a week. Seattle's is held in either January or February, depending on the lunar calendar. Call 223.0623 for more information.

February

Fat Tuesday Pioneer Square jiggles with jazz, rock, and Cajun melodies, plus a waiter/waitress race and a wild (by local standards) parade, as Seattle presents its own spin on Mardi Gras. Events begin Wednesday of the week preceding Fat Tuesday (the day before Ash Wednesday and the beginning of Lent). For details, call 682.4649.

Northwest Flower and Garden Show This veritable Eden of horticulture seems to grow each year, feeding Seattle's much-written-about fondness for gardening. Hundreds of demonstration plots, supply sales booths, statuary displays, and lectures by landscapers and gardening writers round out the schedule. The event takes place at the **Convention & Trade Center;** admission is charged. For information, call 447.5000.

March

St. Patrick's Day Downtown resounds with bagpipe music and the beat of dancing feet as an annual parade follows a special green stripe painted down **Fourth Avenue** from **City Hall** to **Westlake Center;** call 623.0340 for more information. Meanwhile, the popular four-mile St. Patrick's Day Dash leaves from **T.S. McHugh's** (21 Mercer St between First and Queen Anne Aves N) bound for **F.X. McRory's** (419 Occidental Ave S at S King St) in Pioneer Square; call 223.3608 or 865.9134 for details.

Whirligig An indoor, three-week carnival for kids aged two to 10 features rides (including a giant slide), family-oriented performances, and music. The fun takes place at the **Center House** in the **Seattle Center;** call 684.7200.

Mainly Mozart Festival The **Seattle Symphony** schedules three concerts honoring the genius of Wolfgang Amadeus Mozart. Admission is charged and performances take place at the **University of Washington's Meany Theater.** For schedules, call 443.4747.

April

Cherry Blossom & Japanese Cultural Festival This celebration of cherry blossom season features performances of Japanese music, art, and drama, as well as other cultural events. The three-day festival is held at the **Seattle Center;** for more details, call 684.7200.

Daffodil Festival The warm-up act for Skagit Valley's Tulip Festival later in the month, this more-than-60-year-old tradition includes a parade of flower-bedecked private boats along with some Navy craft and a giant floral parade that marches through four towns—**Tacoma, Puyallup, Sumner,** and **Orting**—all in one day. The mid-April event is free; call 627.6176.

Skagit Valley Tulip Festival It is not always easy to gauge precisely when the 1,500 acres of tulip fields north of Seattle will bloom, but it's guaranteed that thousands of Washingtonians will rush to see them when they do. Because **Skagit Valley** roads are regularly jammed with flower lovers during this time, the best plan of action is to find a bicycle and ride casually between the fields, perhaps purchasing a few brilliant bunches along the way. Capitalizing on the floral draw, the adjacent town of **Mount Vernon** celebrates tulip season with parades and a street fair. And **La Conner** almost explodes at the seams as tourists finish off their visit with a stroll through that burg's many small shops. Salmon barbecues, pancake suppers, and formal bike tours may also be on the docket. Watch newspapers for the official blooming announcement. The tulip fields are located outside of Mount Vernon, 60 miles north of Seattle on I-5. Call 360/428.8547 for further details.

May

Opening Day of Yachting Season This is a big deal in a city that claims one boat for every 12 people. On the first Saturday in May there's a ceremonial regatta on **Lake Union,** races to showcase the talents of the **University of Washington** rowing team, and lots of Sunday sailors just trying to steer clear of collisions on **Lake Washington.** Call the **Seattle Yacht Club** at 325.1000 for more about this free event.

Northwest Folklife Festival With booths offering handmade crafts, banjo players, gospel performances, storytelling sessions, and clog-dancing exhibitions, this free four-day hootenanny—said to be the country's largest folk fest—strives to show that Seattle hasn't sold out completely to glitz. Like most major functions at **Seattle Center,** it's dominated by food booths. Attendees are asked to help defray administrative costs by purchasing commemorative event pins. The festival is held every Memorial Day weekend; call 684.7200.

Pike Place Market Festival One of the city's most boisterous neighborhood hooplas, this free festival offers live-music stages, plenty of food and drink, clowns, and an activities area set aside specifically for children. It's held every Memorial Day weekend at **Pike Place Market;** for details, call 587.0351.

Poulsbo Viking Fest Break out your horned helmets and help celebrate the Scandinavian heritage of **Puget Sound's** most deliberately Norwegian village. Expect live music, traditional dancing, and a group of iron-stomached guests engaging in a contest to see who can eat the most *lutefisk* (cod soaked in brine and spices). The free event is held in **Poulsbo,** on the **Kitsap Peninsula,** 12 miles northwest of the **City of Bainbridge Island** (on **Bainbridge Island**) on Highway 305; call 360/779.4848 for further information.

Seattle International Film Festival Founded in 1976, this is supposedly the best-attended film festival in North America, showing more than 160 new works from around the world at several Seattle theaters. Screenings run from mid-May through early June. Series tickets go on sale in January. Call 324.9996 for information.

University Street Fair Fed by a colorful cross section of **University of Washington** students and well woven with curious arts and crafts booths, this free two-day street party, begun in 1970, is always worth a look. There are lots of mimes, musicians, and street eats, plus great people watching. It's usually held the third full weekend in May on **University Way NE.** For more about the fair, call 523.4272.

June

West Seattle Dixieland Jazz Festival An institution in **West Seattle** since 1982, this longstanding two-day event features traditional jazz bands, dancing, food, and beverages. A free shuttle takes attendees from one site to another. A real highlight is the Sunday gospel jazz service, whose site changes from year to year. A modest admission is charged, the proceeds of which benefit services to senior citizens. Call 932.4044 for more information.

Fire Festival More than a century after the Great Fire of 1889, which completely flattened downtown, the city can commemorate that blaze without pangs of loss. Fire equipment parades along **First Avenue,** live entertainment heats up **Occidental Park,** and historical exhibits teach the dangers of pyromania. Pioneer Square marks the center of activity; call 623.1162.

Fremont Arts and Crafts Fair Fremonsters show up by the thousands for this eclectic neighborhood celebration featuring not only food and crafts booths but live music by plenty of street performers. It takes place at **N 34th Street,** just north of the **Fremont Bridge.** For more about the fair, call 548.8376 between January and June.

Out to Lunch Summer is officially declared when the sounds of midday concerts (from jazz to calypso) begin resounding from downtown's canyonlands. The series is free and usually continues through early September. Call 623.0340 for specific locations.

Seattle International Music Festival The two-week schedule includes master classes and open rehearsals, as well as chamber-music concerts. Violinist Dmitry Sitkovetsky, director of the Finnish music festival Korsholm, directs this series. Performances are held at several locations, including **Meany Hall** (Central Plaza, on the University of Washington campus) and the **Seattle Art Museum** (100 University St at First Ave). Admission is charged; call 233.0993 for more information.

Seattle-to-Portland Bicycle Rally (STP) Thousands of cyclists have departed from the **Kingdome** since 1979 on this annual 200-mile pedalthon through the valleys, forests, and farmlands of western Washington on the way to Portland, Oregon. Riders complete this "Tour de Northwest" in one or two days, depending on their exercise history and/or their threshold of masochism (facilities halfway through the course are available to overnighters). Sponsored by the Cascade Bicycle Club, registration is first-come, first-served, with a 10,000-rider limit. For further details, call 522.2453.

July

Bite of Seattle Here's yet another shameless opportunity to eat yourself silly in public, as 50 or more local restaurants serve their specialties from open-air booths. Don't forget the Tums. This food fest takes place at the end of July at the **Seattle Center;** call 684.7200 for details.

King County Fair Enjoy five days of rodeoing, pig racing, and music headliners at the state's oldest county fair beginning the third Wednesday in July. The **King County Fairgrounds** are in **Enumclaw,** just 42 miles southeast of Seattle; take I-5 south to the Auburn exit, then Highway 164. For more about this event, call 825.7777.

Mercer Island Summer Celebration Booths display arts and crafts, jugglers perform, children are invited to participate in distracting building projects, and Saturday night swings with a live band beside the dance floor. This event takes place the second weekend of July at various venues in the **Mercer Island** central business district; call 236.7285.

Olympic Music Festival The rather incongruously named **Philadelphia String Quartet** (which has been based in Seattle since 1966) joins other musicians in an 11-weekend series of chamber-music performances, held in a turn-of-the-century barn on the nearby **Olympic Peninsula** from late June through early September. Bring blankets to sit on. Admission is charged and the festival is held in **Quilcene,** on the west side of Puget Sound, 11 miles west of the **Hood Canal Bridge** on Highway 104; call 527.8839.

Pacific Northwest Arts and Crafts Fair Bellevue upstages Seattle with this exhibition of performing arts, crafts displays, and a juried show of visual arts in **Bellevue Square** and the **Bellevue Square Garage** (at NE Eighth St and Bellevue Way NE, Bellevue). It's free and takes place the last weekend of July; for additional information, call 454.4900.

San Juan Island Dixieland Jazz Festival Ferries chugging to **San Juan Island** are especially full when Dixieland lovers swarm toward one of this area's finest summer musical events. The three-day festival features continuous entertainment presented on three outdoor stages. Music includes traditional jazz, New Orleans–style jazz, swing, gospel, and blues. The shows take place in the town of **Friday Harbor.** Warning: Lodging reservations can be hard to find in the San Juan Islands during this time (late July), so call *very* early to get a room. Individual-day and full-festival passes are available. Catch the ferry at **Anacortes,** 78 miles north of Seattle (take Exit 230 from I-5 and head 20 miles west to the terminal); your best bet is to leave your car there and walk onto the ferry. Call 378.5509 for more about the festival.

Seafair Before Seattle became a politically correct kind of town, the **Seafair Pirates**—a horde of brawny, hard-drinking guys who dressed up once a year like Blackbeard's minions and kidnapped (at least temporarily) prominent Seattleites—were a colorful aspect of the local summer celebration scene. Now they're often considered kitschy. Some humorless critics even say these buccaneers are too frightening for children. But the rest of the festival, at least, maintains the flavor and support it has enjoyed since 1950. Milk carton boat races on **Green Lake,** a torchlight parade, hydroplane races on Lake Washington, and a demonstration of acrobatic flying by the **Blue Angels** are all part of the fun. This event is mostly free and it's held from the third weekend of July through the first Sunday in August at various venues; call 728.0123 for details.

August

Evergreen State Fair Animal shows, stock-car races, a chili cook-off, totem-pole carving, and cow-milking contests are all part of this 11-day show-and-tell in the backwoods hamlet of **Monroe,** 30 miles northeast of Seattle. The fair takes place from late August through Labor Day and there is an admission charge; call 794.7832.

KOMO Kidsfair Jointly sponsored by the local radio station **KOMO** and the **Seattle Center,** this daylong fair presents a roster of outdoor activities for the entire family, including pony rides, face painting, miniature train rides, and the "clown bounce," where kids bounce up and down on a gigantic inflated apparatus. For more information, call 684.7200.

September

Bumbershoot Seattle's premier entertainment event, playfully taking its name from a British slang term for umbrella, is a four-day extravaganza of music, art shows, literary readings, and food, food, food. The **Seattle Center** fills with crafts booths, fortune tellers, balloon artists, and the riffs of nationally known musicologists. Admission is charged and it's held Labor Day weekend; call 684.7200.

The Great Northwest Microbrewery Invitational On the last weekend in September you can sample the breadth of this region's primo craft brews. Admission is charged and the pouring takes place at the **Seattle Center;** for more information, call 684.7200.

Western Washington Fair Most folks just call this country fest the "Puyallup Fair," as in the slogan "Do the Puyallup" (pronounced Pew-*al*-up). For 17 days, children can stuff themselves silly on cotton candy and then try to hold it all down as they bump along on carnival rides. Adults watch rodeos and livestock shows, and listen to well-known country-and-western musicians. The smells of livestock and the grunts of pigs abound. The fair takes place at the **Puyallup Fairgrounds,** 35 miles south of Seattle off I-5. For more information, call 841.5045.

October

St. Demetrios Greek Festival Lovers of bouzouki music and gyro sandwiches take note. This partially covered ethnic tribute to Rain City's 10,000-plus Greek descendants, held at **St. Demetrios Church** (2100 Boyer Ave E at 23rd Ave E), thrives on dancing, heaped plates of Athenian cuisine, wonderfully sticky baklava, and arts-and-crafts exhibits. Long lines form at the food booths, so come early. Admission is charged. The date varies, based on parking availability due to **UW Husky** football games; call 325.4347.

Issaquah Salmon Days This free two-day event, held the first weekend of October, commemorates the annual return of the Northwest's premier sporting fish to its spawning grounds with a parade, salmon bake, hydroplane races on **Sammamish Lake,** and live entertainment. Pony rides and face painting are favorites for children. Events are held all over **Issaquah,** 15 miles east of Seattle on **Interstate 90;** call 392.0661.

November

KING 5 Winterfest A free five-week holiday jamboree beginning Thanksgiving weekend offers entertainment for children, ice skating, symphony concerts, senior dances, holiday music, and, of course, a jolly old St. Nicholas. Sponsored by local TV station **KING,** it runs through early January at the **Seattle Center.** Call 684.7200 for details.

December

Christmas Ships The Christmas Ships sail over **Elliott Bay** and Lake Washington, sparkling with colorful lights and adding a festive spirit to Seattle's holiday season. Bonfires are set up on local beaches to watch the crafts' passage. For site information, call 684.4075.

The Messiah This is one of very few American performances of Handel's celebrated work to employ authentic instrumentation. Call early (323.1040) for reservations, as tickets always sell out. The performances are held from early- to mid-December at **St. Mark's Episcopal Cathedral** (1245 10th Ave E at E Galer St).

The Nutcracker The **Pacific Northwest Ballet**'s rendering of this classic fairy tale might be only vaguely recognizable to Russian Tsar Nicholas II, for whom Tchaikovsky first staged his ballet in 1892. The set designs, by renowned Seattle artist Maurice Sendak, help make this production both more whimsical and more memorable than its competitors. Tickets go on sale in October; call 292.2787.

New Year's Eve at the Space Needle As many as 20,000 chilled and damp celebrants huddle on three levels of the **Needle** (on the observation level, in the **Space Needle Restaurant,** and at the skyline level) to offer toasts and kisses. Local bands hold forth at the tower's base. As midnight approaches, one of the elevators climbs the **Needle,** finally lighting a 12-foot-high set of numbers that heralds the beginning of the new year. Admission is charged; for details, call 443.2100.

Pioneer Square/ International District

In the middle of a parched summer in 1889, when Seattle had been an incorporated city for a mere 20 years, its business district—now known as Pioneer Square— started burning beyond control. Thirty central city blocks, a total of 64 acres, were leveled before the Great Fire of 1889 fizzled amid tidelands where the **Kingdome** stadium stands today. Amazingly, not a single person is known to have perished in the blaze.

No sooner did the smoke dissipate than civic boosters began to see the calamity as a boon for Seattle, a second chance to become a showplace and commercial capital. The fledgling city immediately began to rebuild—this time instituting regulations requiring that all new downtown buildings be constructed of brick, stone, and iron. And the structures were constructed on higher ground.

Ever since claims had first been staked on **Elliott Bay** in 1852, city engineers used dredging and landfill to both expand Seattle's commercial acreage and to lift it above water level. After the fire, this strategy was adopted for Pioneer

Square as well; and much of it was filled in with excess earth graded down from the hills, burying the first stories of many buildings and creating what is now known as **Underground Seattle.**

Thanks in large measure to James J. Hill, who designated Seattle as the western terminus for his **Great Northern Railroad,** the town was back in business less than two years later—more populous and optimistic than ever. Then came the beginning of the Alaskan Gold Rush in 1897, which transformed Seattle into a wealthy embarkation point. Pioneer Square celebrated a commercial heyday until after the turn of the century.

In about 1900, the city began to develop northward and Pioneer Square was left with honky-tonk taverns, bawdy houses, and transient hotels. Opium dens and, during Prohibition, speakeasies sprang up in the shadowy tunnels created by regrading. During the Depression the area became totally decrepit, and by 1966 the proposal was made to level it to make room for more parking lots and new offices.

Architects and preservationists were incensed. So was well-known local newspaper columnist Emmett Watson. "I swear, my friends," Watson lamented in print, "progress is going to be the death of this city yet!" But Pioneer Square escaped death once again. Banks initiated incentive loan programs to revive the neighborhood, and businesses moved in to restore its sturdy buildings. Today, approximately 88 acres of offices, restaurants, art galleries, and specialty stores populate what was the city's first historic district.

The International District (or "I.D.," as locals say), bordering Pioneer Square on the east and encompassing the city's Chinese and Japanese enclaves, has a similarly troubled but far different heritage. Seattle's original **Chinatown** was actually centered at **Second Avenue** and **Washington Street**, smack in what was then the middle of the city. Its inhabitants had come to Puget Sound to work on railroads and in lumber mills or mines. Later, they developed successful cigar-making and dry-goods businesses, but by the mid-1880s, as unemployment rose in the Northwest, white laborers came to resent the Chinese and their "cheap labor." In February 1886 mobs of Sinophobes (including, it's said, many police officers) invaded Chinatown and herded almost all of the city's 350 to 400 Chinese residents to steamships bound for San Francisco. Martial law was declared to halt the expulsion, but at least half of Seattle's Chinese population left anyway, fearful of the consequences should they remain. Only well after the Great Fire of 1889 did the Chinese begin returning to Seattle, and by then new Japanese immigrants had filled up much of the labor vacuum.

Chinatown relocated to the blocks around **King** and **Jackson Streets** in the early 1900s. Meanwhile, the Japanese immigrants had settled in an area just north of there, which they called *Nihonmachi*. By 1910 *Nihonmachi* housed more than 6,000 Japanese residents. But World War II took a toll on both Asian communities. Many Japanese were interned in camps all over the West. Low-income housing subsequently invaded the south end of downtown and condemnation proceedings were brought against a number of older structures. But in the 1970s, a concerted effort went into revitalizing the I.D., and much of it has since been renovated. Families started to move back in, the **Kingdome** was built nearby, parks were laid out, and new businesses—especially Asian restaurants—attract visitors as well as residents from all parts of town to sample dim sum or sushi.

Pioneer Square

1 Pioneer Place Park The spiritual hub of Pioneer Square was once a disregarded and clumsy intersection called Yesler's Corner. Only after the fire of 1889 did it become a landmark. This cobblestoned triangle is home to many panhandlers and pigeons, but it's also a good spot for people watching or studying the surrounding architecture.

A red cedar totem pole has stood on this spot since 1899. The original, carved by Tlingit Indians, was chopped down and taken as a "souvenir" from Alaska's Tongass Island by an excursion party from Seattle. After an arsonist damaged the monolith in 1938, it was shipped back to its home, where local carvers (apparently unperturbed by Seattle's filching of the original) crafted the current replica. A drinking fountain and bust of Chief Sealth designed by James A. Wehn and installed in 1909 are also here. A cast-iron-and-glass pergola was erected at the park's southwestern tip in 1909 (and rehabilitated in 1970) to serve as a shelter for pedestrians waiting to board passing trolleys. The pergola also marked the entrance to Seattle's first public rest room (opened in 1909)—a lavish underground hideaway of Alaskan marble and skylights that offered shoe shines and a newspaper stand until plumbing problems

Pioneer Square

forced its closure in 1939. The facility still exists, but it's accessible now only through a manhole. So far the city has refused all requests to reopen the rest room. ♦ First Ave (between Yesler Way and Cherry St)

2 Pioneer Building Two years after this structure was completed in 1891, the American Institute of Architects labeled it "the finest building west of Chicago." Commissioned by Seattle pioneer and entrepreneur Henry Yesler (whose first home sat on the same property), and designed by Massachusetts emigrant **Elmer Fisher,** the building is a paradigm of this neighborhood's architecture. (Fisher would go on to create some 50 other buildings in and around Pioneer Square, lending it a homogenous but hardly disagreeable look.) Its style is Romanesque Revival, as developed and refined by such visionary architects as **Henry Hobson Richardson** and **Louis Sullivan.** A rusticated stone base and Roman archway give way to progressively different window treatments in the upper stories. The structure was originally endowed with a pyramid-topped central tower, but that was taken down (along with other towers and cornices in the district) as a precautionary measure after an earthquake rumbled up from Olympia to clobber Seattle in 1949. Although the building houses private offices, you can stop in the lobby and take a peek at the Italian red-marble interior and atrium. ♦ 606 First Ave (at James St)

2 Doc Maynard's Public House ★$ This restored pub is high on atmosphere (check out the magnificent carved bar), and on a sunny day, its outdoor tables invite you to take a seat and wet your whistle. The menu is pedestrian, running to sandwiches and bar munchies, but the pub does offer a lively repertoire of rock and R&B bands on Friday and Saturday nights. It's also the jumping-off point to tours of **Underground Seattle,** a long-buried maze of corridors that were once the sidewalks and first floors of Pioneer Square. (See page 10 for tour details.) ♦ American ♦ Cover F-Sa. Daily 9AM-4PM, 8PM-2AM. 610 First Ave (between James and Cherry Sts). 682.4649

The longest and steepest escalator west of the Mississippi is in the Seattle bus tunnel's Pioneer Square Station at Yesler Way and Third Avenue.

3 Mario's Pizza ★★$ Seattle is certainly not short on pizza joints, but few can beat the crust on the pies created in this pizzeria. Ingredients are liberally apportioned and the crusts are thick and chewy. The GASP (a wonderful concoction of garlic, artichoke hearts, sun-dried tomatoes, and pesto) is the house specialty. For more tender palates, there's the soothing Zorba, which is like a flat, open gyro sandwich, with beef, onion, feta cheese, green olives, and homemade *tzatziki* (yogurt, herb, and cucumber sauce). You can get your pizza to go or eat at one of the outdoor tables. And, of course, they deliver. ♦ Pizza/Takeout ♦ Daily. 616 First Ave (between James and Cherry Sts). 621.8500. ⅙

3 Old Timer's Cafe $ The wood-and-brass decor are Pioneer Square clichés, and the boxcar narrowness of this tavern ensures it will seem crowded, even when there are only a few people inside. The draw is the nightly performances by local blues and jazz musicians. The food is of a Southern bent, including gumbo, barbecue ribs, catfish, and mustard greens. Southern ♦ Cover. Daily lunch and dinner; music until 2AM. 620 First Ave (between James and Cherry Sts). 623.9800

4 Lowman Building The only French Renaissance Eclectic-style tower at Pioneer Place, this building (finished in 1900) is quite a standout from the parade of Romanesque piles. The principal designer was **August Heide,** an import from back east who worked primarily in the nearby town of Everett. ♦ 105 Cherry St (at First Ave)

5 Seattle Mystery Bookshop Proprietor Bill Farley carries an abundance of new and used works, paperback and hardcover, including some detective and spy novels that just don't seem to turn up elsewhere in town. There are special sections for Sherlock Holmes and for Puget Sound crime novelists (such as Earl Emerson, J.A. Jance, Robert Ferrigno, and Aaron Elkins). Mailings alert regular patrons to signings by well-known authors. ♦ M-Sa; Su noon-5PM. 117 Cherry St (between Second and First Aves). 587.5737

6 Second & James Parking Garage In an earlier era, one of the city's first and finest hotels occupied this triangular block. The **Occidental Hotel** opened in the 1860s with 30 rooms. But in 1865, as the Civil War was ending, an entrepreneur named John Collins arrived in Seattle, unstrapped $3,000 in gold dust from his waist, and purchased a one-third interest in the ivory-hued hostelry. Collins would go on to write Seattle's first charter, serve on its first city council, develop coal fields on the east side of Lake

Washington, and start the Seattle Gas Light Company, as well as serve a term as mayor. His hotel was no less ambitious.

While Collins was sitting in the first Washington Legislature (1883-84), he had the hotel completely rebuilt in ostentatious style, complete with an elevator; Collins hyperbolically proclaimed the property the "leading hotel in the Northwest," and guest capacity was expanded to 400. But then came the Great Fire of 1889. Collins tried to save his hotel buying up the surrounding clapboard structures and blowing them to smithereens, but the transactions couldn't be made fast enough, and the hotel went up with most of the rest of old Seattle. Collins went on to build a third incarnation of the hostelry, which he later renamed the **Seattle Hotel;** it stood on this site until the early 1960s. Today it's a parking garage shaped like a ship's prow. ♦ Second Ave (between Yesler Way and James St)

7 Smith Tower When it opened on 4 July 1914, this was the tallest building (pictured below) outside of Manhattan—42 floors, 522 feet—and for 48 years thereafter, it remained the highest west of the Mississippi River. (The record was broken officially in 1969 by the 50-story, 609-foot-high **Seattle–First National Bank Tower**—now the **1001 Fourth Avenue Building.**) Bankrolled by Lyman C. Smith, the armaments entrepreneur turned typewriter baron, the building was also Seattle's first fireproof steel structure, decorated with terra-cotta facing and cornices.

Smith was an upstate New Yorker. Visiting Seattle in 1909 to do some real-estate speculation, he saw it as ripe ground on which to demonstrate the depth of his success, and thereby commissioned the firm of **Gaggin & Gaggin** to build a skyscraper that would anchor downtown Seattle once and for all near its starting place. (A forlorn hope: commercial construction moved farther and farther north, fashionably away from the "old city.") Smith also wanted a building that wouldn't be exceeded in height during his lifetime. That wish came true in a twisted way: he died before this

M. BLUM

building was completed.

His "two-stepped" legacy, perhaps inspired by New York City's magnificent Woolworth Building, remains Seattle's best-loved, if not loftiest, construction. An observation deck on the 35th floor provides a marvelous panorama of downtown; and on the same floor can be found the teak-ceilinged **Chinese Room,** which Smith conceived especially for his daughter's marriage and where weddings are still held. The West Coast's only manually operated elevators (complete with original-style levers) are also to be found in this building. And don't miss the enchanting carved Indian heads above the first-floor elevator doors. ♦ 506 Second Ave (at Yesler Way)

Within Smith Tower:

G&G Cigar Store No, this pungent place was not named, as many have supposed, after **Gaggin & Gaggin,** the firm that designed the tower. In fact, the tobacco shop was established elsewhere in 1895 and relocated here only after its completion. Its moniker comes from the initials of former owners Gifford and Good. The cigar selection is rather limited; but with a wooden Indian in the window and aging paraphernalia throughout, it rates high in the historical gem category. ♦ M-Sa. 623.6721

8 Interurban Building (Smith Tower Annex) The exceptional brick masonry, stone carving, and terra-cotta trim make this oft-overlooked office building another excellent example of Pioneer Square's Romanesque-Victorian style. Fenestration carefully orchestrated from floor to floor gives rhythm and a fine scale to the architecture. The corner entrance is ornamented with a lion's head. Not surprisingly, the architect who designed this 1890 building, **John Parkinson,** was a contemporary of **Elmer Fisher.** Until 1920, this was the **Interurban Railway Depot.** And during World War II, Boeing had its headquarters here. ♦ 102-108 Occidental Ave S (at Yesler Way)

9 Madame & Co. This is one of the classier vintage-clothing outlets in town; you'll be lucky to find anything here made after Amelia Earhart disappeared. The pieces are in fine condition, including some 19th-century apparel kept out of harm's way in the back, and there's usually a good pick of antique wedding dresses. ♦ Tu-Sa. 117 Yesler Way (at Occidental Ave S). 621.1728

10 Merchant's Cafe ★$ Originally a wooden drugstore occupied this spot, and upstairs was a gallery displaying work by E.M. Sammis, Seattle's first resident photographer. Then, in the late 1890s, it became a tavern where Klondike gold miners swilled five-cent beers or patronized the high-class brothel upstairs. More wild and uproarious tales and outright whoppers have been swapped in this joint than beer has been spilled on its wooden floors.

The city's oldest tavern, it is also one of its most democratic: down-and-outers occupy bar stools right next to newcomers, but somehow every discussion winds around to "the way Seattle used to be." There's often good live blues music in the evenings, and on summer days black-clad university students gather at sidewalk tables to smoke, eat burgers and other pub grub, and generally cool out. With its wonderful decorative glass and sputtering neon sign out front, this long-time establishment is a genuine spot of Seattle history and style. ♦ American ♦ Daily lunch and dinner. 109 Yesler Way (between Occidental and First Aves S). 624.1515

11 Cow Chip Cookies Only the very hungry or metabolically advantaged snackers will be able to tackle one of the gooey, mammoth munchies served at this chain outlet. Scientific researchers studying the effects of sugar overload are also welcome. ♦ M-Sa. 102 First Ave S (between S Washington St and Yesler Way). 292.9808 &

12 Greetings Trend Shop If you've been in the market for a salmon snout to strap over your nose, try this kooky shop. Other diverting kitsch includes wild-looking earrings, cups bearing *The Far Side* cartoons by Seattle native Gary Larson, and T-shirts with obnoxious messages. ♦ Daily. 106 First Ave S (between S Washington St and Yesler Way) 624.7713

13 Millstream This place takes it to the max in promoting the natural attributes of Seattle and the Pacific Northwest: There are walls of ferry and whale pictures, salmon sculptures, and a trickling fountain just to establish the proper peaceful mood. Even jaded natives have been known to fall under the shop's spell. ♦ Daily. 112 First Avenue S (between S Washington St and Yesler Way). 233.9719

13 Delmar Building (State Hotel) Pioneer Square preservationists managed to save some of the city's classic neon signs and painted billboards. One of the most endearing still hangs from the former **State Hotel,** an excellent brick-and-terra-cotta pile that went up in 1890 and was once a popular stop for gold-seekers coming back from Alaska and lumberers rolling into Seattle on a bender. "Rooms 75 Cents," it reads. Penny-pinchers will be disappointed to learn that the hotel went out of business in 1962. ♦ 114-116 First Ave S (between S Washington St and Yesler Way)

Within the Delmar Building:

New Orleans Creole Restaurant ★$ Internationally recognized jazz bands are generally showcased here on weekends, but this restaurant-cum-honky-tonk is hardly quiet during the remainder of the week. Monday nights feature Dixieland bands, Tuesday is Cajun night, and Wednesday is designated for contemporary jazz. Ragtime, zydeco, and R&B artists all make periodic showings. The food is good but not especially memorable. Gumbo and crawfish are distinctive picks, but the catfish can be oily. An adjoining dark-wood bar is the only place in town where mint juleps ("The South's revenge for losing the war," as one wit put it) are regularly featured on the drinks roster. ♦ Cajun/Creole ♦ Cover F-Sa. Daily lunch and dinner. 622.2563

14 Maynard Building One of the more sophisticated structures in the area, this building illustrates the wide range of possibilities within the Romanesque Revival style. Compared to the bombast of **Elmer Fisher's Pioneer Building,** this structure, designed in **Richardson** Romanesque style by **Albert Wickersham** in 1892, is a whisper of refined detail.

The exterior's handsome sandstone is from Bellingham Bay, to the north of Seattle, and the gray brick was shipped by rail from St. Louis. Window designs in the upper stories show an expressiveness similar to **Louis Sullivan's.** In the lobby, the frame of an elevator shaft flaunts a brilliant bouquet of cast iron, and the staircase shows exquisite wood detailing. For years, the building was a banking center; since its 1975 rehabilitation, however, it has been occupied by many different businesses. ♦ 117 First Ave S (between S Washington St and Yesler Way)

Within the Maynard Building:

Flora & Fauna Books Had Charles Darwin discovered this cloistered basement establishment, he might never have left. The packed stacks are filled with new, used, and rare natural history and life sciences books: approximately 25,000 titles in all. ♦ M-Sa. 121 First Ave S (between S Washington St and Yesler Way). 623.4727

Restaurants/Clubs: Red		**Hotels:** Blue
Shops/ Outdoors: Green		**Sights/Culture:** Black

19

Art by the Foot

Strolling through Pioneer Square is especially popular on the first Thursday of every month, when most of the area's art galleries, plus many specialty clothing stores and crafts shops, stay open late to show off their new displays. It's a chance to cover a lot of ground without the interference of business-people crowding the streets. Some art lovers miss the old days when galleries poured wine for "First Thursday" visitors, but at least there are enough restaurants and taverns here that you won't be without a place to sit beside friends and discuss the nuances of your evening's art grazing.

First Thursday's actual hours vary—they begin around 5:30PM and last until at least 8PM. Start at any gallery in Pioneer Square. There's no central number for First Thursday information, but contact one of the more prominent galleries, such as **Greg Kucera Gallery** (624.0770) or **Foster/White Gallery** (622.2833), if you have questions.

15 Colour Box This club specializes in alternative rock and industrial dance. Just the names of the groups appearing here (from Liquid American to Running with Scissors) are enough to draw you in. Before the shows, the bar runs beer specials the way some establishments have dinner specials. ♦ Cover. Daily 3PM-2AM. 113 First Ave S (between S Washington St and Yesler Way). 340.4101

16 Yesler Building During a flag-waving tour of the Northwest in 1891, President Benjamin Harrison speechified from the balcony of this small, granite-based structure, which stands where Henry Yesler once had a dance hall. Erected in 1890, this **Elmer Fisher** creation was damaged during the 1949 quake, and later repaired. It now houses private offices. ♦ 95 Yesler Way (at First Ave S)

16 WE Hats Remember trying on all the old hats boxed away in your grandparents' attic? You'll recapture that feeling here, where walls are adorned with wacky and delightful chapeaus for men and women, and salespeople don't care if you try on 68 different styles. Many of the works on sale are made in the shop upstairs. Special orders are accepted. ♦ Daily; F-Sa until midnight. 105 First Ave S (between S Washington St and Yesler Way). 623.3409

17 Yesler Way Arriving in Seattle in April 1852, pioneer Henry Yesler was enthusiastically embraced by the town's few inhabitants when he announced his desire to build a sawmill in what is now West Seattle. The enterprise was deemed too important to be located so far away, and Yesler was given this ribbon of property running from the waterfront up to his claim of 320 forested acres.

First called Mill Street, the strip of land eventually assumed the nickname Skid Road, for the skids used to transport the logs from Yesler's property to the sawmill. Then, in the early 20th century, it acquired another nickname: the Deadline, or simply the Line. "Bawdy houses and low theaters were expected to stay south of the Line," explains Murray Morgan in his history *Skid Road*. But the nickname Skid Road predominated. After World War II, when businesses all but abandoned Pioneer Square, the whole quarter came to be known as Skid Road. So did other down-at-heel urban areas throughout the country, although it was paraphrased into *skid row*. Today it's home to various commercial establishments. ♦ Between Alaskan Way and Interstate 5

18 Mutual Life Building Additions can often detract from an architect's vision, but in this case they seem to have enhanced the look of this grand box, which sits where Seattle's first "restaurant"—Henry Yesler's cookhouse—once did business. Most critics agree that the basement and first floor were designed by **Elmer Fisher** and finished around 1892. Upper stories, completed in 1897, are slightly contrasting creations from the partnership of **Robertson and Blackwell.** Another 30-foot hip was added to the west side in 1904, and a 1983 renovation cleaned up the old elevator cars, gave the exterior a swabbing of postmodern hues, and modernized the lobby. ♦ 605 First Ave (at Yesler Way)

Within the Mutual Life Building:

Flying Shuttle The front windows of this shop are filled with lots of handwoven clothing and offbeat jewelry—great for browsing from the sidewalk. Or tempt yourself further: Go in and try on some of the stylish pieces. ♦ Daily. 607 First Ave (between Yesler Way and Cherry St). 343.9762

Magic Mouse This must be where all stuffed animals pray they'll wind up, and hundreds of them do, especially teddy bears. The store's high-quality selection also includes wooden train sets, art supplies, children's books, and more than enough bathtub gizmos to occupy the kids. ♦ Daily. 603 First Ave (at Yesler Way). 682.8097

19 Trattoria Mitchelli ★★$$ Owner Dany Mitchell defies Seattle's reputation for rolling up its sidewalks before 10PM. Late-movie crowds, Pioneer Square's after-theater clientele, and a jolly assortment of famished insomniacs end up at this festive, noisy joint at all hours of the night. Crave a heaping plate of ravioli in butter and garlic at 2AM? A tasty Italian breakfast frittata at 3AM? Step this way, your table's waiting. Plentifully apportioned lunches and early dinners are also served, but people watching before "The Tonight Show" is less interesting. The service is often tardy, but who notices after midnight? ♦ Italian ♦ Daily breakfast, lunch, and dinner until 4AM. 84 Yesler Way (between First Ave S and Western Ave). 623.3885

20 Pioneer Square Hotel $$ The only hotel actually in Pioneer Square, this small, elegant property is a surprisingly good value. Built in 1914, the brick structure has been beautifully restored and offers 75 rooms and suites decorated with period reproductions. The location is convenient, too—within walking distance of all the sights of Pioneer Square. There's no restaurant, but a continental breakfast is included in the rate. ♦ 77 Yesler Way (between First Ave S and the Alaskan Way Viaduct). 340.1234; fax 467.0707

21 Al Boccalino ★★★$$ Gone is Luigi DeNunzio, the former co-owner and effervescent front man who, for so long, made it a pleasure just to walk through this restaurant's door (he walked out that same portal in 1992 to create **La Buca,** on Cherry Street). Chef Tim Roth continues, however, to use the robust recipes that DeNunzio brought over from his Italian hometown. The *gamberoni agli spinaci* (prawns with garlic and spinach) is especially tasty. Intimate rooms and brick walls make this the ideal setting for a romantic rendezvous. ♦ Italian ♦ M-F lunch and dinner; Sa-Su dinner. Reservations recommended. 1 Yesler Way (at the Alaskan Way Viaduct). 622.7688

22 OK Hotel Cafe/Gallery For a déclassé joint hutched away on the noisy back side of this block, in the dread shadow of the Alaskan Way viaduct, this place has scored a lot of good press (it was even featured in the 1992 movie *Singles*). Paintings by local artists were hung on the walls, and an adjoining gallery still features underground cartoons and the like. But what really made the cafe's rep were its live performances, which used to run the gamut from punk rock to avant-garde poetry, but are now mostly jazz and alternative music. The cafe offers a full menu and a bar. ♦ Cover; admission to gallery. Gallery: daily. Cafe: M-Th 7AM-midnight; F-Sa until 4AM; Su until 3AM. 212 Alaskan Way S (between S Main and S Washington Sts). 621.7903

23 J&M Cafe ★$ Pioneer Square's most popular saloon has the longest lines, and no amount of fast-talking will get you past the Gibraltar-sized door sentries. The hamburgers and nachos are worth every cent you fork out for them; but the beer selection is skimpy, and the ambient noise level inside almost requires you to use sign language to communicate. The cafe prospers on its hip rep and the fact that it does have one of the snazziest wooden bars this side of San Francisco. The building and tavern date back to 1900. ♦ American ♦ Daily lunch and dinner. 201 First Ave S (at S Washington St). 624.1670

24 Sound Winds/Air Arts Tiny and whimsical, this shop only *looks* like it sells kites. Actually, it specializes in a bright collection of wind socks and banners. ♦ Daily. 206 First Ave S (between S Main and S Washington Sts). 622.4386

25 Central Tavern and Cafe What kind of place would tout itself as "Seattle's only second-class tavern"? It's got to have a sense of humor, and this joint—dating back to 1889 and looking not quite every year of its age— definitely does. It also has live music seven nights a week starting at 9PM; mostly rock, blues, and R&B. ♦ Cover. Daily 11AM-2AM. 207 First Ave S (between S Main and S Washington Sts). 622.0209

25 Larry's Greenfront This is one of Seattle's best blues clubs, but claustrophobes beware! When one of the regular bands gets its riffs kicking on a Friday or Saturday night, your personal space is guaranteed to be violated— constantly. Table service is legendarily slow, but getting your own beer on a crowded band night is no easier. ♦ Cover. Daily 7AM-2AM. 209 First Ave S (between S Main and S Washington Sts). 624.7665

26 FireWorks Gallery Local artists get to show and sell at this popular shop. Playful bowls and lighthearted jewelry are the specialties, but there are also more serious pieces of furniture for sale. ♦ Daily. 210 First Ave S (between S Main and S Washington Sts). 682.8707. Also at: Westlake Center (at Fourth Ave and Pine St). 682.6462

King Street Station provided the final scene in a particularly bizarre double murder in 1906. The first casualty was one Franz Edmond Creffield, unabashed debaucher and leader of a pseudo-religious cult in Oregon (the Bride of Christ Church), whose followers—almost all women— made a practice of rolling on floors and baying at the moon. On 7 May 1906, during a visit to Seattle, Creffield was shot in the head on the corner of First Avenue and Cherry Street. The killer was George Mitchell, brother of one of Creffield's flock, Esther Mitchell. Shortly after her brother's release from jail, Esther said good-bye to him at the King Street Station. As George turned to leave, Esther drew a gun and executed him in the same way he had Creffield. She was committed to an insane asylum for three years.

27 Grand Central Arcade What a long, strange trip it's been for this site. In the 1870s arms magnate Phil Remington acquired it and several other nearby blocks on speculation. He was subsequently bought out by his entrepreneurial son-in-law, Watson C. Squire, who in 1879 opened the three-story **Squire's Opera House**—Seattle's first *real* theater—on the property. President Rutherford B. Hayes, visiting the West Coast in 1880 (which no sitting president had done before), was given a warm reception at the theater, but he had to shake some 2,000 hands before being released for the evening.

Two years later Squire remodeled the top two floors into the **Brunswick Hotel.** Of course, the Great Fire of 1889 burned it down (an estimated $9-million loss), but Squire was one of the first business leaders in town to announce his intentions to rebuild. In 1890 the new **Squire-Latimer Building** was completed on the same site. The facility supplied central heating and lighting to many other establishments in the district and reportedly made a profit doing so. Yet when the Alaskan Gold Rush took off in 1897, Squire again decided that a hotel would be even more of a moneymaker; he called the new venture the **Grand Central.**

Meanwhile, Squire had become a politician. When Seattle's anti-Chinese riots broke out in 1886, it was Washington Territorial *Governor* Squire who declared martial law. After Washington earned statehood in 1889, Squire was one of its first US senators. The hotel was ultimately less successful. It declined with the rest of the old city and, during the Depression, became a flophouse. Only after 1970, when the Pioneer Square National Historic District was founded, did the hotel again receive attention. It was one of the Square's first major restoration projects, and now bustles with two levels of mall shops. ♦ Daily. 214 First Ave S (at S Main St). 623.7417

Within the Grand Central Arcade:

David Ishii Bookseller Would that everyone in the world could adopt the laid-back demeanor of proprietor David Ishii. At just about any time of the business day, it seems, you can walk by his antiquarian bookstore and see him slouched in a chair, reading his own dusty merchandise. Ishii's two passions are fly fishing and baseball, so if you share his interests you're likely to find just the obscure volume you're seeking in this small, cluttered shop. Books about other subjects are stocked capriciously. ♦ Daily. First floor. 622.4719

Grand Central Baking Co The bakery situated on one side of **Grand Central**'s chandelier-festooned main foyer is famous for its rustic breads and cinnamon rolls; it also supplies the bread that's enjoyed in many of Seattle's best restaurants. Across the way, an affiliated deli does its best work with hearty soups and well-endowed salads (the sandwiches can be somewhat lackluster). Seating is available in the foyer. ♦ Daily. First floor. 622.3644

The Paper Cat On the lookout for greeting cards, comical postcards (yuppies take a clobbering), or rubber stamps? This is a good place to check out. Not all the merchandise follows the cat theme, but there's enough to give this shop "purrsonality." ♦ Daily. First floor. 623.3636

Megan Mary Olander Florist Fresh blooms abound, but it's even more interesting to see how many delicate and beautiful arrangements have been made of dried flowers. Lots of money could be spent here, but the sales staff is also very good at working within minuscule budgets. ♦ M-Sa. First floor. 623.6660

The Blacksmith Shop An ideal anachronism for an area steeped in history, this establishment rings all day long with the pounding of metal upon metal. Owner Mike Linn has been in this business for more than 20 years, designing and making custom furniture, candlesticks, hooks and brackets, and similar pieces. A sign out front, however, makes it clear that whatever else he does, this blacksmith "does not do horseshoes." Visitors can watch Linn work through a glass wall that separates his work area from the retail side of the shop. ♦ Tu-Sa. Basement. 623.4085

28 Ragazzi Upscale womenswear custom-made by Seattle designers beckons the clothes hound. ♦ Tu-Sa. 85 S Main St (between First Ave S and the Alaskan Way Viaduct). 682.6977

29 Bread of Life Mission Victorian in style, with projecting bays but flat fenestrated detailing, this building stands on the site of Seattle's first store, founded in 1852 by pioneer David "Doc" Swinton Maynard. The building is now one of several help centers for elderly and disadvantaged residents of the

Pioneer Square neighborhood. ♦ 301 First Ave S (at S Main St)

30 Earl D. Layman Street Clock Time doesn't stand still, and neither has this fine pedestal timepiece. It used to decorate the sidewalk at the corner of Fourth Avenue and Pike Street, in front of **Young's Credit Jewelers,** but it was moved in 1984 and dedicated to the city's first historic preservation officer (who held office from 1973 to 1982). ♦ First Ave S and S Main St

30 Elliott Bay Book Company Opened in 1973 in what used to be the **Globe Hotel** (and before that was the site of Seattle's first hospital), this is the city's second-largest bookstore; its name is known to bibliophiles across the country. (**University Bookstore,** off the tourist-beaten-path in the University District, is the largest.) The store enjoys a great deal of intellectual cachet, thanks in part to its very popular series of readings by well-known authors. It even publishes its own quarterly paper, *Book Notes,* full of staff reviews.

History, current affairs, cooking, poetry, fiction, and mystery—all are well represented here. Travel books have their very own level; works for children occupy a separate and substantial chamber. Staffers are knowledge-able and wonderfully responsive. If there's anything to quibble about, it's shortages in the architectural history and nature-lit departments. Author readings and/or signings are held several times a week, always at 7:30PM. The readings are free, but seats are limited. ♦ M-Sa until 11PM, Su until 6PM. 101 S Main St (at First Ave S). 624.6600

Inside the Elliott Bay Book Company:

Elliott Bay Cafe ★★$ Could anything be more civil than buying a new book and then trotting downstairs to read it in this brick-and-book-lined retreat? The food runs the gamut, from sandwiches to rather overpriced (or is it just undersized?) desserts; beer and wine are available, as are steaming cups of coffee, just the right brace for a dive into the latest Gore Vidal doorstop. ♦ American ♦ Daily breakfast, lunch, and dinner. 682.6664

31 Bowie & Company, Inc., Booksellers

The only way this shop could survive next door to **Elliott Bay Book Company** is by attracting a completely different audience; and that's what it does, with its shelves of first editions and cases of incunabula. Prices range from under $10 to several thousand dollars. Old maps and postcards are also available, as are mail-order catalogs. ♦ Daily. 314 First Ave S (between S Jackson and S Main Sts). 624.4100

31 Grand Central Mercantile If you're the kind of cook who loves a well-equipped kitchen, then plan to visit this store. Test your connoisseur's skill: Try to figure out the purposes of the many esoteric gadgets that line the walls. ♦ Daily. 316 First Ave S (between S Jackson and S Main Sts). 623.8894

32 The Wood Shop Keepers of this shop like to play with their own toys, which is always a good sign. At least one salesperson has been seen delighting young customers with a dog hand puppet. Shelves of teddy bears and other sturdy toys charm even adults. The goods come from around the world. Check out the Russian stacking dolls (painted like Boris Yeltsin, Mikhail Gorbachev, and other Soviet and Russian rulers) if they're still available. Daily. 320 First Ave S (between S Jackson and S Main Sts). 624.1763

33 Bud's Jazz Records Don't be afraid to open the metal gate and descend the narrow staircase from Jackson Street—there are a lot of ghosts down here (well, in a manner of speaking, anyway). Chicago émigré and jazz aficionado Bud Young has created what must be the largest selection of jazz CDs, tapes, and records this side of the Windy City, some 150,000 titles. Whole afternoons could be spent in the cavelike and cluttered atmo-sphere, flipping through racks of works by John Lee Hooker, Dizzy Gillespie, Stanley Turrentine, Robert Johnson, Lightnin' Hopkins, and an eclectic lineup of other musicians who created the basis of contem-porary jazz and blues. Music searches are accepted and jazz trivia questions are happily fielded by employees. ♦ Daily. 102 S Jackson St (at First Ave S). 628.0445

34 Northwest Gallery of Fine Woodworking For people who thrill to the feel of soft smooth wood, this place is heaven on earth. The gallery showcases local woodcraft in a simple, well-lighted, inviting space without hype or pressuring sales-people. Imagine how the elegant chairs, desks, dressers, and assorted boxes might look in your home—then steel yourself before looking at the price tags. ♦ Daily. 101 S Jackson St (at First Ave S). 625-0542

35 Pacific Marine Schwabacher Building An honest-to-goodness cornerstone of Seattle's development, this was the city's

23

original hardware store. The exquisite brick structure from 1905, by **Leonard L. Mendel** and English-born architect **Charles Bebb** (who later established a partnership with renowned Seattle designer **Carl Gould**), only punctuates the store's success and stature in the community. Notice especially the terra-cotta frieze around the front door, at the southwest corner of First Avenue S and S Jackson Street. Details like this used to be commonplace, decoration to dress up relatively plain-faced commercial buildings. ◆ 401 First Ave S (at S Jackson St)

36 Il Terrazo Carmine ★★★$$$ There's so much deliberate sophistication here you can cut it with a knife … if you aren't already using that particular utensil to slice off pieces of the marvelous venison medaillons. The veal *piccata* has a large number of local fans, and the savory ravioli is pretty good, too. Floor-to-ceiling drapes block out the sun and prying eyes, but on pleasant summer days, the patio out back is available (the nearby Alaskan Way Viaduct, however, often casts too much noise this way to allow for intimate conversation). ◆ Italian ◆ M-F lunch and dinner; Sa-Su dinner. Reservations recommended. 411 First Ave S (between S King and S Jackson Sts). 467.7797

37 A La Francaise One of the best French bakeries in town, this shop has an intimate atmosphere—despite its position on the edge of industrial Seattle—and loaves of French bread that may not make it home untasted. (A few small tables are available for those who can't wait.) ◆ Daily. 415 First Ave S (between S King and S Jackson Sts). 624.0322. Also at: 2609 NE University Village Mall (at 25th Ave NE and NE 45th St). 524.9300

38 Triangle Hotel Building C. Alfred **Breitung** was born in Austria and trained as an architect in Europe before he arrived in Seattle in 1900. Like many other young designers, **Breitung** was attracted to Puget Sound's turn-of-the-century prosperity and the reputations of such people as **Elmer Fisher.** His name is now familiar because of several large constructions in Seattle, including the **Good Shepherd Center** in Wallingford. This hotel was certainly one of his more unusual commissions. When it was completed in 1907 the building housed an eight-room hotel on the second floor, said to be the West Coast's smallest such hostelry. Today it is full of offices. ◆ 551 First Ave S (at Railroad Way S)

Early Indian names for the area we now call Seattle included the far less mellifluous *Duwamps* and *Mulckmukum.* And Pioneer Square was called *Djidjilaletch,* after the Duwamish Indian winter village once located there.

39 Kingdome Newcomers are overwhelmed by some of this stadium's statistics: It claims the largest single-span concrete roof on the planet (seven acres in size), with no posts to interfere with spectator viewing; the top of the dome is 250 feet from the floor; and the concrete used in its construction weighs some 105,600 tons. But such grandeur does not come without problems. In 1994 the stadium was closed for four months for repairs after a few tiles fell from the ceiling; all the tiles have since been removed.

Almost from the moment this round building opened in 1976, Seattleites have criticized it. "Ugly" is one of the nicer epithets used. Many liken it to a huge orange-juice squeezer. One newspaper columnist suggested that its roof should be painted beige, its exterior walls horizontally banded with green, cream, brown, and beige, and the city rent it to **McDonald's** as a huge advertisement for Big Macs. Many other residents wish the city would rip off the roof or replace it with something retractable, so that sunshine might fall on the **Seattle Mariners'** baseball games. (The city argues that a movable roof assembly is "cost-prohibitive.") The stadium's seating capacity varies depending upon the type of event: For **Seahawks'** football games, it seats 64,800 (seating plan pictured below); for **Mariners'** baseball games, 59,600; and for concerts, about 80,000. No matter what event is going on, the "Dome" creates traffic problems when cars spill from its huge parking lots onto the tree-lined streets of Pioneer Square. Tours of the 650-foot–diameter stadium take at least an hour (reservations aren't necessary; just call ahead for times and show up at Gate D). ◆ Tours: M-Sa mid-Apr–mid-Sept. S King St (at Second Ave S). 296.3663, tickets 296.3111

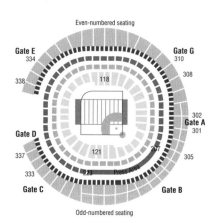

Even-numbered seating

Gate E 334
Gate G 310
338
118
308
302
Gate A 301
Gate D
337
121
305
333
Gate C
Gate B

Odd-numbered seating

40 F.X. McRory's Steak, Chop and Oyster House ★★$$ Talk about a split personality. On one hand, this spot wants to be a high-class establishment, serving grilled meats, succulent bivalves, and substantial dinner salads. On the other hand, it dearly loves being a party place, full of rambunctious college kids and young professionals who drop by after night games at the 'Dome. The latter identity better matches the food, which, while tasty, is not awe-inspiring. And don't wait for a table in the dining room. Eat in the atmospheric high-ceilinged bar, with its full-mirrored wall of liquor bottles and its Leroy Neiman art. There's a good selection of Northwest microbrews and an outdoor seating area for bright afternoons. ♦ American ♦ Daily lunch and dinner. 419 Occidental Ave S (at S King St). 623.4800

41 Great Winds Kite Shop It's like a bigger-than-life kaleidoscope here, with kites, wind socks, and kite-flying accoutrements available in almost as many brilliant colors as styles. ♦ Daily. 402 Occidental Ave S (at S Jackson St). 624.6886

42 Occidental Avenue At the turn of the century, railcars clanked and wobbled down Occidental Avenue, bound for Tacoma. Exclusive parlor cars for spendthrift passengers willing to shell out 85¢, rather than the regular fare of 60¢, brought up the rear. First Avenue (then known as Front Street) was Seattle's oldest thoroughfare, but aged photographs show commercial Occidental Avenue being just as busy during Pioneer Square's post-fire renaissance. Both streets eventually fell on hard times, but after the district earned national landmark status, Occidental Avenue's revitalization was a top priority. Cobblestones were retained, two blocks were closed to cars, and plane trees were planted from S Jackson Street to Yesler Way to lend the new mall, called **Occidental Park,** a leisurely Parisian boulevard atmosphere.Today, food and art vendors gather here on weekends, and starry-eyed couples are often seen strolling the stones, hand in hand. There's a handsome, old-fashioned shelter at the corner of Occidental Avenue S and S Main Street where you can hitch a ride on a streetcar running from the Waterfront up to the International District. And a shady plaza between S Main and S Washington Streets contains totem poles and a horse trough that can be converted to a drinking fountain simply by cupping your hand over it. Sadly, many tourists and even more Seattleites avoid this plaza, fearful of its ubiquitous panhandlers; and the street's northernmost block, between S Washington Street and Yesler Way, has never quite overcome the shabbiness of pre-1970 Pioneer Square. ♦ Occidental Ave S (between S Jackson St and Yesler Way)

Life on the Cutting Edge—Music in the Emerald City

Because Seattle is a relatively young city (nothing here is more than 110 years old), it is perhaps not surprising that avant-garde culture should flourish here. The music scene in particular has an edgy, bohemian feel to it. Although the city has a world-class symphony and a renowned opera company, the "grunge" sound—a blend of rock, heavy metal, and punk popularized by such hometown bands as Pearl Jam and Nirvana—was what put it in the national spotlight. The trend continues with the recent ascendancy of Soundgarden, The Presidents of the United States of America, Foo Fighters, and Alice in Chains; and dozens of clubs and nightspots around town feature up-and-coming local musicians and groups—some of whom have names that would make a sailor blush. But the ambience (which is often rather seedy and literally grungy as well as funky and hip) is as much a part of the overall club experience as the music. Two free publications offer updated listings on who's playing where: *The Rocket,* a biweekly, and *The Stranger,* a weekly. You must be 21 or older to enter most clubs; exceptions are listed in *The Stranger* under the heading "All Ages."

Among the top clubs in town are **Colour Box** (113 First Ave S (between S Washington St and Yesler Way, 340.4101), the **OK Hotel Cafe/Gallery** (212 Alaskan Way S between S Main and S Washington Sts, 621.7903), **Crocodile Cafe** (2200 Second Ave at Blanchard St, 441.5611), and **Lava Lounge** (2226 Second Ave between Blanchard and Bell Sts, 441.5660) for rock 'n' roll; **Dimitriou's Jazz Alley** (Sixth Ave and Lenora St, 441.9729) and **The Backstage** (2208 NW Market St at 22nd Ave NW, 781.2805, box office 789.1184) for jazz; and **Larry's Greenfront** (209 First Ave S between S Main and S Washington Sts, 624.7665) for blues.

43 Pacific Northwest Brewing Company
★$$ Seattle is a pub-lover's town, but this joint—with its shiny brass beer tanks and high ambient noise levels—is not the norm. It's a sleek and upscale place; not surprisingly, it was created by a New Yorker. Bratwurst steamed in ale, fish cakes, and a spicy gumbo are the choice dishes. Crowds are biggest at lunch and after **Kingdome** events. ◆ American ◆ Daily lunch and dinner. 322 Occidental Ave S (at S Jackson St). 621.7002

43 Torrefazione Italia ★$ Quiet, filled with cozy small tables and books on Italian art, and serving potent coffee in colorful earthenware cups, this is one of the most pleasant places in town to wait for a friend. ◆ Coffeehouse ◆ Daily. 320 Occidental Ave S (between S Jackson and S Main Sts). 624.5773

44 Davidson Galleries A changing selection of works by local and international artists is on display, along with a special collection of 19th-and early 20th-century American paintings. ◆ Daily June-Aug; M-Sa Sept-May. 313 Occidental Ave S (between S Jackson and S Main Sts). 624.7684

44 Foster/White Gallery Established Northwest talents, such as Morris Graves and Mark Tobey, are represented here. Some Pilchuck glasswork is also on display. ◆ Daily. 311½ Occidental Ave S (between S Jackson and S Main Sts). 622.2833

45 The Sunday Funnies What looks like a children's store is really for adults who love comics and want cups decorated with Garfield and T-shirts that bear the nostalgic likeness of Popeye. Most of the material is Disney-inspired. ◆ Daily. 312 Occidental Ave S (between S Jackson and S Main Sts). 621.8265

46 Klondike Gold Rush National Historical Park On 17 July 1897 the steamship *Portland* arrived almost empty in Seattle. But after word spread that it was carrying two tons of gold found in Alaska, a full complement of passengers signed up for the return voyage—prospective gold miners who thought they could make a profit from Alaska's biggest gold rush, and prospective gold diggers—women "of questionable virtue" who knew they could mine the pockets of any men who actually struck it rich.This gold rush couldn't have come at a more propitious time for Seattle. Like the rest of the nation, the town was still trying to overcome the hard times that followed the infamous Panic of 1893, so it took full advantage of its position as a principal embarkation point for prospectors (or sourdoughs, as they were called then). Hotels sprang up almost overnight to accommodate the thousands of men funneling through Puget Sound on their way north, and a number of mining schools

also opened. Local outfitters, capitalizing on a Canadian law that required gold seekers to bring along a year's worth of goods, grew rich from the hundreds of dollars each would-be miner had to spend on the provisions. The chamber of commerce even hired Erastus Brainerd, a hucksterish former editor of the *Seattle Post-Intelligencer,* to cement commercial links between this city and the Klondike. Magazines such as *Frank Leslie's Popular Monthly* bought right into Brainerd's game. "The eyes of the civilized world today are turned upon two points—namely the gold fields of Alaska and the City of Seattle," the magazine wrote. A government assay office was established on Seattle's Ninth Avenue in 1898. During its first four years of business, its scales weighed more than $174 million in gold.The **Klondike Gold Rush National Historical Park** is a highfalutin name for what is really a colorful storefront museum (the *real* park is actually divided between Alaska and the Yukon). Through old photographs, walking tours of Pioneer Square, and films, the museum does basically what Erastus Brainerd did so well a century ago: It proves that Seattle was indeed "the gateway to the Klondike." ◆ Free. Daily. 117 S Main St (between Occidental Ave S and First Ave S). 553.7220

47 Waterfall Garden Filled with crashing waterfalls and benches perfect for lunch breaks, this corner plot is a soothing escape from the business world. Yet its very existence is rooted in business, specifically the United Parcel Service. UPS grew from a packaging and delivery enterprise that opened in a basement under this spot in 1907. The company's principal founder, James Emmett Casey, was a Nevada boy who delivered his first parcel on behalf of a Seattle department store in 1899. ◆ Second Ave S and S Main St

48 Washington Court Building What historian Bill Speidel called "the most glorious and sumptuously furnished palace of sin in the city" once operated from this unpretentious, four-story brick Victorian. The madam was Lou Graham, a strong-willed businesswoman who took this site in about 1888, rebuilt it after the Great Fire, and for another dozen years entertained well-to-do gents and their scions. So successful was her business, writes historian Paul Dorpat, that "Graham and her ladies … helped keep the city solvent through the hard times of the mid-1890s." The building is now rented mostly by lawyers. ◆ 221 S Washington St (at Third Ave S)

49 Comedy Underground Nationally known standup comics, as well as local Seinfeld- and Roseanne-wannabes, show up at this joint tucked below **Swannies** bar and restaurant. Monday and Tuesday are "open-mike" nights for amateurs, and the pros entertain Wednesday through Saturday. ♦ Cover. Shows M-Th 8PM; F-Sa 8PM, 11PM. Reservations recommended. 222 S Main St (between Third and Second Aves S). 622.0209

50 Cafe Huê ★★$ Created by a Vietnamese husband-and-wife team, this cafe (whose name is pronounced *way*) serves cuisine that reflects that country's colonial past. Vietnamese dishes display definite French touches, such as escargots seasoned with ginger. And the spring rolls and soups are not to be missed (try the filling crab soup). Chef Kieutuy Nguyen was trained in Saigon by a French baker, so it's no wonder that desserts here (including the wonderful Parisian éclairs, amandines, and traditional napoleons) are so plentiful and rich. Everything is presented with artistry. Service is fast and efficient, and there's no high-turnover mentality here. Despite its proximity to the **Kingdome,** this spot doesn't usually suffer from overcrowding on game nights. ♦ Vietnamese/French ♦ M-Sa lunch and dinner; Su dinner. 312 Second Ave S (between S Jackson and S Main Sts). 625.9833

51 King Street Station Still operating as a railroad depot, this Neo-Classical station was built in 1906 for James J. Hill's **Great Northern Railroad.** In 1910, 62 passenger trains pulled up on the tracks adjacent to this depot every day, disgorging 3,500 passengers. Now, only a handful of **Amtrak** trains arrive here daily. Minnesota architects **Reed and Stem,** who designed the building, created New York City's Grand Central Station in 1913. The brick exterior has hardly changed since day one, but the interior has been sadly modernized. Notice the clock tower; it was modeled after the Piazza San Marco campanile in Venice, Italy. ♦ Third Ave S and S Jackson St

International District

52 Union Station In 1911 Eastern railroad scion Edward Henry Harriman opened this barrel-vaulted stopping point for his **Union Pacific Railroad** above the tidelands of Jackson Street. The last passenger train pulled away from here 60 years later. Ever since, the depot (designed by San Francisco architect **D.J. Patterson**) has been used for antiques shows and a range of catered events. In the 1970s a proposal was made to revitalize it as a "multiuse transportation center," but that didn't fly any better than a later idea to integrate it into a new City Hall complex. The southernmost entry to Seattle's downtown bus tunnel is located next door. ♦ Fourth Ave S and S Jackson St. 622.3214

53 Chau's Chinese Restaurant ★$ The standard Cantonese dishes are okay, but this place really earns its nickel in its seafood. Try the steamed oysters in garlic sauce or the Dungeness crab, and don't be shy about ordering Seattle's favorite bivalve, geoduck (but pronounce it *goo*-ee-duck if you don't want to advertise your tourist status). It's not available everywhere you go, nor is it always so well prepared as it is here. ♦ Cantonese ♦ M-F lunch and dinner; Sa-Su dinner. 310 Fourth Ave S (between S Jackson and S Main Sts). 621.0006

54 Nippon Kan Theater A reminder of Seattle's historic Japantown, opened in 1909 as the **Astor Hotel** and later a performance hall for Kabuki theater, this redbrick building

Hing Hay Park, International District

was renovated in 1981 and is now best known for its Japanese Performing Arts Series, which runs from October through May. ♦ Box office daily. 628 S Washington St (between Kobe Terrace Park and Sixth Ave S). 467.6807

55 Maneki Restaurant ★★$$ It looks rather shabby outside, notched into the ground floor of what used to be the **Northern Pacific Hotel** (built for rail passengers in 1914 by Seattle architect **John Graham Sr.** who later designed downtown's stately **Dexter Horton Building**), but this edifice boasts what may well be Seattle's first sushi bar. The selections are fresh and tasty. ♦ Japanese ♦ Tu-Su dinner. 304 Sixth Ave S (at S Main St). 622.2631

56 Danny Woo International District Community Garden On one side, facing south, these one-and-a-half acres provide an excellent panorama of the old south end, from **Smith Tower** past **Union Station.** On the opposite side, however, at the top of the slope, Interstate 5 charges by in a smelly roar. Luckily, it's possible at most points in this garden to enjoy the former without enduring the latter. Established in 1975 and expanded five years later, the site contains about 120 individual growing areas, each managed by a resident of Chinatown. But passersby are invited to climb the garden's graveled paths, sniff the fragrance of the many fruit trees, and admire a giant stone lantern at the hilltop, given to Seattle by the Japanese city of Kobe during the 1976 US bicentennial. Benches are available for afternoon reading. A few transients hang about, but they're less obtrusive than in Pioneer Square. ♦ Above Sixth Ave S and S Main St

57 Wing Luke Museum Wing Luke was Seattle's first Chinese-American city council representative, elected in 1962, and the first Asian-American elected to public office in the continental United States. He died in a plane crash in 1965, but his interest in meshing the Asian-American experience into Northwest history lives on in this small cultural center, which is full of old photographs, antiques, and Chinese artifacts. ♦ Admission; free Thursday. Tu-Su; Th until 7PM. 407 Seventh Ave S (between S King and S Jackson Sts). 623.5124

58 Linyen ★★$$ The lemon chicken draws much of the clientele to this efficient, well-windowed location in the heart of Chinatown. And the specials, which may include clams in black-bean sauce, pot stickers, and spicy chicken entrées, are likewise delicious. The regular Cantonese menu, however, is not nearly so enthralling. ♦ Chinese ♦ Daily lunch and dinner. Reservations recommended. 424 Seventh Ave S (at S King St). 622.8181

59 Sea Garden ★★★$ In a town jam-packed with great seafood restaurants, this place stands out. The dining room itself is nothing fancy, but the subtly flavored, mildly spiced Cantonese food is wonderful, and the prices reasonable. Top choices include crab with ginger and green onions, clams with black-bean sauce, and braised black cod. ♦ Chinese ♦ Daily lunch and dinner. 509 Seventh Ave S (between S King and S Weller Sts). 623.2100 ♿

60 Phnom Penh Noodle House ★$ It takes some thought to really appreciate this restaurant, since its menu boils down to seven variations of rice-noodle soup. But each bowl has distinctive characteristics that appeal especially to the local Cambodian population, some of whom will almost certainly be waiting in line for a table along with you. ♦ Cambodian ♦ Daily lunch and dinner. 414 Maynard Ave S (between S King and S Jackson Sts). 682.5690

61 Han II ★★$ There's nothing like barbecued meats prepared tableside, and this upscale Korean restaurant puts on a good show for the eyes as well as the palate. Try the short ribs, arranged in a sizzling heap in the middle of your table, or the spicy octopus—the portions are generous. Chicken, pork, and beef are served with a side of pungent *kimchi* (pickled cabbage), a couple of tempura prawns, salad, and rice. ♦ Korean ♦ Daily lunch and dinner. Reservations recommended. 409 Maynard Ave S (between S King and S Jackson Sts). 587.0464

62 Hing Hay Park With its trees and maybe a little rare sunshine, this little park is one of the nicest places to relax in the I.D. The colorful, traditional Chinese pavilion is a gift from the people of Taipei, Taiwan, and the huge dragon mural that decorated the back of the old **Bush Hotel** was designed by John Woo. ♦ Maynard Ave S and S King St

63 Uwajimaya Here is a big, efficient, clean supermarket, where you can even buy live fish that's ready to be sliced and served as sushi. This store (illustrated above) may be the largest Japanese emporium on the West Coast; it's certainly the hub of Seattle's Japanese community. Founded in 1928 by Fujimatsu Moriguchi, the business moved into this huge location in 1970 but is still owned by the Moriguchi family. It's a great cultural experience, even if you don't purchase any of the innumerable fresh vegetables, porcelain pieces, or appliances on sale. Most of the

---

Restaurants/Clubs: Red   Hotels: Blue
Shops/♣ Outdoors: Green   Sights/Culture: Black

second floor is occupied by a branch of **Kinokuniya Books** (587.2477), Japan's second-largest book chain. ♦ Daily until 8PM. 519 Sixth Ave S (between S Weller and S King Sts). 624.6248

64 Adams/Freedman Building Elaborate facades, with cast-stone canopies at the entrances and an intriguing hierarchical arrangement of windows, make this one of the neighborhood's more elegant structures. Raised in 1910 as a hotel, it's been rehabbed with apartments and commercial space. ♦ 515 Maynard Ave S (between S Weller and S King Sts)

Within the Adams/Freedman Building:

Choy Herbs A native of Hong Kong, Kai Chiu Choy has been in this country since 1974, dispensing herbal medicine in a state where such a specialty is neither generally recognized by physicians nor licensed. Choy's diagnoses include taking a patient's pulse, looking at his or her tongue, and carefully examining the face and eyes for signs of internal disorders. (The eyes, it seems, are more than windows on the soul; according to Choy, they reveal kidney or liver problems.) ♦ M-Sa 2PM-5PM. 624.8341

65 Honey Court Seafood Restaurant ★$$ Octogenarian Luk Sing Hing used a term of endearment for her late husband as the name for this much-written-about restaurant. Surely he would have approved of the 160-plus menu items here. Cantonese and Hong Kong styles are integrated to produce inexpensive curries of chicken or beef with rice, as well as the favored plates of barbecued pork over vermicelli with scallions and slivered ginger. ♦ Chinese ♦ Daily lunch and dinner. 516 Maynard Ave S (between S Weller and S King Sts). 292.8828

66 International District Children's Park If your offspring need a break from touring the city, give them some time out at this quiet corner with its long curving slide and a bronze dragon sculpture designed by Seattle artist George Tsutakawa. ♦ Seventh Ave S and S Lane St

During the Great Fire of 1889, Judge C.H. Hanford, conducting a murder trial at Pioneer Square's old courthouse while flames were spreading in the nearby streets, refused to adjourn and release his jury, which was about to be sequestered. Only when smoke finally billowed through his courtroom windows and a witness on the stand became too flustered to answer questions did Judge Hanford let the jurors flee—those, at least, whom he didn't press into service to save the courthouse from being destroyed.

Bests

Mindy Cameron
Editorial Page Editor, *Seattle Times*

Take a walk around **Green Lake,** centerpiece of Seattle's busiest park in the city. Any time of day, any weather, enjoy the ambience provided by an always eclectic collection of Seattleites of all ages—walking, jogging, cycling, skating, in-line skating, pushing baby strollers. Plenty of nearby spots for coffee, bagels, pizza, ice cream, breakfast, lunch, or dinner.

Shop for fresh flowers and fresh fish at **Pike Place Market.** Get a barbecued-pork humbow for lunch and stroll the market, **Post Alley,** and **First Avenue** for the Seattle most loved by tourists and locals alike.

University Village is a mall with a difference—fresh air. Inviting plaza surrounded by unusual mix of chain stores—**Eddie Bauer, Gap, Barnes & Noble**— and local shops. Check out **Pasta and Co.** for gourmet food items, **Viva's** for casual Northwestern women's apparel.

Best late-evening ambience is a glass of Port at the elegant, all-wood, in-the-round lobby of **Sorrento Hotel,** on **Madison Street** in the hospital district.

Salvatore Ristorante Italiano, just north of the **University District,** is classic Seattle neighborhood dining. Regulars keep coming back for friendly atmosphere, superb Italian food.

Bud Young
Owner, Bud's Jazz Records

Pioneer Square Area—Preserved turn-of-the-century downtown—nightlife, art galleries, bookstores.

Pike Place Market—Farmer's Market—seafood—craftspeople—street performers (big stretches, for four to five blocks).

Waterfall Park—A manmade waterfall with sculptures—a wonderful escape from the hustle and bustle in only a quarter block.

Waiting for the Interurban in **Fremont** neighborhood—outdoor sculpture, well loved by neighbors.

The Troll—A monstrous, whimsical ogre that is really amusing in a surprising site—Fremont.

Walker Rock Garden—A 30-year project in a middle-class home that is a spectacular array of structures. Private but available by appointment.

The Music Scene—Symphony, ballet, opera, *jazz,* blues, chamber music, choral.

Theater—About nine Equity theaters.

Clouds—Come to Seattle to see the beautiful cloud cover—fascinating. (Who wants to see monotonous blue skies?)

Bud's Jazz Records—Extraordinary inventory of jazz in all its forms.

Business District

"Downtown" Seattle is a geographical ambiguity. Technically, the center of town is at University Street and Fourth Avenue. But the city's true heart is split between **Pike Place Market** and **Pioneer Square.** What lies between the two sites is a high-tide area bounded on the south by **Yesler Way,** on the north by **Virginia Street**, on the west by **Second Avenue,** and on the east by **Interstate 5.** Seattle's financial, shopping, and entertainment operations moved here after the Great Fire of 1889 destroyed the original city center. Downtown's post-fire move north can be tracked through the age and character of its architecture. The area first developed along Second Avenue, dropping enough banks in its wake to create the closest thing Seattle had to a real financial district. A building boom during World War I brought many of the magnificent terra-cotta structures that still stand on Second and **Third Avenues** (for more about these buildings, see "Terra-cotta Town" on page 74). After development of the boxy, modern **Seattle–First National Bank Tower** (now called **1001 Fourth Avenue Plaza**) in 1969, a great fence of high-rises ascended north along **Fourth Avenue,** and the area declared itself Seattle's new financial district.

Walt Crowley, a local TV commentator and longtime civic activist, pointed out some years ago that Seattle "is really a confederacy of neighborhoods. People don't identify so much with downtown as they do with the specific area in which they live. In Portland, Oregon, downtown is everybody's neighborhood. But in Seattle, everybody's neighborhood is their downtown."

Seattleites venture downtown to work, of course. And they come here to shop for special presents and to show out-of-town visitors the sights. But efforts to keep the business core thriving 24 hours a day by transforming old hotels or commercial buildings into condominiums have seen only limited success.

Explore the central Business District on a weekday, when street musicians perform, espresso carts steam, and people watching is at its best. Weekend activities gravitate to the Waterfront and Pioneer Square, with some spillover into **Westlake Center,** while "downtown" goes into siesta mode until Monday morning.

1 Old Public Safety Building Young Seattle took a long time to erect a City Hall to match its optimism and ambition. (For that matter, the city still lacks such a centerpiece, tolerating instead that glass-walled Kennedy-era monstrosity on Fourth Avenue known as the **Municipal Building.**) But in the early days of the 20th century, local burghers hired architect **Clayton Wilson** to erect a new administration building on this triangular block. Comparisons with New York City's Flatiron Building are inevitable, but **Wilson** did more than just copy it. His five-story structure with a penthouse, faced with brick and sandstone and boasting a curved copper roofline, was properly formal without being pretentious. City government moved in immediately, but only seven years later it had to relocate again to larger digs in the **King County Courthouse** on Third Avenue. **Wilson**'s structure subsequently housed a hospital, a jail, and a police station. Still later, after abuse as a parking garage and as an unofficial sanctuary for the homeless, it was converted back into office space. ♦ 400 Yesler Way (at Fourth Ave)

2 City Hall Park Seattle's **City Hall** stood on this tiny treed triangle until 1909. When that was leveled, Mayor George Dilling established this historic but now rather seedy site as the city's first downtown park, originally known as **Court House Park.** The surrounding area was the site of the "Battle of Seattle," an 1856 skirmish during the Indian War in which the frigate *Decatur* peppered the area east of Third Avenue with cannonfire to root out some natives who were hiding there. This conflict was the culmination of years of tension between white settlers and the Klickitat, Muckleshoot, and Nisqually people who were here originally. Cannonballs from this episode have been uncovered in the park as recently as 1995. ♦ Jefferson St and Yesler Way

3 King County Courthouse From the 1890s until 1916 the county's center of legal activity was several blocks east of this intersection at Third Avenue and James Street. Where **Harborview Hospital** now perches atop its bluff, an old "cruel castle" of a courthouse then loomed, its imposing pillared mass lifting to a dome visible from all over town. The current courthouse was designed by

A. Warren Gould, another of early Seattle's prolific designers. His concept broke away from the old notion of a monumental temple of justice, calling instead for a 22-story, H-shaped skyscraper with a pyramid-topped tower in the center. Only six stories were erected initially, with another five added in 1930 under the direction of **Henry Bittman** and **John L. McCauley.** The planned tower and additional floors were never built. ♦ Third Ave and James St

4 521 Cafe ★$ At lunchtime on weekdays, this spot looks like an annex to the **King County Courthouse** across the street. Judges, lawyers, cops, and more than a few quavering defendants are the core clientele, supplemented by other city employees and a few down-on-their-luck types looking decidedly uncomfortable amidst all the designer suits. Burgers (best with grilled onions) are the signature fare at this home-cooking joint. But sometimes it's a hard choice between the burgers and the meat-loaf special. The milk shakes are sublime. Try to grab one of the two tables in the windows up front—they're the best spots for people watching. ♦ American ♦ M-F breakfast and lunch. 521 Third Ave (between Jefferson and James Sts). 623.2233 ♿

5 Ruby Montana's Pinto Pony Who would have thought that the kitschware of the 1950s and 1960s would someday become so chic? Lava lamps, pink flamingos, ant farms, and Elvis can all be found here. The array of retro-cultural effluvia salvaged from the Jazz Age to the Information Age is amazing. Just across the street, the **Pinto Pony II** (602 Second Ave between James and Cherry Sts, 621.9426) features vintage furniture. ♦ Daily. 603 Second Ave (between James and Cherry Sts). 621.7669

6 Greg Kucera Gallery It's a small space, but this gallery has a big reputation. Exhibits range from the works of nationally known artists—photographs by William Wegman, paintings by Jennifer Bartlett or Terry Winters, prints by Motherwell or Frankenthaler, sculpture by Deborah Butterfield—to the work of such local artists as Alden Mason. The exhibits are always thought-provoking, and sometimes controversial. ♦ Tu-Su. 608 Second Ave (between James and Cherry Sts). 624.0770

7 Alaska Building Opened in 1904, this 14-story structure (designed by the St. Louis firm of **Eames & Young**) was the first in Seattle to employ steel-frame construction. That technology, developed in Chicago office towers as early as the 1880s, allowed exterior masonry to be ornamental rather than strictly load-bearing. Thus, buildings could be made bigger and taller without becoming as heavy as the Romanesque piles of Pioneer Square. The penthouse here was once home to the

Alaska Club, a social circle for Last Frontier emigrants, many of whom came south after the 1897 gold rush. Today the building houses municipal offices. ♦ 618 Second Ave (between James and Cherry Sts)

8 Bakeman's Restaurant ★$ Tucked beneath the historic **Hoge Building,** famous for a pride of lion heads along its cornice, is a no-frills lunchtime fave among office workers. Sandwiches (especially the turkey and meat loaf varieties) are thick enough to defy easy gripping (or biting), and the soups are renowned. ♦ American ♦ Restaurant: M-F breakfast and lunch; bar: M-F until 7:30PM. No credit cards accepted. 122 Cherry St (between Second and First Aves). 622.3375 ♿

9 Cherry Street Parking Garage While it isn't usually on the city tour, this arch-windowed structure was showman John Cort's **Grand Opera House,** the "finest theater in the city" when it opened in 1900. Where cars now puff and park, Seattleites used to gather along two huge balconies to take in turn-of-the-century culture. (Note what looks like the vestige of a grand entrance.) ♦ Third Ave and Cherry St

10 Arctic Building The tusks of the 25 terracotta walrus heads (see the illustration on page 75) that stud the handsome facade here are not the same ones that garnered public attention in 1917, when the prestigious old Arctic Club first opened this classically decorated building. It seems the original tusks were removed during the 1950s, owing to public fear that they'd break off and spear passing pedestrians. Not until the early 1980s, when a loving restoration of this **A. Warren Gould** edifice took place, did the walruses get their tusks back, this time cast of a special epoxy. Unfortunately, the life-size polar bear that formerly crowned the building's Third Avenue entrance was not replaced. Inside, the restored **Dome Room,** a gold-leafed space once used as a restaurant for club members and now rented for special events, is worth a peek. ♦ 700 Third Ave (at Cherry St)

11 Chamber of Commerce Building An Italian Romanesque basilica notched into the contemporary downtown area? Leave it to the local chamber of commerce to plumb ostentatious associations. This 1924 design was allegedly inspired by a trip to Europe that the principal architect, **Harlan Thomas,** took to view 12th-century Lombardy churches. The chamber moved out of its faux cathedral years ago and the structure is now occupied in large part by the architectural group **TRA,** which rehabilitated the building in 1970 and is the direct descendant of **Schack, Young & Myers,** the firm that assisted **Thomas** in the structure's conception. A sculptural frieze called *Primitive & Modern Industries* by Morgan Padelford extends to the left side of the main entrance and refers to aspects of

Northwest history. ♦ 219 Columbia St (between Third and Second Aves)

12 McCormick's Fish House and Bar
★★$$ Decorated with lots of polished wood, brass, and greenery, this restaurant tends to attract an older, conservative, and loyal clientele. Younger drop-ins usually come from City Hall or one of the other government beehives nearby and wind up in the convivial bar. The offerings are pretty reliable and the quality consistent—the menu features simple preparations of seafood, with selections changed daily. Service is almost always efficient. ♦ Seafood ♦ M-F lunch and dinner; Sa-Su dinner. Reservations recommended. 722 Fourth Ave (at Columbia St). 682.3900

13 Columbia Seafirst Center
Seattleites love to hate this 76-story cloud-ripper that is so out of scale with the rest of downtown. You can't help but notice this exclamation point of steel and glass; built in 1985, it's the tallest building in town. **Chester L. Lindsey Architects** achieved an unusual vertical and monumental sense by sheathing the center in black glass; a lighter face would have revealed individual floor levels and thus perceptually diminished the building. Alternating concave and convex exterior surfaces, as well as the skyscraper's stairstepped arrangement, create more complex light patterns than would be possible on a straight-sided tower. Forget the lower-level shopping floors, which are a bit dingy. An observation deck on the 73rd floor, however, provides a broad panorama of the city and is in many ways superior to the **Space Needle**—it's higher and more private, its view is better, and its admission charge is much less. ♦ Fee to observation deck. Observation deck: M-F. Columbia St (between Fifth and Fourth Aves). 386.5151

COURTESY OF CHESTER L. LINDSAY ARCHITECTS

14 First United Methodist Church
Interstate 5 severed this church from First Hill, to the east, the neighborhood it had served for most

of this century. Now it sta[...] handsomely domed anac[...] field of central city skyscr[...] **James Schack** and **Danie[...]** latter served as city archit... ...many years), this 1907 building combines Roman and Palladian Renaissance qualities, a departure from the Gothic cathedral designs then so popular in America. In addition to its usual religious activities, the church also occasionally serves as a lecture hall. ♦ 811 Fifth Ave (between Columbia and Marion Sts). 626.7278

15 Rainier Club
Architect **Kirtland Cutter** is not as well known here as in his adopted hometown of Spokane, Washington (where he designed, for instance, the eclectic old Davenport Hotel). Yet this building, opened in 1904, is indeed one of the most startling and handsome juxtapositions to the skyscrapers of Seattle's central business district. **Cutter** modeled this males-only club after English men's clubs, with rustic brickwork and curvilinear gables drawn from Jacobean, or late English Renaissance, style. (A separate guest entrance for women was tucked away on the Marion Street facade.) In 1929 the prestigious partnership of **Charles Bebb** and **Carl Gould** added 54 feet to the south end of the building, all in character with the original design. The club was created as a haven for the city's meritocracy, a place for them to gather and chat over cigars and brandy. Today it's still private, though the membership is no longer restricted to men. From the outside, little has changed: Many Seattleites don't even know what goes on inside these brick walls, for there's no sign outside announcing the building's use. ♦ 810 Fourth Ave (between Columbia and Marion Sts)

16 Metropolitan Grill
★★★$$$ Proving that not all Seattleites are worried about their fat and cholesterol intakes, this restaurant turns out thick mesquite-grilled steaks accompanied by baked potatoes or pasta. The clam chowder makes a good starter, and the burgers and onion rings are tasty, too. An adjacent big-windowed bar is comfortable until 5PM, when financial district habitués start streaming in. "The Met" is popular with Japanese businesspeople, who can request a special translated menu. ♦ American ♦ M-F lunch and dinner; Sa-Su dinner. Reservations recommended. 818 Second Ave (at Marion St). 624.3287 &

Restaurants/Clubs: Red   Hotels: Blue

Shops/ ♀ Outdoors: Green   Sights/Culture: Black

right Lights, Small City: Seattle's Theater Scene

Seattle has always been known for its lively and often provocative artistic community. Originally called *New York Alki* (meaning "New York By-and-By" in the Chinook language), the city offers theater that is as vibrant, interesting, and multifaceted (if not more so) than that of its former namesake. Productions range from revivals of classic Chekhov and Shakespeare, recent Broadway hits on tour, and cabarets, to new works by up-and-coming local playwrights and avant-garde shows. And the settings are equally variant: plush modern theaters, dimly lit church basements, funky warehouse spaces, a former bathhouse—even a laundromat. In any given week, there's bound to be something worth checking out.

Several mainstream theaters are clustered inside the **Seattle Center** (bounded by Fifth and First Aves N, and Denny Way and Mercer St). Among the best are the **Bagley Wright Theater** (443.2222), home of the renowned **Seattle Repertory Theatre,** nicknamed "The Rep"; the **Intiman Playhouse** (626.0782), where the troupe of the same name performs; and the **Charlotte Martin Theater** (441.3322), which hosts productions by the popular **Seattle Children's Theatre (SCT).**

In the downtown area are two beautifully restored showpieces: the **Paramount** (901 Pine St at Ninth Ave, 682.1414), designed in 1929 by **B. Marcus Priteca;** and the **Fifth Avenue Theatre** (1326 Fifth Ave between University and Union Sts, 625.1900), a former vaudeville house whose interior resembles the imperial throne room in the Forbidden City. Both of these venues host touring productions of blockbuster shows such as *Phantom of the Opera* and *Sunset Boulevard.*

New works—some of which are rather daring and experimental—are featured at **A Contemporary Theatre (ACT),** which recently moved from **Queen Anne** to the **Eagles Auditorium** (1416 Seventh Ave between Union and Pike Sts, 285.5110) in the **Business District.** Other adventurous local theaters include the **Bathhouse Theatre** (7312 W Green Lake Dr N between N 76th St and Aurora Ave N, Greenlake, 524.9108), which specializes in innovative updates of classic works (such as a 1950s rock 'n' roll version of *A Midsummer Night's Dream*); and the **Empty Space Theatre** (N 35th St and Fremont Ave N, Fremont, 547.7500), which puts on new works (a recent production was *A Perfect Ganesh* by Terence McNally). Productions with a multicultural theme are presented at the **Group Theatre** (441.1299) at the **Seattle Center** and the

Northwest Asian American Theater (409 Seventh Ave between S King and S Jackson Sts, 340-1445) in the **International District.**

And theatergoers who really want to take a walk on the wild side should check out Seattle's abundant "fringe" theater, featuring offbeat and colorful offerings. Although some productions are less successful than others, there's something for every taste, and ticket prices are much lower than at mainstream venues. Every March, the **League of Fringe Theaters (LOFT,** 325-5446), a coalition of small troupes, puts on the very popular **Fringe Theater Festival,** a 10-day event during which avant-garde productions are held at several different venues on **Capitol Hill.**

The grande dame of fringe is the **New City Theater** (1634 11th Ave at E Olive St, 323.6800) on Capitol Hill, whose specialty is performances of daring new works by nationally known playwrights such as Caryl Churchill and Sam Shepard. The **Annex** (728.0933) puts on musicals by local playwrights; and **Greek Active** (516.4125) features campy takes on classic plays (recent examples include *Mourning Becomes Electra* and Gore Vidal's *The Best Man*).

Named for Gertrude Stein's lover, **Alice B. Arts** (322.5423) bills itself as "a gay and lesbian performing arts organization for all people"; the group presents theater, music, comedy, and dance programs at various locations all over the city. Recent productions include *Jeffrey,* a gay adaptation of *Hamlet,* and *Alice Unchained: High Art and Cheap Acts.* **AHA!** (2222 Second Ave between Blanchard and Bell Sts, 728.1375) puts on continuing episodes of the ingeniously named satire *Star Drek: The Musical;* and the **Velvet Elvis Art Lounge Theater** (107 Occidental Ave S between S Washington St and Yesler Way, 624.8477) in **Pioneer Square** performs wacky original works and small touring productions. And undoubtedly the most unusual place to see a show is the tiny theater in the back of the **Sit 'n' Spin** laundromat (2219 Fourth Ave between Blanchard and Bell Sts, 441.9484 &), where you can see a wide variety of material (alcohol is served here, so you must be 21 or over to enter).

Inexpensive (or even half-price) tickets at Seattle's major venues are often available on the day of the performance; check with **Ticket/Ticket** (324.2744; cash only) and **TicketMaster** (628.0888). Smaller and fringe theaters feature low-cost previews, rush tickets, senior discounts, and pay-what-you-can performances.

17 1001 Fourth Avenue Plaza When this modernist bronze monolith (pictured at right) was completed in 1969, professional journals hailed it as among the most technologically advanced buildings of its time. **Don Winkelmann,** a partner in the **NBBJ Group** who was responsible for the design, rhapsodized for the *Seattle Times:* "You see a jet move across the horizon above this building and [the] two are compatible. It all fits with rockets to the moon." Many Seattleites took a dimmer view of the 50-story corporate headquarters for Seattle–First National Bank. One popular derisive comment was that the building was the box that the **Space Needle** came in. Others criticized it as a dark birthmark on the predominantly white terra-cotta hand of Seattle, and they didn't like the fact that it so overwhelmed the beloved **Smith Tower,** which is only 42 stories tall. But time has quieted the cavil, as did a 1986 revitalization that added small shops and a glass-enclosed **Wintergarden,** making the building more people-friendly. English sculptor Henry Moore's bronze *Three-Piece Sculpture: Vertebrae* is the most prominent feature of the plaza. ♦ 1001 Fourth Ave (at Madison St)

18 Seattle Public Library This plain-visaged International Style building from 1959 replaced one of the most imposing of the 10 libraries in the Seattle area paid for by iron-and-steel-magnate Andrew Carnegie. (Only one other of the bunch faced the wrecking ball; eight more are still scattered in various neighborhoods, from Auburn to Fremont and Ballard.) The city's earliest library collection was housed in Henry Yesler's mansion at Third Avenue and James Street (now the site of the **King County Courthouse**); but when that burned down in 1901, taking 25,000 volumes with it, the editor of the *Seattle Post-Intelligencer* convinced Carnegie to build the city a *real* book repository. The answer to that wish opened in 1906, a big muscle of gray Tenino sandstone columns and giant arched windows, designed by Chicago architect **P.J. Weber,** that might have pleased even Emperor Nero. Cramping and construction problems finally doomed the Carnegie building. There's also a rooftop cafe, but it's usually noisy and the view of Puget Sound is blocked by other buildings. ♦ M-Th 9AM-9PM, F-Sa 9AM-6PM,

Su 1-5PM Sept-May; M-Sa June-Aug. 1000 Fourth Ave (at Madison St). 386.4636.

19 Madison Renaissance Hotel $$$ Despite its proximity to the Interstate 5 gully, this property (formerly the **Stouffer Madison**) manages to project a sense of quiet. Maybe it's the regal color scheme, or the muted lighting, or the marble and rich wood that decorates the 554 guest rooms. Perhaps it's the peaceful views from both sides (Elliott Bay on the west, the Cascade Mountains on the east). Luxury addicts can book rooms on the **Club Floors** (25th and 26th), which offer special check-in services, a complimentary continental breakfast, and even a library. A 40-foot-long rooftop pool and Jacuzzi will work out the jet-lag kinks. Indoor parking (for a fee) and free in-town transportation are also available. And there's a soothing piano bar right off the lobby. ♦ 515 Madison St (at Sixth Ave). 583.0300; 800/468.3571; fax 622.8635 ♿

Within the Madison Renaissance Hotel:

Prego ★★★$$$ With views of the bay and the mountains from its 28th-floor location, this is a choice romantic spot and one of the city's better restaurants. It's known for its combinations of Northern Italian dishes and seafood. Try the black linguine with sautéed Maine lobster, shrimp, and scallops. ♦ Italian ♦ M-F lunch and dinner; Sa-Su dinner. 583.0300 ♿

20 Hotel Vintage Park $$$ Well-known San Francisco hotelier Bill Kimpton has given the formerly disheveled **Kennedy Hotel** a refurbished lobby, some elegant furnishings, and a too-quaint-for-words Washington wine theme (the 129 guest rooms are named in honor of wineries and vineyards throughout the state). It's all part of Kimpton's usual "discount luxury" package. Rooms are decorated in splashy textiles but subtle colors, and if they offer some unnecessary accoutrements (direct-dial phones in the bathroom?), their general comfort, as well as the hotel's convenience to downtown, is undeniable.

As at other Kimpton properties on the West Coast, complimentary local wines are poured each afternoon in the fireplaced lobby. Ask for a room on a high floor or on Spring Street, as Fifth Avenue is a funnel for rush-hour traffic. On-site parking and 24-hour room service are available. ♦ 1100 Fifth Ave (at Spring St). 624.8000, 800/624.4433; fax 623.0568 ♿

Within the Hotel Vintage Park:

Tulio Ristorante ★★★$$ In the midst of high-rise downtown, patrons here enjoy the pleasant conviviality of an Italian

neighborhood gathering spot. The ambience suggests a Mediterranean villa, with cream-colored walls, wood paneling, and white tablecloths. Tables are set out on the sidewalk in warm weather. Chef Walter Pisano directs a kitchen staff which cures its own meats, makes its own bread and pasta, and even stretches its own mozzarella. The smoked-salmon ravioli is a delicate mating of Northwest and Mediterranean cuisines, but many regulars favor the roasted chicken stuffed with caramelized garlic and sage, and served with a lemon risotto. ♦ Italian ♦ Daily breakfast, lunch, and dinner. 624.5500 ♿

21 Pacific Plaza Hotel $ An older property (built in 1929, refurbished in 1989), this is a pleasant surprise in the middle of "Big-Bucks Hotel Land." The 159 rooms aren't luxurious, and they're often too small for families, but the hotel's central location (only five blocks from **Westlake Center**) is real hard to beat at the price. The rate includes a complimentary continental breakfast. The hotel's restaurant also serves lunch and dinner. ♦ 400 Spring St (at Fourth Ave). 623.3900, 800/426.1165; fax 623.2059

22 Holiday Inn Crowne Plaza $$$ What it lacks in architectural character, this 415-room hotel tries to compensate for in its services. Upper-level rooms, dressed up in appealing reddish hues, have access to a special lounge and their own concierge, and receive free newspapers. Guests staying on some of the lower floors, unfortunately, find less distinctive accommodations. There's a cafe that serves breakfast, lunch, and dinner. The lobby is comfortable and the staff helpful, but in a downtown full of historic establishments, this hotel just isn't all that interesting. ♦ Sixth Ave and Seneca St. 464.1980, 800/521.2762; fax 340.1617

23 Freeway Park How better to defy noisy freeway canyons than to cover them with something as peaceful as this five-acre park? Developed in 1976 under the direction of Lawrence Halprin, this $13.8-million greensward on a large overpass atop Interstate 5 features small ponds, flower beds, an engagingly irregular array of stairs leading from level to level, and a concrete abstraction of a waterfall that audibly separates the park from its hectic surroundings. Relax with a good book and imagine the blood pressures escalating on the freeway below you. ♦ Sixth Ave and Seneca St

24 Financial Center The designer of this 1972 rough-concrete tower, with its appealing, punch-cardlike fenestration, was **Don Winkelmann**—the same man who did the dark **1001 Fourth Avenue Plaza** building three years before. In the 1970s the architect was sometimes called "Mr. Fourth Avenue" because of the towers he was lining up along that thoroughfare. Despite his influence on the

Seattle cityscape, **Winkelmann** appreciated the city's old architecture as much as he did his own. So taken was he with the nearby **Seattle Tower**, for instance, that he insisted his new financial center not block any of its views. His solution, unfortunately, was to lay down a fairly lifeless plaza to one side of the center. ♦ 1215 Fourth Ave (between Seneca and University Sts)

25 Seattle Tower Being surrounded by more contemporary skyscrapers only enhances the nobility of this 26-story Art Deco tower (pictured at right), completed in 1929. Faced with earth- and rock-colored gradations of brickwork—darker at the bottom, becoming lighter as the building ascends—the tower was intended to remind viewers of Northwest mountains. Principal designer **Joseph Wilson** tapered the structure upwards to emphasize its verticality and made the most of setbacks to bring light to a maximum of offices. At one time, those setbacks were filled with more than 200 floodlights, which simulated an aurora borealis across the building face. The Third Avenue lobby continues the mountain theme, achieving a cavernlike ambience with its dark marble walls and gilt ceiling. Look for such interior details as Indian headdresses, stylized evergreens, and abstract Chinese characters. ♦ 1218 Third Ave (between Seneca and University Sts)

M. BLUM

26 1201 Third Ave For a while, this tapered, 55-story eye-grabber (formerly known as the **Washington Mutual Tower**) was wildly popular in Seattle. The much-ballyhooed New York firm of **Kohn Pedersen Fox** had bundled it up with historical references: a cruciform floor plan, for instance, harking back to Greek cross churches of the Renaissance, and a stepped-back profile that reminded critics of the Empire State Building. No one seemed to care that it barely related to the surrounding architecture and presented nothing better than a cliff face at sidewalk level. With an exterior of pink Brazilian granite, its playful pyramidal top (inspiring jokes about this being Seattle's largest pencil), and a lobby resplendent in mahogany, the 1988 structure seemed a significant and relieving departure from decades of almost featureless glass boxes. ♦ 1201 Third Ave (between Seneca and University Sts)

27 Brooklyn Cafe and Oyster Bar Lounge
★$$$ When land was being cleared to erect **1201 Third Ave,** this splendidly refitted brick building that houses this dining spot somehow survived the wrecking ball. The interior finishings are quite handsome—lots of wood and shiny metal, plenty of big booths, and chic cafe tables surrounded by stools. But the menu—given to steaks and seafood— isn't innovative or consistent enough to make a special trip here. Appetizers tend to be too small, too expensive, or both, and service can be slow. ♦ Steak/Seafood ♦ M-F lunch and dinner; Sa-Su dinner. Reservations recommended. Valet parking. 1212 Second Ave (between Seneca and University Sts). 224.7000

28 Cobb Building This august imposition of brick and terra-cotta, completed in 1910, is the last survivor of a once-grand midtown scheme. In 1861 Seattle pioneers Arthur and Mary Denny and Charles and Mary Terry dedicated this corner, along with the surrounding 10-acre knoll (all of which were on the outskirts of town at that time), as the site of a territorial university. Thirty years later, school regents determined that their original clapboard-and-cupola institution was no longer sufficient, and moved the burgeoning **University of Washington** to its present site at the north end of Lake Union. The city then proposed to develop this knoll as a park. But **UW** had other ideas: Regents signed a 50-year agreement with the Metro-politan Building Company to improve the acreage for commercial use.

The New York architectural firm of **Howells & Stokes** was engaged, and a comprehensive program was developed to raise uniform, 11-story facades along both sides of Fourth Avenue, with a central plaza and residential apartments on Fifth Avenue. Both this building and the **White-Henry-Stuart Building,** on an opposite corner of Fourth Avenue and University Street, were completed before the plan began to unravel. Later neighboring structures, such as the **Olympic Hotel** (now the **Four Seasons Olympic Hotel**) and the **Skinner Building,** were compatible with the architectural plan but deviated from its uniformity. In the 1960s a contrasting design scheme took control of the tract, and the **White-Henry-Stuart Building** was razed to make room for the popsicle-ish **Rainier Tower** (see below). But the **Cobb** (believed to have been the first medical-dental office

building on the West Coast) remains, and it is still very impressive. Note the Beaux Arts– inspired ornamentation, particularly the Indian heads attributed to sculptor Victor G. Schneider. ♦ 1305 Fourth Ave (between University and Union Sts)

29 Seattle Pendleton If consumption of woolen goods has tapered off over the past 20 years owing to the increased use of synthetic materials, it has only made Oregon's Pendleton Woolen Mills more determined to promote its durable line of jackets, sweaters, scarves, and accessories beyond the Beaver State. Hard as it is to believe, this entire business evolved from the lowly Pendleton blanket, first crafted in eastern Oregon by Thomas Kay, an Englishman who'd studied in the textile mills of Philadelphia and came out west in 1863 to "borrow" native blanket designs for his own products. ♦ M-Sa. 1313 Fourth Ave (between University and Union Sts). 682.4430. Also at: Bellevue Square Mall (NE Eighth St, between Bellevue Way NE and 100th Ave NE), Bellevue. 453.9040

30 Rainier Tower First-time visitors are often caught staring up at this striking white high-rise, alternately wondering how it balances on its 12-story pedestal and whether it might topple down upon them. Not to worry. The principal designer, **Minoru Yamasaki,** knew what he was doing. Born in Seattle, the architect presented his hometown not only with this building, but another landmark: the

Rainier Tower

Pacific Science Center complex at **Seattle Center.** His reputation spread beyond Puget Sound, and he designed the Century Plaza Towers in Los Angeles, the World Trade Center in New York, and corporate offices worldwide. In all his work, **Yamasaki** once said, he strove to offer "delight, serenity, and surprise." He certainly succeeded here in this upside-down pencil of a skyscraper, locally known as the "beaver building" because it looks as if a beaver had chewed it. Two levels of shops, collectively known as **Rainier Square,** anchor the pedestal. ◆ 1200 Fourth Ave (between University and Union Sts) ⑤

Within Rainier Square at Rainier Tower:

Biagio Pricey but excellent leather accessories for the status-conscious shopper can be found at this emporium, where the smells alone are worth a stop. ◆ M-Sa. Lower level. 223.0469 ⑤

Crepe De Paris For an evening of musical comedy, book a table at this cozy cabaret, which puts on six to eight shows a year, from humorous productions like *Waiter, There's a Fly in my Latte* to Gershwin reviews. ◆ Cover. Shows Th-Sa 8PM. Reservations required. Second level. 623.4111

FOUR SEASONS OLYMPIC
Seattle

31 Four Seasons Olympic Hotel $$$$
Seattle newspapers printed special photo sections touting this hotel's virtues when it opened in 1924. Men and women showed up in fancy cars and fancier dress, anxious to celebrate their city's newfound sophistication. The hotel's designers—**George B. Post, Carl Gould,** and **Charles Bebb**—had created an Italian palazzo, with a base of rusticated stone, a terra-cotta face, and such details as Roman arches and dentils. It was a landmark by which Seattle could judge its general prosperity.

After half a century, though, the declining hotel only narrowly escaped demolition. Sale to the Four Seasons chain and a 1982 rehabilitation by **NBBJ** brought grandeur back to both the interior and the exterior. Public rooms, including the cavernous lobby, now showcase lots of marble, thick carpeting, comfortable armchairs, and giant potted plants. A balcony around the lobby features some delightful historical photos of the hotel. The 450 guest rooms are somewhat less ostentatious, but they're still large and attractively appointed with 1920s reproduction furniture. Valet parking, 24-hour room service, and complimentary shoe shines all add to that pampered feeling.

Laura Ashley has a stylish outpost inside the hotel, peddling its demure line of dresses, blouses, nighties, and signature-print home decorations. **Shuckers,** a clubby oyster bar on the Fourth Avenue side, is excellent for winding down after work. The refurbishment added the large-windowed **Garden Court,** above the University Street entrance, where you can enjoy a light lunch or high tea, or dance to swing bands on carefree weekend evenings. ◆ 411 University St (between Fifth and Fourth Aves). 621.1700, 800/223.8772; fax 682.9633 ⑤

Within the Four Seasons Olympic Hotel:

The Georgian Room ★★★★$$$$ With its chandeliers and tall windows, this restaurant looks like a ballroom in a French manor house. Into this classically elegant space chef Kerry Sear has introduced an unexpected menu catering to diners who are health-conscious yet still want sophisticated presentation. Originally an artist, he often draws his meals before preparing them in the kitchen. There is, for example, a dazzling five-course vegetarian chef's menu which *Bon Appetit* has called "brilliant." Popular entrées include a baked vegetable stew with a mixture of rice sausage and mustard sauce, and green bean fritters with red onion cream and parsnip chips. While Sear is a vegetarian, diners can also find plenty of fresh seafood, fowl, and meat dishes here as well. For about $20 extra, the sommelier will select wines that complement each course, adding to the delights of your meal. ◆ Continental/ Vegetarian ◆ M-Sa dinner; Su breakfast and dinner. Reservations recommended. 621.7889 ⑤

32 Skinner Building What does this blocklong, tile-roofed Mediterranean palazzo from 1926 have to do with the monumental Old Faithful Inn in Yellowstone National Park and the Canyon Hotel at the Grand Canyon? They were all designed by **Robert C. Reamer.** Born in Ohio in 1873, **Reamer** started with an architectural firm in Detroit and moved from there to Cleveland, Chicago, San Diego, and Wyoming. He came to Seattle during World War I to become chief architect for the Metropolitan Building Company. Considered at one time to be a supreme practitioner of his art—a Richardsonian in his architectural aesthetics and a romantic by inclination—**Reamer** has all but disappeared from Seattle history books. Yet his buildings (this structure, the **Meany Tower Hotel** in the University District, the **Seattle Times Building** on John Street, and the **1411 Fourth Avenue Building** downtown) are some of the most intriguing around. ◆ 1326 Fifth Ave (between University and Union Sts)

Within the Skinner Building:

Fifth Avenue Theater The **Skinner's** Wilkeson sandstone exterior hides Seattle's loveliest performance space, said to be patterned after the imperial throne room in Beijing's Forbidden City. Gustav Liljestrom, a Norwegian artist trained in China, was responsible for the interior of this former vaudeville house, which features a coiled dragon painted on the ceiling. The theater was restored in 1980 and now hosts touring Broadway shows. Don't miss a chance to venture inside. ◆ Box office M-F. 625.1900

33 Fox's Gem Shop This is a sophisticated and refined environment that's all glittering stones, a finely tailored clientele, and steep prices. There's lots of sterling silver jewelry and a boutique selection of Tiffany products. ◆ M-Sa. 1341 Fifth Ave (between University and Union Sts). 623.2528

34 Eddie Bauer, Inc. Eddie Bauer was born to Russian immigrant parents on Orcas Island, northwest of Seattle, in 1900. Always enchanted with fishing and hunting, it seemed natural that he would move into sporting-goods sales for a career and be wildly successful at it. He finally opened his own store in Seattle in 1922, attracting customers with his demanding policies about quality and his interest in improving what was already on the market. It was the latter that led him to invent the down jacket.

While fishing on Washington's Olympic Peninsula in 1934, Bauer almost froze to death because he didn't bring along an appropriate jacket. He started thinking about how to make both warmer and lighter outerwear and remembered a tale his uncle had told about surviving the Russo-Japanese War of 1904 by wearing goose-down quilted undergarments. Bauer took some of the down he was already importing from China for use in flyties and shuttlecocks, quilted a few jackets for himself, and when friends declared them a hit, patented both the jackets and their manufacturing process. There are now about 200 stores across the country that bear his name.

Although it's now owned by **Spiegel Inc.,** the company still sells the well-known goose-down fashions, as well as sleeping bags, backpacking equipment, knives, sunglasses, and some of the coziest wool socks available anywhere. The store is known for offering hefty price reductions on the Bauer line. ◆ Daily; F until 8PM. Fifth Ave and Union St. 622.2766 ⅃

35 Seattle Hilton $$$ It's rather confusing that this hotel's lobby sits on the ninth floor rather than at ground level (to make way for a parking garage). But that may be the only unusual thing in this cookie-cutter member of the Hilton chain. Furnishings are tasteful, but hardly memorable, and color schemes in the 237 rooms are benign, reflecting the aesthetics of a 1980s redo. A view restaurant, the **Top of the Hilton,** specializes in local seafood and attracts a mostly business clientele to its lounge. (As with most view restaurants, the prices are as high as the elevation.) Very convenient for conventioneers, an underground passage even connects the hotel to the **Washington State Convention & Trade Center, Rainier Square,** and the **Fifth Avenue Theatre.** ◆ 1301 Sixth Ave (at University St). 624.0500, 800/542.7700; fax 682.9029

36 Kreilsheimer Place/Eagles Auditorium When completed in 1925, architect **Henry Bittman's** Renaissance Revival–style home for the Fraternal Order of Eagles was among the country's most distinguished fraternal buildings. The block, a fine example of Seattle's ornate terra-cotta facades, is the new home of **A Contemporary Theatre** (see plan below), which recently moved here from Lower Queen Anne. This Equity theater company puts on a wide variety of 20th-century works. Their annual holiday performances of *A Christmas Carol* are popular. The season runs from May through December. ◆ Box office: daily noon to 6PM. 700 Union St (at Seventh Ave). 285.5110. A Contemporary Theatre

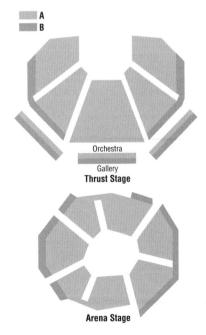

A
B

Orchestra

Gallery
Thrust Stage

Arena Stage

37 Washington State Convention & Trade Center Too chunky, gray, and cold to be appealing, this 370,000-square-foot convention center can at least accommodate the sort of large-scale get-togethers that Seattle couldn't easily host before. Reception rooms are designed for groups numbering 50 to 4,000 people. Indoor parking is available for some 900 cars. There's a **Visitors' Center** on the galleria level that provides the usual tourist information. ♦ Visitors' Center M-F. 800 Convention Place (at Eighth Ave and Pike St). Convention Center 447.5000, Visitors' Center 461.5840

38 Seattle Sheraton Hotel and Towers $$$$ This modern hotel is a convenient retreat for businesspeople attending events at the **Washington State Convention & Trade Center,** just up Pike Street from here. An expansive lobby is decorated with Dale Chihuly glass art. Meeting rooms are plentiful. Most of the 840 guest rooms are cramped by comparison, lacking all but the most essential components. Four VIP floors (31-34) offer more elaborate rooms and a separate concierge. A health club and pool on the 35th floor are open to all guests. **Banners,** a casual, well-lighted restaurant off the lobby, offers a sumptuous buffet luncheon; there's also the outstanding **Fuller's** (see below). **Gooey's** (named, they say, after that bizarre long-necked mollusk, the geoduck) is a rather small disco with a decent bar. Parking is available for a fee. ♦ 1400 Sixth Ave (at Union St). 621.9000, 800/325.3535; fax 621.8441 ♿

Within the Seattle Sheraton Hotel and Towers:

Fuller's ★★★★$$$ Named for Dr. Richard Fuller, founder of the **Seattle Art Museum,** this restaurant is a showplace for some of the city's best cuisine *and* best contemporary art (paintings by Morris Graves and Mark Tobey, and glasswork by Dale Chihuly). Chef Monique Barbeau pairs Northwest ingredients with Asian-inspired reductions and marinades, eschewing fat-laden cream and butter sauces; the results are light and flavorful. Consider for starters the sautéed salmon on cornmeal pancakes with a tomato jam, or a salad of wilted spinach and smoked duck in a honey-sesame dressing. Similarly inspired entrées include a caramelized, pan-seared cod served with jasmine rice and greens. Barbeau was named Best Chef of the Pacific Northwest in the 1994 James Beard Awards. ♦ Northwestern ♦ M-F lunch and dinner; Sa dinner. Reservations recommended. 447.5544 ♿

39 Butch Blum Sophisticated, high-fashion men's clothing by classically influenced, contemporary European and American designers (such as Donna Karan, Ermenegildo Zegna, and Calvin Klein) is the specialty of this upscale boutique. The service is warm, personal, and attentive without being

intrusive. ♦ M-Sa or by appointment. 1408 Fifth Ave (at Union St). 622.5760; fax 622.6664

40 US Bank Centre Although it's a hefty hunk of California glitz and post-Postmodernist doodads staked into downtown Seattle, this building (formerly the **Pacific First Centre**) draws Seattleites with its nationally known retailers in **City Center.** The smaller shops here are also worth a browse. ♦ 1420 Fifth Ave (between Union and Pike Sts) ♿

Within the US Bank Centre:

Ann Taylor In the same way that **Brooks Brothers** purveys timeless fashions for men, so this fine chain courts the women's trade. It's conservative and expensive, but reliable. ♦ Daily. First floor. 623.4818 ♿

Design Concern With high-design office supplies and tableware, Japanese clocks, and a broad selection of obscure gadgets, this is a great place to browse and shop for gifts. ♦ Daily. Second floor. 623.4444 ♿

Boxer Bay When you weren't looking, men's Skivvies became fashion statements, and here is one store that makes the most of that trend. In addition to silk drawers and Hugh Hefneresque lounge attire, the store also sells comfy cotton robes and, somewhat incongruously, ties. ♦ Daily. Second floor. 625.9418 ♿

Palomino ★★★$$ Leave your jeans and T-shirts in the closet. Like owner Rich Komen's other restaurants (**Cutter's Bayhouse** in **Pike Place Market, Triples** on Lake Union, and **Palisade** in Magnolia), this gleaming, highly stylized spot draws a beautiful crowd of designer-suited gents and women in fancy dresses. Dale Chihuly glassworks sparkle under the directional lights. The unwalled kitchen and open oven produce excellent king salmon, garlic chicken, and pork loin. Pizzas are thin-crusted and, alas, also thinly covered. The bar fills up quickly with an after-work crowd, but the people watching is even better here than in the dining area. There's a decent selection of microbrews on tap; have the knowledgeable bartenders help you try some new varieties. ♦ Mediterranean ♦ M-Sa lunch and dinner; Su dinner. Reservations recommended. Third floor. 623.1300 &

41 Brooks Brothers "BB" has had to make some changes in the last few years to maintain its commercial position, but this corner store (the clothier's only outpost north of San Francisco) doesn't seem to have lost a smidgen of traditional demeanor. A wealth of inventory, including some elegant women-swear, is presented in a refined manner; the salespeople are helpful but not intrusive, and the guys working the men's suits department might have learned their manners from valets to the Duke of Windsor. It's worth waiting until June and right after Christmas for the annual sales. ♦ M-Sa. 1401 Fourth Ave (at Union St). 624.4400

42 1411 Fourth Avenue Building Textural details spun from Celtic motifs and Art Deco flourishes enliven the facade and lobby of this **Robert C. Reamer** office tower which opened in 1929. The stone facing represented a move away from the brick and terra-cotta that were so common to other structures in the neighborhood. Note the elegant entrance sign created by Lloyd Lovegren (who went on during the 1940s to design the Lacey V. Morrow Bridge across Lake Washington). ♦ Between Union and Pike Sts &

Within the 1411 Fourth Avenue Building:

JoAnn's Cookies A must-try here are the chocolate-chip dippers: great disks made all the more dangerous to weight-conscious adults by their half-coatings of chocolate. The bagels here, made fresh daily, are another sure-fire hit. ♦ M-F from 6:30AM. 623.8853 &

43 Fourth and Pike Building Designed by the architectural firm of **Lawton and Moldenhour,** this 1926 skyscraper of cream-colored terra-cotta was one of the last commercial high-rises built before the Great Depression brought downtown construction to a screeching halt. The impressive lobby here somehow survived relatively intact, while other downtown buildings were having theirs regretfully "modernized." ♦ 1424 Fourth Ave (at Pike St)

Within the Fourth and Pike Building:

Dashasa Studio Jeweler Daniel Shames has a fondness for intensely colored opaque stones, and he crafts them into gorgeous pendants and rings. Pieces are hand-assembled to order; the prices are high (starting from $500), but considering the labor involved, not unreasonably so. ♦ Daily by appointment only. Suite 807. 623.0519

Dance legends Mark Morris, Merce Cunningham, and Robert Joffrey all lived and worked in Seattle, as did the famous stripper Gypsy Rose Lee.

Seattle Pen

Seattle Pen This intimate shop sells only writing instruments—new models and exquisitely kept older specimens. Repairs and engravings are available, too. ♦ M-F; Sa until 3PM. Suite 527. 682.2640

44 Sharper Image Across from the **Westlake Center** in the **Century Square Building** is a browser's delight and a gadgeteer's dream. This catalog-come-to-life is full of high-tech sound equipment, full-body massage tables, adult toys, and fancy watches. ♦ Daily. 1501 Fourth Ave (at Pike St). 343.9125

45 Banana Republic This used to be the **Coliseum Theater,** an Italian Renaissance relic. The first theater in the world designed specifically to show motion pictures, it was commissioned by Joe Gottstein, an ambitious 23-year-old Seattle native who believed people would flock to the movies if they could enjoy them amidst some class and comfort. So in 1916 **B. Marcus Priteca,** personal architect to vaudeville magnate Alexander Pantages, took on the assignment of creating an opulent film palace. The resulting 1,700-seat theater, with its terra-cotta facade detailed with grotesque masks, festoons of fruit, and bullock's heads, was a huge success. But later in its life the venue fell on hard times, languishing in virtual disuse. In 1994, the theater was purchased and faithfully renovated by **Banana Republic,** and it has reopened as the flagship store of this international chain. The shop occupies the entire lower level, including the former lobby, and guided tours of the restored theater upstairs are offered. ♦ Daily. 1506 Fifth Ave (at Pike St). 622.2303

46 Nordstrom The department-store chain may have spread nationwide, but Seattleites still consider this locally owned store very much theirs and the Nordy's label a symbol of cachet. The store is famous for its generous customer service policy. This is one place where returns are no big deal—in fact, unscrupulous people reportedly return things that they didn't even buy here and the merchandise is accepted without complaint. Salespeople are attentive without being cloying, and they're knowledgeable about current fashion trends. A personal-shopper service accommodates people who haven't the time or the inclination to browse through all the racks themselves. Valet parking is also available.

Because **Nordstrom** was originally a shoe store, the footwear department here is one of its largest. Women's clothes take up several floors and a series of departments, each with a character (and often age bracket) of its own. Men enjoy a large casuals section, a broad selection of ties, and suits for any occasion. Gifts and some gourmet foods can be found in the **Boardwalk** department. Several annual sales are much anticipated: the store's anniversary (July), and the two semiannual sales for women (June and November) and men (June and January). In 1998, the shop plans to move one block east, to the elegant 1919 building that once housed the **Frederick & Nelson** department store. The six-story landmark (on Pine St between Sixth and Fifth Aves) will contain a 300,000-square-foot shop, as well as **Nordstrom**'s corporate headquarters. ♦ Daily. Fifth Ave and Pine St. 628.2111

47 Meridien West and Meridien East The newest addition to the Business District is this super-glitzy megamall that occupies an entire square block. Some Seattleites think it's a sign that the city has come of age, while others see it as an ostentatious harbinger of Seattle's imminent decline. The complex, comprised of the 65,000-square-foot **Meridien West** and the 96,000-square-foot **Meridien East** across the way, boasts mostly chain shops and restaurants, including **Niketown** (447.6453), **Planet Hollywood** (287.0001), and **The Original Levi's Store** (467.5152). Future additions (set to open at press time) include the **Wolfgang Puck Cafe,** an informal pizzeria run by the eponymous LA chef; **Sega Gameworks,** featuring high-tech, interactive, and virtual reality entertainment; and **Cineplex Odeon,** with 16 screens and seating for 3,200 people. ♦ Daily. Bounded by Seventh and Sixth Aves and Pike and Pine Sts

48 WestCoast Roosevelt Hotel $$ When this 20-floor hotel (then the tallest in town) originally threw open its doors in 1930, the *Seattle Daily Times* could hardly contain its enthusiasm. The building's entryway received particular attention: "The ornately furnished lobby was virtually a tower of flowers as guests and well-wishers trooped into it last evening. Visitors were given the freedom of the house and were enabled to inspect the lounge, decorated in French Moderne style and furnished in highly polished ebony and hardwood, and saunter up a winding staircase past the orchestra balcony to the mezzanine." Unfortunately, that lobby—with its strip skylight and several levels—was lost during a 1987 renovation. The present low-ceilinged space, appointed pleasantly with light gray decor and glass blocks, was at one time the **Rough Rider Lounge,** sporting a disco dance floor where a baby grand piano now rests.

Designed by architect **John Graham Sr.,** the hotel used to be a warren of 234 small rooms. The floors have since been redivided to allow for only 151 larger accommodations, each decorated with subtle and comfortable furnishings. Superior-class rooms also boast Jacuzzis. The 19th floor (with a skylight

enclosing the outdoor landing on that floor) is a town house for one of the building's owners. The top level has a single deluxe guest room, with what is perhaps the structure's best view of the city. ♦ 1531 Seventh Ave (at Pine St). 621.1200, 800/426.0670; fax 233.0335 ♿

Within the WestCoast Roosevelt Hotel:

Von's Grand City Cafe ★★$ Occupying the hotel's old main lobby space, this clubby restaurant serves an assortment of sandwiches, fish, and steaks. But it's best known for dispensing quality martinis—and lots of them. ♦ American ♦ Daily breakfast, lunch, and dinner. 619 Pine St (at Seventh Ave). 621.8667 ♿

49 Paramount Theater This theater and its smaller sister space in Portland, Oregon, were modeled after the Paramount in New York City. Again, **B. Marcus Priteca** was the architect, but here, 13 years after construction of the **Coliseum,** he played a more reserved hand. Its monumental proportions—from the high-rise brick facade to the tall arched windows out front and roofline decorations—were all meant to emphasize the theatricality and fantasy of screen and stage drama. Where vaudeville performers used to trod the boards, the spotlights now fall mostly on rock musicians.

A group of deep-pocketed investors, headed by former Microsoft marketing exec and arts-management consultant Ida Cole, purchased the theater in early 1993, renovated and added to the structure, and replaced low-income housing units in the upper stories with commercial spaces. ♦ Box office opens one hour prior to show time (cash only). 901 Pine St (at Ninth Ave). 682.1414, TicketMaster 628.0888

50 WestCoast Camlin Hotel $ Money to finish this brick-and–terra-cotta tower in 1926 was actually embezzled by a pair of hyper-ambitious bankers, Adolph Linden and Edmund Campbell, who were subsequently prosecuted and sent to Walla Walla State Penitentiary in eastern Washington. The architect was **Carl J. Linde** of Portland, Oregon, a onetime brewery designer from Wisconsin who had worked under noted Oregon architect **A.E. Doyle.** Most of **Linde**'s efforts were concentrated on the hotel's Ninth Avenue facade. The basic style was Gothic, complete with lions' heads and other decorative gargoyles. Interestingly, the 11-story structure is only *half* a hotel. A second, 14-story establishment, to have been built just north of the existing hotel (where a parking lot now stands), never made it past the drawing board.

This hotel was isolated to the northeast of downtown when it opened in 1926, but it has since been engulfed by the expanding city. A $2-million restoration in 1985 brought in double-paned windows, so that noise (even from the **Paramount Theater** across the street) isn't a problem in the 136 large guest rooms, each of which is decorated in various shades of beige, with exposed pipe fixtures in the bathrooms and overstuffed chairs. Just try to avoid the gloomier cabanas. ♦ 1619 Ninth Ave (between Pine St and Olive Way). 682.0100, 800/426.0670; fax 682.7415

Within the WestCoast Camlin Hotel:

The Cloud Room ★$$ This restaurant turns out acceptable meals (particularly pasta), but the real attraction of the 11th floor is one of the city's most enjoyable and delightfully kitschy piano bars. ♦ Continental ♦ Restaurant: M-F breakfast, lunch, and dinner; Sa-Su breakfast and dinner. Lounge: M-F 11AM-1:30AM; Sa-Su 5:30PM-1:30AM. 682.0100

51 Westlake Center Downtown's $250-million version of a suburban shopping mall is over-sanitized, overlighted at night, and offers little in the way of a downtown park—a component that its creators, the Maryland-based **Rouse Company,** promised their center would go out of its way to provide. Overall, the glitzy mall feels little connected to the architectural and social character of Seattle's nexus. And it seems aggressively unconnected to the town's history, even though it stands at what has long been an important hub, which, until 1931, held a glorious flatiron building called the **Hotel Plaza.** Yet, because Seattle has no real civic center, this complex has succeeded in becoming a focus of activity. The third floor's carnival of food counters is awash during weekday lunchtimes with workers from the surrounding office hives. A rather stark public plaza out front stays lively with T-shirt vendors, street musicians, hellfire-and-brimstone preachers, and a fountain that you can actually walk through. And it doesn't hurt business any that the monorail from **Seattle Center** has its endpoint here, or that one of the downtown transit tunnel's five stations sits beneath the center. ♦ Fourth Ave and Pine St ⑂

Within Westlake Center:

Monorail This is the beginning (or end) of the 1.2-mile overhead journey to **Seattle Center.** Trains depart every 15 minutes, and the 90-second trip is over before you know it. Still, how many other cities have monorails? ♦ Fee. Daily. Third floor. 441.6038 ⑂

Jessica McClintock Boutique Characters from a Barbara Cartland novel might shop at this store, which is filled with lots of frills and puffs of lace and flouncy skirts. ♦ Daily. Lower floor. 467.1048 ⑂

Crabtree & Evelyn The shelves are filled with dozens of different soaps, and jar after jar of bath scents, potpourri, sachets, and room fresheners. Combine a few of these tension-relieving nostrums with a good book and a glass of wine and you could poach in the tub for hours. ♦ Daily. First floor. 682.6776 ⑂

FireWorks Gallery This downtown branch of the Pioneer Square store is even more devoted to artsy souvenirs and jewelry. ♦ Daily. First floor. 682.6462. Also at: 210 First Ave S (between S Main and S Washington Sts). 682.8707 ⑂

Monorail

Williams-Sonoma The French porcelain, chrome gadgets, glassware, and cookbooks look so good in this pristine location that it's a shame to mess them up in your own kitchen. But this is a great place for people who care as much about how their kitchenware works as how it looks. Beware of the crowds of shoppers here at Christmastime. ◆ Daily. First floor. 624.1422 ♿

Brentano's Efficiently run and impressively well stocked, this is one of downtown's best bookstores. Look for large selections of general fiction, mystery, science fiction, self-help books, travel, and history. The children's department could be beefed up some, but the magazine racks are amply stocked: if there were any more titles, Seattleites would never return to work from their lunch hours. ◆ Daily. Second floor. 467.9626 ♿

Victoria's Secret Sift through a variety of tasteful lingerie, suggestive nighties, sports bras, come-hither scents, and comfortable bathrobes, all at reasonable prices. ◆ Daily. Second floor. 623.6035 ♿

Boston Sox For those who appreciate wildly designed stockings and socks, this is a shoppers' paradise, and a great place for Christmas stocking stuffers. ◆ Daily. Second floor. 625.1663 ♿

The Disney Store Everything here, from *Lion King* lunchboxes to *Sleeping Beauty* pajamas, is based on Disney movies, but at least it's cheaper than a trip to Disneyland. Daily. Second floor. 622.3323 ♿

52 Metro Bus Tunnel It's not exactly the London Underground, but Seattle's 1.3-mile transit tube isn't a gloomy bat cave, either. Buses passing through here are converted temporarily from diesel to electric power. On a cold or rainy day, shoppers appreciate the interior walkways (just above the bus platform level) that connect **Westlake Center** with **Nordstrom** and **The Bon Marché.**

About $3 million was spent by **Metro** on public art for the five bus stations. At the **Westlake** stop, check out the multicolored terra-cotta tiles that carry leaf and vine patterns. (The **Pioneer Square Station** features large clocks made from masonry remnants and a mural that captures aspects of Seattle history in tile. Origami designs spark up the **International District** bus terminal.) ◆ Ticket window: M-F 5AM-7PM; Sa. Pine St (between Fourth and Third Aves). 553.3000

53 The Bon Marché Upholding the tradition of department stores, "The Bon" wants to be everything to everybody. Clothes, cosmetics, china, shoe repair, furniture, candy, liquor—they're all here. Merchandise is well selected and stocked, and prices are often more moderate than at similar stores in town. ◆ Daily; M-F until 8PM. Third Ave and Pine St. 344.2121

54 Key Bank Tower (Olympic Tower) This 1929 Art Deco specimen features a polygonal crown and restored terra-cotta facing. It was the creation of local architect **Henry Bittman.** ◆ Third Ave and Pine St

55 A.E. Doyle Building Built as a department store in 1915, this unobtrusive terra-cotta edifice, designed in the Venetian Renaissance palazzo style, was remodeled in 1973 and now carries the name of its original architect, a prominent figure in early 20th-century Portland, Oregon. ◆ Second Ave and Pine St

Within the A.E. Doyle Building:

M. Coy Books More selective than comprehensive in his selection of books, proprietor Michael Coy is usually on top of the latest best-sellers and new regional publications. General fiction is well represented, and there's a mind-engaging array of nonfiction available, but the range within any genre (particularly mystery and science fiction) is fairly narrow. Fortunately, employees are helpful and ready to take special orders. A small coffee shop in the back contributes a relaxed and contemplative atmosphere. ◆ Daily. 117 Pine St (at Second Ave). 623.5354

Most cities have only one sister city (if any) elsewhere in the world; Seattle has quite a few, including Beersheba, Israel; Bergen, Norway; Chongqing, China; Christchurch, New Zealand; Galway, Ireland; Kobe, Japan; Limbe, Cameroon; Managua, Nicaragua; Mazatlán, Mexico; Mombasa, Kenya; Nantes, France; Reykjavik, Iceland; Tashkent, Uzbekistan; and Taejon, South Korea. And there are local committees for each one of them; for more information, call City Hall at 386-1511.

Restaurants/Clubs: Red   **Hotels:** Blue
Shops/ ❦ Outdoors: Green   **Sights/Culture:** Black

Pillars of the Community

That tourists regard Seattle as home to so many totem poles is an odd quirk of taste and history. Native Americans of the Seattle area, after all, did not create this detailed form of columnar art, but Seattleites took a shine to it way back in the 19th century. Ever since, totem poles have been imported, duplicated locally, or stolen for their aesthetic attributes rather than for their regional relevance. Poles around town are generally the work of the Tlingit people of southeastern Alaska, the Haida of the Queen Charlotte Islands, or the Kwakiutl and Tsimshian Indians of southwestern **British Columbia.** They symbolize this city's reputation as the Gateway to the North.

Totem poles originated as memorials, grave posts, and architectural supports. Their designs included creatures of nature transformed into specific mythological figures—Raven, Frog, Coyote, and others—each with its own temperament, style, and power. The representations were stacked on a totem pole in ways that retold bits of Native American history or legends, with the top figure identifying the clan whose story was being told.

The 50-foot-tall western red cedar pole in **Pioneer Place Park** (First Ave between Yesler Way and Cherry St) is Seattle's best-known totem. The original monolith, a Tlingit pole stolen by a Seattle expeditionary party during the 19th century, stood in that park from 1899 until it was damaged by dry rot and arson in 1938. What exists today is a replica, also carved by Tlingit. This totem symbolizes not one but three myths, the predominant legend involving the cunning Raven (a figure depicted at the top of the totem at right), who stole the sun and the moon from Raven-at-the-Head-of-Nass and brought them to the world. In addition, this totem tells how intermarriages between Raven and Frog clanspeople, who have been transformed into humans, are complicated when their offspring are shaped like frogs. The obelisk also recalls a sea voyage taken by Mink and Raven in the belly of Killer Whale. During the trip, the two passengers feast on their host's body until they reach the heart, at which point Killer Whale dies and washes ashore. The adventure leaves Raven with a sleek sheen, while Mink has become dirty from rolling in rotten wood in an attempt to rid himself of the oily residue.

In **Pioneer Square**'s peaceful **Occidental Park** (Occidental Ave S between S Jackson St and Yesler Way) is a totem called *Sun and Raven,* a 32-foot pole carved by artist Duane Pasco for the 1974 World's Fair in Spokane. Three other Pasco pieces—*Man Riding on Tail of Whale, Tsonoqua* (a mythical giant of the deep forest), and *Bear*—are also in the park. And at **Seattle Center** (bounded by Fifth and First Aves N, and Denny Way and Mercer St), near the **Center House**, you can see a 30-foot Pasco pole with four main figures: Hawk, Bear (holding a salmon), Raven, and Killer Whale.

The carved cedar pole at the intersection of **Alaskan Way S** and **S Washington Street** was commissioned by the Port of Seattle to commemorate links between Seattle and Alaska. This 1975 piece, created at the Alaska Indian Arts Center in Haines, Alaska, includes several symbols of the 49th state. Eagle, representing the main Tlingit tribe, sits at the top; below him is Brown Bear holding a coin, symbolizing Alaska's great size and wealth, and Killer Whale, representing tenacity and strength; and at the pole's base is the figure "Strong Boy," which stands for the state's youth and vigor.

The more traditional of the two poles in **Victor Steinbrueck Park** (Western Ave at Virginia St), at the north end of **Pike Place Market,** does not depict a legend but includes mythical figures inspired by Haida Indian designs, which stand for qualities of strength and abundance. The other, a nontraditional unadorned totem pole, was apparently inspired by a pole found near Ketchikan, Alaska, that features Abraham Lincoln; Seattle's version is topped by two figures of a farming couple standing back to back. These pieces were designed by Quinault Indian artist Martin Oliver and Seattleite James Bender.

A 1937 example of the art, carved originally for a fish cannery in Waterfall, Alaska by a Haida Indian, can be seen just east of the **Montlake Bridge** on **E Shelby Street.** After many years of greeting fishers returning to Alaska, this pole was stored in a Seattle warehouse until it could be purchased and reassembled by philanthropic locals. The obelisk tells about a very old woman whose brother, a Haida chief, considered her worthless. When the chief moved his people, he ordered that his sister be left behind without food or fire. She, however, called upon the spirits for help, and her prayers were answered by an eagle that brought her food each day. When a bear tried to steal the raptor's gifts, the woman again appealed to the spirits, who sent someone to kill the thieving bruin.

Two other fine examples of totem art are located in **Vancouver**'s **Stanley Park** (at the foot of Georgia St). Charles James carved the turn-of-the-century house posts, both of which depict Thunderbird at the top. They were designed to serve as architectural supports for communal homes.

M. BLUM

56 Mayflower Park Hotel $$ The 173 rooms here are furnished in antiques, but they're sometimes small—that's the trade-off for accommodations right in the heart of the downtown shopping district. Just be sure to ask for a room high up in this handsome 1927 tower (illustrated above), where you'll see a slice of the city past surrounding building walls. An antiques-filled lobby provides access to a commodious, high-ceilinged bar and to the neighboring **Westlake Center. Clippers**, just off the lobby, serves three meals daily, but it is best for breakfast and lunch, when its big windows let in plenty of natural light. ♦ 405 Olive Way (at Fourth Ave). 623.8700, 800/426.5100; fax 382.6997

57 Times Square Building It was no coincidence that this flatiron structure and the irregular intersection to its immediate west came to be known as Times Square. First off, the building housed the *Seattle Times* newspaper from 1916 until 1931. Second, the intersection bears a strong resemblance to Manhattan's Times Square. Constructed of terra-cotta and granite, with fine Beaux Arts detailing (note the elegant eagles decorating the roofline), it was one of the earliest downtown works by architect **Carl Gould.** A graduate of the Ecole des Beaux Arts in Paris who apprenticed with the famous New York City firm of **McKim, Mead & White** before heading west for his health, the architect would eventually give Seattle a series of landmarks, including the original **Seattle Art Museum** on Capitol Hill and the **Suzzallo Library** at the **University of Washington.** ♦ Bounded by Olive Way and Stewart St, and Fifth and Fourth Aves

58 WestCoast Vance Hotel $ Built in 1926 by the Vance Lumber Company as a stopover for visiting lumber brokers and other dealmakers, this hotel was pretty seedy when the WestCoast chain decided to spend $7 million in 1990 on its restoration. The exterior was never meant to be breathtaking, but it does include fine terra-cotta detailing near street level and a nicely polished dark lobby. The 165 rooms tend to be smaller than normal but still pleasant, with the best views of the **Space Needle** from above the fifth floor on the north side. ♦ 620 Stewart St (at Seventh Ave). 441.4200, 800/663.1144; fax 441.8612

Within the WestCoast Vance Hotel:

Salute in Città ★$$ Although far less romantic than the funky original **Salute,** which is north of the University District, this trattoria makes the cut for its excellent and inexpensive designer pizzas. They're on the small side, but are ideal nighttime bar fare. ♦ Italian ♦ Daily breakfast, lunch, and dinner. 728.1611. Also at: 3410 NE 55th St (at 35th Ave NE). 527.8600

59 Westin Hotel $$$ You can't miss this place: it's the one with the round twin pillars of guest rooms that look like corncobs. Each of the 865 rooms features a balcony (though the best vistas are from above the 20th floor). Guests enjoy spacious and well-lighted accommodations but contrasting plain furnishings. Some of the rooms are "Guest Offices," equipped with such handy business features as a combination laser printer/ fax/copier, speakerphone with dataport, printer cables, and office supplies; in addition, local, 800-number, and credit card calls are free. Room rates include a complimentary breakfast. The convention facilities are plentiful and spread over several levels. There's a large pool, a supervised exercise room, and three lounges. ♦ 1900 Fifth Ave (at Stewart St). 728.1000, 800/228.3000; fax 728.2259 &

Within the Westin Hotel:

Nikko ★★★$$$ Recently renovated to the tune of $1.5 million, this stylish, multilevel Japanese dining room is better than ever. Traditional Japanese art hangs on the walls, adding an exotic touch, and the food is an equally potent draw. Sit at the enormous sushi bar and order the wonderful Nikko Roll—seven kinds of raw fish rolled with avocado and rice. The *robata* (shish kebab) bar serves every kind of grilled item imaginable, including oysters, short ribs, scallops, vegetables, and mushrooms, and the multicourse dinner special (which changes monthly) features both familiar dishes and more unusual choices. This is definitely one of the best restaurants of its kind in the Northwest. ♦ Japanese ♦ M-F lunch and dinner; Sa dinner. 322.4641 &

60 Dahlia Lounge ★★★$$$ This eatery is a very colorful place, with bright red walls and rice-paper fish lamps that "swim" above the dining tables. The inventive menu by executive chef John Sundstrom features Northwestern meat and produce prepared with Pacific Rim accents. To start, try the shrimp, lobster, and shiitake mushroom pot stickers with a sauce of sake and chili oil. The crab cakes, a favorite entrée here, are

legendary in Seattle; almost as popular is the grilled salmon with ginger-sake butter. Be sure to go all the way and order dessert: The only dilemma is whether to have a pear tart with caramel sauce or the coconut cream pie. The waitstaff are friendly and helpful; don't hesitate to ask for their suggestions.
♦ Northwestern ♦ M-F lunch and dinner; Sa-Su dinner. Reservations recommended. 1904 Fourth Ave (between Stewart and Virginia Sts). 682.4142 &

61 Annex Theatre This interesting fringe theater is operated by ambitious, thoughtful twentysomethings. The experimental offerings can sometimes be pretty dreadful, but even then they almost always have a spark of creativity. If you're looking for a sure bet, stop in for the late-night Friday improvs (11PM). ♦ Box office daily 6:45PM-8PM. 1916 Fourth Ave (between Stewart and Virginia Sts). 728.0933

62 Moore Theater and Hotel For many years pioneer Arthur Denny had reserved six acres here in hopes that Seattle might one day capture the Washington state capitol building (which was eventually built in Olympia). But in 1888 he went ahead and filled the site with a first-class hotel—something the city desperately needed after the Great Fire of 1889. The national depression of 1893 stalled construction of this multitowered edifice, and it was finally completed a decade later by Seattle superdeveloper James A. Moore. (President Teddy Roosevelt was the first guest at the new hotel when it opened in 1903.) Almost immediately, Moore had bigger dreams for this area. He wanted to enlarge his hotel and to erect the most artistic and beautiful theater in the West.

Sure enough, the hotel and an adjoining playhouse (both designed by prolific Seattle architect **E.W. Houghton**) went up in 1908. But in the meantime the hotel was razed to make possible the regrading of Denny Hill. James Moore fell on hard times not many years later and so did his theater. Its vaguely Egyptian Revival-style interior is still intact, but the likes of Marie Dressler and John Barrymore no longer perform here. Now the hall is used only sporadically, mostly for concerts. ♦ Box office hours vary, call ahead. 1932 Second Ave (at Virginia St). 443.1744

Bests

Ruby Z. Montana
President/Ruby Montana's Pinto Pony, Ltd.

A Ruby Montana ideal weekend would begin with: breakfast at the **Twin Teepees** followed by a walk along **Elliott Bay** at **Myrtle Edwards Park.** Jump on the **Waterfront Trolley** and ride to the end of the line to the **International District** to visit the flour-coated **Fortune Cookie Factory** and **Liem's Pet Shop,** home of exotic fish and fowl. Lunch at the **Iron Horse,** where your meal is delivered by a real toy train that runs around the restaurant. After lunch, a stroll through **Pioneer Square** with a quiet moment at **Waterfall Garden** followed by an exhilarating ride in a vintage cage elevator to the top of **Smith Tower** for a walk around the catwalk adjacent to the elegant **Chinese Room.** Next a short hike up **First Avenue** to the **Pike Place Market** for a frosty beer at the **Athenian.** Dinner at the **Queen City Grill** (reserve booth #3); don't miss the wild mushroom appetizer. After a sumptuous meal, waddle over to **Dimitriou's Jazz Alley** for an intimate live music experience. After the show, drive up the the **Highland Drive Overlook** and enjoy the beautifully twinkling city and the ferries silently crossing the dark sound. Nightcap at **Sorry Charlie's** to the strains of 65-year-old Camay girls singing show tunes at the piano bar. Check into the **Sorrento Hotel** (Room 608) and have many technicolor dreams. Wake up to a room service breakfast with a view of the **Space Needle** and go downstairs to a massage from Yasuo Mori, followed by a hearthside tarot reading in the lounge by Tarotmancer Alexa Robbins (wife of writer Tom Robbins—so you know that she is quite magical). Next pack a picnic and take a field trip to the **Walker Rock Garden** for a contemplative pause on how lucky you are to live in such a rich environment. Cap it all off with a fried chicken dinner (served family style) at the historic **Alki Homestead** and a moonlit walk on the sandy beach at **Alki Point,** site of Seattle's first settlers.

Other favorites. . .

Going to the **Children's Museum** with my twin nephews and hanging out in the pipe of the volcano.

A visit to the *Fremont Troll*—great photo opportunity.

A walk through the verdant fern-lined ravine of **Ravenna Park** (you can borrow our cocker spaniel Dale Evans aka Bubby the Wonder Dog).

A roundtrip ferry ride to **Bremerton** at sunset to watch **Mount Rainier** turn a rosy peach.

Councilmember Martha Choe
Seattle City Council

Wide World Books. Great place for tour and guide books. Next door is a great tea house **(Teahouse Kuan Yin).** Easy way to spend two or three hours.

Discovery Park. You can walk, jog, fly a kite, ride a bike—spectacular views of Puget Sound.

Esther "Little Dove" John
Flutist, composer, record label owner/Dove-Paloma Music

Cafe Flora—Gourmet vegetarian restaurant.

Volunteer Park Conservatory—public hothouse.

Mecca Cafe—chess, tea, live poetry, and jazz.

The Japanese gardens at the **Arboretum**—peace and beautiful horticulture.

Pike Place Market / Waterfront

The market is a kinetic profusion of people, energy, and individual enterprise. Flowers for sale. Pottery. Pastries. Scarves. Cigars. Seascapes. T-shirts. Teacups. Fish peddlers toss huge flounder above the heads of awed customers. A ragtag band coaxes a lively rendition of Jimmy Buffett's "Pencil-Thin Mustache" from time-distressed instruments. A hawker at the **Read All About It** newsstand shouts, *"P-I! Seattle Post-Intelligencer! Seattle Times! New Yo-o-o-rk Times! LA Times! We've got the Times!"* Shoppers jockey with automobiles along the two-and-a-half block stretch of **Pike Place**, with drivers almost invariably losing out. As many as 40,000 people visit this bazaar daily.

There's no guarantee you'll find the freshest produce here, but for urban color, **Pike Place Market**—the oldest continuously operating farmer's market in the country—is unbeatable. *New York Times* correspondent Timothy Egan called it the "Marrakech of the Northwest." Artist Mark Tobey, who haunted the market frequently, beginning in the 1920s, once described it as "a refuge, an oasis, a most human growth, the heart and soul of Seattle."

The market began in 1907, when food wholesalers formed a "Produce Row" along **Western Avenue**. Farmers who couldn't take the time off to sell their crops relied on wholesalers to do the job for them. But local growers suspected (quite rightly, in many cases) that these intermediaries were cheating them of a fair price for their goods and, at the same time, gouging customers with excessive fees. The city's response was to establish a *true* farmer's market. The location was based primarily on convenience (aggressive regrading had recently leveled the land at **Pike Street**'s western end, and newly planked **Western Avenue** connected it with the Waterfront). On opening day, 17 August 1907, fewer than a dozen wagons showed up (and one of those, driven by a Japanese farmer, was ransacked), but thousands of Seattleites came eager to buy. The next week, 70 wagons took positions on the Pike Place curb. Fishmongers soon infiltrated the neighborhood, as did other small businesses. Stall sizes had to be reduced to fit everybody in and canopies were built to keep commerce chugging along through the Seattle rains. Several proposals called for **Pike Place Market** to grow into a grandiose commercial complex spilling down from its bluff on **Elliott Bay** into a railroad and marine terminal on the Waterfront. But residents voted to keep the market small and personable: exuberant with Italians, Japanese, and Sephardic Jews hawking their goods; replete with local characters like Horseradish Jerry, who ground roots into relish, or the old-timers who droned tall tales of the Klondike Gold Rush. Within 10 years the market had become Seattle's funky equivalent of a community square.

The 1929 Depression exacted its toll on **Pike Place Market.** So did World War II's internment of Japanese farmers; the decline of **First Avenue**, from a worker's mall to a strip of peep shows and honky-tonks; and the insurgence of supermarkets. By 1963, with the market and indeed all of Seattle in wan condition, planners encouraged the city to bulldoze the market in favor of a parking and high-rise development. Only a concerted effort by preservationists, politicians, local architects (among them the persistent **Victor Steinbrueck**, who had designed the **Space Needle**), and eventually voters saved the heart and soul of Seattle. A seven-acre Market Historical District was established in 1974.

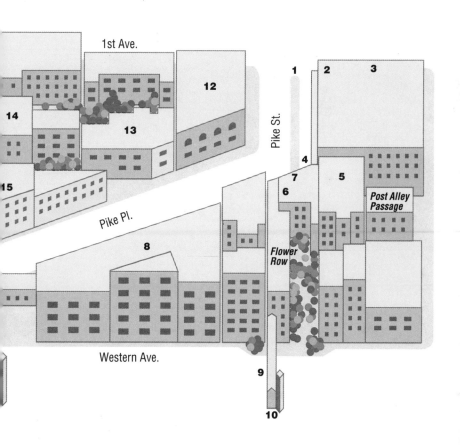

Regular guided tours will give you an overview of the market, but the best way to get a feel for it is to wander about its well-preserved edifices, exploring the alleys, stairways, and ramps where the many buildings have been strung together throughout the years. However, it would take years to fully appreciate all the attractions and rhythms of the place; in fact, even most natives know it only in passing. **Pike Place Market** (which is also referred to as the "Public Market") is open daily early May through December, and Monday through Saturday the rest of the year. Individual shop hours vary, as do the seasonal schedules of businesses not contained completely within market buildings.

Since **Pike Place Market** achieved historic status, every one of its buildings has been renovated or reconstructed. Unfortunately, less attention has been paid to Seattle's Waterfront. This was once the center of local commerce, a strip alive with the shouts of merchants and the jibs of the **Mosquito Fleet**, an early ferry service. But several decades ago the Waterfront was severed from the rest of downtown by the **Alaskan Way Viaduct** and—except for the estimable **Seattle Aquarium** and the too small **Waterfront Park**—has since been all but completely given over to fast-food joints and kitschy emporiums. Hope for its revitalization is now centered on the **Bell Street Pier**, an 11-acre span of urban shoreline that has recently been developed as a convention center, dining complex, marina, and museum.

Pike Place Market

1 Market Information Booth Market maps and other visitor info are happily dispensed here. This is the starting point for tours of the neighborhood. ♦ Daily. First Ave and Pike St. 682.7453

2 Economy Market Promoter and investor **Frank Goodwin** was an eccentric who played heavily with penny stocks, put together an early steam-powered automobile, and practiced a strict vegetarian diet. He bought heavily into Pike Place real estate and was the man who finally brought the market in out of the rain in 1907, when he constructed the **Main Arcade**. An amateur architect, **Goodwin** designed and built a multistory expansion of the market down Pike Place bluff to Western Avenue. In 1916 he obtained a lease on the **Bartell Building** (completed in 1900) at the corner of First Avenue and Pike Street, transforming it into today's **Economy Market**. Look for his design work in this building's Doric columns and the plaster garlands of fruit and flowers. Preservation architect **George Bartholick** headed a rehabilitation of the market in 1978. The angled ramps in the atrium used to be trodden upon by horses, which were checked through here on their way to the main market. ♦ Pike St and First Ave

Within the Economy Market:

Read All About It One of the two best-stocked newsstands in this city (the other contender is **Bulldog News** in the University District), the inventory here reflects a walloping diversity of American and international periodicals. Expect everything from *Popular Mechanics* to *Sassy*. Looking for the *International Herald Tribune* or the *Nome Nugget?* They're here, too. ♦ Daily. 7AM-7PM. Main floor. 624.0140

Stamp Happy Children of all ages could spend hours here testing out the available and often comic rubber stamps, but buyers are also welcome. ♦ Daily. Main floor. 682.8575

Daily Dozen Doughnuts Snag a baker's dozen sack of miniature doughnuts—plain, powdered sugar, or cinnamon. Then hope nobody witnesses your abject gluttony. ♦ M-Sa. No credit cards accepted. Main floor. 467.7769

DeLaurenti's Specialty Foods Exotic Mediterranean canned goods, meats, and wines are shoehorned into a space barely big enough to contain them all. Though the history of this shop is commonly traced back to owners Pete and Mamie DeLaurenti in the 1940s, Mamie's very Italian mother, Angelina Mustelo, had opened a small store on the market's lower level in 1928. ♦ M-Sa. Main floor. 622.0141. Also at: 317 Bellevue Way NE (between NE Second and NE Fourth Sts), Bellevue. 454.7155

The Great Wind-Up Follow the noise of barking dogs, growling dragons, and hopping bunnies to this toy-filled corner shop. While children gather ideas for Christmas, adults will enjoy a tableful of windup kangaroos, chattering teeth, and mince-stepping eyeballs. ♦ Daily. Atrium. 621.9370

Sasquatch Whether descended from prehistoric primates or born from human imagination, Sasquatch (or Bigfoot, if you prefer) has become the Northwest's signature monster. Its appearances hark back to the tribal mythology of virtually every native people from coastal British Columbia to northern California. The name Sasquatch comes from *sas-kets,* a term used by Salish-speaking tribes of southwestern British Columbia to describe the hairy, humanlike giants they said lived in the Fraser River Valley and communicated via whistles and shrill screams. More than 2,500 Sasquatch sightings have been recorded since the 1960s, most of them in Washington State. This brooding sculpture was carved by artist Richard Beyer. ♦ Atrium

Tenzing Momo Come to this herbal apothecary to buy a stick of incense or some bulk herbs. You can also pick up fluid extracts, Chinese nostrums, ear-wax candles, or books on witchcraft. The store's name, translated from Tibetan, means "illustrious dumpling." This is holy ground for worshipers in the temple of natural health. ♦ M-Sa. Atrium. 623.9837

3 Liberty Malt Supply Company/Pike Place Brewery The **Liberty Malt Supply Company** has sold fresh hops, malted barley, and home-brewing supplies since 1921. Beer-making classes are offered several times a year, covering the basics as well as fermentation, bottling, and stylistic variations. Nearby, the **Pike Place Brewery** has been producing fine-quality beers, carried by some of the best taverns in town, since 1989. Brewery tours are available daily; call for times. ♦ Daily. Liberty Malt Supply Company: 1419 First Ave (between Union and Pike Sts). 622.1880; Pike Place Brewery: 1432 Western Ave (near the Hillclimb Corridor). 622.3373

4 Lower Post Alley This was once a major commercial route connecting the market with Western Avenue's Produce Row, the Waterfront, and Pioneer Square. Guttering beneath the main market sign and clock, the alley is now pretty much ignored, yet it is supposedly the only completely restored cobblestone street in the Northwest. The glass-walled bridge above the alley's entrance off First Avenue was known historically as the Bridge of Sighs. Apparently, from here south, the alley used to be lined with bars, and sailors would stop in at each of them for a nip before shipping out of town. It's said that from the bridge women would watch their men

amble slowly away and, presumably, sigh. ♦ Between Pike and Union Sts

Along Lower Post Alley:

Il Bistro ★★$$$ Trimmed in dark woods and set off by arches, this quiet dining spot is like a European *cave* or wine cellar. People come here after work to decompress, sipping wine or whiskey in the jazz-filled bar or chatting over dinner in the more secluded reaches. Italian dishes got this place off the ground, and, while a variety of seafood plates have been introduced with varying degrees of success, pasta is still instrumental in keeping it popular. Both the tortellini with garlic, pine nuts, and tomatoes and the linguine *carrettiera* (with seasonal mushrooms, hot pepper flakes, tomato, cream, and vodka) will satisfy your appetite. The cioppino is also a standout. ♦ Italian ♦ M-Sa lunch and dinner; Su dinner; bar until 2AM. 93A Pike St (on Lower Post Alley). 682.3049

5 LaSalle Hotel This bay-windowed building beside the **Public Market** sign was the first bordello north of Yesler Way and survived to become the last of this city's big-time bawdy houses. Erected in 1909 as the **Outlook Hotel,** prior to World War II it was owned by a Japanese family who catered to frugal workers and the elderly. After the 1942 internment of Japanese residents, the hotel was taken over by Nellie Curtis (née Zella Nightengale), who had run orderly disorderly houses across Canada before moving to Seattle in 1931. Small and birdlike, she drove Cadillacs, kept her money in drawers rather than banks, wore ermine shawls, and collected hats with the same superfluousness with which Imelda Marcos would later gather shoes. As Alice Shorett and Murray Morgan recall in their jolly history, *Pike Place Market: People, Politics, and Produce,* the hotel even had "enough rooms so that some could be used for legitimate purposes, thus providing a cover for more profitable activities."

Shortly after business got under way here, some of Nellie's "girls" went down to the Waterfront to meet incoming ships and hand out business cards: "LaSalle Hotel—Friends Easily Made." That night hundreds of libidinous wharf rats and sailors tried to anchor in one of the hotel's 57 berths, attracting attention not only from the local military but from reform Mayor William Devin, who ordered a prostitution crackdown. But Nellie's fortunes went undisturbed.

It was only in 1949, after her nephew botched a temporary management of the place and Seattle had been shaken by its first major earthquake, that Nellie decided to sell the hotel. The buyers were a Japanese-American couple, George and Sodeko Ikeda, who had trouble convincing some of Nellie's old clients that there were no longer any "working girls" in the hostelry. The Ikedas subsequently sued Nellie for overstating profits to be made from the property. Not only did Nellie lose $7,500 in court, but she finally attracted the attention of the Internal Revenue Service. The hotel was rehabilitated in 1977 and now contains commercial space as well as low-income housing. ◆ Lower Post Alley (off First Ave, between Union and Pike Sts)

6 Market Clock Rising from the elbow that connects the **Economy Market** to the **Main Arcade,** this timepiece and the **Public Market** sign that surrounds it are supposed to be the oldest examples of public neon in Seattle, dating back to the 1920s or 1930s. The clock is a favorite among visiting photographers, and on New Year's Eve, crowds of happily tipsy Seattleites gather below it to celebrate at the stroke of midnight. ◆ Pike Pl and Pike St

7 Rachel, the Market Pig This overgrown piggy bank is the Market Foundation's friendliest fund-raiser. More than $35,000 has been dropped into her belly since she took up her position below the **Market Clock** in 1986. ◆ Pike Pl and Pike St

8 Main Arcade Frank Goodwin's first market building, dating from 1907, reflects a simpler architectural style than he applied to his reworking of the **Economy Market.** About 50 percent of the market's fish and produce stalls are located here, with many others just across the street. Take a look at the engraved floor tiles covering the arcade's main level, laid out as part of a fund-raising project in the mid-1980s. Seattleites paid $35 apiece to have their names imprinted on these tiles; Ronald and Nancy Reagan are also represented here, although they didn't pay anything for the privilege. Two floors (making up what used to be called the **Labyrinth**) descend from street level and are known simply as "First Floor Down Under" and "Second Floor Down Under." ◆ Pike Pl (between Pike and Pine Sts)

Pier 54, now the Waterfront home of Ye Olde Curiosity Shop, is remembered by old-timers as the place where, in 1940, Two-Ton Tony Galento, a 350-pound boxer, climbed into a tank of seawater to wrestle a 75-pound octopus. Brokered by the late Seattle restaurateur Ivar Haglund, the bout ended in a draw.

Restaurants/Clubs: Red   **Hotels:** Blue
Shops/🍴**Outdoors:** Green   **Sights/Culture:** Black

Within the Main Arcade:

Athenian Inn ★★$ Opened in 1909 as a Greek bakery/luncheonette, and later operated as a bar (it received one of Seattle's earliest liquor licenses, in 1933), this is among the market's most democratic restaurants. Fishers hunker up to the bar counter while designer-suited sales reps wait in line for tables with views of Puget Sound. The menu hits all the local standards—from grilled oysters to fat burgers—with the breakfast faves being red-flannel hash (with beets, corned beef, green peppers, and potatoes) and sweet-potato turkey hash. The breakfast menu is available all day long, and the bar has 16 beers on tap and stocks more than 300 brews. ◆ American ◆ M-Sa breakfast, lunch, and dinner until 6:30PM. Main floor. 624.7166 &

City Fish This busy stall was started by the city in 1918 to offer Seattleites fresh fish at reasonable prices. Newspaper reports of overcharging had led Mayor Hiram Gill to make his health commissioner responsible for setting up a market space stocked with dirt-cheap hatchery fish. Prices began at one-third to one-quarter of what was being charged elsewhere for fish. For four years, this operation was profitable, but as sales waned, the city sold out. David Levy, one of the first Sephardic Jews to arrive in Seattle, bought the stall in 1926 and quickly earned the nickname "Good Weight Dave" for keeping his thumb off the scale. The business, still in Levy family hands, continues to sell high-quality fish and also offers overnight shipping to any location in the continental US. Look for the well-preserved **City Fish Market** sign on Pike Place. ◆ Daily from 7:30AM. Main floor. 682.9329

Lowell's Restaurant $ Substantive, though not surprising, dishes (try the fried oysters and the Monte Cristo or Reuben sandwiches) are served at this classic cafeteria and restaurant. It was opened as a coffee shop in 1908 by brothers Edward and William Manning, who did something early on that much later would become a Seattle signature: They started selling roasted coffee beans in bulk. ◆ American/Seafood ◆ Daily breakfast, lunch, and dinner until 5PM. Main floor. 622.2036

Market Spice Olfactory overload! More than a hundred flavors of tea, bulk coffee beans, and giant jars of seasonings can be found here, as can tea-brewing paraphernalia and boxes of fine sweets. Head first to the free-tea dispenser, just beside the cashier's counter and usually filled with the popular house blend (developed by the wife of a pharmacist in the 1970s). Then roam the aisles with an open mind … and an open nose. Mail orders accepted. ◆ Daily. Main floor. 622.6340 &

Maximilien-in-the-Market ★★$$$
You've got to admire the ego of a restaurant that showcases a review written in French. Are you just to *assume* that the report is favorable, or should you simply allow yourself to be seduced by the old-fashioned charm and exceptional Puget Sound views here? Owned by Francois and Julia Kissel, this restaurant is proud of its "Frenchness," but that doesn't translate to hautiness; in fact, the staff is pleasant and attentive. Entrées include boneless chicken baked with apples and sausage in cider, fresh salmon and mussels, as well as the more pedestrian (but well prepared) fish-and-chips. The bar is a fine redoubt from winter chills. ◆ French ◆ M-Sa breakfast, lunch, and dinner; Su brunch and dinner. Reservations recommended. Main floor. 682.7270 &

Pike Place Fish In 1947 the Seattle City Council forbade singing by market vendors. But wait until you hear the bellowing hawkers here, whose voices positively explode from beneath the **Market Clock.** Crowds of tourists gather to observe the iced beds of crab and to gape as fishmongers hurl salmon over customers' heads for weighing behind the counter. Founded in 1930, the store ships fresh fish anywhere in the US. ◆ Daily from 6:30AM. Main floor. 682.7181, 800/542.7732; fax 682.4629

Place Pigalle ★★$$ Early in this century, this place was essentially a bar frequented by men (many were patrons of the **LaSalle Hotel** bordello) who drank with their hats on. Now it's one of the most pleasant dining spaces in the market—the floor is covered in alternating black-and-white tiles, and the outlook on Puget Sound is wondrously unobstructed. The menu includes whatever is seasonally fresh, leaning heavily toward such seafood as Dungeness crab, hazelnut-covered red snapper, and steamed mussels Pigalle (dressed with bacon, celery, shallots, and balsamic vinaigrette). Another worthy choice is the open-faced chicken sandwich with chipotle pepper aioli. The only disappointment is the oyster stew, which, while rich and flavorful, can be skimpy with the bivalves. A porch is available for outdoor dining during the summer. ◆ Continental/Northwestern ◆ M-Sa lunch and dinner. Reservations recommended. Down the staircase behind Pike Place Fish. 624.1756

Golden Age Collectables This crowded corner store carries the city's largest selection of comics, everything from standards such as *Spiderman, Legends of the Dark Knight,* and the *Green Arrow* (the last now drawn by local talent Mike Grell and set in Seattle), to *Aliens, Swamp Thing, Bikini Confidential,* and some of the more obscure titles from the Dark Horse publishing house of Portland, Oregon. There's a wide array of vintage comics, too, plus science-fiction novels, models, sports cards, and binders full of classic, movie-star publicity stills. Special orders are taken. ◆ Daily. First Floor Down Under. 622.9799

Market Magic Shop Common thrills here are the impromptu performances by owners Darryl Beckmann and Sheila Lyon, who always seem willing to open their bags of tricks. With professional paraphernalia and joke props, replicas of old Houdini posters, and juggling clubs, this is an ideal spot to conjure up an afternoon's escape—mental, if not physical. ◆ Daily. First Floor Down Under. 624.4271

Old Seattle Paperworks With the feel of a richly cluttered attic, this is a narrow storehouse of old postcards for sale, classic black-and-whites from Seattle's early years, and piles of dusty *National Geographic* magazines like the ones your grandparents have held onto for half a century. ◆ Daily. First Floor Down Under. 623.2870

MisterE Books

MisterE Books This store is tiny but caters nicely to both best-seller addicts and readers who collect first-edition mysteries, science fiction, and Westerns. ◆ Daily. First Floor Down Under. 622.5182

Grandma's Attic One of several collectibles outlets on the arcade's lowest level, this one is filled with delicate, feminine vintage outfits and knickknacks. ◆ Daily. Second Floor Down Under. 682.9281

Yesterdaze Intriguingly cluttered with well-kept old hats, ties, and jewelry but especially known for its period military clothing, this shop is a perfect stop for collectors. ◆ M-Sa. Second Floor Down Under. No phone

---

The late journalist and broadcaster Alistair Cooke once characterized Seattle as "a rain-soaked fishing village midway between San Francisco and Alaska."

Bertha Landes elected mayor of Seattle in 1913, was the first woman in the US to hold that office.

During the Klondike Gold Rush of 1897, Seattle's pawn shops took in as much as $1000,000 day.

In the Market for a Good Time?

Think of **Pike Place Market** as a separate village within a city, one that claims its own rules of conduct, its own traditions, its own unique style and pace. You really need a kindly old uncle or aunt to show you the ropes, but barring that option, here are a few tips for getting the most out of Seattle's spiritual nexus.

Show up here early in the morning (between 7AM and 8AM) to see the farmers and craftspeople setting up their colorful stalls. If your goal is to find the best choice of fresh foodstuffs, come between 8AM and 11AM, before lunchers descend upon the market. And if you're hoping to score last-minute discounts on the day's still-unsold edibles, arrive at about 4:30PM.

Vendors new to the market don't have enough seniority to earn display space on weekends, so they tend to bring their novel works to the market Monday through Friday. You'll find more familiar, longtime craftspeople here on weekends.

Just as it is impolite in foreign countries to bargain for goods and then choose not to buy them, it also is considered gauche in the market to listen to street musicians for any length of time without contributing at least a few coins to their buckets or violin cases.

Despite ongoing discussions about making **Pike Place** a car-free zone, the market just wouldn't be the same without the constant jockeying of humans and autos here. If you're happy to move at slug speed, stay on the crowded sidewalks. Otherwise, step right onto the brick-covered street and walk with the cars. Just keep a wary eye out for drivers wheeling in and out of the angled parking spaces.

The odds of finding a parking spot around **Pike Place** are poor at best. Try, instead, the 550-space **Market Garage** just west of the **North Arcade,** off Western Avenue, which allows free parking with shopping validations from many market merchants. On-street parking is easiest to find heading north of the market, between Bell Street and Denny Way. Avoid parking lots along First Avenue, as they tend to be overpriced.

Do not depend on market merchants to choose your produce. The best way to get the quality you pay for is to paw lightly over the foodstuffs yourself—no matter how much sellers try to discourage this practice.

Two sets of public rest rooms are available in the market. One is at the south end of the **Main Arcade,** downstairs from **Pike Place Fish.** The other can be found at the **Main Arcade's** north end, by descending the ramp adjacent to **City Fish.**

One-hour tours of the market are scheduled on Saturday mornings, at either 9AM or 10:30AM, depending on the availability of guides. They set out from the **Market Information Booth,** at the corner of First Avenue and Pike Street. The charge is $5 per person and reservations are required. Call 682.7453 for weekly schedules and to sign up for an informative walk.

---

9 Kasala A glass-walled corner location provides a cheery showplace for contemporary and high-style (but surprisingly comfortable) furniture for office and home. There are lots of high-tech floor lamps and other European accessories. Salespeople are readily available but usually leave you alone to browse. ◆ Daily. 1505 Western Ave (near the Hillclimb Corridor). 623.7795. Also at: 1014 116th Ave NE (between Bellevue Redmond Rd and NE 12th St), Bellevue. 453.2823

KASALA

10 Hillclimb Corridor In the market's early days, a wooden pedestrian overpass (built in 1912) connected Pike Place with Waterfront piers, an essential link. Many sellers at the market arrived by boat, often on craft belonging to the old **Mosquito Fleet,** an armada of 70 small steamers that hustled people and products to 350 ports on Puget Sound. In 1973, after the market gained historical status, those rickety steps were replaced with these landscaped stairs

(designed by **Calvin/Gorasht and Sanders**) down to the Waterfront and the **Seattle Aquarium.** The incline is steep (some refer to it as Cardiac Gulch), yet the **Hillclimb** has proved a magnet for both shops and shoppers. ◆ Between Western Ave and Alaskan Way

In the Hillclimb Corridor:

El Puerco Lloron ★$ It looks like a cafeteria decorated by cheesy Tijuana trinket collectors, but the handmade tortillas, tamales, and exceptional *chiles rellenos* more than make up for the decorative deficiencies. Beware of the salsas: It's always best to taste first before pouring them over your meal. ◆ Mexican◆ Daily lunch and dinner. 624.0541

Procopio Treat yourself to a delicious homemade gelato sans artificial anything. Appropriately enough for this city, flavors include cappuccino and mocha. ◆ M-Th until 10PM; F-Sa until midnight. No credit cards accepted. 622.4280

Chicken and Egg Northwestern style is showcased here: canopied beds, well-stuffed sofas, and rush-woven bench seats, all showing the knots and unique bulges of the

Douglas fir trees from which they were shaped. Logs used to make this furniture are peeled to their cambium layers and then cured in late summer sunshine until they achieve a palomino gleam. Knots are sanded and hand-rubbed with beeswax. The warmly natural, unmanicured results fit surprisingly well into even the most modern settings. Profits from sales go to funding child-abuse prevention efforts and school programs through the Children's Trust Foundation and Cities in Schools. And don't worry that forests are being devastated; the firs used are culled only from overgrown stands. Also available are decorative accoutrements (dried flowers, small sculptures) and interior-design books supporting the natural look. ◆ Daily. 1426 Alaskan Way. 623.6144

11 North Arcade This has become one of the slowest-moving pedestrian areas in the market, as everybody stops to look at the tables piled with handknit sweaters, homemade jellies and jams, and arrangements of dried flowers. On warm days merchants even stretch out north along the sidewalk, selling some of the more interesting T-shirts available here, as well as jewelry and pottery. ◆ Pike Pl (between Pine and Virginia Sts)

12 Corner Market Building One of the things about **Pike Place Market** that most fascinates architects is that so little of the development here can be ascribed to professional designers. An exception is this formal structure built in 1912, and conceived by **Harlan Thomas,** designer of the **Sorrento Hotel** and **Harborview Hospital,** both on First Hill, and the Byzantine **Chamber of Commerce Building** downtown on Columbia Street.

A three-story brick structure, this building is best recognized by its graceful arched top-level windows. The first tenant was **Three Girls Bakery,** which now operates in the **Sanitary Market Building.** Also housed here was the Northwest's first homegrown grocery chain: Herman Eba moved from the **Main Arcade** stall he'd occupied since 1910 to the **Corner Market** in 1929, and six years later adopted the business name **Tradewell,** a label that later became familiar to supermarket shoppers around the region. This was the first market landmark to be rehabilitated (1975). ◆ Pike Pl and Pike St

Within the Corner Market Building:

The Crumpet Shop ★$ This cozy dining room prepares its own spongy crumpets, which are great topped with raspberry jam, marmalade, or even ricotta cheese. This is a wonderful choice for a unique and inexpensive breakfast; lox or ham on crumpets are available at lunch, as are more conventional sandwiches. The space can be packed with take-out patrons early on weekday mornings, but it's a comforting crowdedness—really.

◆ Teahouse/Takeout ◆ Daily breakfast, lunch, and afternoon tea. First floor. 682.1598 ♿

Left Bank Books It takes a while to acquaint yourself with the categorization (books written by men, for instance, are separated from books by women), and the array of new and used volumes tends to be more funky than complete. But there's an endearing, antiquarian nature to this place, buttressed by a lack of computerization and pack-rat mentality. The bent is toward liberal, sometimes revolutionary works. ◆ Daily. First floor. 622.0195

Cafe Counter Intelligence ★$ You've got to appreciate the decor in this long narrow joint, where the artwork along one wall may be a series of dinner plates decorated with desperado mug shots and where the counter-top is a mosaic of tiny tiles spelling out the shop's moniker. Noshes include toasted crumpets, seasonal fruits, sandwiches, and special soups. But the true culinary stars here are the coffee (in a dizzying array of permutations) and the milk shakes (especially the peppermint and the Dutch chocolate varieties). ◆ Coffeehouse ◆ Daily. No credit cards accepted. Second floor. 622.6979

CHEZ SHEA

Chez Shea ★★★$$$$ This restaurant is especially romantic late at night, when candlelight is the principal illumination, torch songs are the featured entertainment, and the half-moon windows allow a softened perspective on the market below and the ferries gliding over Puget Sound. A dinner here might begin with a caramelized onion phyllo tart with black olive chevre, followed by a rosemary butternut bisque. Another good entrée choice is pan-roasted oysters with a pumpkin seed crust. The mixed greens pale by comparison, but the scrumptious lemon almond buttermilk tart makes up for the deficiency. The wine list represents both top West Coast and European vintages. There's also a lounge serving libations and a bistro-style menu. ◆ Continental/Northwestern ◆ Tu-Su dinner; lounge until 2 AM. Second floor. 467.9990

Pike Place Bar & Grill ★$ Sandee and Gordy Brock's joint is a market standard, not flashy but satisfying. Newcomers usually wind up at the restaurant end, filling themselves with sandwiches (thumbs up, especially for the French dip) or pleasing pasta and fish specials. Seattleites gravitate to the noisier bar, which has the best views of the market. Piano players keep the bar's resident instrument well exercised. ♦ American ♦ M, Su lunch; Tu-Sa lunch and dinner. Second floor. 624.1365

13 Sanitary Market Building The name derives from the fact that this was the first building in the market that didn't allow horses inside. It was four stories tall when erected in 1910, but the upper floors were destroyed by a fire 31 years later, one of several conflagrations to sweep through the market since its inception. City architect **Daniel R. Huntington** redesigned it in 1942 as a two-story edifice with rooftop parking. The building was rehabilitated again in 1981 by **Bassetti/ Norton/Metler.** ♦ Pike Pl (between Pike and Pine Sts)

Within the Sanitary Market Building:

Jack's Fish Spot $ Behind the fresh shellfish tanks (the only ones in the market) is a walk-up seafood bar. Try the cioppino or the fish-and-chips. ♦ Seafood ♦ Restaurant: daily lunch; fish market: daily from 7:30AM. Lower floor. 467.0514

Rasa Malaysia ★$ This is the first in a popular chain of restaurants where the emphasis is on noodles, usually sautéed with very fresh veggies, peanut or another mildly spicy sauce, and a variety of fish, shrimp, or meat. Try a fruit smoothie or some of the fresh and not overly sweet lemonade. ♦ Malaysian/Takeout ♦ Daily lunch and dinner until 6PM. No credit cards accepted. Lower floor. 624.8388. Also at: Broadway Market (401 Broadway E at E Harrison St). 328.8882 ৬; 7208 E Green Lake Dr (between NE 72nd St and Maple Leaf Pl). 523.8888

Three Girls Bakery ★$ Its roots are in the **Corner Market Building,** where it opened in 1912, but this bakery is now an institution at its current location. You can tell by the crowded lunch counter and the line weaving from its take-out window down the sidewalk. In addition to the baked goods, a delicious assortment of soups and sandwiches are featured; the corned beef and the ham are savvy buys. ♦ Deli/Bakery ♦ M-Sa breakfast and lunch. Lower floor. 622.1045

Ace Loan This pawnshop is packed with wristwatches, cameras, and other hocked possessions. ♦ M-Sa. Upper floor. 682.5424

14 Post Alley Market Designed in 1983 by **Bassetti/Norton/Metler,** this building is strictly functional (unlike some of the other nearby structures). Shops at the bottom give way to offices on top. ♦ Post Alley (between Pike Pl and Pine St)

Within the Post Alley Market:

Made in Washington Locally made jams, coffee cups that sport rigid whale-tail handles, and similar souvenirs are sold here. ♦ Daily. 467.0788

SBC ★$ It's the rare Seattleite who would remember this, but Jim Stewart began selling roasted coffee in 1970, when he had an ice-cream parlor called the **Wet Whisker** in Coupeville on Whidbey Island. He opened his first location with his brother, Dave, in 1971 at Pier 70 on the Waterfront. Ten years later, **Stewart Brothers Coffee** began business in Bellevue Square. By 1989, when the name changed to **SBC Coffee** (defined archly as "Seattle's Best Coffee"), Jim Stewart had locations on both sides of Lake Washington, including the **Westlake Center.** This contemporary corner shop in **Pike Place Market** was

Post Alley

designed by architects **Olson/Walker.** On warm days the alleyside wall opens and patrons spread onto sidewalks. Both bulk coffee beans and cups of espresso variations are available. ♦ Coffeehouse ♦ Daily from 7AM. 467.7700

Sisters ★$ In summer the glass front opens to the elements so patrons sitting along the counter can eavesdrop on alley strollers. And year-round, this is a bright and warm-hearted establishment, specializing in sandwiches served on a focaccia roll. The Corsica (Black Forest ham, artichoke hearts, fontina cheese, and tomato) and the Gesundheit (sun-dried tomato, cream cheese, avocado, and alfalfa sprouts) are faves. Black-bean chili and borscht are good winter warmers. Breakfast waffles, selected deli meats, and cheeses are served all day. ♦ European deli ♦ Daily breakfast, lunch, and dinner until 5PM. No credit cards accepted. 623.6723 &

15 Triangle Building When it was constructed in 1908 as home to the South Park Poultry Company, shoppers used to browse here among the stripped chickens that hung from the ceiling. The structure was rehabilitated in 1977 by architect **Fred Bassetti,** along with the adjoining **Silver Oakum Building** to the north. ♦ Pike Pl and Pine St

Within the Triangle Building:

Cinnamon Works The signature cinnamon rolls here may be filling, but the chocolate-chocolate-chip cookies are some customers' secret weakness. ♦ Daily from 7AM. No credit cards accepted. First floor. 583.0085

Mr. D's Greek Deli ★$ Fast food, Aegean style, with *spanakopita* (spinach and feta cheese wrapped in phyllo), juicy gyro sandwiches, and Greek pastries to go. There are a few tables in the back where you can chow down. ♦ Greek Deli/Takeout ♦ Daily. No credit cards accepted. First floor. 622.4881

Mee Sum Pastries The service can be a bit surly, but it's a small price to pay for the fine Chinese pot stickers and *hum baos* (meat- or vegetable-filled doughy buns) here. ♦ Daily. No credit cards accepted. First floor. 682.6780

Copacabana Cafe ★$ This restaurant was opened in 1963 by Ramon Pelaez, a writer, former owner of Bolivia's largest radio station, and longtime political activist. Pelaez died in 1979, but his daughter and son-in-law continue to run the city's only Bolivian restaurant, using many Pelaez family recipes. Look up one level as you stride the bricks of Pike Place and you're likely to spot the crowded, two-tables-wide deck that surrounds this place—a favorite summer dining option. Service here can be abysmal; don't be surprised if your beer order is forgotten or if the check comes before your lunch. But the food is worth missing a meeting or two. Best choices from the regular menu are the filling paella and the *pescado a la Española,* a delicate halibut steak in a sauce of onions and tomatoes. Order the shrimp nachos (with a side of beer) as an appetizer. ♦ Bolivian ♦ Daily lunch and dinner. Second floor. 622.6359

16 Inn at the Market $$ What finer location for a Seattle hotel than smack dab in the midst of its famous market district? And in most aspects, this 65-room hotel, wrapped about a surprisingly peaceful courtyard, will live up to your expectations. There's a well-respected restaurant located right downstairs, a large deck overlooking the market and Elliott Bay, blessedly little chance that you'll be surrounded by conventioneers (thanks to a shortage of facilities in the hotel for their use), separate floors for nonsmokers, and a warm, European personality. The rooms are good-sized and attractively decorated with sculptures and flowers. Though the hotel doesn't have a kitchen, the restaurant provides room service. The downside is that the same thing that makes the market a wonderful place to be—the bustle and the attendant noise—can also detract from the intimacy and comfort. Rooms on the west side have the best views, but there's disruptive noise for most of the day; those on the east, or First Avenue, side suffer traffic noise. This is a hotel for lovers of the urban experience. ♦ 86 Pine St (at First Ave). 443.3600; fax 448.0631 &

Within the Inn at the Market:

Campagne ★★★$$$ Romantically appointed, with Oriental rugs and a satisfying view of Elliott Bay, this restaurant's Provençal menu enchants its patrons with such dishes as calamari dusted with ground almonds, sautéed in olive oil, and served with fresh thyme and lemon; foie gras terrine with fruit chutney and thyme-scented brioche; and pan-roasted scallops served on a potato puree. For dessert, try the fresh fruit tarts. On the level beneath the restaurant is the stylish **Cafe Campagne,** serving bistro cuisine (such as cassoulet, garlic mashed potatoes, and poulet rôti) in an informal setting. ♦ French ♦ Restaurant: daily dinner; lighter fare served until midnight; bar daily until 2AM. Cafe: M-Sa breakfast, lunch, and dinner; Su brunch. Reservations recommended. Jacket required. 728.2800 &

Dilettante Chocolates Formulas for making this shop's sweet temptations were passed down from Julius Rudolph Franzen, who created pastries for Emperor Franz Josef of Austria and was master candy maker to Nicholas II, the last czar of Russia. Just before the czar was assassinated, Franzen immigrated to the US, where he educated his American brother-in-law, Earl Davenport, in the chocolatier's art. Now, Davenport's grandson produces some of the most tempting truffles, butter creams, and dragées (nuts or dried fruits dredged through dipping chocolate) you'll ever try. ♦ Daily. 728.9144. Also at: 416 Broadway E (at E Republican St). 329.6463 &

DeGraff Books This bookshop is cozy, with helpful salespeople and a good assortment of contemporary fiction, especially mysteries. ♦ Daily. 441.0688 &

17 Garden Center Originally an egg market, this building became the place for flowers and plants in 1946. ♦ Pike Pl (between Pine and Stewart Sts)

Within the Garden Center:

Seattle Garden Center Potted plants decorate the sidewalk outside, and indoors are planters, tools, birdhouses, and more seed packets than most people would think to use in a lifetime. Polish up that green thumb. ♦ Daily. 448.0431

Sur La Table Shirley Collins's hillside lodestone for butchers, bakers, and candy-stick makers represents the height of kitchen chic. Even amateurs can appreciate the shiny and varied wealth of gadgets, dishware, picnic baskets, and kitchenware here. The staff is knowledgeable, and there's a wide assortment of pricey cookbooks to further expand your culinary expertise. Just watch out for weekends and lunch hours, when the cramped aisles seem to become all feet and elbows. ♦ Daily. 448.2244, 800/243.0852

18 Upper Post Alley Horse-drawn hearses once clattered down this uneven brick path to deposit corpses in the basement crematorium of the Butterworth Mortuary, now home to

Kell's Restaurant & Pub (see below). This is still the only section of Post Alley open to vehicular traffic. ♦ Between Stewart and Virginia Sts

Along Upper Post Alley:

Glass Eye Gallery Mount St. Helens's volcanic eruption in 1980 proved a big boon to some of the Northwest's novelty glass makers. The co-owners of this shop, Rob Adamson and Dale Leman, caught on early to the possibilities (they're still riding the trend) and incorporated the peak's ashen and slightly iridescent detritus into their hand-blown glass pieces. Look here for dishware, blown-glass fruit, and shapely vases. ♦ Daily. 782.6548

The Perennial Tea Room For all the coffee talk in Seattle, there is the occasional tearoom, and this is one to remember. It features lovely teapots, ranging from what you'd expect in the parlor of a proper English home to outrageous and funky. The shop also is well-stocked with biscuits, teas, tea cozies, and all manner of things to accessorize your afternoon sip. Daily. 448.4054 &

Kell's Restaurant & Pub ★$$ This hidden-away pub is easy to miss, but don't. It's everything a pub should be: Aged and full of smoke-darkened woods and sporting prints, this is a place where patrons aren't afraid to argue and maybe fight for their politics. Guinness is available on tap, or dip into a pint of one of the Northwest's assertive brews. The menu complements the Irish ambience with homemade stews and meat pies. And live Irish music is featured Wednesday through Saturday nights. In summer a small outdoor dining area is cordoned off in the alley. ♦ Irish ♦ Cover F-Sa nights. Daily lunch and dinner. Bar open daily until 2AM. 728.1916

The Pink Door ★★$$ Although some summer visitors know this place solely for its alfresco dining, this high-ceilinged trattoria serving inexpensive Italian fare is romantic year-round—at night candles illuminate the surroundings. Service can be forgetful and sometimes you have to wield sharp elbows to find lunchtime seating, but such dishes as fettuccine with clam sauce and lasagna are hard to beat. ♦ Italian ♦ Tu-Sa lunch, afternoon antipasto, and dinner; bar Tu-Th until 11:30PM, F-Sa until 1:30AM. 443.3241

19 Stewart House A workingperson's hotel, built in stages between 1902 and 1911, this place closed in the 1970s for failure to meet city housing codes. A 1982 renovation by **Ibsen Nelsen & Associates** rehabilitated the wooden structure and included a four-story brick-faced addition. Studios for senior citizens and people with disabilities are located above the street-level shops. ♦ Stewart St and Pike Pl

Within the Stewart House:

Cucina Fresca Stop by for exceptional pasta salads, entrées to warm in the oven or consume picnic-style, and other Italian deli take-out goodies. ♦ Daily. 448.4758

Le Panier Warm, fragrant French breads are the main attraction, but once you're inside, the pastries are no less an enticement. This is no place to be worried about your waistline. ♦ M-Sa from 7AM. 441.3669

Market Tobacco Patch Owner Bill Coulson defies political correctness to maintain Seattle's premier pipe and cigar emporium. Pipe tobacco is available in a splendid variety, and Coulson keeps 60 to 80 types of cigars in stock. But the real treat here (for smokers, at least) is stepping inside the climate-controlled cigar humidor and inhaling deeply. ♦ Daily. 728.7291

20 **Soames-Dunn Building** Two adjoining structures from 1918—one held Dunn's Seeds, the other the Soames Paper Company, which peddled paper bags to market merchants—were combined to make this building. A 1976 rehabilitation was accomplished by architect **Arne Bystrom**. ♦ Pike Pl (between Stewart and Virginia Sts)

Within the Soames-Dunn Building:

Emmett Watson's Oyster Bar
★★$ A former semipro baseball player, Watson is now the city's curmudgeonly veteran columnist (with the *Seattle Times*, after an early stint with the competing *Post-Intelligencer*). He was the journalist who discovered and notified the world that Ernest Hemingway's 1961 death in Ketcham, Idaho, was a suicide. More recently he's led the "Lesser Seattle" movement, endorsing slow or no growth for the city and railing against the influx of Californians.

This oft-crowded restaurant named in Watson's honor has earned institution status for its consistently fresh and varied selection of oysters. Salmon soup and hearty helpings of fish-and-chips can also be had, if you're not keen on bivalves. Wash your food down with something from the ample beer roster. One warning: Niched beside a courtyard at the back of the **Soames-Dunn Building,** the restaurant can be hard to find. ♦ Seafood ♦ Daily lunch and dinner. 448.7721

The Soap Box Indulge your inner child with the bath oils and the rubber duckies that are sold here. ♦ Daily. 441.5680

The Souk Foods and spices from the Middle East, Pakistan, India, and Africa stock these shelves. ♦ Daily. 441.1666

Starbucks ★$ According to an old Turkish proverb, "Coffee should be black as Hell, strong as death, and sweet as love." Well, the ancient Turks would be shocked at the way their heady brew is treated around here. The ol' black magic has all but disappeared from the coffee in the Seattle area, where ordering a cup of regular, "unmilked," unadorned java will earn you the kind of bug-eyed stares usually reserved for asylum escapees. The caffeine craze in Seattle can mostly be attributed to this chain, which grew to ubiquity (not only in Seattle, but throughout the country) after this storefront opened in 1971. It's always crowded on weekends, when classical violinists regularly perform just outside the front door. ♦ Coffeehouse ♦ M-Sa from 7:30AM; Su from 8:30AM. 448.8762 ఉ. Also at: Numerous locations throughout the city

21 **Louie's on the Pike** While most market shops specialize, here is a general-interest grocery store—*the* place to shop if you're looking for something so pedestrian as a bottled soft drink or an ice-cream bar. There's also a decent deli counter inside. ♦ Daily. 1926 Pike Pl (between Stewart and Virginia Sts). 443.1035

22 **Pike & Western Wine Merchants** This shop stocks a wide range of wines, specializing in vintners from the Northwest; the selection of French and German vintages is also well chosen. ♦ Daily. 1934 Pike Pl (at Virginia St). 441.1307 ఉ

23 **Victor Steinbrueck Park** It's fitting that such a lively spot (designed in 1982 by both **Steinbrueck** and **Richard Haag**) should be dedicated to an architect who sought to maintain the vibrancy of **Pike Place Market.** This grassy viewpoint bustles on warm days with businesspeople lunching, tourists pondering the passage of ferries on the Sound, and the usual Seattle complement of panhandlers. A pair of Northwest Indian totem poles designed by Quinault tribe member Marvin Oliver were carved with the assistance of James Bender. The bad news is that right below the park rushes the interminably noisy Alaskan Way Viaduct. ♦ Western Ave (at Virginia St)

There are about 500 floating houseboats docked in and around Lake Union, but the most famous of all is the fictional one Tom Hanks and his son lived in in *Sleepless in Seattle*.

Funny thing about Seattle: Cartoonists Lynda Barry and Gary Larson have put the city on the map, and local outfit Fantagraphics is avant-garde cartoonist Robert Crumb's favorite publisher.

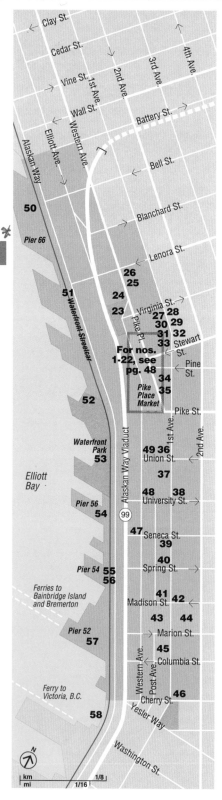

24 Cutter's Bayhouse ★$$$ People either love this place or they would sooner swear off *lattes* for life than dine here again. The problem isn't the food; like its sister establishments (**Triples** on Lake Union, **Palisade** in Magnolia, **Palomino** downtown), this one shows skill in the kitchen. So what if the menu is all over the map—a little Chinese, some Cajun, a dash of Italian—as long as the pasta, seafood, and the garlicky focaccia remain impressive. No, the problem here is the clientele: lots of competitive yuppies (and wannabes), lots of fatless body fanatics, and everybody checking out everybody else's vital stats. ♦ International ♦ Daily lunch and dinner; bar (serving light meals) daily until 1:30AM. 2001 Western Ave (between Virginia and Lenora Sts). 448.4884

25 Seattle Club On the edge of the **Pike Place Market,** this 2,400-member health club features all the usual exercise equipment and free weights, as well a pool, indoor track, basketball, racquetball, and squash courts, and aerobics classes. A number of downtown hotels offer their guests temporary club memberships here. ♦ Daily. 2020 Western Ave (between Virginia and Lenora Sts). 443.1111

◆

PHOENIX RISING GALLERY

◆

26 Phoenix Rising Gallery Simultaneously playful, pricey, and *very* crowded with merchandise, this shop is decorated with table after table of contemporary glassworks, jewelry, business gifts, and home accessories. ♦ Daily. 2030 Western Ave (at Lenora St). 728.2332

27 Virginia Inn A favorite hangout for newspaper and magazine types, the "V.I." (originally the **Virginia Bar**) has anchored this corner of First Avenue and Virginia Street since about 1908. Unlike many similar pubs, it never closed during Prohibition but was converted temporarily into a card- and lunchroom. Knife-scarred wooden booths hug a corner near the door, leaving the remaining floor space to a maze of little round tables and a long elegant bar that can barely be seen through the mass of revelers on weekdays after 5PM. The choice of craft beers and wines, while not extensive, is select.

There's not much in the way of pub grub, although the platter of smoked salmon and bread provides a reasonable light lunch. Art on the brick walls changes frequently. The rest rooms are worth a peek: *True Detective* motif in the men's john, and lip prints next door for women. ♦ Daily until 2AM. 1937 First Ave (at Virginia St). 728.1937

27 The Kaleenka ★$$ Seattleites may be most familiar with this Russian restaurant because of the popular food stands it sets up at such city fairs as Bumbershoot and the Northwest Folklife Festival, from which it purveys hot, hearty piroshkis (meat and cheese wrapped in soft baked dough). But the sit-down menu here is far more extensive and no less satisfying; it includes a terrific multivegetable borscht, chicken Kiev, and *galubtzi* (cabbage leaves filled with beef, pork, and rice and then baked in a sour cream and tomato sauce). ♦ Russian ♦ M-Sa lunch and dinner. 1933 First Ave (between Stewart and Virginia Sts). 728.1278 &

28 Peter Miller Books
Specializing in architecture and design books (new as well as out-of-print titles), with such nifty accessories as build-it-yourself paper replicas of the **Space Needle,** this bookstore is a great place to while away an hour. There's a mail-order catalog, too. ♦ Daily. 1930 First Ave (between Stewart and Virginia Sts). 441.4114

29 Labuznik ★★$$$ Owners Peter and Susan Cipra defy current wisdom that says restaurants must continually change in order to remain interesting. For more than two decades, this has been a comforting holdout of traditional Central European cuisine (Cipra, himself, is from the former Czechoslovakia). The menu is built around roast pork, veal chops, and rack of lamb, with side dishes of sweet-and-sour red cabbage, sauerkraut, and dumplings. The goulash and the fish soup are remarkable. The windowless dining room's look is understated and subdued, featuring taupe walls and plenty of fresh flowers; there's also sidewalk seating in summer. ♦ Central European ♦ Tu-Sa dinner. Reservations recommended. 1924 First Ave (between Stewart and Virginia Sts). 441.8899

30 Pensione Nichols
$ Prices at Lindsey Nichols's bed-and-breakfast establishment are extremely reasonable for the location—just a block off Pike Place and convenient to a superfluity of restaurants and

shops. It's easy to miss the entrance: It's just a single doorway off the sidewalk that opens onto a cliff of stairs. The *pensione* occupies two floors up the stairs; check in at the desk

on the third floor. The eight guest rooms and two suites are brightly painted, cozy, and overlook either First Avenue or Elliott Bay; the latter are slightly quieter, but the former seem more intimate. A large third-floor sitting room embraces views of Elliott Bay and is replete with soft couches for reading or clandestine romancing. Guests (save for those in the suites) must share bath and rest room facilities, but they are quite comfortable and well maintained. A continental breakfast is included in the room rate.

While the establishment has collected national raves, local attention has been far more stingy. Overshadowing it has been the nearby **Inn at the Market,** a higher-priced and more expensively retailed hostelry. Also weighing against it may be the fact that the *pensione* is located directly above a porno-movie house. Whatever the reason, the slight is unfortunate, for Nichols manages a secret uptown gem. ♦ 1923 First Ave (between Stewart and Virginia Sts). 441.7125

30 Cafe Sophie $$ If the stone gargoyles, decorative angels, and cathedral ceilings inside give you an oddly sepulchral feeling, it's not without cause: the gaudy (and reportedly haunted) dining room was originally the chapel of a three-story funeral parlor built by undertaker Edgar Ray Butterworth. Architect **John Graham Sr.** designed the stone-footed, Victorian-Romanesque building—his first commercial structure in Seattle—in 1903, before venturing on to create such landmarks as downtown's **Bon Marché** and **Frederick & Nelson** stores. The continental fare has gone downhill recently, but the stunning architecture alone makes this place worth a visit. ♦ International ♦ Tu-Sa lunch and dinner. 1921 First Ave (between Stewart and Virginia Sts). 441.6139

31 du jour ★★$ The lowercase moniker should not suggest lower-class cuisine. Indeed, this cafeteria-style eatery serves dishes suitable for a "downtown business-person's lunch," as one employee describes it. Included are thick, delicious sandwiches, hearty soups, and a spread of tempting salads. (Try the chicken-pecan salad if it's available.) This is also a great find for lovers of morning baked goods. A dining area at the rear, aggressively white in its decor, provides agreeable views of Puget Sound. Takeout is also available. ♦ Cafeteria ♦ M-F breakfast, lunch, and dinner until 6PM; Sa until 5PM. 1919 First Ave (between Stewart and Virginia Sts). 441.3354 &

32 Fast Forward Owner Harry Green focuses on works created by local designers of jewelry, eye-catching shirts, and dresses that can be tucked into a bag no larger than your fist. ♦ M-Th, Sa; F 10AM-8PM; Su noon-6PM. 1918 First Ave (between Stewart and Virginia Sts). 728.8050

Carefree (and Car-Free) Sightseeing: Seattle by Bus

One of the most convenient and least expensive ways to tour Seattle is by taking the regular commuter buses operated by **Metro Transit** (553.3000). You can cover a lot of ground in a short time, and you don't have to worry about navigating through traffic or getting lost. The routes cover most of the city, and several offer spectacular views of both Seattle's glorious natural surroundings and its architectural splendors. Traveling by bus is also a great way to get in touch with the daily routine of local residents, making you feel less like a stranger. All of the routes listed below leave from downtown, and maps and schedules can be found at libraries, hotels, the ferry terminal, and tourist offices. Your journey will be much more relaxing if you avoid the morning and evening rush hours (7 to 10AM and 4 to 6PM Mondays through Fridays). To save money, purchase an All-Day Pass (allowing a day's unlimited travel on weekends and holidays on all **Metro Transit** buses) from the driver.

West Seattle:

Two bus routes cover this area. **No. 37** travels high over the **Duwamish River** for a view of the harbor and downtown skyline before heading out along the shoreline around **Duwamish Head** and along the beach past **Alki Point;** stunning vistas of the **Pacific Ocean,** offshore islands, and the **Olympic Mountains** unfold before you. **No. 56** goes over the West Seattle ridge, showing off the **Space Needle, Queen Anne Hill, Magnolia,** the harbor, and downtown.

Magnolia:

No. 19 reverses the West Seattle routes by going north, then west up a steep viaduct to the crest of **Magnolia Bluff.** As the bus travels along the bluff, you can see downtown, West Seattle, **Puget Sound, Bainbridge** and **Vashon Islands,** and, in clear

weather, the stunning sight of **Mount Rainier** filling the southeastern horizon.

West Queen Anne/Madrona Park:

No. 2 gives you a choice of two different views: from downtown, up the steep **Counterbalance** to the top of Queen Anne Hill for fabulous views of the city in all directions; or up over **First Hill** (affectionately called "Pill Hill" because of the many hospitals and clinics here) and out through the **Madrona** neighborhood to **Lake Washington.** A sign on the front of the bus indicates which destination it's going to.

Madison Park/Ferry Terminal:

No. 11 runs in a straight diagonal line along the four-mile width of the city, from the harbor to Lake Washington. Passing over hills and through valleys, it takes you through commercial and residential areas, including the trendy, newly gentrified **Madison Valley** area, the **Washington Park Arboretum,** the exclusive **Broadmoor** residential enclave, and the charming Madison Park neighborhood.

Colman Park:

No. 27 goes from downtown across **Yesler Way,** then descends precipitously to the shoreline of Lake Washington. From the lake, it continues past **Leschi Park** to Colman Park. Along the way, you'll get to see the **Evergreen Point** and **Lacey V. Morrow Floating Bridges,** the wooded **Seward Park** peninsula, **Mercer Island,** and Mount Rainier, as well as several long beachfront stretches of the Olmsted green belt.

U-District/Sand Point:

No. 75 begins on the freeway, then it takes a scenic tour of the **University of Washington** before heading east and north on **Sand Point Way** along the Lake Washington shoreline. Eventually, it ends up at the world's first shopping mall, the **Northgate Shopping Center,** which was erected in the early 1950s.

33 Zebra Club This unisex store carries sporty and lightweight street attire for those who favor the ultracasual look. Ubiquitous video equipment heightens the youth-oriented tone. An espresso cart out front is particularly popular. ♦ Daily. 1901 First Ave (at Stewart St). 448.7452

34 Local Brilliance There's playfulness in owner/designer Renata Tatman's affordable assortment of locally created womenswear

and accessories. Note especially the fluid works of Sara Campbell, whose designs in contemporary fabrics take their inspiration from styles of the 1920s through the 1940s. ♦ Daily. 1535 First Ave (between Pike and Pine Sts). 343.5864

34 Ragin' Cajun ★★$$ This tiny eatery with four booths, a couple of tables, and counter service is owned by chef Danny Delcambre, who learned traditional Cajun cooking from his mother and later interned with Paul Prudhomme. Try the blackened catfish or the red beans and rice with andouille sausage—they're all top-notch. The restaurant serves beer and wine and offers outdoor seating in the summer. Delcambre is deaf and blind, and believes he is the only similarly disabled restaurateur in the country. ◆ Cajun ◆ Tu-Sa lunch and dinner. 1523 First Ave (between Pike and Pine Sts). 624.2598 ♿

Retro Viva

35 Retro Viva Everything old is new again, as they say. Vintage jewelry, jazzy bras, men's shirts, and hats that barely escaped the pages of early fashion mags—this shop is full of attire (at fair prices) for the funky fashion plate. ◆ Daily. 1511 First Ave (between Pike and Pine Sts). 624.2529. Also at: 4515 University Way NE (between NE 45th and NE 47th Sts). 632.8886; 215 Broadway E (between E John and E Thomas Sts). 328.7451

36 South Arcade This tower, a jarring, neon-highlighted contrast to the sedate **Pike Place Market,** was designed in 1985 by **Olson/Walker.** ◆ 1411 First Ave (at Union St)

Within the South Arcade:

Undercover Quilts This store has a lot of authentic antique quilts, some dating as far back as the 1850s, as well as a large collection of new quilts made by artists from all over the US. Owner Linda Hitchcock will even make a quilt to your specifications. Also in stock here are fabrics, one-of-a-kind dolls, and Christmas decorations made from vintage quilts. ◆ M-Sa; open occasional Sundays as well. 622.6382

World Class Chili ★$ Arguments about what chili is and what it isn't could (and do) fill whole cookbooks. Joe Canavan, who collected recipes for years before he opened this small place, has decided to give purists and bean lovers something to sink their spoons into. Here the Texas-style bowl, dense with beef and chilies, leads the herd. Other versions mix beef and pork with ingredients like chocolate and cinnamon, substitute chicken for red meat, or throw out the meat altogether in favor of lentils and veggies (sacrilege!). ◆ Chili ◆ No credit cards accepted. M-Sa lunch and dinner until 6PM. 623.3678

37 Un Deux Trois ★★★$$$ At this cozy, intimate retreat owned by Judy Schocken, the emphasis is on contemporary French cuisine. The dining room is bright and airy, with floor-to-ceiling windows that look out onto the huge *Hammering Man* sculpture in front of the **Seattle Art Museum.** Chef Astolfo Rueda's specialties include ragouts, roasted meats (venison, rabbit, duck), fresh local seafood, and braised vegetables. Rueda is locally famous for his exquisite sauces and his wonderful soups (especially his bisques). The restaurant validates parking in the lot next door for dinner guests. ◆ French ◆ M lunch; Tu-Sa lunch and dinner. 1329 First Ave (between University and Union Sts). 233.0123; fax 623.2213 ♿

38 Seattle Art Museum (SAM) Asked to explain the intent behind his firm's design of the **Seattle Art Museum** (pictured below), which was relocated downtown in 1991, Philadelphia architect **Robert Venturi** said he wanted to create a "current urban art museum that is popular yet esoteric, closed but open, monumental yet inviting, an accommodating setting for the art, but a work of art itself." In other words, a little bit of everything: a

Seattle Art Museum

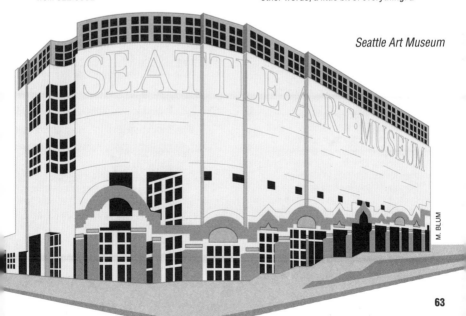

M. BLUM

sophisticated but unimposing juxtaposition of convex and concave curves, all faced in fluted limestone and terra-cotta ornament.

The main entrance on First Avenue is enlivened by sculptor Jonathan Borofsky's *Hammering Man*, a black, 48-foot-tall mechanical piece that took a spill during its installation and had to be repaired before final placement.

Working within zoning requirements that dictated view corridors to Puget Sound, **Venturi**, his partner **Denise Scott Brown,** and their associates created a waterfall of an outdoor staircase along the south wall that's almost mirrored by a processional stair inside, leading from the lobby to second-floor galleries and punctuated by sculptures of Chinese military guardians, camels, and rams. Brightly hued arches hang majestically over those inside stairs. It's a bit disappointing, however, after this elaborate staircase, to deal with the narrow twisting flights of stairs and elevators that continue the escalation within the building. The loftlike galleries are pleasant, if spare, and broad, curving hallways are well lighted from view windows at either end.

The second-floor exhibition space hosts special shows. Native American, African, Chinese, and Near Eastern treasures occupy the third floor. The fourth level contains a history of European and American works, including pieces by such Northwest artists as Morris Graves, Jacob Lawrence, and Kenneth Callahan. A cafe providing refreshments (open the same hours as the museum) is located on the mezzanine level. ♦ Admission; free for children 12 and under, members, and the first Tuesday of each month; discount for senior citizens and students. Tu-Su; Th until 9PM. 100 University St (at First Ave). 654.3100

39 Grand Pacific Hotel Displaying a stone and arched face that would have been more familiar in Pioneer Square than this far north on First Avenue, this building (known upon opening in 1898 as the **First Avenue Hotel**) was at no time a luxury inn. Its tenants were miners, sailors, and businessmen of modest means, in the early years many of them blowing through town on their way to the gold fields of the Klondike. But the structure, with its Romanesque stone footing, arched windows along the third floor, and fine detailing over most of its brick upper facade, doesn't lack class or style. Now restored, it's been joined internally to the neighboring **Colonial Hotel,** and divided into residential units. ♦ 1115-1117 First Ave (between Spring and Seneca Sts)

40 Watermark Tower This sculpted 20-story edifice (designed by **Bumgardner Architects** in 1983) bursts upward from the preserved terra-cotta facade of the 1915 **Colman Building** (conceived by **Carl Gould** and

Charles Bebb). Pay special attention to the dynamic entry arch on Spring Street. ♦ First Ave and Spring St

Within Watermark Tower:

McCormick & Schmick's ★★$$ Waiters in black bow ties add a touch of class to this restaurant that specializes in seafood and grilled meats. The lamb chops don't disappoint, nor do the salmon dishes. Enjoy a preprandial cocktail in the comfortable, dark-wood barroom. The Irish coffees served here are better than most. ♦ Seafood ♦ M-F lunch and dinner; Sa-Su dinner. Reservations recommended. 1103 First Ave (at Spring St). 623.5500

41 Alexis Hotel $$$ Designed in 1901 by architect **Max Umbrecht,** this building was renovated in 1982 as part of a large-scale, privately funded project that also fixed up several nearby edifices. The property was refurbished again in 1996, doubling in size. Convenient to **Pike Place Market,** the **Seattle Art Museum,** and Pioneer Square, the hotel now boasts 109 guest rooms, two restaurants, a fitness center, and spa services.

Trapped between the revolting Alaskan Way Viaduct and noisy First Avenue, there are no views to speak of here, but a handful of balconied rooms face an interior courtyard and thus provide the most peace and quiet. Suites are outfitted with Jacuzzis, wood-burning fireplaces, and marble fixtures. Complimentary services include shoe shines, Sherry in your room, continental breakfast, and a morning newspaper. "Discount luxury" hotel operator Bill Kimpton, who also owns the **Hotel Vintage Park** in the business district, is now at the helm. Parking around here can be a problem. ♦ 1007 First Ave (at Madison St). 624.4844, 800/426.7033; fax 621.9009

Within the Alexis Hotel:

The Bookstore Bar This is actually a better taproom than it was a bookstore. With its shelves full of literature, the place still maintains a bit of the feeling of its previous incarnation. The atmosphere is conducive to political discussions and after-work jousts with colleagues. Appetizers from the **Painted Table** restaurant (see below) are available as bar snacks, and there are microbrews on tap. ♦ M-Th until midnight, F-Su until 2AM. 624.4844

The Painted Table ★★★$$ Chef Tim Kelly exhibits his skill and creativity in such Northwest and Asian specialties as layered goat cheese and vegetable salad, risotto with mussels, shrimp, and scallops, and pan-roasted Alaskan halibut with grilled portobello mushrooms. Twice a week in summer and twice a month the rest of the year, Kelly also gives shopping tours of **Pike Place Market,** followed by a special three-course lunch here. ♦ Northwestern♦ M-F breakfast, lunch, and dinner; Sa-Su breakfast and dinner. Reservations recommended. 624.3646, tour information and reservations 340.6710

The Legacy The collection of historic baskets, masks, and carvings from Northwest Indians and Eskimos here is rounded out with newer native merchandise. ♦ M-Sa. 624.6350

42 Warshal's Sporting Goods An anachronism on increasingly chic First Avenue, this store has occupied the same post–Great Fire edifice for half a century. In addition to its broad selection of hunting, fishing, and other sports equipment, there are also photography and darkroom supplies. Look for the frequent specials. ♦ M-Sa. 1000 First Ave (at Madison St). 624.7300

43 Old Federal Office Building Looking very much like a snowcapped mountain range, what with its brick facing topped by terra-cotta detailing, this memorable stepped-back Art Deco structure (which just received an extensive renovation) was one of the few projects raised in downtown during the Depression. The architect was **James A. Wetmore.** ♦ 909 First Ave (between Marion and Madison Sts)

44 Henry M. Jackson Federal Office Building The original building on this site was the **Frye Opera House.** With a mansard roof and brick-walls, featuring 1,400 seats and a stage with seven trapdoors, the theater was once Seattle's most ostentatious landmark. The Great Fire of 1889 began at this intersection, in a woodworker's basement, and the **Frye** went up in smoke. After the fire, **Elmer Fisher** designed the Victorian-style **Burke Building** here, which in turn was torn down in 1974 to make room for the current structure, boasting a hipped and tiled roof and a fenestration of interlocking prefab concrete segments. This tower (designed by **Fred Bassetti,** along with **John Graham & Company**) gives off a Mediterranean palazzo feel. The lobby appeals with its wood finishes, but the star of this building is its outdoor cascading hillside stairs, which include remnants from the **Burke Building.** Sculptor Isamu Noguchi contributed an abstract grouping of pink granite blocks, called *Landscape of Time,* to the Second Avenue plaza here. ♦ Bounded by Second and First Aves, and Marion and Madison Sts

45 Colman Building Scottish immigrant James M. Colman's namesake structure had trouble getting off the ground in more ways than one. A mechanic and a steam-mill operator, Colman first acquired this property by running a ship aground here long enough to earn legal title; he planned simply to build over the hull. But Colman's original, very ornate design (conceived by architect **Stephen Meany** before the Great Fire of 1889) was stunted by his business caution after the blaze. He went ahead with only the concept's first two stories, waiting to see what demand there was for more office and commercial space in the rapidly rebuilding city. Not until about 1904 did architect **August Tidemand** completely revamp these two floors in brownstone style; he then added four more austere brick stories above those to form the basic edifice you see today. In 1930 Seattle architect **Arthur B. Loveless** performed another remodeling that incorporated several Art Deco elements into the glazed street canopy and lobby. ♦ 811 First Ave (between Columbia and Marion Sts)

Ferry Tales

The **Washington State Ferry System**—the largest in the country—calls itself the state's number one tourist attraction, and its boast seems justified: It affords the ideal vantage point for taking in the sunlit waters and salt air of **Puget Sound,** the snowcapped **Cascade Mountains,** the stunning Seattle skyline, and wildlife. Each year, it carries more than 23 million people to 20 ports of call throughout Puget Sound, its inland waterways, and the **San Juan Islands.** The 25 vessels that make up the fleet range from small, sleek, passenger-only boats to massive car ferries. Many of their names, such as *Hyak, Elwa, Cathlamet,* and *Sealth,* come from local tribal languages. Some passengers use the ferry to commute to or from work; others ride it for purely recreational purposes.

The options are almost endless, from sightseeing trips that last only a few hours to longer trips to the beautiful San Juan Islands or the charming cities of **Vancouver** and **Victoria** in **British Columbia.** If you want to avoid crowds, don't travel during peak commuter hours (7 to 10AM and 4 to 6PM Mondays through Fridays) or on summer weekends.

No matter when you go, however, you may have to wait for a place on a boat, so bring something to keep yourself entertained. (By the way, the food sold on board is mediocre, so bring your own snacks if you think you'll want to eat.) The schedule varies by season; for information on departure times and ticket prices, call the **Washington State Ferry System** (464.6400 or 800/843.3779).

Maps Joseph Conrad captured the [gr]aps in *Heart of Darkness*, when [Marl]owe explained: "Now, when I was a little chap, I had a passion for maps. I would look for hours at South America, or Africa, or Australia, and lose myself in all the glories of exploration." Marlowe might have begun many a voyage at this shop, which sells hundreds of maps as well as guidebooks and assorted travel paraphernalia to satisfy the hunger of wanderlust. ♦ M-Sa. 702 First Ave (at Cherry St). 623.8747

46 La Buca ★★$$ Another Italian restaurant—just what Seattle needs, right? But with a couple of familiar powerhouses behind it (Luigi DeNunzio, formerly of **Al Boccalino** in Pioneer Square, and Raffaele Calise, who helped create the popular **Salute** restaurants), this dining spot has survived the glut. Stuck below street level (the name means "The Hole") in an orange-walled space, the restaurant specializes in Southern Italian cuisine. There's lots of whole-wheat pasta, calamari, chicken, and veal. Favorite dishes include the *risotto di mare* (*arborio* rice bobbing with prawns, mussels, and clams, all accented with saffron) and the tenderloin of pork sautéed and served with red-pepper sauce and olives. The kitchen also turns out some savory fish specials, particularly halibut. Forget the grilled and marinated prawns, though. And two cautions: main-course portions are small and the ambient noise level can be high. ♦ Southern Italian ♦ M-Sa lunch and dinner; Su dinner. Reservations recommended. 102 Cherry St (at First Ave). 343.9517

47 Current The high-style Moderne furniture that turns up in these expansive showrooms is unquestionably elegant. There are pieces for every room in the house, with a special focus on sconce lighting. The prices, unfortunately, can be quite steep. ♦ Daily. 1201 Western Ave (at Seneca St). 622.2433

48 Seattle Bagel Bakery Lines are long on weekends, as at-home brunchers slip in for supplies of pumpernickel, onion, or salt bagels. Even topped with lox or cream cheese, the chewy dough dominates the taste buds. This is one of Seattle's top bagelries. ♦ Daily from 7:30AM. 1302 Western Ave (at University St). 624.2187

Restaurants/Clubs: Red   **Hotels:** Blue

Shops/ ♥ Outdoors: Green   **Sights/Culture:** Black

49 Wild Ginger ★★★$$ The satay bar here was the first of its kind in the nation and continues to be a main event. You can just hang out, enjoying the grilled chunks of chicken, beef, prawns, or veggies on skewers that are served with a zingy peanut or soy and black-vinegar sauce, or take a place in the antique-filled dining room and order them as appetizers. The fragrant Wandering Sage soup is another house specialty. The seafood, particularly the scallops, is delicious, as are the beef curry and a sweetly flavored duck. Specials are influenced by cooking from around the Pacific Rim and are based on what's seasonally fresh. Paintings by local artists hang on the white walls. ♦ Asian ♦ M-Sa lunch and dinner; Su dinner; satay bar until 2AM. 1400 Western Ave (at Union St). 623.4450

50 Bell Street Pier Seattle's latest effort to reclaim its forgotten north waterfront area is this enormous complex, a combination of convention space, marina, museum, and restaurant. The **Bell Harbor International Conference Center,** cunningly designed to look and feel like a part of the "working waterfront" that surrounds the pier, has full conference facilities geared to international business (including a multilingual staff and five simultaneous translation booths). Above the center is a public viewing space complete with comfortable benches and free telescopic sights; it's a great spot to sit and watch the harbor and street activity. Visitors' gastronomic needs are satisfied by **Anthony's Pier 66 & Bell Street Diner** (448.6688), a complex of three restaurants that comprise the newest link in the **Anthony's Homeport** chain of seafood eateries. Other facilities here include a small short-stay marina and a cruise ship dock; and **Odyssey, The Maritime Discovery Center,** an interactive maritime museum, was scheduled to open at press time. ♦ Odyssey: daily. Odyssey: admission. Pier 66 (at Alaskan Way and Bell St) ♿

Waterfront

51 Waterfront Streetcar Seattle's original trolleys were stripped from service decades ago, but, for nostalgia's sake, **Metro Transit** imported these vintage machines from Australia to make the clattering 15- to 20-minute run from Pier 70 through Pioneer Square to the International District. ♦ $1.10 at peak times (M-F 6 to 9AM and 3 to 6PM); 85¢ off-peak; children under five free. Daily. Off Alaskan Way (from Pier 70 to the International District). 553.3000

52 Seattle Aquarium Designed by **Fred Bassetti and Company** in 1977, this Waterfront institution attracts visitors with its more-than-generous complement of tanks holding marine exotica, its "discovery lab" where children can pet starfish and peer

through microscopes, and the playful clans of seals and sea otters that occupy its upper reaches. (Look for feeding-time notices: it's the best time to watch these jesters.) Farther inside, visitors walk under a 4,000-gallon glassed-in pool where sharks and myriad other Puget Sound creatures swim. One of the latest additions is a six-foot-long water monitor lizard in a naturalistic environment. The lizard, a native of Malaysia, is a descendant of dinosaurs. Expect to spend at least two to three hours at the aquarium.
♦ Admission; children age 2 and under free; discount for senior citizens, disabled persons, children ages 3 to 5, King County residents, and groups of 10 or more. Daily. Pier 59 (off Alaskan Way). 386.4320

53 Waterfront Park A soothing "boardwalk" hugging Elliott Bay, the elevated walkways here give visitors a better perspective on the city and the Sound. It's a good place for picnics, offering a superfluity of fish, hot dogs, and ice-cream parlors nearby. Long gone is adjacent Pier 58, where the first cargo of tea from the Orient arrived in 1896 and where the steamer *Portland* anchored in 1897 with the first news that gold had been discovered in the Klondike; a plaque here recalls the beginning of Alaska's gold rush. The minipark was designed in 1974 by the **Bumgardner Architects.** ♦ Pier 57 (off Alaskan Way)

54 Elliott's Oyster House & Seafood Restaurant ★$$$ Water views, fast service, and some of the best oysters in town are featured here. ♦ Seafood ♦ M-Sa lunch and dinner. Pier 56 (off Alaskan Way). 623.4340

55 Ye Olde Curiosity Shop A mecca for tourist-trinket junkies, founded in 1899, this carnival-flavored shop sells rubber slugs, Seattle T-shirts, Russian nesting dolls, seashells, scrimshaw, and shrunken heads—they're all here, alongside such Barnum-esque oddities as a bottled pig with eight legs, three eyes, three mouths, and a pair of tails. Most popular is Sylvester the Desert Mystery: a mummified murder victim found in the Arizona sandflats in 1895 with a bullet through his stomach and with mustache and fingernails still intact. ♦ Daily; Th-Sa until 9PM. Pier 54 (off Alaskan Way). 682.5844

56 Ivar's Acres of Clams and Fish Bar ★$ Ivar Haglund, who died several years ago, was Seattle's quintessential promoter. He's remembered for his corny commercial slogan (Keep Clam), his guitar playing and storytelling, and the carp wind sock that he ran up the flagpole on **Smith Tower** when he owned that building, beginning in 1976. This full-service restaurant offers a variety of seafood; best choices are usually the clam nectar and the cod-and-chips. The outdoor seating can hardly be beat for Seattle charm. A sentimental statue of Ivar feeding gulls holds court nearby. ♦ Seafood ♦ Daily lunch and dinner. Pier 54 (off Alaskan Way). 624.6852

57 Colman Dock Elliott Bay's worst docking collision occurred here in April 1912, when the ocean liner *Alameda* charged right into this pier, toppling its previously elegant clock tower into the drink. The *Alameda* suffered barely a scratch. The clock from the tower was retrieved after the collision, and restored; you can see it inside. It wasn't the first time this dock was rebuilt, nor would it be the last. The original wharf went up by order of Scottish immigrant James Colman in 1882. The current modern incarnation is its sixth and least interesting form, dating only to 1966. **Washington State Ferries** leave from here many times daily, bound for Bainbridge Island and Bremerton (call 464.6400 for the schedule). ♦ Pier 52 (off Alaskan Way)

58 Washington Street Public Boat Landing Built in 1920 from a design by city architect **Daniel R. Huntington,** this iron-and-steel pergola—much less ornate than the older Pioneer Place pergola only two blocks to the east—was intended to house Seattle's harbor master and be the entry point for visiting seamen. Now rehabilitated, it is more a curiosity than anything else, being located near Pier 48 but away from other Waterfront landmarks. Watch for it on the **Waterfront Streetcar** ride. ♦ Alaskan Way (at Washington St)

Bests

Pat Arthur
Project Director, Institutions Project/Columbia Legal Services

The troll under the bridge in **Fremont.** A life-size troll "street sculpture" that has captured a real Volkswagen in its hands.

Kayaking on **Lake Union.**

A ferry ride to **Lopez Island** from **Anacortes** to watch the resident whale pods.

Private gatherings in the **Chinese Room** at the top of the **Smith Tower.**

Feeding time at the **Aquarium** when the sea otters are fed.

Shopping for vegetables and fish at **Pike Place Market.**

While in **Pioneer Square,** don't miss the **Elliott Bay Book Company.** It's what a neighborhood bookstore should be—complete with author's readings.

km
mi

1/4 1/8 1/4 1/2

N

W Prospect St.

W Kinnear Pl.

W Olympic Pl.

Kinnear
Park

W Mercer Pl.

Pier 86

Elliott
Bay Park

Elliott Ave. W

W Roy St.

W Mercer St.

W Republican St.

5th Ave. W

3rd Ave. W

1st Ave. W

Queen Anne Ave. N

1st Ave. N

Warren Ave. N

2nd Ave. N

3rd Ave. N

Nob Hill Ave. N

60

61

62 63

59   **57 64**
        55 56   58
           54
           53

65

Opera
House

**45
Seattle
Center**

W Harrison St.   **52**

Key Arena

W Thomas St.

51

Spa
Nee

Myrtle
Edwards
Park
50

W John St.

49

48

47
46

Pacific
Science
Center

Elliott
Bay

Bay St.

Eagle St.

Pier 71

Broad St.

3rd

2nd Ave.

1st Ave.

BELLTOW

13
Pier 70

14

Clay St.

Cedar St. **12**

Western

11

Ferry to Victoria, B.C.
(passengers only)

Pier 69

Waterfront Streetcar

Elliott Ave.

Alaskan Way

Pier 66

Belltown/Seattle Center

No matter what you call it—Belltown or the **Denny Regrade District**—
this area just north of downtown is Seattle's boulevard of forgotten dreams,
at least those of an urban development nature. During the late 19th century,
one of Seattle's first settlers, William Bell, hoped to create a commercial center
here, but he died before his plans could amount to much. Between 1906 and
1911, city engineer Reginald H. Thomson ordered that 300-foot-high **Denny
Hill**, which loomed up from the corner of Second Avenue and Virginia Street,
be sluiced into **Elliott Bay.** The regrading was supposed to inspire business
development by making the neighborhood flatter and thus easier to traverse.
That notion, however, fell upon deaf ears.

In 1911 engineer Virgil Bogue unveiled a plan that would have made the
intersection of **Fourth Avenue** and **Blanchard Street** the nexus of a new and
improved downtown Seattle. Bogue proposed the construction of a civic

uld stretch from this intersection all the way to **Lake Union.** re boulevards, federal buildings, a courthouse, library, art tory memorial tower, and subway, all of which would transform dowdy Seattle into a major metropolitan center. Bogue was an urban visionary and, like most visionaries, his ideas were rejected.

It wasn't until 1962, with construction of the Century 21 Exposition and the landmark **Space Needle,** that Belltown made the leap into the future. This World's Fair was "The Jetsons" incarnate, a spectacle that *Life* magazine called "out of this world." Attorney General Robert Kennedy, actors John Wayne and Danny Kaye, Prince Philip of Britain, and even Lassie showed up to take a gander. Elvis Presley arrived amid a wail of shrieking teenagers to shoot a mediocre movie called *It Happened at the World's Fair.*

The fairgrounds have now become the **Seattle Center** (freshly renovated to the tune of more than $200 million), the closest thing the city has to a community center. Thousands of people crowd in here year after year for events such as the Northwest Folklife Festival and Bumbershoot. Parents bring their children to visit the museums; teens hang out with friends at the amusement park, gobble pizza in **Center House,** and attend dances and karaoke competitions; and the **Space Needle** remains a popular upscale dating destination. Sporting events, ranging from professional basketball (the **Seattle SuperSonics**) to high-school football, take place in the **Key Arena** (formerly the **Coliseum**) and at **High School Memorial Stadium.** Several stages deliver theater and musical productions.

Belltown still inspires dreams, but now they're more of the bohemian and artistic sort. Secondhand shops, bookstores, art galleries, and coffeehouses have sprung up in buildings vacated long ago by more conventional businesses, and Belltown has become a focus of Seattle's dance-club scene, attracting a wide roster of rock bands. Restaurants, which once eschewed the neighborhood as just too far from the city's critical office mass, have moved in. And while drug dealing and some violence encourage caution at dusk, the growth of this arty fringe area has not been stemmed.

1 Gravity Bar ★$ Founded in 1986 by local ceramic artist Laurrien Gilman, this chic establishment has literally moved up in the world, from a slope just above **Pike Place Market** to more spacious quarters in the **Terminal Sales Building.** But the move seems not to have affected the menu—or the laid-back attitude. Healthy vibes positively emanate from the place, what with all the pine nuts, carrot-based libations, sun-dried tomatoes, tofu, and brown rice being dished up. If you're feeling adventurous, try the signature wheat-grass juice or the hot apple, lemon, and ginger drink. The atmosphere and clientele are distinctly artsy. ♦ Vegetarian ♦ M-F lunch and dinner; Sa-Su brunch and dinner. No credit cards accepted. 113 Virginia St (between Second and First Aves). 448.8826. Also at: Broadway Market (415 Broadway E at E Harrison St). 325.7186

2 Vogue Variety is the key word that keeps this dance club happening. On any given night the dark interior and silver walls become the background for a different theme—reggae, gothic, industrial rock, and fetish music that sometimes extends to the dancers' outfits, makeup, and jewelry. ♦ Cover. Daily until 2AM. 2018 First Ave (between Virginia and Lenora Sts). 443.0673 ⅖

3 Jet City Vintage Take a neon-illuminated trip down memory lane, complete with tables full of ceramic ashtrays and chrome toasters, walls covered in old movie posters and Marilyn Monroe images, and a smattering of bubblegum and pinball machines. This shop makes for terrific browsing and offers reasonable prices. ♦ Daily. 2200 First Ave (at Blanchard St). 728.7118

4 Queen City Grill ★★$$ A rich mahogany bar, several small booths, and burnt sienna walls all combine to create a chic yet casual atmosphere. Credit for the success of this stylish grill goes to co-owners Peter Lamb (also responsible for **Il Bistro** in **Pike Place Market**) and Steven Good, as well as to chef Paul Michael, who does marvelously simple but wonderful things with grilled fish or meats and garlic. Now, if only the portions were as large as the owners' ambitions … ♦ American ♦ M-F lunch and dinner; Sa-Su dinner. 2201 First Ave (at Blanchard St). 443.0975 ⅖

Child's Play

After the requisite trip on the **Monorail,** what's a parent to do on those rainy Seattle days? Here are 10 tips for keeping the kids entertained:

1 Visit the **Tropical Rain Forest** at the **Woodland Park Zoo** and check out the poison-dart frogs.

2 **Prick up** your ears for Saturday morning story time at the **Elliott Bay Book Company.**

3 **Rent** a paddleboat and churn up the waters of **Green Lake.**

4 **Climb** into a space capsule at the **Pacific Science Center.**

5 **Walk** under the sea at the **Seattle Aquarium.**

6 **Attend** a performance of the **Seattle Children's Theater.**

7 **Take** a guided nature walk with the park rangers at **Discovery Park.**

8 **Build** a miniature sailboat at the **Center for Wooden Boats.**

9 **Browse** among the shrunken heads (and peek at Sylvester the Mummy) at **Ye Olde Curiosity Shop.**

10 **Check out** the model ships at the **Museum of History and Industry.**

5 **Uno-Duo** This combination of two shops (one for womenswear, one for menswear) features clothes that are dressy and a bit daring. Refreshingly, shoppers don't have to drop a month's salary on an outfit here. ♦ Daily. 2209 First Ave (between Blanchard and Bell Sts). 448.7011

6 **Casa-U-Betcha** ★★$ A gift from Portland, Oregon, where the first **Casa** opened to raves in the mid-1980s, this ultrahip "tacoria" has two things going for it. One is the blue margaritas (stupid looking but quite tasty), which help you forget that the food here, while filling and usually good, bears only a passing resemblance to anything served south of the border. The other is its reputation as a happening place full of people sidling up to the bar and crowding into the too-loud dining room with their beautiful *compadres.* A DJ spins dance records from early evening until closing time. ♦ Southwestern/Mexican ♦ Tu-Su lunch and dinner; bar daily until 2AM. Reservations recommended. 2212 First Ave (between Blanchard and Bell Sts). 441.1026 ა

7 **Flying Fish** ★★★$$ The January 1996 issue of *Bon Appetit* magazine includes this place on its short list of the hottest new restaurants in the country. Co-owners Christine Keff and Paul Mackay present an imaginative, frequently changing menu of mainly seafood dishes. Keff's fusion cuisine shows influences and flavors drawn from all over the world, particularly Thailand, Mexico, and Catalonia. Especially recommended are the Thai crab cakes, lobster risotto, and grilled escolar. The vibrant decor, featuring bright, tropical colors and hand-painted tables, nicely complements the food. Catering to late-night diners, the kitchen stays open until midnight. ♦ Seafood ♦ Daily dinner (until midnight).

Reservations required. 2234 First Ave (at Bell St). 728.8595 ა

8 **Odd Fellows Hall/Austin A. Bell Building** The connected brick structures you see here, plus the **Hull Building** kitty-corner across First Avenue, are about all that remain of an ambitious 19th-century scheme to develop Belltown as a commercial hot spot. The architect was **Elmer Fisher,** who put his stamp all over Pioneer Square, but the plan was the brainchild of pioneer William Bell and his son, Austin Americus Bell.

In 1883 William Bell erected the impressive four-story, mansard-roofed **Bell Hotel** (subsequently renamed the **Bellevue Hotel**) at the corner of Battery Street and what's now First Avenue. Four years later Bell died from a "softening of the brain" that had brought on fits and confusion. His son came north from his home in California to attend the funeral and claim his inheritance. In 1888, while architect **Fisher** was working on a new hall for the Odd Fellows fraternal group two doors south of the hotel, Austin commissioned him to design a compatible apartment building that would fit between the hall and the hotel. This was to be Austin's first big mark on Seattle and, though he'd suffered from periodic depression, he seemed enlivened by the project. But in the spring of 1889, after a hearty breakfast and a stroll to his office, he wrote a shaky note to his wife and shot himself in the head. He was 35, the same age his father had been when he carved out the clearing that would become Belltown. His wife, Eva, completed Austin's handsome structure and named it in his honor.

The **Bellevue Hotel** has long since vanished, and the **Odd Fellows Hall** is now the **2320 First Avenue Building,** its upper stories warrened with offices. But the **Austin A. Bell Building** has been boarded up, a disheveled ghost of a tormented man's dream. 2320 First Ave (between Bell and Battery Sts)

9 Lampreia ★★★$$$ This sleek, spare restaurant seems even more elegant compared to its gritty Belltown surroundings. Chef Scott Carsberg marries highly seasoned Italian oils and sauces with fresh Northwest produce to create such appetizers as *pizzelle* (crisp little waffles with thin slices of marinated tuna and pesto). Entrées are similarly inspired: think cannelloni stuffed with Dungeness crab or braised saddle of rabbit wrapped in pancetta. Dessert lovers will not want to pass up the chocolate *feuilleté* (thin alternating layers of chocolate and praline). ◆ Italian ◆ Tu-Sa dinner. Reservations recommended. 2400 First Ave (at Battery St). 443.3301 ♿

10 Cyclops ★★$$ If "funky" is not your style, don't come within a mile of this place, cluttered inside and out with heaps and piles of kitschy detritus. Its walls glow purple, green, and yellow from a perverse series of paintings, and torrents of seemingly bizarre music wash out of the sound system. But some surprisingly good fare is on the menu: Italian, Russian, French, vegetarian—the proprietors aren't afraid to experiment and are incapable of botching anything. Their credo is: "We *Never* Serve French Fries." The help can be a little surly, but the food is worth the abuse, and the weekend hours accommodate night owls. ◆ International ◆ M-F lunch and dinner; Sa-Su brunch and dinner; F-Sa open until 4AM. 2416 Western Ave (at Wall St). 441.1677 ♿

THE EDGEWATER
A NOBLE HOUSE HOTEL

11 Edgewater Inn $$$ Several of the 235 rooms here literally hang out west over Puget Sound, affording marvelous scenery during the day and fresh salt air at night. At one time this hotel rented fishing poles to guests who wished to wet a line from their rooms (the Beatles were supposed to have indulged in this sport during an early visit here). But too many people made a mess while cleaning their catches, so the service was discontinued. In 1988, the hotel was remodeled to give a mountain-lodge ambience. Waterside rooms are the quietest, but city-view rooms are also fine—and cheaper. Parking is free, and there's a good restaurant with a piano lounge, **Ernie's Bar & Grill.** ◆ Pier 67 (at

Alaskan Way and Wall St). 728.7000; 800/624.0670; fax 441.4119

12 Center on Contemporary Art (COCA) Featuring works by local, national, and international artists, this organization features "risk-oriented" programs with controversial exhibits. "Modern Primitives," **COCA**'s most famous show to date, made national news and is credited with starting the recent tattooing and body piercing craze among young Americans. ◆ Tu-Sa. 65 Cedar St (between Western and Elliott Aves). 728.1980

13 Pier 70 The **Ainsworth & Dunn Wharf** has stood at the north end of the Waterfront for nearly a hundred years—a marvelous building, with wide-plank flooring, rough-hewn log walls, and cavernous open spaces. (A history of this fine structure is mounted just inside the entrance.) It now houses a variety of curio, candy, and T-shirt shops for tourists, as well as some restaurants. ◆ Off Alaskan Way (at Broad St) ♿

Within Pier 70:

Panos ★★$$ Back in the 1980s, when it sat high atop Queen Anne Hill, this restaurant was a mecca for lovers of Greek cuisine. Many foodies mourned owner Panayotes Marinos's decision to close shop and depart for Europe. But he returned, and his restaurant re-creation—in a bright Waterfront location—happily lives up to its past glories. The rich moussaka is the primo menu pick, but the *keftedes* (a seasoned meat dish made with milk and bread) and *spanakopita* (spinach pie) are not to be missed either. The lightly fried squid rings here may be the best in Seattle. Another worthwhile pick is the Greek chicken, marinated in olive oil and wine; however, skip the overly rich *aginares politikes* (a sort of soup with artichoke hearts, potato chunks, and carrots in an olive oil, lemon, and dill sauce). Overall the service is responsive, but the bouzouki music tends to blare, and both the wine and beer lists could be expanded and improved. ◆ Greek ◆ M-F lunch and dinner; Sa-Su dinner. Reservations recommended. 2815 Alaskan Way (at Broad St). 441.5073 ♿

14 Waterfront Streetcar Seattle's original trolleys were stripped from service decades ago, but for nostalgia's sake, **Metro Transit** imported these vintage machines from Australia to make the clattering 15- to 20-

minute run from Pier 70 through Pioneer Square to the International District. ◆ $1.10 at peak times (M-F 6 to 9AM and 3 to 6PM); 85¢ off-peak; children under five free. Daily. Pier 70 (off Alaskan Way and Broad St). 553.3000

15 Shiro ★★★$$ Chef Shiro Kashibo, who originally opened the outstanding **Nikko** restaurant at the **Westin Hotel,** brings his highly acclaimed talents to the menu here. Naturally the sushi and sashimi are superb, and so are the appetizers (particularly the soft shell crab and asparagus salad). There are even a few exotic items to tempt the more adventurous palate, like squid tentacles and cured seaweed. The place itself seems rather formal, with its blondwood paneling and immaculate linen tablecloths and napery, but the staff is warm and friendly. ◆ Japanese ◆ M-F lunch and dinner; Sa-Su dinner. Reservations recommended. 2401 Second Ave (at Battery St). 441.5073 ₺

16 Rendezvous The primary battleground for the hearts and minds of Belltown, the bar here is worth a look, but in general steer clear of it unless you're into knocking back triple scotches. Instead, head straight to the **Jewelbox Theater** in back, which is somewhat shabby, but elegant and comfortable. The entertainment consists of a wildly uneven menu of live music. ◆ F-Sa 6AM-2AM. Cover. 2320 Second Ave (between Bell and Battery Sts). 441.5823 ₺

17 2-11 Billiard Club Once upon a time this fine old establishment (with roots back to 1936) was located downtown. But, to Belltown's eternal benefit, the club was forced to move north during construction of the Metro Bus Tunnel. Its regular clientele moved with it; they're the ones decorating the bar with their personal billiards equipment. But don't be intimidated—pool-playing expertise is not required. The tables are adequate, although the cue sticks are less so. The club's best feature is its laid-back atmosphere, conducive to hours of chasing balls across a field of green felt. ◆ Daily. 2304 Second Ave (between Bell and Battery Sts). 443.1211

17 Speakeasy Cafe $ The cybercafe trend, which has been sweeping through major cities all over America, has arrived in Seattle. Tagged "the coffeehouse of the computer age" by co-owner Tyler Apgar, this eatery offers 12 terminals that allow patrons to access the Internet for free, as well as more advanced graphics terminals for rent. There is a menu of snacks and sandwiches, but it's only incidental. The atmosphere is bright and open, the decor sparse but comfortable. There are poetry readings and live music in the front room, and there's a theater in back. Cybercafe ◆ Daily lunch and dinner. 2304 Second Ave (between Bell and Battery Sts). 728.9770; fax 782.2172; E-mail http://www.speakeasy.org, cafe @ speakeasy.org

18 Mama's Mexican Kitchen ★$ Every inch of wall space here is a witty adventure, overdecorated with Mexicana; there's even an "Elvis Room," with some memorabilia of the singer and videos of his movies. Is there a stick of furniture in the place that matches any other? Probably not. Food comes in huge portions, with lots of taco and burrito plates and rice and beans on the side—a carboloader's fantasy. Little on the menu will blow you away, though. Come here on a warm summer's night when you get a table outside and eat basket upon basket of the saltless tortilla chips, washing it all down with Corona beer. ◆ Mexican ◆ Daily lunch and dinner. 2234 Second Ave (at Bell St). 728.6262 ₺

19 Lava Lounge If you're in the mood for a dry martini or an exotic drink in a hip, trendy nightclub, this is the place for you. This lounge is a popular hangout for young Seattleites, who come to sit in the plush red booths, drink, and listen to live performances by up-and-coming artists and groups. There's also a menu of bar-type munchies. ◆ Daily until 2AM. No credit cards accepted. 2226 Second Ave (between Blanchard and Bell Sts). 441.5660 ₺

19 Dingo Gallery Aficionados of World's Fair–era kitsch will find plenty of it here, artfully displayed in about 10 rooms. The prices aren't bad, but the real fun is soaking up the owner's impressive aesthetic in mounting and arranging each separate room. ◆ Tu-Sa 1-6PM. 2222½ Second Ave (between Blanchard and Bell Sts). 443.6935

19 Signature Bound The stock of this tiny bookstore is skimpy but well-chosen, running toward bohemian tastes of the 1980s and 1990s—selected classics, a smattering of science fiction, banned and obscure material, feminist tracts, poetry, and self-published 'zines. Both new and used books are sold. ◆ M-Sa. 2222 Second Ave (between Blanchard and Bell Sts). 441.3306

20 Crocodile Cafe During the day this cafe is an only moderately successful diner. But at night it turns into one of Seattle's most adventurous and intriguing rock clubs, booking cutting-edge acts from the city and elsewhere in the country. Kitsch art crams every cranny and literally drips off both the ceiling and walls, even in the rest rooms. One of the more creative displays is the salad-fork mélange in the men's room. ◆ Cover. Tu-F 7AM-2AM; Sa 8AM-2AM; Su 9AM-3PM. 2200 Second Ave (at Blanchard St). 441.5611

The Odd Fellows Hall (now the 2320 First Avenue Building) once played host to comedian W.C. Fields. Novelist Tom Robbins lived in the building in the mid-1980s; he says he was once visited there by Timothy Leary, who declared the place haunted.

Terra-cotta Town

The raging fire that destroyed early Seattle in 1889 was a tragic event, but this very same fire also had a lot to do with how the city's architecture developed over the following five decades. Just trace the growth northward from **Pioneer Square.** Starting at **Smith Tower,** the handsome but weighty Romanesque Revival style of brick and stone gives way to paler, more gracefully ornamented terra-cotta towers that were believed (correctly) to be more structurally sound than their precursors. These buildings were also a kind of insurance policy for Seattle: terra-cotta, it had been proved, was more fire-resistant than many other building materials. Perhaps more significant, however, is that for most of this century these towers would characterize Seattle as a great white city on the water.

Terra-cotta became an accepted building material for Chicago's large-scale projects shortly after that city suffered its own skyline-devastating blaze in 1871. The enriched clay eventually became the facing of choice among early American skyscraper builders, including such architects as **Louis Sullivan** and **Daniel Burnham,** who discovered they could use it to create higher and slimmer towers. They achieved this by assembling steel skeletons to bear most of a building's weight, and then sheathing the structure with a lighter skin of terra-cotta (which weighs about 70 pounds per cubic foot, compared to 170 pounds for granite).

It could also be modeled easily into an infinite variety of shapes before it was hardened by firing—a bottom-line plus during a period when the expense of traditional ornamental stonework was on the rise. As architect **Frank Lloyd Wright** later remarked, terra-cotta "takes the impression of human imagination. . . . It is in the architect's hand what wax is in the sculptor's hand." The material allowed designers to more fully express themselves in the sort of Beaux Arts embellishments popular during the early 20th century. Gargoyles, cartouches, French nymphs, or a ribbon of walrus heads could all be produced cheaply and quickly and in numerous shades to enhance a structure.

Of course, the Northwest's damp climate forced special requirements on terra-cotta manufacturing. More porous versions might have been fine for California, but here the clay renderings had to be highly glazed, a fact that contributed greatly not only to their waterproofing but also to their general longevity. (The Capitol Theater in Yakima, Washington, for instance, was hit by a fire some years back that destroyed the interior but left the distinguished terra-cotta facade standing.)

One of the earliest architects erecting terra-cotta–sheathed edifices in Seattle was **Charles H. Bebb,** an Englishman who'd worked in Chicago with **Louis Sullivan**'s firm. In about 1890 he moved to Seattle to serve as an engineer for an early terra-cotta company owned, at least in part, by pioneer Arthur Denny. **Bebb** formed his own architectural practice in 1898, subsequently linking up with **Leonard L. Mendel** and the talented New Yorker **Carl F. Gould** to create some of Seattle's most significant terra-cotta structures. They were joined in their taste for terra-cotta by local architects **John Graham Sr., Henry Bittman, A. Warren Gould,** and theater designer **B. Marcus Priteca,** an experimental stylist who created molds for classical ornamental motifs that became catalog items and eventually detailed buildings all down the West Coast.

Not until 1930 did the demand for terra-cotta suffer a decline, brought on by the Depression, escalating production costs, and changes in architectural taste. By then, however, Seattle—as well as Portland, Oregon, and San Francisco—displayed a rich diversity of terra-cotta works. Unfortunately, some of the finest examples have been victims of the wrecking ball (including the old **Rhodes Building** and the **Orpheum Theater,** both once in downtown Seattle), but others are still standing and are definitely worth seeing. A few of the more interesting examples are listed below.

Alaska Building Downtown's first steel-girdered high-rise, it was designed in 1904 by **Eames & Young.** 618 Second Ave (between James and Cherry Sts)

Arctic Building Designed in 1917 by **A. Warren Gould,** this ivory-colored terra-cotta structure has "confectioner's touches of aquamarine and rose," as one architectural guide puts it. The walrus heads lining the edifice speak well of the artistic possibilities in this clay construction. 700 Third Ave (at Cherry St)

Banana Republic Formerly the **Coliseum Theater,** a 1916 structure by **B. Marcus Priteca,** this is one of downtown's most beautifully detailed buildings despite its decline over the last two decades. Although it now houses the flagship branch of **Banana Republic,** it has been completely restored to its original appearance. 1506 Fifth Ave (at Pike St)

Corona Hotel When designing this 1903 structure, **Bebb & Gould** paid homage to **Louis Sullivan,** who inspired the facade's woven floral ornamentation of unglazed terra-cotta. 608 Second Ave (at James St)

Dexter Horton Building Like the **Arctic Building** before it, this 1922 tower (by **John Graham Sr.**) is ivory-hued—a nationally popular color at the time. But it's more sternly businesslike in conception, with giant Doric columns of granite on the north side that express the original height of its lobby. 710 Second Ave (at Cherry St)

Fischer Studio Building Bebb & Mendel designed the building in 1912; two years later, **Bebb** and his new partner **Gould** added five stories onto the original three and integrated the facade into a continuous whole. The seventh and eighth floors, blank on the exterior except for Venetian-inspired detail, were built to house a Renaissance Revival–style music hall. 1519 Third Ave (between Pike and Pine Sts)

Four Seasons Olympic Hotel Designed in 1929 by **George B. Post,** an important New York architect, with **Bebb & Gould** administering the construction, this brick-clad building has terra-cotta ornaments. 411 University St (between Fifth and Fourth Aves)

Medical-Dental Building In 1925, **John Graham Sr.** designed this building as a physical and spiritual extension of his 1919 **Frederick & Nelson** department store. But while the drama of the former **F & N** is apparent at all heights, most of the building's interest doesn't begin until the 14th floor, where Venetian filigrees and a series of setback penthouses and towers are located. 505 Olive Way (between Sixth and Fifth Aves)

Sailors Union of the Pacific A creation of **T. Bohannon** and **K. Better,** this 1954 edifice is a particularly late and simplistic example of terra-cotta design. 2505 First Ave (at Wall St)

Seafirst Bank A former department store, this building designed in 1908 by **J.J. Baillargeon** has an arched entrance, lion heads decorating the corners, and shell-patterned window frames adorning the ground level. 1100 Second Ave (at Spring St)

Securities Building This **John Graham Sr.**–designed 1912 structure has a Greco-Roman design, executed in terra-cotta. Pay special attention to the ornamentation, including playful green cartouches, along **Third Avenue.** 1904 Third Ave (between Stewart and Virginia Sts)

Smith Tower Due to terra-cotta's light weight, this early skyscraper (designed in 1912 by **Gaggin & Gaggin**) could be built taller than was previously possible. 506 Second Ave (at Yesler Way)

Terminal Sales Building This 1923 building by **Henry Bittman** has tan brick and terra-cotta facing, with English Gothic ornament that stands out pleasantly against its Art Deco profile. 1934 First Ave (at Virginia St)

Woolworth Building The designer, **Harold B. Hamhill,** built this Moderne-style structure around 1935 using Woolworth's standard design. It was the only new terra-cotta building constructed in downtown Seattle during the 1930s and 1940s. 301 Pike St (at Third Ave)

The Arctic Building's walrus heads (like the one pictured here) had their tusks rmoved more than 30 years ago for fear they'd fall off and mortally wound passerby. During a 1980s restoration, however, the walruses got their tusks back.

M. BLUM

21 Bethel Temple Erected around 1915, this elegantly appointed terra-cotta edifice originally housed the ritzy **Crystal Swimming Pool**; it's now a Pentecostal church. Where the corner of this structure now drops back to glass doorways and a lighted sign at Second Avenue and Blanchard Street, a huge metal dome used to rise over a pillared base. Model T's would drive up and drop youngsters here for an afternoon dip. The only hint of this building's early purpose may be the stylized green dolphins that decorate its roofline.
♦ 2033 Second Ave (at Lenora St)

22 Bushell's Auctions Owner Mary Bushell deals mostly in estate sellouts and private offerings, and some of the goods are real finds. There are lots of household items, including dishware and bedroom sets.
♦ Auctions are held almost every Tuesday (with previews on Monday); call ahead for details. 2006 Second Ave (between Virginia and Lenora Sts). 448.5833

23 Caffè D'Arte ★$ One of the better finds for Seattle caffiends, this establishment anchors the most exposed corner of what used to be the nine-story **Calhoun Hotel** (constructed in 1918), now an apartment property called the Palladian. ♦ Coffeehouse ♦ M-Sa. 2000 Second Ave (at Virginia St). 728.4901. Also at: 125 Stewart Ave S (at Second Ave). 728.4468

23 The Poor Italian Cafe ★★$ This *caffè* serves hearty calamari and creamy homemade pasta, including a rich ravioli guaranteed to commit criminal acts against your best shirt or blouse. Owner Gregory Pesce maintains a friendly, open atmosphere. The wine list gets only a passing grade, but the service is cheery and the bread, terrific.
♦ Italian ♦ M-F lunch and dinner; Sa-Su dinner. Virginia St and Second Ave. 441.4313 &

No history of Seattle would be complete without a mention of Mercer's Maidens. In 1864, a young entrepreneur named Asa Mercer offered to travel across the country to New England to procure brides for a number of lonely local bachelors. After collecting a large sum of money from these men, he sailed away to Boston, returning that May with 11 young women. He repeated the feat two years later. Unfortunately, he overstepped himself a bit: He had promised to come up with 500 brides, but he could find only 100 or so. The firestorm created by all this caused Mercer (who had married one of the young women himself) to leave Seattle for the Rocky Mountains, where he lived the rest of his life as a rancher. This tale was the basis of the TV series "Here Come the Brides."

24 Sub-Pop Mega Mart When this tiny music store with the rather facetious name began its slow climb to preeminence on the Seattle landscape a few years ago, its goal was to carry all the latest, trendiest records. And although the place is about the size of the average bathroom, it has succeeded. The stock here features new releases of independent labels, with the music styles ranging from grunge and hip-hop to blues and bubblegum pop. If you want to find out what's happening in music today, this is the place to start. ♦ Daily. 1928 Second Ave (between Stewart and Virginia Sts). 443.0322

25 Pacific Galleries Here's an auction house that specializes in liquidating estates. Like all such places, it's a crapshoot—sometimes a gold mine, sometimes mediocre goods. ♦ Call ahead for dates and details. 2121 Third Ave (between Lenora and Blanchard Sts). 441.9990

26 Fourth and Blanchard Building
Affectionately known by locals as the "Darth Vader Building" for its resemblance to the *Star Wars* villain, this dark, 440-foot-tall glass monolith was designed by the same folks who brought you the **Columbia Seafirst Tower** downtown **(Chester L. Lindsey Architects).** It's all astonishing surfaces, with dramatic angles at the top that make it eerily reminiscent of New York architect **Philip Johnson's** Pennzoil Place in Houston. In the nearby courtyard, adorning two benches across from each other, are *He* and *She*, two life-size bronze statues by Howard Garnitz.
♦ 2101 Fourth Ave (between Lenora and Blanchard Sts)

27 Warwick Hotel $$$ Too large to be considered intimate, but too small to feel so corporate, this hotel is an odd beast. The 229 rooms are comfortable and large, with balconies that offer decent downtown views. There's a pool (albeit a shallow one) in the health club, and the piano lounge provides entertainment nightly. Front desk personnel are friendly and efficient, and a 24-hour courtesy van will whisk you to downtown engagements. Room rates, however, are steep for accommodations so far from the heart of the city; even the reduced corporate tariffs aren't exactly a bargain. The **Liaison** restaurant serves breakfast, lunch, and dinner. ♦ 401 Lenora St (at Fourth Ave). 443.4300, 800/426.9280; fax 448.1662

28 Monorail Walking along Fifth Avenue just north of Pine Street after dark, when the ghostly monorail flashes by overhead, is one of Seattle's finest urban experiences. The monorail is very quiet, with faces peering out of the lighted windows. The slingshot-shaped concrete supports make for a fine Hitchcock scenario, with generous geometric lines and shadows. Locals who've pushed for the

Restaurants/Clubs: Red   Hotels: Blue
Shops/ ♥ Outdoors: Green   Sights/Culture: Black

monorail's removal—so a clear view of the **Space Needle** can be opened along Fifth Avenue—don't appreciate the drama of this silver-skinned dinosaur. Director Alan Rudolph did, however, and he made plentiful use of it in his 1985 film *Trouble in Mind*. Be on your guard, though, especially at night: This stretch of Fifth Avenue is not heavily populated. ♦ Fifth Ave (between Pine St and the Seattle Center)

29 Dimitriou's Jazz Alley Longtime jazz producer John Dimitriou owns this club, a genuine treasure for blues and jazz fans alike. Some of the most significant names in the genre have graced the room: Harry Connick Jr. used to play here before he was famous, and Diane Shuur has been a regular performer throughout the years. Expect to see such entertainers as Charles Brown, Ray Brown, Maynard Ferguson, and Betty Carter, seven days a week, every week. The food is nothing special, but the room is excellent, with comfortable seating. If you're a music fan, don't miss this place. ♦ Cover. Tu-Su. Reservations recommended. Sixth Ave and Lenora St. 441.9729

30 Sixth Avenue Inn $ One step above a motel (some rooms even have brass beds, and room service is available), this 166-room hostelry is reasonably priced and centrally located, fairly convenient to both the downtown core and the **Seattle Center**, and it has a basic restaurant for quick meals. Street noise can be a problem, though, especially on the Sixth Avenue side. ♦ 2000 Sixth Ave (at Virginia St). 441.8300; fax 441.9903

31 Art/Not Terminal After four initial years operating in a space converted from a **Trailways** bus station (hence the name), this co-op gallery/shop moved into more upscale digs. Shows change each month, though some stay longer. Exhibits draw from the work of about 200 member artists, including sculptors, photographers, and painters. The nonprofit gallery is good to its artists, taking an uncharacteristically small percentage from the sales, and customers can even work out layaway plans with individual artists. New show openings, with live music and refreshments, are scheduled the Saturday immediately following the first Thursday of each month. ♦ Daily. 2045 Westlake Ave N (at Lenora St). 233.0680 ♿

32 Elephant Car Wash Sign A tacky fave among locals, this blinking and revolving pink sign won a 1956 design contest held by car-wash owners. It has since proliferated (several replicas now adorn branches from here to Puyallup) and become almost as renowned a symbol of Seattle as the **Space Needle**. *Cosmopolitan* magazine even suggested that single women of the 1990s should be on the lookout for this pink pachyderm, as the establishments it decorates tend to be hangouts for eligible men. ♦ 616 Battery St (at Seventh Ave)

33 Group Health Building (P-I Building) The New York firm of **Lockwood-Greene** was responsible for most of the architecture of this three-story block, and the landscaped top level was added in 1978 by Seattle's **Naramore, Bain, Brady & Johanson** (now the **NBBJ Group**). The *Seattle Post-Intelligencer* newspaper moved out of the building in the late 1980s, taking along the giant revolving globe that had capped the rounded tower. The *P-I* now operates from a glass cliff on the Waterfront, while Group Health Cooperative has taken over this structure. ♦ 521 Wall St (at Sixth Ave)

34 Ditto Tavern A Belltown focus for the disgruntled, this tavern attracts those inclined to read, write, and recite poetry. Recently expanded to three times its previous size, it now also contains a literary museum with over 250 typewriters on display in one room. The place is charming enough, particularly when it's full of would-be writers hammering away at the manual typewriters scattered about. The owner claims (probably accurately) that it is the only tavern in the country that sells paper and has a photocopier for its customers to use. Live alternative rock is often scheduled, beginning at 10PM. ♦ Cover for live music (call ahead for schedule of performers). T-Su until 2AM. 2303 Fifth Ave (between Bell and Battery Sts). 441.3303 ♿

35 Two Bells Tavern ★★$ Belltown's great altar of burger worship is almost impossible to get into at lunchtime, when the suits mix with the bohemians in the booths and at the bar. Come for one of the Paul Bunyan–size decks of beef covered in fried onions, with a sidecar of chunky potato salad. It's messy but worth the dry-cleaning bill. The lemonade and the salads are also recommended. Small rock groups or solo singer/songwriters appear here on Monday nights, beginning at 10PM. All in all, it's a good place to see and be seen.

◆ American ◆ Restaurant: daily lunch and dinner. Bar: daily until 2AM. 2313 Fourth Ave (between Bell and Battery Sts). 441.3050

36 Sit 'n' Spin ★$ If you find you're running out of clean clothes, consider it an opportunity to visit one of Seattle's most unusual hot spots: a standard laundromat combined with a restaurant/nightclub. Along with the usual coin-operated washers and dryers, there's a dining area that serves a menu of tasty sandwiches, focaccia, beer, wine, and espressos. In addition, you can entertain yourself by playing board games, listening to music from the jukebox, and watching the hip, fashionable people who seem to hang out here even if they don't have laundry to do. The back room was recently converted to a 200-seat theater catering to avant-garde tastes (alcohol is served, so you must be over 21 to enter). ◆ American ◆ Daily lunch and dinner; F-Sa until 2AM. No credit cards accepted. 2219 Fourth Ave (between Blanchard and Bell Sts). 441.9484 ⅁

37 Engine House No. 2 A fire station has occupied the corner of Fourth Avenue and Battery Street since 1890, although the original wooden building—**Engine House No. 4**—sat across Battery Street from where architect **Daniel R. Huntington**'s 1920 brick structure now stands. Unlike **No. 4**, which had to depend on horse-driven fire engines, the new **No. 2** was the talk of the town during the Jazz Age for its "motor-powered apparatus." ◆ Fourth Ave and Battery St

38 Exotique Records The selection at this interesting and offbeat record store runs toward the adventurous. What the stock lacks in range, it makes up for in depth: There is plenty to riffle through here, especially independent releases in acid jazz, underground dance, and alternative music. ◆ Daily. 2400 Third Ave (at Battery St). 448.3452

39 Taki's ★$ Though this restaurant specializes in pizza and pasta, the lasagna is particularly good. Prices are very reasonable, and the room is a nice place to sit and visit—a great lunch spot. ◆ Italian ◆ M-Sa lunch and dinner. 425 Cedar St (between Fourth and Fifth Aves). 448.7750

40 Chief Seattle Fountain This bronze memorial to the city's namesake (who was actually called Chief Sealth, not Seattle, by the way) was the first public artwork commissioned by the City of Seattle. With the Alaska-Yukon-Pacific Expo approaching in 1909, local business leaders prevailed upon the city to set aside a triangle of property where they proposed to commemorate the friendship between the white settlers and Native Americans of Elliott Bay. The symbol of that friendship was to be a life-size rendition of Chief Sealth, the leader of the Duwamish and Suquamish tribes who had negotiated the

treaty that gave up title to what's now much of northwestern Washington state. The sculptor was James A. Wehn, who two years later would design the fountain and bust of Chief Sealth at **Pioneer Place Park** and go on to establish the sculpture department at the **University of Washington.**

Disputes over which foundry should cast the work delayed the statue's unveiling, but it was finally put on view in 1912. For many years after that it stood green from advanced oxidation. In 1989, the city discovered while cleaning that the statue had a very thin gold plate which now lends it an extra sheen. ◆ Tilikum Place (between Fifth Ave and Cedar St, at Denny Way)

41 Denny Park In 1884, pioneer David Denny and his sister Mary donated the land on which this two-block-size oasis of trees was established. It is the city's oldest park. Previously, it had been **Seattle Cemetery.** (The dear departed are now at **Lake View Cemetery** on Capitol Hill.) ◆ Denny Way (between Ninth and Dexter Aves N)

42 13 Coins ★$$ While other swankier joints have failed, this culinary institution just keeps going and going. What's the secret? Probably a combination of the fact that it stays open 24 hours; has a huge menu of pasta, grilled meats, and fish entrées; and serves a dynamite Caesar salad. The portions are generous and the people watching in the wee small hours is some of the best around. ◆ American ◆ Daily 24 hours. 125 Boren Ave N (between Denny Way and John St). 682.2513 ⅁

43 Seattle Times Building The city's afternoon newspaper occupies a lesser-known building among those designed by architect **Robert C. Reamer** (who was also responsible for the **Skinner Building** and **1411 Fourth Avenue Building** downtown). Completed in 1930 but added to since, this Moderne-style headquarters is notable for the grillwork at its entrance and the understated sign cut along its facade. ◆ Fairview Ave N and John St

44 Cafe Lôc ★$ Good, basic, inexpensive Vietnamese fare is served quickly, unpretentiously, and abundantly. There's another outlet in the **Seattle Center,** but for atmosphere and comparative tranquillity, this venue is much preferred. ◆ Vietnamese ◆ Daily lunch and dinner. 407 Broad St (between Denny Way and John St). 441.6883. Also at: Center House, Seattle Center. 728.9292

SEATTLE CENTER

45 Seattle Center Site of the 1962 Century 21 Exposition, this sprawling complex of buildings (for a map of the center, see below) on 74 acres of land just north of Belltown has recently emerged from a five-year, $204-million refurbishing. Much of that money has gone toward the renovation of the pyramid-shaped **Coliseum** (now called the **Key Arena**), featuring a larger seating capacity, a state-of-the-art video scoreboard, and a new parking garage. Other improvements include a total

redesign of the facade of **Center House,** including the construction of a colorful outdoor plaza leading to the south entrance; the expansion of the **Children's Museum;** the addition of several pieces of modern art; and the enhancement of the lighting and sound systems. Future projects include repairs to the **Opera House,** the construction of a second performance space at the **Bagley Wright Theatre,** and the **Frank Gehry**–designed **Experience Music Project,** dedicated to Northwestern musicians (particularly local guitar wizard Jimi Hendrix). ♦ Bounded by Fifth and First Aves N, and Denny Way and Mercer St. 684.8582

Within the Seattle Center (the letters preceding each entry refer to the map below):

Pacific Science Center

A **Space Needle** "Back when we were in school, if you wanted attention, you put up your hand. That is what the Space Needle will do for the [1962 World's] Fair and Seattle." Those words were spoken by Joe Gandy, used-car salesman and president of the Century 21 Expo. His enthusiasm was not unfounded: In its three-plus decades, the **Space Needle** has become the supreme symbol of Seattle, the city's equivalent to San Francisco's Golden Gate Bridge. If it seems perfectly absurd at first, don't worry, it will grow on you.

This monument was the brainchild of World's Fair organizer Eddie Carlson. He scribbled his idea on a napkin one night, an image that looked like a flying saucer on a tripod. Architects **Victor Steinbrueck** and **John Graham Jr.** gave it a kind of "Amazing Stories" reality. Construction proved to be an enormous project. Consider some of the stats: The foundation is 30 feet deep and weighs 5,850 tons; what you see above ground weighs 3,700 tons; the legs are anchored by some 74 bolts, the dimensions of which are 4 inches by 32 feet; the tower claims 24 lightning rods and can endure winds of up to 150 miles per hour; and it stands more than 600 feet high. The elevator takes 43 seconds to reach the peak (and is literally a breath-taking experience). The restaurant floor at 500 feet turns a single revolution every hour, thanks to a one-horsepower motor. And the view is magnificent from the **Observation Deck,** particularly on clear days. Check it out. ♦ Fee for the Observation Deck. Daily until midnight. 443.2111, 800.937.9582 ᪲

Within the Space Needle:

Space Needle Restaurant $$$ It's sad to say, but this casual restaurant and the swankier Emerald Suite ($$$$; 443.2150 ᪲) don't measure up to their lofty positions on the **Needle.** It's understood, of course, that you're paying for the view, and it is a very fine one. But the cost is just too steep for the meals served here, which have a reputation for dipping to mediocre and barely rising to good. Both restaurants specialize in Northwestern fare, especially seafood. Diners ride the elevator free of charge. A dress code (no T-shirts, tennis shoes, or jeans) is enforced at the **Emerald Suite.** ♦ Northwestern ♦ M-Sa breakfast, lunch, and dinner; Su brunch and dinner. Reservations recommended. 443.2100 ᪲

B **Fun Forest Amusement Park** Originally called the **Gayway** in World's Fair days, this facility is only so-so, although kids in the middle of their second Sno-Cone and fifth Tilt-a-Whirl ride won't care. For the old-at-heart there's a carousel and classic bumper cars. Call ahead for hours and special offers. ♦ Fee for rides. Daily noon-11PM Memorial Day—Labor Day; hours vary off-season. 728.1585

C **Monorail** The **Seattle Center** marks this train's northern terminus. From here, it departs every 15 minutes to **Westlake Center.** ♦ Fee. Daily. 441.6038

D **Pacific Science Center** It's an interesting stop for adults, but with the hands-on exhibits and full slate of activities and programs (about dinosaurs, for instance, and whales), this place is even better for children. It's a sort of mini-campus with six interconnected buildings. Designed for the World's Fair by well-known Seattle-born architect Minoru Yamasaki, along with Naramore, Bain, Brady & Johanson, it claims a wonderfully tranquil and inviting space outside, full of pools and soaring arches. ("It is as if Venice had just been built," crowed Alistair Cooke when the complex opened.) But the inside all too often feels cramped and constricted. There's a fine planetarium, a laser theater, and an IMAX theater. ◆ Admission. Tu-Su. 443.2880, recorded information 443.2001

E Charlotte Martin Theater Designed by **Mahlum & Nordfors McKinley Gordon,** this $10.4-million building is the home of the popular **Seattle Children's Theatre (SCT).** Artist Garth Edwards's functional art delights the eye even as it serves a structural purpose: Images from smiling cacti to fanciful sea creatures adorn handrails, archways, even heating grills. ◆ Box office: M-Sa. 441.3322

F Center House A $6-million facelift has given this center a much more contemporary look. The plaza on the south side of the building is inlaid with brightly colored bricks and ribbons of steel; there's also a new walkway from there to **Center House** itself. On the side of the building is a quartet of acrobats created by sculptor Timothy Siciliano. Many cultural festivals are held here throughout the year. The inside of the center is less interesting—mostly overpriced fast-fooderies—but there is the newly expanded **Seattle Children's Museum** (441.1768), located on the lower level. With its exhibit space tripled in size, the museum provides special multicultural programs as well as a permanent **Playcenter,** a supervised play area for the little ones. Also on the lower level is the **Group Theater** (441.1299), which performs multicultural plays. ◆ Daily. 684.7200

G International Fountain From its inception, this fountain possessed an endearing hideousness (John Wayne, looking it over in 1962, asked, "What's that? An airplane crash?"). With its long, pointed water spouts on a metal hill, sharp marble and granite boulders, and steep-sided cement crater, it was not only aesthetically displeasing but also dangerous to the many children who played around it. In addition, many of the spouts were broken. But the city has recently given the entire structure a makeover: Its metal hill is now smooth, the spouts have been repaired, the concrete crater has a less steep grade, a computerized sound and lighting system has been added, and the boulders are gone. There's even a curving ramp leading to the foot of the fountain—great for wheelchair users and stroller-pushing parents. The result is a safer and far more inviting attraction.

H Opera House Some of the finest cultural offerings to be found in Seattle cross the stages of this large structure along Mercer Street. The building used to be Seattle's **Civic Auditorium** but was remodeled for the World's Fair by **B. Marcus Priteca** and **James Chiarelli.** It is now home to the **Seattle Opera,** the **Seattle Symphony,** the **Seattle Youth Symphony,** and the **Pacific Northwest Ballet.**

James Fitzgerald's refurbished and graceful *Fountain of the Northwest* stands in front of the **Intiman Playhouse,** home to the theater troupe of the same name, and the **Bagley Wright Theatre** hosts the **Seattle Repertory Theatre** company. The quality of productions at these venues ranges widely, but they are all first-rate houses. ◆ Mercer St (between Fourth and Warren Aves N). Seattle Opera 389.7676, Seattle Symphony 443.4747, Seattle Youth Symphony 362.2300, Pacific Northwest Ballet 441.9411, Intiman Playhouse 626.0782, Bagley Wright Theatre 443.2222

46 Caffè Minnie's ★$$ While most of the city's restaurants still shut down pretty early (9PM during the week and 11PM on

International Fountain

weekends), this informal eatery decorated in a funky style (pink walls with maroon trim, glass-topped tables) dares to go its own way, serving a full menu of international specialties 24 hours a day. So, if you're dying for a bowl of gazpacho or a Dutch Baby (a puffy baked pancake with custard reportedly invented in Seattle) at 3AM, **Minnie's** is the place to go. ♦ International ♦ Daily 24 hours. 101 Denny Way (at First Ave). 448.6263 ♿

47 Champion Wine Cellars The selection of wines here is both imported and domestic, and staffers are helpful, knowledgeable, and bewilderingly happy to answer your every oddball query. The store also stocks a selection of imported beers. ♦ M-Sa. 108 Denny Way (between Warren and First Aves N). 284.8306

48 Romper Room This funky dance club is unafraid to throw house, rave, industrial, and even good old grunge music into the stew. Live acoustic sets are scheduled on Monday night, and Tuesday is open-mike night. Look for occasional drink specials. There may be too much black-light ambience here for some dancers, but a pool table and art gallery in a side room provide a momentary escape from the fashion parade. ♦ Cover. Su-Th 4PM-2AM; F-Sa 4PM-3AM. 106 First Ave N (between Denny Way and John St). 284.5003 ♿

49 P-I Globe At least as tacky as the **Elephant Car Wash**'s pink proboscidean is this revolving neonized world atop the *Seattle Post-Intelligencer's* offices. It's easily visible from many points on Elliott Bay (including the ferry routes and harbor tours), as well as, suddenly and unexpectedly, from many parts of Belltown, **Seattle Center,** and the Queen Anne neighborhood. Locals have come to rely so much on the regularity of this landmark's spin that when mechanical problems cause a halt, you can almost see the psychological pall it casts. ♦ 101 Elliott Ave W (at Denny Way)

50 Myrtle Edwards Park Situated on the Waterfront just north of downtown and west of the **Seattle Center,** this spot makes for a spectacular city stroll. On nice days, catch an unmatched view of the Olympic Mountains, Mount Rainier, the Seattle skyline, and more along the rolling greensward's two-mile-long walkway. On less nice days (for which a rain slicker is strongly recommended), it offers a moody sky and coal-gray churning waters. This is a favorite place for picnickers, in-line skaters, and lunchtime runners. ♦ Alaskan Way (between Bay and W Thomas Sts)

51 Pottery Northwest Most of this building is devoted to studio space for local artisans. A small gallery lets visitors in on what residents are up to, which is often interesting, brightly colored work. Some classes are held here, too. ♦ Tu-Sa. 226 First Ave N (at Thomas St). 285.4421

Kaspar's

52 Kaspar's ★★★$$ Owner/chef Kaspar Donier earned his culinary credentials at the Four Seasons in Vancouver, BC, and this restaurant pays further tribute to his talents. The interior is bright and airy, with neutral shades of tan, cream, and taupe complemented with lush plants. Some of the dinner attractions include crab-and-salmon hash cakes topped with a mushroom sauce; seasonal asparagus spears in a marinade of olive oil, herbs, and garlic; and duck with a Port wine and dried cherry sauce. The before-and after-theater crowd can choose from a good selection of smaller offerings from the bar menu. ♦ Continental ♦ Tu-Th, Sa dinner; F lunch and dinner. Reservations recommended; valet parking available. 19 W Harrison St (between Queen Ave N and First Ave W). 298.0123 ♿

53 Inn at Queen Anne $ Former studio apartments have been converted into 37 suites with small kitchens—nothing fancy, but very functional. Long-term rentals are available as well. It's located within two blocks of the **Seattle Center** and a major grocery store, **QFC,** which is good because there's no restaurant here. ♦ 505 First Ave N (at Republican St). 282.7357; fax 282.7619

CHUTNEYS

54 Chutney's ★★★$$ This friendly Indian restaurant is named after the spicy condiment, which comes to your table in two varieties—cilantro and mint, and garlic and tomato—along with a complimentary appetizer called Papadum, a lightly fried sheet of pressed lentils. (Those with sensitive palates be warned: These chutneys are pretty fiery.) Standouts on the generally excellent menu include rack of lamb and *Aloo Gobi* (potatoes and cauliflower prepared in a rich and heavily spiced yogurt sauce). There's also a bargain all-you-can-eat lunch buffet, whose dishes are much milder than their counterparts at dinner (but you can ask for extra chutneys to spice things up, if you wish). The decor features traditional fabrics and 39 bas-relief images of Indian gods on the walls. ♦ Indian ♦ Tu-Th, Sa dinner; F lunch and dinner. Reservations recommended. 519 First Ave N (between Republican and Mercer Sts). 284.6799 ♿

Restaurants/Clubs: Red	**Hotels:** Blue
Shops/♟ Outdoors: Green	**Sights/Culture:** Black

55 Uptown Espresso ★$ One of the best cups of espresso available in Seattle (and that's saying a lot) is served with pizazz and cutting-edge attitude. The **Uptown Bakery,** offering great baked goods, was recently added to the premises. ◆ Coffeehouse ◆ Daily. 525 Queen Anne Ave N (between W Republican and W Mercer Sts). 281.8669

55 Sorry Charlie's $ The food and drink are only marginal attractions here, the real draw being the piano bar, where talented singers and tin ears alike hold forth with enthusiasm. This place had karaoke-type singing before the high-tech version became fashionable. And as with karaoke, piano sing-alongs always risk painful embarrassment for both listeners and crooners, but no one seems to mind. ◆ American ◆ Restaurant: daily breakfast, lunch, and dinner. Bars (regular and piano): daily until 2AM. 529 Queen Anne Ave N (between W Republican and W Mercer Sts). 283.3245

56 Mecca Cafe ★$ Originally opened 1 July 1930, this eatery used to be popular with older people and working-class residents. Lately, however, it's become the meeting place of choice for grunge rockers and other young Seattle bohemians, who come for late-night eating and drinking and early-morning hangover cures. It tends to be rather loud, and the staff and regulars can get quite vehemently opinionated when discussing local issues. There's also a bar. It's a good place to hang out, enjoy well-prepared (if standard) American diner food, and people watch. ◆ American ◆ Daily lunch and dinner (until 2AM). 526 Queen Anne Ave N (between Republican and Mercer Sts). 285.9728 ♿

57 Keystone Corner Cards Baseball and other sports-card aficionados share a deep respect for this place. ◆ M-Sa. 534 Queen Anne Ave N (at Mercer St). 285.9277

57 Titlewave The selection is small at this general-interest used-book store, but it's put together with excellent taste, which means you might spend less than 15 minutes browsing here but still turn up something you've wanted for a while. Unfortunately, the stock tends to be pricier than you'd expect. ◆ Daily; F until 10:30PM. 7 Mercer St (between First Ave and Queen Anne Aves N). 282.7687

58 T.S. McHugh's Restaurant & Pub ★$$ Owned by formula restaurateur Mick McHugh, this is an American place masquerading as a British pub, with the required (but faux) time-darkened facade outside and the rich wood appointments inside. There's an Old World conviviality at the bar, where the bartenders chat up the customers and help them expand their knowledge of liquors and local micro-brews. Skip the dining room and stay at the bar where you can order a hefty sandwich or burger, accompanied by terrific fries, and sample the plentiful stash of beers. ◆ American ◆ Daily lunch and dinner; bar until 1AM. 21 Mercer St (at First Ave N). 282.1910

59 Ozzie's ★$ A burger joint with attitude for the 1990s (they call it vegetarian-friendly), this place boasts chrome and neon fixtures, shimmering color schemes, design angles so acute you don't want to bump against them, neo-1950s and 1960s kitsch decor, and a pool table. If you don't want a hamburger, try a nut-burger (they're actually better). The fries are fine and so are the desserts and break-fasts. ◆ American ◆ Daily breakfast, lunch, and dinner. 105 W Mercer St (at First Ave W). 284.4618 ♿

60 Mediterranean Kitchen ★$ Vampires will want to keep clear of this garlic-heavy Middle Eastern restaurant, but budget diners will praise the ratio of price per pound of food. It's unusual *not* to see patrons exiting here with a carton or more of leftovers, maybe the remains of the superb Farmer's Dish (tart lemon chicken on a hillock of rice) or a helping of lamb shank with couscous, carrots, and potatoes. Dinners come with a bowl of soup (lentil, if you're lucky) and a soothing romaine salad with mint leaves. Owner Kamal Aboul-Hosn, who also runs **The Oven,** a Middle Eastern eatery on Capitol Hill, offers several tempting appetizers (the *baba ganooj* and hummus both deserve plaudits), but only those with ambitious appetites could eat all this and an entrée too. ◆ Middle Eastern ◆ Daily dinner. 4 W Roy St (between Queen Ave N and First Ave W). 285.6713

61 Cinema Espresso ★$ A fine little corner spot, this coffee shop is decked out in movie memorabilia and peopled by drifting screen-writers and actors just back from or about to go to LA. Usually not crowded, it's a good place to spend an afternoon reading a book. Desserts here are worth a shot. ◆ Coffeehouse ◆ Daily. 600 Queen Anne Ave N (at Roy St). 286.0866

62 Tower Books Stuffed to overflowing, this outlet of the national chain is up to snuff in fiction standards, with an especially large selection of sci-fi and mysteries. There's also a large children's literature department and a huge array of magazines. Browsers are welcome. ♦ Daily until midnight. 20 Mercer St (at First Ave N). 283.6333. Also at: 10635 NE Eighth St (between 108th and 106th Aves NE), Bellevue. 451.1110

63 Larry's Market The Belltown link in this chain of upscale food emporiums offers a staggering selection of the freshest produce, meat, seafood (including sushi), and other grocery items. The decor is quasi-industrial, with exposed ventilation pipes, rafters, and metal racks. There's also a huge underground parking garage. ♦ Daily 6AM-midnight. 100 W Mercer St (between Warren and First Aves N). 213.0778. Also at: 10008 Aurora Ave N (between N 100th and N 103rd Sts). 527.5333

64 The Pacific Dessert Company ★★★$ This late-night place makes a great evening finale for sugar lovers. The cafe features exquisite chocolate confections, fruit pies and tarts, espresso, and herbal teas. It's decorated with changing exhibits of local art ranging from mediocre to very good (and whoever does the chalkboards is positively gifted). Warning: This place fills to overflowing after theater performances at **Seattle Center.** ♦ Dessert ♦ Daily until midnight. 127 Mercer St (between Warren and First Aves N). 284.8100 ♿

65 Bamboo Garden ★$$ A decidedly odd vegetarian experience, but one not to be missed, this restaurant (aka the "fake-meat palace") lists items on its Hong Kong–style menu according to which meats they simulate. The only thing to avoid is the faux "beef"—trust us on this one. ♦ Vegetarian/Chinese ♦ Daily lunch and dinner. 364 Roy St (between Fourth and Nob Hill Aves N). 282.6616 ♿

66 Bahn Thai ★★$ Zestful but not overpowering Thai fare is served in an ornately overdecorated setting within a converted house. The curry of the day is usually an excellent choice, as is the chicken satay. Only menu listings with more than two or three stars are hot. ♦ Thai ♦ M-F lunch and dinner; Sa-Su dinner. 409 Roy St (between Fifth and Fourth Aves N). 283.0444

67 Jillian's Billiard Club This pool hall, in what was once a Toyota showroom, offers 33 tables and a munchies menu, along with beer, wine, champagne, and the ubiquitous espresso drinks. A bar at one end of the club provides a windowed retreat. It's a dress-up joint, not your classic dark pool hall like the **2-11 Billiard Club** (see page 73). Billiards lessons are available. ♦ M-Th, Su until 2AM; F, Sa until 4AM. 731 Westlake Ave N (between Valley and Aloha Sts). 223.0300

68 Wawona Harking back to Seattle's maritime heritage is this tri-masted, 468-ton schooner built in 1897. For three decades, beginning in 1914, the ship sailed north to hunt for cod in the Bering Sea. Ironically, those fish that ended

their lives on the *Wawona* actually helped extend this ship's own life, preserving the inner hull with their oils. In 1970 it was the first US ship to be declared a national historic site. ♦ The $1 fee goes toward the ship's upkeep. Daily. Northwest Seaport Dock (near the corner of Westlake Ave N and Valley St, just west of the US Naval Reserve station). 447.9800

69 Center for Wooden Boats A historical museum and boat-rental dock are rolled into one, with many vintage and replica craft on view. The center also offers classes in sailing, sail repair, boat-building, and other maritime skills. ♦ Fee for boat rentals. Museum/gift shop: M, W-Su. Boat rentals: daily. 1010 Valley St (at Lake Union). 382.2628

70 Chandler's Crabhouse and Fresh Fish Market ★$$$ One in a series of glitzy nosheries that round the southern end of Lake Union and attract a libidinally active clientele, this spot does its best with crab (no surprise here) in a multitude of variations. There's also a daily fresh-fish roster and a satisfying Sunday brunch. ♦ Seafood ♦ M-Sa lunch and dinner; Su brunch and dinner. 901 Fairview Ave N (at Lake Union). 223.2722 ♿

70 Duke's Chowderhouse and Outrageous Canoe Club ★$ Stuck into the lower corner of the **Chandler's Cove** retail complex, this spot is rather hard to find. But the view of Lake Union can't be beat, even when the sun is bright enough to pierce your retinas, and the deck dining area makes a terrific after-work hangout. (The interior, by contrast, is often too noisy for a pleasant chat.) Fresh seafood is available daily, but the sandwiches and fries fit equally well with the yacht-club atmosphere. ♦ American ♦ Restaurant: daily lunch and dinner. Bar: daily until 2AM. 901 Fairview Ave N (at Lake Union). 382.9963 ♿

Being a town of the Old West, Seattle was no stranger to mob justice. The first lynching here, on 18 January 1882, was of two men who had robbed and killed a store clerk. Unlike in many other Wild West communities, however, this event was a civic embarrassment in Seattle. To avoid portraying the city in an unfavorable, dangerous light, the coroner's office listed the men's cause of death as "irate citizens."

Alice B. Toklas, the longtime companion of Gertrude Stein, attended the University of Washington in 1893 and 1894.

70 Cucina! Cucina! ★$$ Being seen is the important thing here—it's a good thing, since it's so noisy no one can hear you anyway—so dress smartly, for you will be checked out. This restaurant is big on pasta, focaccia, and designer pizzas (try the smoked-chicken pie), with deck seating out back where you can watch boats and pontoon planes on Lake Union. ♦ Italian ♦ Restaurant: M-Sa lunch and dinner; Su brunch and dinner. Bar: daily until 1:30AM. Reservations recommended. 901 Fairview Ave N (at Lake Union). 447.2782 ♿. Also at: the MGM Bldg, Bellevue Pl (10500 NE Eighth St at 105th Ave NE). 637.1177 ♿

71 I Love Sushi ★★$ The beloved menu of the popular sushi palace of the same name in Bellevue is now offered at this outpost. Tuna, eel, and Dungeness crab remain ever-popular selections. Hara-San, one of the master chefs from the original restaurant, wields the knives here. ♦ Japanese ♦ M-Sa lunch and dinner; Su dinner. 1001 Fairview Ave N (at Lake Union).

625.9604. Also at: 11818 NE Eighth St (near 118th Ave NE), Bellevue. 454.5706

72 Lincoln Towing "Toe Truck" Another stop on the official "Outrageous, Never to be Sanctioned by the Chamber of Commerce" kitsch tour features this company's pink, pickup truck with a gargantuan toe protruding from its roof. Get those cameras ready! ♦ Mercer St and Fairview Ave N. 622.0415

73 St. Spiridon Orthodox Church The city's first Russian Orthodox church was established in 1898, the same time Americans were rushing through Seattle on their way to gold fields in the old Russian outpost of Alaska. This tiny church, conceived by architect **Ivan Palmov** (who also designed **St. Nicholas Russian Orthodox Church** on Capitol Hill), came along much later—in 1938—yet it contains all of the arresting clichés of Eastern churches. Drivers racing down Interstate 5 are often bewildered to see its white-and-blue onion domes. ♦ Yale Ave N (at Harrison St). 624.5341

Charity Begins Away from Home: Helping Seattle's Homeless

Despite its explosive growth in recent years, Seattle has not been able to escape the problem of homelessness. By conservative estimates, the number of homeless people on the streets of the city each day ranges from 3,000 to 5,000 (and workers in the field will tell you that it's more like 7,000). But like many of America's major cities, Seattle has developed several innovative programs to help people make the transition from life on the streets to the life that most of us take for granted. Two of these are of particular interest to the visitor: **Real Change Magazine** and **Common Meals.**

Real Change Magazine is a monthly newspaper run, written, and distributed by homeless or formerly homeless members of the community. Started in 1994, its circulation has grown to nearly 25,000. The paper offers interesting articles, fiction, and poetry, as well as the occasional investigative piece or interview. The $1 "suggested donation" is well worth it, as 75¢ of it goes directly to the vendor. A much more viable alternative to panhandling, selling **Real Change** has allowed many of Seattle's homeless to work their way off the streets.

Opened in 1992, **Common Meals** (in the Josephinum Hotel, 1902 Second Ave

between Stewart and Virginia Sts, 448.6422) is run completely by the homeless community. All of the staff—from the hostess who seats you to the dishwasher in the kitchen—are formerly homeless people receiving job training that may well allow them to make a living for themselves. The atmosphere is informal, the decor catch-as-catch-can (the plates and furnishings don't match, etc.), but the food is very good. The place is open daily for lunch (with a menu of burgers, fries, and other basic American fare), but the best time to visit is on Thursday nights. That's when there's a special prix-fixe dinner menu planned and prepared by one of the city's top chefs; the culinary talents who have donated their time and expertise here include Charles Ramseyer of **Ray's Boathouse** and Tim Kelly of **The Painted Table.** The schedule of chefs is planned several weeks in advance; for information and reservations, call the office manager at 443.1233. At **Common Meals,** you can enjoy a gourmet meal worthy of Seattle's finest restaurants for much less money—and support a good cause at the same time.

It's a rare charity that benefits both the giver and the receiver, but **Real Change** and **Common Meals** are two of them.

km 1/2   1
mi 1/4   1/2

N

Union
Bay

Montlake
Bridge

Foster
Island

520   Evergreen Point Floating Bridge

Fuhrman
Ave. E

Montlake

E Hamlin St.

Portage
Bay

E Roanoke St.

EASTLAKE

5

E Lynn St.

24th
Ave. E

Washington Park
Arboretum

MADISON
PARK

Eastlake Ave. E

E Blaine St.

E Garfield St.

43rd Ave. E

Louisa Boren
View Park

Lake Washington Blvd. E

Arboretum Dr. E

Broadmoor
Dr. E

10th Ave. E

E Galer St.

Volunteer
Park

23rd Ave. E

Parkside Dr. E

McGilvra Blvd.

E Prospect St.

CAPITOL
HILL

E Aloha St.

For nos 1-80,
see pg. 88

Bellevue Ave. E

Belmont
Ave. E.

E Republican St.

E John St.

E Thomas St.

E Madison St.

E John St.

Florence
Ct.

E Denny Way

E Denny Way

31st Ave.

Broadway

12th Ave.

E Pine St.

CENTRAL

E Union St.

FIRST
HILL

Madison St.

15th Ave.

19th Ave.

23rd Ave.

M.L. King Jr. Way

34th Ave.

35th Ave.

Madrona Park
Bathing Beach

E Cherry St.

Lake
Washington

83

Cherry St.

James St.

MADRONA

81

Boren Ave.

E Alder St.

Lakeside Ave. S

Leschi
Park

82

E Yesler Way

86

84

16th Ave. S

S Jackson St.

Frink
Park

85

S Dearborn St.

YESLER
TERRACE

90

Mercer
Island

900

12th Ave. S

S Holgate St.

BEACON
HILL

Rainier Ave. S

Colman
Park

Airport Way

5

S Lander St.

87

88

Lake Washington Blvd. S

S McClellan St.

West Seattle
Fwy.

S Spokane St.

Beacon Ave. S

Jefferson
Park
Golf
Course

M.L. King Jr. Way S

167

34th Ave. S

Rainier Ave. S

89

Stan Sayres
Memorial
Park

Industrial
Way

900

Genesee
Playfield

93

S Genesee St.

S Columbia Way

Columbia
Park

38th Ave. S

42nd Ave. S

MT. BAKER

Andrews
Bay

Lake Washington Blvd. S

94

15th Ave. S

92

51st Ave. S

91

90

Seward
Park

Capitol Hill to Seward Park

In a city of diverse neighborhoods, those areas lying just east of downtown—along the hilly ridge that separates downtown skyscrapers from placid **Lake Washington**—are by far the most diverse. The wealth of old Seattle is entrenched here, but these streets are also home to penniless refugees, leather-clad punks with Jello-bright hair, and, in August, crowds drawn to Seafair's annual hydroplane competition.

The 1990 census identified two dozen distinct racial and/or ethnic groups in this enormous area, including European-Americans, African-Americans, and Asian-Americans. Latinos and Native Americans also appear in significant numbers. Diversity reaches its apex on Capitol Hill, where any given block may be home to young singles, blue-collar Boeing workers, members of the gay and lesbian community, and émigrés from a half-dozen nations. If there is a minority group in this part of town, it might be the white families with children that predominate throughout the rest of the city.

There's no real central focal point here, and indeed the neighborhood boundaries are ill-defined; even City Hall may find itself divided as to whether a given residence is located in, say, **Leschi** or **Madrona**. Outside of boisterous **Broadway** on Capitol Hill and a few neighborhood pubs, a visitor will not find much nightlife on these tree-lined streets. But there are other diversions. **Madison Park** hosts an impressive enclave of stately and well-preserved mansions, surpassed only by **Millionaires' Row** and the **Harvard-Belmont Historic District** on Capitol Hill.

First settled by Italian farmers, the nearby **Central District** became more urban and residential during World War II, as African-Americans from the South arrived to work in Seattle's booming economy. In recent years, much of the neighborhood has fallen into disrepair, and vice and violence have crept in. But there's also a closeness felt by the residents here, people bravely fighting modern urban plagues.

There are a plethora of parks in the area—from the traditionally styled **Volunteer Park** on Capitol Hill to the urban wilderness of Seward Park on Lake Washington. The lake draws flocks of citizens to its shores in warm months and is used year-round for fishing and boating. **Washington Park Arboretum** will captivate both the casual stroller and the professional botanist. And these are just the largest greenswards; perhaps a dozen smaller (but no less charming) acreages—such as the **Louisa Boren View Park**—are tucked away, known to neighborhood residents and waiting to be discovered by the visitor.

Madison Park

1 Nellie Cornish Memorial Sculptures
Artist Parks Anderson's 1989 stylized windmills, jutting up from the waters of Lake Washington at the western end of the Evergreen Point Floating Bridge (Highway 520), were installed in honor of longtime Seattle arts advocate Nellie Cornish, founder of Capitol Hill's **Cornish College of the Arts.** Each tower consists of four steel legs rising from a concrete base and topped with two bronze wind-wheels that rotate in opposite directions. Above these, and not visible except from boats that can get closer than cars to these sculptures, is a tiny bear, balanced whimsically on a golden ball, with another smaller ball perched on its nose. When the Northwest isn't experiencing a drought, fountains shoot eight-foot-tall sprays of water up the legs; they're lighted at night and create an eerie spectacle. ♦ West end of the Evergreen Point Floating Bridge

2 Museum of History and Industry (MOHAI) Opened in 1952, the city's premier repository of the past had a long gestation period. In 1911 historians began efforts to erect a permanent museum, but sufficient funds weren't gathered until the late 1940s. After locating choice property on the current site, however, museum backers faced opposition from the **University of Washington,** which owned the land—or thought it did, anyway. It turned out that a

portion of the property was under federal control; museum supporters lobbied for its use and won.

The museum now chronicles the city's heritage with displays of fire engines, a cable car, and numerous artifacts from the lumber, shipping, and fishing industries. Seattle is the birthplace of the Boeing Company, so it's no surprise to find a 1920s Boeing mail plane here. The museum also boasts a rich maritime collection—the model ships and figureheads are popular with children—and one of the state's most extensive arrays of historic photographs from the region. ♦ Admission. Daily. Reservations required to visit the photo archives. 2700 24th Ave E (at E Hamlin St). 324.1125

2 Foster Island Walk At the bottom of MOHAI's parking lot is the start of the largest wetlands trail system left in Seattle. A 20-minute nature walk starts off along wooden plankways and winds through a tangle of tall grasses, marshland exposed after the opening of the Lake Washington Ship Canal lowered the lake by 20 feet. The trail leads to tiny Foster Island, a historic burial ground for the Union Bay Indians, now a pleasant picnic spot. From this point, you may gaze at the regular parade of boats crisscrossing the canal from Lake Washington to Lake Union. It's very soothing here—walk at water's edge past the white water lilies, yellow irises, and cattails and listen to the sounds of song sparrows, red-winged blackbirds, and marsh wrens. Dreamy as it is, your powers of reverie must be able to block out the discordant howl of traffic and the unsightly concrete of nearby Highway 520. No pets or jogging are allowed on this quiet trail, which continues past Foster Island another half-hour to the **Washington Park Arboretum.** ♦ 2700 24th Ave E (enter from the MOHAI parking lot)

3 Montlake Bridge Built in 1925, with distinctive Gothic-inspired towers (visually linking it to the nearby **University of Washington**), this span was designed by the university's architect, **Carl Gould.** At that time, the need for a bridge had only existed for eight years, since the ship canal, finally linking Puget Sound with Seattle's "inland sea," plowed through what had originally been an isthmus. An earlier, more easily crossed canal (about a hundred yards south of the present Montlake Cut, and filled long ago) had been completed in 1884 but was used only for logs and the occasional canoe, as it was too narrow to carry ships.

Completion of the **UW** stadium in 1920 initiated interest in a bridge; in fact, in preparation for the stadium's first football game (**UW** and **Dartmouth**), a graduate manager at the school tied a row of barges together near this point to allow fans easy passage north from the Montlake neighborhood. Three elections later, this bridge was built. A pleasant walkway runs along the south side of the canal and beneath the bridge. ♦ Montlake Blvd NE (off Hwy 520)

4 Seattle Yacht Club A water-oriented city, Seattle has a long list of yacht clubs—some spiffy, some not. This 3,000-member organization is the largest, the oldest (founded in 1892), and the hardest to get into (you must be nominated by a current member). It sponsors Seattle's traditional raft of events revolving around the opening day of yachting season, which is the first Saturday in May. The clubhouse was designed around 1920 by architect **John Graham Sr.** Facilities also include four docks full of well-oiled teak and mahogany. ♦ 325 E Hamlin St (on Portage Bay). 325.1000

5 Café Lago ★★$$ The chefs at this cozy bistro pride themselves on their gnocchi, but the real prize here is the antipasti selection. One top choice is the eggplant marinated in garlic and olive oil. Arrive early, as reservations are not accepted. ♦ Italian ♦ Tu-Su dinner. No reservations; no credit cards accepted. 2305 24th Ave E (between E Lynn and E McGraw Sts). 329.8005 ♿

5 The Daily Grind ★$ Expansive and well-lighted, this corner cafe is redolent with the scents of fresh baked muffins and scones. It's great for extended planning sessions (nobody ever kicks you out of this place) and very early morning good-byes. ♦ Coffeehouse ♦ Daily. 2301 24th Ave E (at E Lynn St). 322.9885 ♿

Arboretum

6 Washington Park Arboretum This 200-acre woodland, planned in 1936 and stretching south from Lake Washington's Union Bay, is the city's jewel in a necklace of parks designed by the Olmsted Brothers landscaping firm of Massachusetts.

The arboretum was a long time in the making. After putting the area aside as parkland in 1904, the city developed Lake Washington Boulevard East (the narrow, curving thoroughfare that cuts through the park) as a scenic entryway to the 1909 Alaska-Yukon-Pacific Exposition, held on the **UW** grounds. But it didn't develop the park until the university agreed to help manage it. The arboretum first featured native plants (despite the Olmsteds' historical antipathy toward Northwest flora), but in the 1940s, it expanded to include species from all over the globe. Today more than 5,500 kinds of trees, shrubs, and flowers flourish on the grounds.

Visitors to the park can find a spot to fit almost any mood: toss a Frisbee across the broad, open meadows; stroll through the ornamental gardens; or enter into the serene, otherworldly atmosphere of the tea garden. A harmonious collaboration of natural elements and human stewardship prevails throughout the park. Many plants have identification tags, but the thickly wooded grounds have none of the fussy feeling of some public gardens. There are several hours' worth of trails to explore. Dogs love to romp in this park, but the city's leash laws should at least be acknowledged, if not followed to the letter. ♦ Bounded by E Madison St and Hwy 520, and Arboretum Dr E and 26th Ave E

Within the Washington Park Arboretum:

Graham Visitors' Center The park's focal point offers trail maps, botanical pamphlets, and a small gift shop and bookstore. The center schedules two large sales during the year, one of plants (in April) and another of bulbs (in October), when you may see normally serene local gardeners locked in combat for possession of a bewildered baby rhododendron. Just outside the front door, several hiking trails lead to wooded areas. ♦ Daily. Group tours of the park Sunday at 1PM and every second Wednesday of the month at 10AM (except in December). 2300 Arboretum Dr E (off Lake Washington Blvd E). 543.8800

 Winter Garden Plants that thrive in the mild Northwest climate and bloom between October and March are displayed here. Witch hazel and viburnum are prominent attractions. In early spring, the tall cornelian cherry shrubs burst forth with their small yellow flowers, set against an underplanting of Lenten roses. ♦ Adjacent to the Visitors' Center. 543.8800

Azalea Way This wide, grassy three-quarter-mile path was the site of a raceway for harness horses in Seattle's pre-auto era, but is now considered too fragile to withstand even joggers—it's for walkers only. Crowds gather along the path on weekends from April through June to see flowering cherry trees, azaleas, and dogwoods. Farther along is the **Rhododendron Glen,** where a pond reflects a riot of colors. ♦ Between Arboretum Dr E and Lake Washington Blvd E

 Japanese Tea Garden Designed in the Momoyama style in 1960 by Japanese architect **Juki Iida,** this 3.5-acre garden is a tranquil world of Asian and Northwest

plantings, rookeries, bridges, granite lanterns, waterfalls, and glassy pools. Believed to be one of the most authentic outside of Japan, construction of the garden required transporting more than 500 massive granite boulders, each wrapped in bamboo matting to prevent scratching, from high in Washington's Cascade Mountains. The original cypress-and-cedar teahouse, hand-constructed in Japan, was destroyed by fire in 1973, then rebuilt following the original plans. The teahouse offers monthly demonstrations in Chado, the highly ritualized Japanese tea ceremony. ♦ Admission. ♦ Daily Mar-Nov. 26th. Ave E (off E Lee St). 684.4725, tea ceremony demonstrations 324.1483

7 Madison Park Hardware Yes, there are lots of standard supplies here, plus a frosting of kitchen paraphernalia, toys, and baskets. But the bonus is proprietor Lola McKee, the unofficial mayor and historian of Madison Park, who has become a tenacious advocate for preservation of this community's many charms. ♦ M-Sa. 1837 42nd Ave E (off E Madison St). 322.5331

8 Red Onion Tavern This is a classic neighborhood joint where the never-rowdy clientele grows younger as the night wears on; by closing time young singles predominate. The pool tables are bumpy, and the pizza is filling but mediocre. However, a fireplace does much to promote lingering conversation. ♦ Daily until 2AM. 4210 E Madison St (between 43rd and 42nd Aves E). 323.1611

8 Cactus ★★$$ Popular Spanish and Mexican specialties are served here, authentic right down to the use of fish flown in from the Yucatán. But the primo draws are the invitingly displayed and spicy tapas. ♦ Spanish/Mexican ♦ M-Sa lunch and dinner; Su dinner. Reservations recommended for groups of five or more. 4220 E Madison St (at 43rd Ave E). 324.4140

9 Madison Park and Beach Not a component in the Olmsted Brothers' greenbelt scheme but linked to it by later planners, this is the northernmost in a continuous string of parks that lines Lake Washington's western banks. There are roped-off swimming areas and lighted tennis courts, and on steamy summer afternoons droves of sunworshipers jam the beach.

In the 1890s the **Madison Street Cable Car Company** ran a line out here to a small amusement park with a 500-seat pavilion, boathouse, ballpark, and racetrack. Boat cruises around the lake began from this spot,

and summer vacationers came to mount big canvas tents on specially constructed platforms.

In preparation for the AYP Exposition, $30,000 was spent on improvements to the amusement park, which was then called **White City,** and a ferry line to Mercer Island and other nascent Eastside communities was added. But it all fell into disuse after the Expo ended. One remaining remnant of those days is **Pioneer Hall,** which is listed on the National Register of Historic Places. Built in 1910, the structure now houses a museum (with very limited hours) that displays pioneer artifacts, period costumes, and 19th-century photographs. In 1919 the city bought the streetcar line, along with the park and its entertainment facilities. Twenty years later the city initiated a WPA landscaping program to take advantage of new waterfront space created here after the ship canal lowered Lake Washington by 20 feet. ♦ Pioneer Hall: open 1-4PM on the second Sunday of the month. Pioneer Hall: free. E Madison St (on Lake Washington)

10 Alexander Pantages House Lying south of Madison Street and north of where Lake Washington Boulevard dips down to the lake from the **Washington Park Arboretum** is a wooded and palatial residential canton called Washington Park. Although it only began to develop after the 19th century, the neighborhood has the classic weight of a much older subdivision. One of the most impressive architectural statements made here is the home of impresario Alexander Pantages, who owned vaudeville theaters all over the West. His half-timbered mansion, designed in 1909 by **Wilson & Loveless,** carries overtones of California Mission Revival style. It's a private residence. ♦ 1117 36th Ave E (between E Prospect and E Madison Sts)

11 Lake Washington Boulevard Those landscaping Olmsted Brothers, and their father before them, were great believers in contouring human developments to the land. Their comprehensive plan for Seattle included this scenic and meandering boulevard along the west side of Lake Washington, running south from the AYP Exposition grounds (now the **UW** campus) to **Seward Park.** Today, some parts of this 1910 contoured drive have been bypassed by straighter Lakeside Avenue South (especially the famous curves through **Colman Park,** just south of the Lacey V. Morrow Floating Bridge/I-90). But you can still follow the old route; watch closely for signs. ♦ Between S Orcas and E Calhoun Sts

12 Walker-Ames House Architects **Charles Bebb** and **Leonard L. Mendel** designed this stately Colonial Revival manse in 1907. It is now the residence of the **University of Washington**'s president. ♦ 808 36th Ave E (between E Valley and E Ward Sts)

Eastlake

13 Roanoke Park Place Tavern This is a prime watering hole for the just-over-21-and-frisky set down from Capitol Hill. It's lively and good for people watching but definitely *not* the place to go if you're feeling your age. Burgers and beer are the two essential food groups. ◆ Daily until 2AM. 2409 10th Ave E (near E Miller St). 324.5882

14 Romio's Pizza ★★$ A relatively young entry in the pizzeria chain, this branch is more spacious but less homey than its brethren. It's hard, though, to dis a joint that serves pizza as fabulous as this. ◆ Pizza/Takeout ◆ Daily until 11PM. 3242 Eastlake Ave E (at Fuhrman Ave E). 322.4453. Also at: 2001 W Dravus St (between 20th Ave and 21st Ave W). 284.5420; 8523 Greenwood Ave N (between N 85th and N 87th Sts). 782.9005; 917 Howell St (between Terry Ave and Ninth Ave). 622.6878

15 Tio's Bakery & Cafe ★$ This place serves omelettes for breakfast and red snapper at dinnertime, but the real draw is the baked goods—coffee cakes, muffins, cinnamon rolls, and breads. Late-night or early weekday morning visits provide the most peaceful environment; there are huge crowds on Saturday and Sunday mornings. ◆ Spanish/Bakery ◆ M-Sa breakfast, lunch, and dinner (W-Sa until 10PM); Su breakfast. 2379 Eastlake Ave E (at E Louisa St). 325.0081 ◇

16 Carrot Cafe ★$ It's a popular place and on weekends you may have to cool your heels outside the front door with a newspaper. The menu features such dishes as vegetarian lasagna and self-designed omelettes. ◆ American ◆ Daily breakfast and lunch. 2305 Eastlake Ave E (at E Lynn St). 324.1442 ◇

17 Serafina ★★$$ A few taverns have always been present in Eastlake, plus the odd used-books outlet and some totally forgettable office buildings, but such refined establishments as this place have greatly enhanced the neighborhood's profile in recent years. Begin your meal with a few small appetizers in the tapas style—the *crostini* with Tuscan olive spread and goat cheese are particularly good. The entrées, including penne with smoked mozzarella in a spicy tomato cream sauce; blue cheese chicken salad with pears, grilled walnuts, and Sherry vinaigrette; and *salsiccia*

toscana (sausage braised with caramelized onions and cabbage and served over polenta) are all delicious.

This popular place is often crowded, and on busy nights the service can be slow. When there aren't a lot of patrons, it can be a romantic setting, especially with the occasional addition of live piano music. There's a wonderful patio out back, where diners at a handful of tables can relax and eat in a tranquil garden setting. ◆ Italian ◆ M-F lunch and dinner; Sa-Su dinner. Reservations recommended. 2043 Eastlake Ave E (at E Boston St). 323.0807 ◇

18 Interlaken Park This park is really just a serpentine, tree-lined street with a few shady footpaths that are frequented by neighborhood residents. It was originally the route of a short-lived bicycle path, built during a Seattle bike craze around the turn of the century. Interlaken Boulevard now connects the **Washington Park Arboretum** and Lake Washington Boulevard East with Capitol Hill, before heading west into Highway 520 and Interstate 5. ◆ Interlaken Blvd (from Lake Washington Blvd E to Hwy 520)

Capitol Hill

19 Louisa Boren View Park Pike Place Market hero **Victor Steinbrueck** designed this small park in 1975. Looking north, it commands views of Portage Bay, the **UW** campus, Lake Washington, and the Cascade Mountains. The park was named after Louisa Boren Denny, the last survivor of the 1851 Alki Point settlers. The large untitled Cor-Ten steel sculpture, composed of 10 interlocking blocks rusted to an even brown color, was created by artist Lee Kelly. ◆ 15th Ave E and E Garfield St

The Big Snow of 1880 marked the worst winter this city ever experienced. Snow began to fall on 5 January and within a week was heaped in six-foot-high drifts. The *Seattle Post-Intelligencer* confessed that "we shall have to admit hereafter that snow does occasionally fall in this country.The 64-inch snow total from that week brought the city (including vital railroad lines) to a complete standstill.

"The streets were so steep that members of the Seattle Symphony, who had to climb three blocks to reach their practice hall from the place where they stored their instruments, arrived winded, and sometimes rehearsals were over before all the horn players had caught their breath. The musicians rigged a pully to carry the instruments uphill, so that strangers in town were sometimes startled to have a cello or a tuba swoop past them on the street."

Murray Morgan, Skid Road

20 Lake View Cemetery Before **Volunteer**
Park could begin to grow in the 1890s, the city had to relocate one of its principal graveyards from what is now the park's north end. Regrettably, most of the dead residents had already been moved once before, in 1885, when the city turned its pioneer cemetery into **Denny Park,** south of Lake Union. Two years later Leigh S.J. Hunt, owner and editor of the *Seattle Post-Intelligencer,* convinced the city council that the graves should be moved again, just a few hundred feet north. This final site is now the **Lake View Cemetery,** with perhaps the best views of any graveyard in the city.

People come from as far away as Japan and China to visit the gravesites (near the summit) of kung fu star Bruce Lee, a former Seattleite who died in 1973, and his son Brandon, who was killed in a shooting accident during the making of the 1994 film *The Crow.* And there are some wonderful old tombstones here, dating back to the 1850s. Pioneer David Swinton "Doc" Maynard, who perished in 1873, is buried here beside one of his two wives, Catherine, whose epitaph reads, "She did what she could." Nearby is a rugged headstone under which Princess Angeline, the daughter of Chief Sealth, the city's namesake, lies in a canoe-shaped coffin. ♦ Bounded by 15th and 11th Aves E, and Volunteer Park and E Howe St. 322.1582

21 John Leary House When completed around 1904, this stone and half-timbered manse was one of the largest and most lavish in the city. The architect was Seattle's **J. Alfred Bodley.** The owner, John Leary, arrived in Seattle in 1869 and founded the West Coast Improvement Company, which was primarily responsible for the development of Ballard. In 1882 Leary became principal owner of the *Seattle Post,* which he soon merged with the competing *Intelligencer* to create what is still the city's morning daily, the *Seattle Post-Intelligencer.* He also opened and operated a coal mine, was partly responsible for supplying Seattle with its first natural gas, and set up a waterworks system that brought in water from Lake Washington for the first time.

Not content with his accomplishments, Leary was elected mayor of Seattle in 1884 and served two terms in office. It seemed John Leary could have anything he wanted. But he died at the age of 68 before he could move into his dream house. The mansion is now home to the Episcopal Diocesan offices. A stained-glass window designed for the house by New York's Tiffany & Company is now at UW's Burke Museum. ♦ 1551 10th Ave E (between E Garfield and E Howe Sts)

22 St. Mark's Episcopal Cathedral This graceful but somewhat chilly Episcopal temple for the Diocese of Olympia was designed by **Bakewell and Brown,** a noted San Francisco architectural firm. Built between 1926 and 1930 in a Neo-Byzantine style, the church has an interior that one critic described as "an immense masonry box." Inside is a world-renowned, 3,744-pipe Flentrop organ, acquired in 1965, which draws musicians from all over the world to perform in the cathedral's annual recital series. ♦ 1245 10th Ave E (at E Galer St). 323.0300

23 Egan House Wedged into a wooded glen, this triangular oddity may well be the most unusual residence in Seattle. Built in 1958, the house is the work of **Robert Reichert,** a local architect well known for unconventional designs. This building's form, write Sally B. Woodbridge and Roger Montgomery in *A Guide to Architecture in Washington State,* "expresses its interior organization, in which levels, like graduated trays, diminish in size as they rise." It's a private residence. ♦ 1500 Lakeview Blvd E (near E Highland Dr)

24 Sam Hill House Designed by the Washington, DC, architectural firm of **Hornblower & Marshall,** this mansion was built in 1909 for the son-in-law of **Great Northern Railroad** magnate James J. Hill. The five-story fortress is a concrete variation of an 18th-century manor house, resembling in many respects the Petit Trianon at Versailles. Hill supposedly built it in order to be able to properly receive Crown Prince Albert of Belgium, who, despite two planned trips to Seattle, canceled both times. It's still a private residence. ♦ 814 E Highland Dr (between Broadway E and Harvard Ave E)

25 C.J. Smith House This beautiful brick mansion, with lead-glass windows and an elegant low brick wall separating the front yard from the sidewalk, was built in 1907, though it's been renovated and altered recently. The design, by Spokane architect **Kirtland K. Cutter** and his frequent partner **Karl Malmgren,** was influenced by the work of English architect **Richard Norman Shaw,** who was much in favor in America at the time. Born in 1854, Charles Jackson Smith, a native of Kentucky, was president of the Dexter Horton National Bank, a forerunner of today's Seafirst Bank. The house remains a private residence. ♦ 1147 Harvard Ave E (between E Prospect St and E Highland Dr)

26 Brownell-Bloedel House Architect **Carl Gould** departed from his usual style by sheathing this 1910 Georgian Revival residence in natural wood shingles. It's a private residence. ♦ 1137 Harvard Ave E (between E Prospect St and E Highland Dr)

Coincidence or karma? The electric guitar was invented in Seattle. Jimi Hendrix was born in Seattle. You be the judge.

27 R.D. Merrill House Built in 1909, this modified Georgian mansion, complete with formal garden and carriage house, is the only West Coast structure designed by famed New York architect **Charles A. Platt,** who is best known for his Freer Gallery in Washington, DC. Merrill was born in Michigan in 1869 to a lumber family from Maine. Continuing in the family tradition, he moved to the Pacific Northwest in 1898 to manage the Washington and British Columbia properties of Merrill and Ring, a leading lumber firm of the era. ♦ 919 Harvard Ave E (between E Aloha and E Prospect Sts)

28 Volunteer Park During the 1880s this 43-acre plot was known simply as **City Park.** But in 1901 it was renamed to honor Seattle men who fought in the Spanish-American War of 1898. The same year a 20-million-gallon reservoir was carved from the park's southern flanks, and around 1906 a 75-foot-tall water tower (pictured below) was put up to increase water pressure in the mansions sprouting nearby. The Olmsted Brothers engineered the final refinements. As part of their comprehensive plan, they decided that this should be one of several "neat and smooth" central parks (as opposed to such "wild" outlying greens as **Seward Park**). Second-growth fir trees were felled and replaced by a more ordered regiment of blue spruce, flowering cherry trees, and Port Orford cedar. A carriage concourse was laid, fountains and a giant bandstand were built, and a semicircular concert grove was pruned out of the undergrowth. With only a few exceptions, the park today looks much as it did when the Olmsteds completed their work.

Volunteer Park Water Tower

M. BLUM

Fine clear-weather views of the **Space Needle,** Puget Sound, and the Olympic Mountains are available from this 445-foot elevation. Climb to the top of the brick-faced water tower—a tricky ascent, given its steep stairs—for an even better perspective. The park fills with people during summer theater performances and weekend festivals. Two outdoor tennis courts are well maintained but underused. A popular children's playground and wading pool lie in the northeastern corner.

Despite the tranquillity, a few cautions should be exercised here. Behind the concrete bandstand, situated just north of the reservoir, is a public rest room where various criminal activities have occurred despite frequent police patrols; it's best to avoid it after nightfall. It seems quite safe at all other hours, however. ♦ Bounded by E Prospect and E Galer Sts, and 15th and 11th Aves E. 625.8901

Within Volunteer Park:

Conservatory Constructed for $20,000 in 1912, this conservatory was patterned after London's spectacular Crystal Palace exhibition hall. It was a prefab building: Manufactured in New York, the components were shipped to Seattle and put together by parks department employees. Capitol Hill's landed gentry of the time readily embraced the conservatory, calling it the finest structure of its kind west of Chicago and contributing plant specimens to its collection.

During the Depression, however, the conservatory fell upon hard times, its humid environment rotting the Southern swamp cypress frames and rusting some of the iron supports. By the 1970s the greenhouse was beginning to list to one side and visitors weren't allowed on the premises during windy weather because panes of glass tended to pop out of their frames. A $500,000 restoration program in the early 1980s re-created the building's graceful roof and sides using steel, cast iron, and Alaska cedar. During refurbishment, a colorful etched-glass canopy—*Homage in Green*—was installed over the entrance. Created by Richard Spaulding, a former artist-in-residence with the Seattle Arts Commission, *Homage* is enlivened with lilies, passion flowers, and morning glories, all of which are familiar from Victorian designs. Inside, more than a quarter-million visitors each year study an incredible array of orchids, cacti, and tropical species in three crowded wings. Sadly, the abundant foliage permits no room for wheelchairs. Admirers periodically lobby the city for expansion, but the park's neighbors, fearing more traffic, object. ♦ Daily. North side of park. 684.4743

Monument to William H. Seward The weathered bronze statue is a likeness of the former US Secretary of State and real-estate tycoon who bought Alaska from the Russians in 1867 for two cents an acre. New York artist Richard Brooks created this piece for the **1909 Alaska-Yukon-Pacific Expo.** This statue, which was originally intended to be moved to **Seward Park** after the exposition was over, has been in its current "temporary" location for close to 90 years. ♦ In front of the Conservatory

Seattle Asian Art Museum This beloved building (the old **Seattle Art Museum**) was given new life in 1994 as a showcase for the museum's extensive assembly of Asian art, which ranks in the top 10 collections outside of Asia; its Japanese collection is one of the top five in the US. The works here reflect a span of many ages and cultures in India, China, Japan, Korea, and Southeast Asia. The museum is also an education venue for scholarly exchange about Asian art and culture.

Designed by **Carl Gould,** the building is a Moderne gem. It was completed in 1933 and was a gift to the city from Dr. Richard Fuller, philanthropist and president of the Seattle Fine Arts Society, and his mother, Mrs. Eugene Fuller. At the time of its construction the museum was a fresh Protomodern design—with rounded corners, curved walls, and a foyer flowing gracefully toward side galleries and stairways. ♦ Admission; children under 12 free; discount for seniors and students. Tu-Su. 1400 E Prospect St (at 14th Ave E). 625.8900

Black Sun One of the park's focal points is this massive black granite sculpture—nine feet in diameter—created in 1968 by artist Isamu Noguchi (who also did *Landscape of Time,* a collection of carved granite boulders at Second Avenue and Marion Street). Area residents call it either "The Doughnut" or "The Black Hole." Not to discourage anyone, but if you choose to frame a photograph of the **Space Needle** through the hole in the middle, you won't be the first to do so. ♦ Across from the Seattle Asian Art Museum

29 Parker House A vast Colonial Revival mansion was built in 1909 for George H. Parker, the West Coast fiscal agent for the United Wireless Company. Parker's $150,000 home, supported by Corinthian columns, boasted five covered porches, 12 bedrooms and 16 other rooms, seven fireplaces, five bathrooms, hardwood floors, muraled walls, and an adjoining coach house. Parker, however, was not to enjoy his mansion for long. In 1910 he was convicted of stock and mail fraud and given a two-year sentence at

the federal prison on McNeil Island in south Puget Sound. It's a private residence. ♦ 1409 E Prospect St (at 14th Ave E)

30 Roberta's Bed & Breakfast $ This B&B (pictured above) offers five rooms with private baths and queen-size beds. The breakfast is a full, family-style vegetarian affair. There are lots of books for the borrowing, and *The New York Times* is available every day. Ask for the mountain view room. It's a one-block walk from here to **Volunteer Park.** No off-street parking is available. ♦ 1147 16th Ave E (between E Prospect St and E Highland Dr). 329.3326

31 Capitol Hill Addition Many of the comparatively modest residences found just east of **Volunteer Park** were part of the **Capitol Hill Addition,** a residential development begun around 1905. Spearheading that project was James A. Moore, the real-estate promoter who later built the **Moore Theater** downtown and created the University Heights district. Moore already had an interest in this neighborhood; in 1901 he'd acquired a good portion of it. Moore's wife, Eugenia, named the development after an exclusive section of Denver, her hometown.

Before opening the area to occupants, Moore spent $150,000 on improvements (cement sidewalks, paved streets, sewers, and water), "a previously unheard-of procedure," wrote the *Seattle Times.* The subdivision attracted the construction of many Colonial Revival homes—a style now commonly referred to as the Classic Box—along a nearby streetcar line. The houses here still delight with intricate details, such as squared-off corner bay windows, leaded glass, and Moorish keyhole windows. It's worth walking these thoroughfares to observe Moore's early legacy. One of the finer examples of the Classic Box can be found at **747 16th Avenue East** and is identified by its shallow ground-floor bays. ♦ Bounded by E Mercer and E Galer Sts, and 23rd and 15th Aves E

At 1.4 miles long, Evergreen Point Floating Bridge is the longest floating bridge in the world.

Chief Sealth

A pivotal figure in Seattle's early history was Chief Sealth, leader of the Suquamish and Duwamish people. Born around 1786 on **Blake Island,** in **Puget Sound,** Sealth is said to have witnessed the 1792 arrival in Puget Sound of Captain George Vancouver, the first European explorer of the area. The young boy's fascination with these foreign visitors marked the beginning of his lifelong relationship with the white newcomers.

At the age of 20, already proficient in the arts of warfare and persuasion, Sealth was named *tyee* (chief) of the Suquamish and Duwamish tribes. As more and more whites began to explore the area, Sealth, who ruled with a firm, benevolent hand, continually advocated a peaceful coexistence between his people and the settlers. (In fact, he went so far as to convert to Christianity in the 1830s, taking the baptismal name of Noah.)

In 1851, when settlers arrived in what is now **West Seattle,** the Suquamish and Duwamish people welcomed them warmly. Sealth soon befriended one of them, a young pioneer from Ohio named Dr. David Swinton "Doc" Maynard. He persuaded Maynard and his companions to move to the **Pioneer Square** area, where the forests were thicker and the land was better suited to development. He also encouraged his people to help the white men build houses and lay out streets. Maynard opened a shop here and quickly became prosperous; grateful for the chief's friendship and helpful advice, he suggested that the founding fathers call their new town "Seattle," a more pronounceable version of Sealth's name. They agreed, preferring it to its original name, "Duwamps."

As Seattle grew, tensions began to develop between the whites and many of the native groups in the region. In 1854, Congress proposed the Point Elliott Treaty, which stipulated that the US government would purchase two million acres of land in the region for $150,000, which would be paid over 20 years. The agreement also allotted 2,600 acres to be used as reservations and promised to provide services such as education and medical care to the natives. In January 1855, Chief Sealth addressed a crowd of natives and settlers, including territorial governor Isaac Stevens. While he expressed a willingness to go along with the government's proposal, he also touched upon several other themes, including sensitivity to nature, the sanctity of the landscape, the inevitable decline of the tribal peoples, and the danger that "civilization" could wreak havoc on the environment. He also warned the white men that they were not invincible—they were no less susceptible to conquest than the natives. The speech is still remembered today for its eloquence and wisdom.

Many of the tribes followed Sealth's lead in signing the treaty, but some refused, including the Muckleshoot, the Nisqually, and the Klickitat. Their attacks on the settlers ultimately led to the Indian War of 1855-56. During this conflict, the natives fired on the settlers from the cover of the forest, and the settlers barricaded themselves in the stockade and returned fire, assisted by the battle sloop *Decatur.* At last, the settlers prevailed, and Governor Stevens ordered that the remaining natives be placed in the reservations that had been created by the treaty.

After the war, things were never the same for the Native Americans, even the peace-loving Sealth and his people. Despite the chief's history of friendly relations with the white settlers, many of them still distrusted and disliked him. And the government did not adhere to its part of the Point Elliott Treaty: Not only were services denied to the residents of the reservations, but the government did not even make the entire $150,000 payment for the land. As Seattle continued to grow and expand, the Suquamish, Duwamish, and other native groups grew smaller and poorer. Throughout, however, Maynard and Sealth remained fast friends.

Chief Sealth died in June 1866 and was buried in **Suquamish Village** on the **Port Madison Reservation** in **Kitsap County.** His funeral was attended by a large crowd of his native followers and a few older settlers (including Maynard) who remembered him fondly. Today, the towers of his namesake town are visible from his gravesite, and there are several monuments to his memory; the largest and most prominent is a statue of the chief in **Tillicum Place,** at the junction of **Fifth Avenue** and **Denny Way**.

Chief Sealth Statue

32 Isaac Stevens School Early school district architect **James Stephen,** whose institutional artistry is also on display at **Summit Grade School** on First Hill, and **Latona Elementary** and **Interlake School** in Wallingford, designed this huge wooden Colonial Revival edifice in 1906. ◆ 1242 18th Ave E (between E Highland Dr and E Galer St). 281.6760

33 Holy Names Academy Beaux Arts styling receives grand exposition in this domed Catholic girls' school, designed by **C. Alfred Breitung,** who also created the tiny **Triangle Hotel Building** in Pioneer Square and Wallingford's **Home of the Good Shepherd.** ◆ 728 21st Ave E (between E Roy and E Aloha Sts). 323.4272

34 St. Joseph's Catholic Church Pay close attention to the tall, tapering belfry of this stripped-down Gothic house of worship, for it's there that you can find some relationship between this 1932 building and a still-more-impressive structure also designed by architect **Joseph Wilson:** downtown's **Seattle Tower.** The facing of the church was apparently intended to be something grander than cast concrete, but the Depression forced **Wilson** to simplify his dreams. Don't miss the stained-glass window on the entrance face. ◆ 732 18th Ave E (between E Roy and E Aloha Sts). 324.2522

35 Salisbury House $ A Victorian charmer owned and operated by Mary Wiese and her daughter Catheryn, this bed-and-breakfast can accommodate eight guests in four rooms, with queen-size beds and private baths. Family-style vegetarian breakfasts are served here, the library is comfy and well stocked, and **Volunteer Park** is two short blocks away. Off-street parking is not available. ◆ 750 16th Ave E (at E Aloha St). 328.8682

36 Millionaires' Row This tree-lined cluster of Xanadus extends south from **Volunteer Park** along 14th Avenue East to East Roy Street. Seattle's most prominent families once found status and security here, as this mini-neighborhood was protected from mere mortals by a private gate. The gate is now gone, but the district retains much of its earlier elegance. As in other affluent Seattle neighborhoods, however, many of the mansions have been converted from single-family residences to apartments. ◆ 14th Ave E (between E Prospect and E Roy Sts)

Along Millionaires' Row:

Thomas Bordeaux House The builder of this house was a Canadian who arrived here in 1852 and later ascended to the presidency of the Mason County Logging Company and the Mumby Lumber and Shingle Company. Thomas Bordeaux was also a director of the First National Bank of Seattle. His home, complete with a decorated tower, was built in 1903. Designed by Seattle architect **W.D.**

Kimball, it reflects the half-timber style then in vogue. ◆ 806 14th Ave E (between E Valley and E Aloha Sts)

Cobb House Built in 1910, this house—"a fusion of the spirit of the German Black Forest and the English Arts & Crafts movement," as *A Guide to Architecture in Washington State* so eloquently puts it—was designed by the prestigious early-20th-century firm of **Bebb & Mendel.** It has lovely lead-glass windows and a sizeable second-floor balcony secluded by a parapet. The first owner was C.H. Cobb, a native of Maine, who moved west to California in 1876, then headed north to Seattle, where by the 1890s he had incorporated four logging and timber companies and the Marysville and Arlington Railroad Company. ◆ 1409 E Aloha St (off 14th Ave E)

37 Landes House $ This turn-of-the-century establishment—two adjacent houses connected by a garden courtyard—features a nice garden, a hot tub, off-street parking, and nine guest rooms (some with decks, some with private baths) and a two-bedroom apartment that can be rented for a minimum stay of three days. Fresh-baked goodies are served as part of the expanded continental breakfast. And resident owners Tom Hanes, David Sakstrom, and James Swanson are excellent and informative hosts. ◆ 712 11th Ave E (between E Roy and E Aloha Sts). 329.8781

38 Anhalt Apartments Dating to the late 1920s, these units are fine representations of the stylish but practical sort of brick apartment houses designed and constructed by developer/builder **Fred Anhalt.** Some apartments here have nine rooms, two baths, and a fireplace. To ensure soundproofing, **Anhalt** used double floors and double interior walls. The lovely landscaped courtyard and picturesque round-stair tower (an interesting and space-saving alternative to stairways) are Anhalt trademarks. ◆ 1005 E Roy St (at 10th Ave E)

Longtime Seattleites seem surprisingly undaunted by the precipitation here. Many don't carry umbrellas on wet days, and chances are they don't even *own* one, preferring for some reason to make mad dashes from the car to the office and back. And is it wishful thinking or downright denial that leads locals to buy more sunglasses per capita than residents of any other city in the United States? Probably neither. More likely they stash their old pairs away during rainstorms and, after a while, forget where they put them.

Restaurants/Clubs: Red   **Hotels:** Blue
Shops/ ♈ Outdoors: Green   **Sights/Culture:** Black

39 Harvard-Belmont Historic District Many of Seattle's top industrialists, financiers, and business leaders, including **Great Northern Railroad** heir Sam Hill, lived in this venerable Capitol Hill enclave. Horace C. Henry, another railroader, who'd moved to Seattle in 1890 from his native Vermont to build the original belt line around Lake Washington for the **Northern Pacific Railroad,** also lived here.

Most of the mansions in the district were built between 1905 and 1910, with the predominant architectural styles being Tudor, Colonial, and Georgian Revival. In the 1920s a second wave of building brought a number of elegant brick apartment complexes to the area, many of them designed by **Fred Anhalt.** Unlike most of the city's old neighborhoods—which have largely succumbed to modern development—this area has remained a gracious retreat of tree-lined streets, professionally tended gardens, and majestic residential and institutional buildings. It is on the National Register of Historic Places. ♦ Bounded by E Roy St and E Highland Dr, and Broadway E and Belmont Ave E

39 Rainier Chapter House of the DAR City architect **Daniel R. Huntington** designed the chapter house of the Daughters of the American Revolution in 1924 as a replica of George Washington's Mount Vernon estate. The building is rented out for parties, chamber-music concerts, and the like, and it is a favorite for wedding receptions. ♦ 800 E Roy St (at Harvard Ave E). 323.0600

39 Bacchus Restaurant ★★$ The atmosphere here may remind you of an old wine cellar, although the walls are muraled over with an Alexander Pushkin folktale, painted by Russian artist Vladimir Pavlovich Shkurkin. (They're left here from an earlier restaurant.) The *paidakia* (lamb chops broiled with lemon, olive oil, and garlic) is a fine treat, as is the panfried baby squid appetizer (lots of onions and chopped almonds for crunch and color), and the *kefthethes* (meatballs served on pita and sprinkled with feta cheese). The Greek burger, buttermilk pancakes, and similarly shameful bows to American tastes could all be done without, but those are minor annoyances. Service is efficient, if somewhat overly familiar, and it's surprisingly quiet. ♦ Greek ♦ Daily lunch and dinner. 806 E Roy St (between Broadway E and Harvard Ave E). 325.2888

In a backlash against the Seattle hype of the 1980s, Emmett Watson, the *Seattle Times*'s longtime columnist and curmudgeon, resorted to half-truths and a few pointed prevarications regarding Seattle's resolute smugness, its notorious rainfall, and its general backwardness. "Plainly," Watson stated, "only a fool would want to live in Seattle, fools like me...."

39 Loveless Building Designed in an English cottage vein by architect **Arthur B. Loveless,** this graceful block of first-floor shops and second-floor apartments arranged around a concealed courtyard was built in 1933. In his book *Seattle Past to Present,* Roger Sale refers to the "enchanting Loveless Block, stores and apartments of an elegance that Arthur Loveless alone among traditional Seattle architects seemed to have." **Loveless** was a master of well-sited period revival designs. His houses are dotted over Capitol Hill, and in 1930, he remodeled the Colman Building on First Avenue in an Art Deco style. ♦ 711 Broadway E (between E Roy and E Prospect Sts)

40 Cornish College of the Arts This "quietly elegant building of Mediterranean persuasion," as it is described in *A Guide to Architecture in Washington State,* was designed in 1921 by the Seattle architectural firm of **Albertson, Wilson & Richardson.** Nellie Cornish, the piano-playing daughter of a Tennessee sheep farmer who moved to Seattle in 1900, founded the school without any initial support from the city. But with programs in art, music, theater, and dance, the institute has since played an important part in Seattle's cultural life. Renowned choreographer Martha Graham and painter Mark Tobey were members of the faculty. Nellie Cornish lived in an apartment on the top floor of this terra-cotta–ornamented edifice. ♦ 710 E Roy St (between Harvard and Boylston Aves E). 323.1400

41 Harvard Exit Seattle's first luxury art theater makes its home in a building that once held a ladies' club. From the crowded entryway, pass through what must have been an elegant drawing room or living room but is now a very comfortable, old-fashioned space to meet your moviegoing partners. Checkers are available for extended waits. The theater schedules some of the better flicks passing through town, and entries in the annual Seattle International Film Festival often play here. ♦ Box office opens one hour before show time. 807 E Roy St (at Harvard Ave E). 323.8986

41 Deluxe 1 Bar and Grill ★$ Amidst the Broadway area's fervid grab for glitz and its increasing dependence on patrons from beyond Capitol Hill, this spot has managed to retain its down-home feeling—there are no bow ties behind the bar, no leather-skirted waitresses, no Art Deco menus. Warm a stool or pull up a chair and order a bacon, onion, and avocado burger that's guaranteed to put permanent frown lines in your doctor's fore-head. Or try the pesto potato skins with a pint of microbrewed beer. In summer a retractable wall out front allows for a maximum of people watching with a maximum of comfort. ♦ American ♦ Daily lunch and dinner until 2AM. 625 Broadway E (at E Roy St). 324.9697

41 Dancer's Series: Steps Look down as you're strolling either side of busy Broadway between East Pine and East Roy Streets. Periodically, you will spot arrangements of bronze footprints, accompanied by dance instructions, by Seattle artist Jack Mackie. Mackie, with assistance from artist Charles Greening, created these eight street-level artworks to be used, not just observed. He even mixed a few steps of his own creation (the Busstop, for instance, and the Obeebo) in with the classic rumba, waltz, and tango. Mackie gave special treatment to the heels, imbedding parking tokens in those footprints outside a parking lot, and offering a simplified view of the skyline in a set near a bus stop.
♦ Broadway E (between E Pine and E Roy Sts)

42 Byzantion ★$ You'll find Greek food (and lots of it) at this place that's renowned for the quality of its *spanakopita* (spinach pie) and lamb dishes. Try the feta-cheese omelette at breakfast. ♦ Greek ♦ Daily breakfast, lunch, and dinner. 601 Broadway E (at E Mercer St). 325.7580 &

43 Siam on Broadway ★★$ Regulars don't even consider sticking around here to eat—there's generally a 10- to 20-minute wait for a table. Instead, they call ahead, then fly by to pick up steaming orders of garlicky orange beef, *pad thai* noodles, or panfried butterfish. Be forewarned: the spice heat ratings of the dishes should be taken seriously. ♦ Thai/Takeout ♦ M-F lunch and dinner; Sa-Su dinner. 616 Broadway E (between E Mercer and E Roy Sts). 324.0892 &

43 Orpheum With compact discs galore, from heavy metal rock to old jazz, this store may be noisy, but it's ideal for browsing after a movie at the **Harvard Exit** or on a lazy weekend afternoon. ♦ Daily until midnight. 618 Broadway E (between E Mercer and E Roy Sts). 322.6370 &

44 Olympia Pizza and Spaghetti House III ★$ Comfy booths, room for small parties, and killer pizza—what else do you need? ♦ Pizza/Takeout ♦ Daily. 516 15th Ave E (between E Republican and E Mercer Sts). 329.4500 &

44 City Peoples' Mercantile This small store somehow includes something for everyone. There's a well-stocked hardware department for the neighborhood wall-bangers, along with housewares, art supplies, and a trendy selection of clothing. The espresso cart out front provides nourishment and newspapers. Four women began this emporium in the 1970s and have since expanded their operations to include **City Peoples' Garden Store,** an upscale shop for gardeners (2939 E Madison St, between Martin Luther King Jr. Way E and Lake Washington Blvd E, 324.0737) ♦ Daily. 500 15th Ave E (at E Republican St). 324.9510. Also at: 3517 Fremont Ave N (between N 35th and N 36th Sts). 632.1200

45 Jalisco ★$ A small, family-run Mexican operation, this restaurant is patronized almost exclusively by Hill residents. The standard dishes—especially enchiladas and burritos—are well done, and servers will help you design a combination plate. Or you could just order the delicious quesadillas. There are great margaritas and a wide selection of Mexican beers, but entertainment is limited mostly to the clientele, who seem anxious to practice their dubious Spanish on the patient and extraordinarily efficient staff. ♦ Mexican ♦ M-Sa lunch and dinner. 1467 E Republican St (between 15th and 14th Aves E). 325.9005. & Also at: 122 First Ave N (between Denny Way and John St.). 283.4242 &; 12336 31st Ave NE (between NE 123rd St and Lake City Way NE). 364.3978 &; 115 Park Lane St (at Lake Washington Blvd). 822.3355 &

Who invented the Happy Face, that lemon-yellow symbol of goodwill that was ubiquitous during the Vietnam War years and continues to make passersby smile. . . or cringe, depending on their kitsch threshold? There's something of a debate about that (though we're pretty sure it wasn't Forrest Gump). A San Francisco button-store owner once tried to take the credit. Other wags say the noseless, browless, guileless character with the vapid grin has no single parent but rather a variety of folk sources. Seattle advertising exec David Stern contends, however, that he was actually responsible for making the Happy Face the world's third-most-recognizable symbol (the red octagonal traffic STOP sign is the most recognizable, while the circle with a bar through it that silently screams "don't, don't, don't" takes second place).

46 Horizon Books An old house has been converted to a used-book cavern, where intrepid literati wander labyrinthine passageways in search of affordable reading. Your best bet is to ask for directions upon entering the maze. The science-fiction section is out of this world. ♦ M-F until 10PM; Sa-Su until 9PM. 425 15th Ave E (between E Harrison and E Republican Sts). 329.3586

47 Hopscotch ★★$ This clean, brightly lit, contemporary eatery boasts no fewer than 60 varieties of scotches, as well as a wide assortment of tasty American dishes at reasonable prices. Entrées range from light (chicken salad, Caesar salad, and an open-faced Dungeness crab sandwich) to hearty (roast chicken and tenderloin steaks). The sinful desserts (brownie with ice cream, hot fruit crumble, and a variety of pies) are available in huge portions or half-size "slivers." ♦ American ♦ M-F lunch and dinner; Sa-Su brunch and dinner. 332 15th Ave E (at E Thomas St). 322.4191 &

48 Dilettante Patisserie & Cafe ★$ A chocoholic's fantasy, this place carries some of the most tempting truffles, butter crèmes, and dragées (nuts or dried fruits dredged through high-quality dipping chocolates) you will ever try to resist. There's a small menu offering such things as Romanian borscht and sandwiches. They also operate an imperfect-chocolates outlet store (2300 E Cherry St at 23rd Ave E, 328.1955). ♦ Cafe ♦ M-Th, Su until midnight; F-Sa until 1AM. 416 Broadway E (between E Harrison and E Republican Sts). 329.6463 &. Also at: The Inn at the Market, 86 Pine St (at First Ave). 728.9144

48 Bailey/Coy Books Covering a lot of area in a fairly confined space means that this bookstore, for all its efforts, must be very selective. Look for current best-sellers, a wide selection of gay and lesbian studies, and respectable depth in the gardening and fiction categories. ♦ M-Th until 10PM; F-Sa until 11PM. 414 Broadway E (between E Harrison and E Republican Sts). 323.8842

48 Pagliacci ★$ Seattle boasts three branches of this popular pizzeria chain. Top choices include Pizza Centioli, which features an extra-thin crust coated with olive oil, fresh garlic, peppers, and mozzarella and fontina cheeses; the South Philly, a pizza topped with Italian sausage, mushrooms, and onions; calzones; and pasta dishes. By the way, if somebody here tries to sell you the Brooklyn Bridge, it's not a scam—they're talking about a pizza with pepperoni, Italian sausage, mushrooms, black olives, and green peppers. You can either eat here (though the surroundings are rather unprepossessing) or get an order to go; delivery service is also available to most neighborhoods after 5PM. ♦ Pizza/Takeout ♦ Daily lunch and dinner. 426 Broadway E (at E Republican St). 324.0730, delivery 726.1717 &. Also at: 4529 University Way NE (between NE 45th and NE 46th Sts). 632.0421 &; 550 Queen Anne Ave N (at Mercer St). 285.1232 &

49 Broadway Market The market first came to life in 1928. The 32 stalls and shops with their fine prepared foods, fresh produce, and gift items served as the community center for Capitol Hill area residents for almost 50 years. In 1987, with a sense of history in mind, a **Fred Meyer** store was gutted and revamped into a new market housing a delightful florist, cafes, movie theaters, and a variety of shops. Musicians often entertain in the main gallery. There's a parking garage on East Harrison Street. ♦ Daily. 401 Broadway E (at E Harrison St). 322.1610 &

Within Broadway Market:

B&O Espresso ★$ Located right in the middle of the arcade, this is home to the hippest crowd and some of the best desserts and espresso in Seattle. ♦ Coffeehouse ♦ Daily; F-Sa until 10PM. First floor. 328.3290 &. Also at: 204 Belmont Ave E (at E John St). 322.5028

Bulldog News This little sibling of the expansive University District store carries a diverting array of magazine titles, from *Working Woman* to *Cigar Aficionado*. ♦ Daily until 10PM. First floor. 322.6397 &. Also at: 4208 University Way NE (between NE 42nd and NE 43rd Sts). 632.6397

Gravity Bar ★$ The setting is right out of *Star Wars*—futuristic and chromey with high-tech lighting. As with its larger Belltown branch, it's heavily into healthy juices and brown rice, and, of course, espresso. The staff is trendy, but then, so's the clientele. Still, you can do lots of sidewalk watching from the tall windows. ♦ Vegetarian ♦ Daily breakfast, lunch, and dinner. First floor. 325.7186 &. Also at: 113 Virginia St (between Second and First Aves). 448.8826

Rasa Malaysia ★$ Another in a popular chain of take-out or eat-in spots, this restaurant specializes in noodles, usually sautéed with fresh veggies; peanut or another mildly spicy sauce; and a variety of fish, shrimp, or meat dishes. Malaysian/Takeout ◆ Daily lunch and dinner. First floor. 328.8882. Also at: 7208 E Green Lake Dr (at NE 72nd St). 523.8888; Pike Place Market (Sanitary Market Bldg). 624.8388

Ticket/Ticket This counter operation offers day-of-the-show, half-price tickets (there's a service charge for each ticket, however) to music, theater, and dance performances. ◆ Daily. Cash only. Second floor. 324.2744

Urban Outfitters Totally hip apparel and housewares for the modern urban dweller are for sale here. ◆ Second floor. 322.1800

50 The Oven ★$ This is an affiliate of Belltown's **Mediterranean Kitchen.** In large part, the menu here is the same (including the renowned Farmer's Dish—tart lemon chicken on a hillock of rice), but there are also gyro sandwiches and beef or chicken *shawarma* (marinated and broiled on a vertical rotisserie) plates. ◆ Middle Eastern/Takeout ◆ Daily lunch and dinner. 213 Broadway E (between E John and E Thomas Sts). 328.2951 &

51 TestaRossa ★★$ Thick and flavorful Chicago-style pies are turned out by this second-floor pizza joint. The garlic, spinach, and mushroom pie is everyone's favorite. ◆ Pizza ◆ Daily. 210 Broadway E (between E John and E Thomas Sts). 328.0878 &

51 Steve's Broadway News Steve Dunnington, formerly a mustachioed fixture at **Read All About It** in **Pike Place Market,** has brought his love of magazines and other periodicals to hyperkinetic Broadway. The usual mix is available here, as well as some oddball foreign papers. ◆ Daily; F-Sa until midnight. 204 Broadway E (between E John and E Thomas Sts). 324.7323

51 Espresso Roma ★$ Here is a perfect spot to sip and read all those papers you bought next door at **Steve's.** Small and quiet, this is one coffeehouse where no one will disturb you. Students and artists camp out here. ◆ Coffeehouse ◆ Daily. 202 Broadway E (at E John St). 324.1866 &. Also at: 4201 University Way NE (at NE 42nd St). 632.6001 &

52 Hill House $ Owners Ken Hayes and Eric Lagasca have lovingly restored a 1903 Victorian home. The five guest rooms (three with private baths) are individually decorated, and all have queen-size beds and down comforters. The location is excellent—close to Broadway and on bus routes to both downtown and the **University of Washington.** A full gourmet breakfast is included in the rate. This is a nonsmoking place. ◆ 1113 E John St (between 11th and 12th Aves E). 720.7161

53 Prince of Wales $ Try to secure the Prince's Retreat (the attic suite), with its westward deck view of the city, Puget Sound,

and the Olympic Mountains. There are four rooms, all with private baths. Owner Carol Norton serves a full breakfast and welcomes well-mannered children. The bus stops across the street, and it's only a one-mile walk to downtown's Washington State Convention Center. ◆ 133 13th Ave E (at E John St). 325.9692; 800/327.9692; fax 322.6402

54 Group Health Cooperative of Puget Sound In their efforts to find affordable medical care, farmers, union members, secretaries, and a handful of professional people defied the medical establishment of the 1940s to establish this cooperative in 1947. Today **GHC** is the nation's largest consumer-governed health-care organization, serving nearly a half-million residents of Washington and Idaho, and a model for accessible, cost-effective, quality health care. This central facility is Seattle's largest hospital and the neighborhood's major employment center, spawning an attendant flock of shops and restaurants on 15th Avenue East. Park in the underground garage. ◆ 200 15th Ave E (at E John St). 326.3000

55 Kidd Valley ★$ Unlike some other chain burger joints, this one succeeds at being both fun for children and culinarily satisfying for the adults who accompany them. Hamburgers here are flavorful fistfuls of juicy meat and bun, best accompanied by the thick and not-too-greasy fries. The milk shakes are some of the best in town (order the chocolate or the root beer). Lines are common at the counter. ◆ American/Takeout ◆ Daily breakfast, lunch, and dinner. 135 15th Ave E (between E Denny Way and E John St). 328.8133 &. Also at: 4910 Green Lake Way N (between Stone Way N and N 49th St). 547.0121 &; 14303 Aurora Ave N (at N 143rd St). 364.8493 &; 531 Queen Anne Ave N (at W Mercer St). 284.0184 &

56 The Corner House $ Of special note in this bed-and-breakfast are the beds themselves, guaranteed to rival or surpass your own in comfort. There are only two rooms (each with a private bath), but the atmosphere is warm and inviting. Owners Julianne Nason and Oliver H. Osborn serve a continental breakfast and offer off-street parking. ◆ 102 18th Ave E (at E Denny Way). 526.9859

"Seattle is a moisturizing pad disguised as a city."
Jerry Seinfeld

57 Gaslight Inn $ This bed-and-breakfast (illustrated above) is a good choice if you want easy access to downtown: The *No. 10* bus stops right out front and goes all the way to the Waterfront. Antique Mission-style furniture graces the dining room, parlor, living room, and library. During the summer, guests can enjoy the heated pool surrounded by beautiful plantings and container gardens. Five of the nine rooms have private baths. One guest room has a city-view deck, and another has a fireplace. A continental breakfast is served. ♦ 1727 15th Ave (between E Olive and E Howell Sts). 325.3654

58 Globe Cafe & Bakery ★$ Soy-milk *lattes* might seem too healthy for some, but the vegan tilt here is balanced by a relaxed atmosphere and outrageously good gingerbread. Toys are on hand for the young-uns. ♦ Coffeehouse ♦ Daily until 7:30PM. 1531 14th Ave E (at E Pine St). 324.8815

Hoping to shed the raw wooliness of its frontier roots, in 1903 Seattle hired the Olmsted Brothers landscaping firm of Massachusetts to develop a comprehensive city plan. Like their firm's founder, the renowned Frederick Law Olmsted (who designed Boston's park systems and New York's Central Park), Frederick Law Olmsted Jr. and his cousin, John Charles Olmsted, believed that the most beautiful cities integrated natural areas with commercial and residential ones. Building on earlier parkland purchases, the Olmsted plan called for a 20-mile long greenbelt from **Seward Park** north and then west across the city to **Discovery Park.** Although the plan never made it to fruition due to budget problems, the Olmsted legacy lives on in the treed boulevards and long, thin stretches of forested land that connect many of the city's 300 parks today.

The regrading of Seattle's streets after the Great Fire of 1889 made use of some rather unusual items. A broken water main in the 1930s released a number of objects from beneath the pavement—including a rowboat.

Restaurants/Clubs: Red   **Hotels:** Blue
Shops/ ♥ Outdoors: Green   **Sights/Culture:** Black

59 Comet Tavern This pub's clientele is a Whitmanesque sampler of politicians, aspiring artists, writers, and escapees from nearby **Seattle University.** There's lots of graffiti but zero video games; it's just an honest drinking joint. ♦ Daily until 2AM. 922 E Pike St (at 10th Ave E). 323.9853

60 Egyptian Theater One of the city's classiest moviehouses is within an old Masonic temple that also serves as headquarters for the Seattle International Film Festival, held each May. Inside is **Cafe Cairo,** an espresso bar operated by Craig Donarum, who gave this city its first espresso cart. ♦ Box office opens one hour before show time. 801 E Pine St (at Harvard Ave E). 323.4978

61 Neighbours By day, it's a mediocre restaurant, but at night it's a happening disco, catering mostly to a gay crowd. Very-late-night patrons may be treated to a galley of over-fried foods just to keep up their strength to find their way around this truly cavernous space. ♦ Cover. M-Th, Su until 2AM; F-Sa until 4AM. 1509 Broadway (between E Pike and E Pine Sts). 324.5358 &

First Hill

62 Stimson-Green Mansion As Seattle began to establish itself in the mid-19th century, the city's captains of industry all competed furiously to build grander mansions than those of their rivals. The first such examples graced First Hill, just east of downtown. It became Seattle's earliest status neighborhood, but the reign was brief, lasting only a generation or two before developments more remote from the city were settled. This baronial house is a fine reminder of those times.

Built between 1899 and 1901 from designs by architects **Kirtland K. Cutter** and **Karl Malmgren** (whose efforts were heavily influenced by the European Arts and Crafts movement), the house was occupied from its completion until 1914 by the family of Ballard mill owner Charles D. Stimson. From then until 1975, it was the property of the Joshua Green family (Green was a prominent early Seattle banker). Today the mansion is a full-service catering facility. ♦ Business office M-F. 1204 Minor Ave (at Seneca St). 624.0474

63 Summit Grade School/Northwest School One of the finest among architect **James Stephen**'s many Seattle schools, this 1905 wood structure is a catalog of brick-and-stucco facing, stepped parapets, and decorative ironwork, with an octagonal bell tower. The local school district closed this building in 1965, but more than a decade later it was bought and rehabilitated by operators of the **Northwest School,** a private institution for grades six through 12. ♦ 1415 Summit Ave (between E Union and E Pike Sts). 682.7309

64 Cafe Sabika ★★$$ This bistro certainly deserves its rep for homey friendliness (it's not uncommon to hear chef/owner John Rios singing in the kitchen) and classic, elegant meals. Rios's background in the food preparations of Provence has added an interesting dimension to all the dishes—from pork burritos to duck linguine to tender beef Wellington. ♦ International ♦ Tu-Sa dinner. 315 E Pine St (between Bellevue and Melrose Aves). 622.3272

65 Re-bar Probably the best danceteria in Seattle, this club certainly boasts the liveliest disc jockeys (don't miss Queen Lucky if she's in town). The crowd is mixed straight and gay, but mostly gay on the signature **Queer Disco Nights.** You'll hear lots of Diana Ross and industrial dance—it all depends on the DJ. Live bands and theater performances are scheduled irregularly; call ahead for information. ♦ Cover. Daily until 2AM. 1114 E Howell St (off Boren Ave). 233.9873

66 REI Founded in 1938, **Recreational Equipment Inc.** has become a Seattle institution, as well as the nation's largest consumer cooperative, with 30 stores across the US and more than one million active members worldwide. In 1996, it moved from its original 11th Avenue East location to this huge flagship store with 80,000 square feet of retail space. Everything you'll need for your next expedition to the Himalayas or just a jog around the block is here: gear and clothing for backpacking, climbing, water sports, cycling, and skiing. The new space also features a 65-foot freestanding indoor climbing pinnacle (the world's largest), an indoor trail where you can "test walk" your hiking boots before you buy them, and a 20,000-square-foot courtyard that boasts a mountain bike trail, a stream, vegetation, and a waterfall. There's even an adventure-travel booking service and a mail-order catalog that is circulated around the world. ♦ Daily. 222 Yale Ave N (between John and Thomas Sts). 223.1944

67 Reiner's ★★★$$$ Hans Abbersold has taken over from original chef/owner Reiner Gruebel, but this small, elegant restaurant continues to serve the same excellent French fare. The menu changes frequently, depending on what ingredients are available, but the tender veal and fish dishes are always good. The service is somewhat slow but very courteous. ♦ French ♦ Tu-Sa dinner. Reservations recommended. 1106 Eighth Ave (between Spring and Seneca Sts). 624.2222

68 Sorrento Hotel $$$ Built in 1908, this hotel boasted the city's first rooftop restaurant. (The architect was **Harlan Thomas.**) Restored to its original elegance, it's small by comparison with today's hotels; it does, however, have an unusual intimacy. Some of the 76 guest rooms are small (a few have only narrow views), but all are comfortably appointed and feature an Asian decor. Try to reserve a room with a view over Puget Sound. The lobby's **Fireside Lounge** has an appealing clublike atmosphere, and complimentary sedan service is available within the downtown area. There's also a fitness center. ♦ 900 Madison St (at Terry Ave). 622.6400, 800/426.1265; fax 343.6155 ₺

Within the Sorrento Hotel:

Hunt Club ★★★$$$ The executive chef, Eric Lenard, prepares a variety of seasonal game and seafood dishes combined with a Northwestern flair in this elegant, intimate dining room. The menu changes daily, depending on what is in season and what can be found at the local markets. At lunchtime try Dungeness crab cakes with steamed Asian greens and a lemon-butter sauce. For dinner, the classic braised osso buco is a winner. Lenard also prepares ostrich and pheasant periodically. ♦ Northwestern ♦ Daily breakfast, lunch, and dinner. Reservations recommended. 343.6156; fax 343.6155 ₺

69 St. James Cathedral Imagine what this astonishing Neo-Baroque church, with its twin 175-foot-tall towers, would look like with a copper dome above its entrance. That was its appearance from 1907 until January 1916, when the canopy collapsed beneath the weight of 30,000 pounds of snow. "A roar like the boom of a heavy gun brought priest and layman to the cathedral," wrote the *Seattle Post-Intelligencer.* "They saw a huge jagged hole where the massive dome had soared and poured great clouds of mortar dust and flying snow." Months later, the church was reopened with a flat roof that lessened the building's visual impact (it was designed by **Heins & LaFarge** and **John Graham Sr.**) but actually improved interior acoustics. ♦ Ninth Ave and Marion St. 622.3559

69 Trinity Parish Episcopal Church This handsome, rough-cut stone landmark near the **Harborview Medical Center** and overlooking Pioneer Square is in the style of English-country parish churches. **John Graham Sr.** restored the building and gave it a new rectory after a terrible fire in 1901. ♦ 609 Eighth Ave (at James St). 624.5337

70 Temple de Hirsch Sinai Built in 1960 as a stylized mountain with exquisite stained glass, this Jewish sanctuary is a commanding presence on the hill. There is some disagreement about the architect, but the prevailing opinion is that it was **B. Marcus Priteca.** ♦ E Pike St and 16th Ave. 323.8486

Central District and Madrona

71 Mount Zion Baptist Church This over-a-century-old church is a prominent feature of the Central District community. It seats a thousand people, and is packed to the rafters every Sunday. The church's 100-member gospel choir has become nationally famous through several acclaimed gospel recordings. The more than 2,000 members include several of the city's major politicians, and its pastor—the Reverend Samuel B. McKinney—is an assertive voice for African-Americans in Seattle. ♦ 1634 19th Ave (at Madison St). 322.6500

72 Madison Street Seattle's only waterfront-to-waterfront thoroughfare, this street stretches from Elliott Bay through the Central District to Lake Washington. Look at it as a core sample of local history and economics, taking in affluent neighborhoods, poverty-stricken pockets, new condominiums (especially in the area known as Madison Valley, from 23rd Avenue East to the lake), and old, single-family residences. ♦ Lake Washington to Elliott Bay

73 All the Best This upscale pet-supply store is typical of the stores now opening along a once slumlike stretch in the Madison Valley area which has undergone extraordinary gentrification in recent years. The pet foods sold here pack natural ingredients. Indulgent pet owners will appreciate the diversity of neat toys and books in stock here, too. ♦ Daily. 2713 E Madison St (at Martin Luther King Jr. Way E). 329.8565

74 Cafe Flora ★★★$$ Bright and airy, this vegetarian eatery has an energetic, lively atmosphere. Dishes are presented in a stylish fashion; highlights include Portobello Wellington (mushroom-pecan pâté and grilled portobello mushrooms wrapped in pastry) and Oaxaca Tacos (which come filled with spicy mashed potatoes and cheddar, mozzarella, and feta cheeses and served with black bean stew and sautéed greens on the side). The menu also offers nondairy items for the strict vegan, as well as a good selection of beers and wines. For dessert, there's always fresh fruit and a number of pastries, such as cheesecake, nondairy fruit crisps, and cakes. The large outdoor dining area is wonderful to linger in during warm weather. ♦ Vegetarian ♦ M-F lunch and dinner; Sa-Su brunch and

dinner. Reservations required. 2901 E Madison St (at 29th Ave E). 325.9100 &

75 Rover's ★★★★$$$$ Chef Thierry Rautureau's small, semiformal, and exquisitely intimate establishment in its frame-house setting is a French restaurant par excellence. Perhaps it's because he gives familiar Northwestern fare a French accent, rather than simply producing Gallic classics. Rautureau specializes in generous servings of seafood, including Columbia River sturgeon and halibut, the latter served with an embarrassment-of-riches lobster sauce. Ellensburg lamb, rabbit, and game entrées also make appearances on the menu. The chef's talents may be sampled best by ordering the eight-course chef's grand menu, which can also be ordered with vegetarian components. Wines from the Northwest and France complement the meal. There's also a courtyard for warm weather dining. ♦ Northwestern/French ♦ Tu-Sa dinner. Reservations recommended. 2808 E Madison St (between 29th and 28th Aves E). 325.7442 &

76 Denny-Blaine Park Here is a tranquil little public beach on Lake Washington; note, however, that there's no bathhouse and no lifeguard on duty. ♦ Lake Washington Blvd (at 40th Ave E)

77 Madrona Park Bathing Beach Change in the bathhouse and then hit the beach. The water is pristine here (thanks to a major civic cleanup of Lake Washington back in the 1960s), but it's painfully cold, even in summer. For a less Arctic experience, take a seat in one of the usually unoccupied lifeguard perches and watch the joggers, dog-walkers, and picnickers do their thing. In clear weather, there is no better place from which to view 14,410-foot Mount Rainier, which (although 50 miles away) dominates the southern horizon. Clear skies also reveal other snowy peaks in the Cascade mountain range to the east, and the sharp-eyed may spy 10,778-foot Mount Baker north of the lake. It would be easy to forget that you're in a city, were it not for the jagged profile of Bellevue across the lake. ♦ Lake Washington Blvd (at E Marion St)

79 Hi-Spot Cafe ★$ This revitalized old-time coffeehouse is in a Madrona home where the meal of choice is breakfast (hearty omelettes and terrific cinnamon rolls). Lunch, however, brings sumptuous burgers, terrific BLTs, and good vegetarian soups. The dinner menu, which changes monthly, includes pasta, seafood dishes, and salads. ♦ American ♦ M breakfast and lunch; Tu-F breakfast, lunch, and dinner; Sa breakfast and dinner; Su breakfast. 1410 34th Ave (between E Union and E Pike Sts). 325.7905

79 Sam's Super Burgers ★$ This unpretentious joint is a required stop on the hamburger lover's tour of Greater Seattle. The sandwiches are big, with lots of meat. Burgers topped with hot link sausage are a tasty (if not healthy) favorite. ♦ Soul food ♦ M-Sa lunch and dinner. 2600 E Union St (at 26th Ave). 329.4870 ♿

80 Catfish Corner ★★$ Talk about ultra-specialization: Though this eatery does have other things on the menu, the breaded catfish is so superb that there's no reason to choose anything else. The potato salad is a bit mustardy, but still excellent. ♦ Soul food ♦ Daily lunch and dinner. 2726 E Cherry St (at Martin Luther King Jr. Way). 323.4330 ♿

81 Ezell's Fried Chicken ★★$ This is the take-out place that talk-show hostess Oprah Winfrey calls to have out-of-this-world fried chicken shipped to her overnight (no matter what the status of her weight loss program). ♦ Fried Chicken/Takeout ♦ Daily lunch and dinner. 501 23rd Ave (at Jefferson St). 324.4141 ♿

82 R&L Home of Good Barbeque ★★$ A Central District culinary landmark since Robert and Louise Collins opened the pit in 1952, this place serves excellent alder-smoked pork ribs, hot links, and baked beans. ♦ Barbecue ♦ Tu-Sa lunch and dinner. 1816 E Yesler Way (between 19th and 18th Aves). 322.0271 ♿

83 Frye Art Museum Dominated by the 19th-century European salon paintings of patrons Charles and Emma Frye, this small museum also includes Wyeth works and some by non-native Alaskan artists. The International Style building was designed in 1952 by **Paul Thiry** and is similar to his **Museum of History and Industry** in Montlake. ♦ Free. Daily. 704 Terry Ave (at Cherry St). 622.9250

84 New Hong Kong Seafood Restaurant and B.B.Q. ★★$ Southeast Asians (mainly Vietnamese, but Cambodians, Laotians, and Thais as well) have recently made their mark in Seattle, just as the Chinese and Japanese did a century ago. The result is a new version of the International District, centered around the intersection of South Jackson Street and 12th Avenue South. You need only glance at the native-language storefront signs to know that these places draw their customers from the Asian community. This restaurant has a 200-item menu featuring Chinese, Vietnamese, and Thai dishes; word is that it serves some of the best wonton soup in town. ♦ Southeast Asian ♦ Daily lunch and dinner.

212 12th Ave S (between S Jackson St and Boren Ave S). 324.4091

85 Tabernacle Missionary Baptist Church Certainly one of the most exuberant African-American churches in Seattle, the congregation here is inspired by Reverend Robert Manaway. The choir is loaded with energy and with talent. ♦ 2801 S Jackson St (at 28th Ave S). 329.9794

You Wanna Bet?

Unlike Reno or Vegas, Seattle is not a gambling destination per se. In town, there's not much legal gambling aside from the state lottery and the occasional bingo game for charity. But not far outside the city limits are several Vegas-style casinos, all operated by local Indian reservations as a way to earn revenue. Exempt from local and state laws prohibiting casino gambling, these establishments have become very popular in recent years.

The standard table games are featured—poker, blackjack, baccarat, craps, and roulette—as well as bingo (but no slot machines; they're illegal in Washington State). In most cases, the minimum bet is $3. Most casinos are open from 10AM to 6AM and have gift shops, restaurants, and bars. In keeping with their Native American heritage, almost all of them also have a museum-like area displaying cultural artifacts (so you can enrich your mind, if not your wallet). You must be 21 or older to enter a casino.

The gaming places closest to Seattle are the **Tulalip Casino** (whose name is pronounced Too-lay-lup; 360/651.1111 ♿) in **Marysville,** about 30 miles north on **I-5;** the **Muckleshoot Casino** (206/804.4444 ♿), 30 miles southeast on **Highway 164;** and the **Puyallup** (Pew-al-lup) **Casino** (206/597.6200 ♿) in **Tacoma,** 32 miles south on **Highway 167.** On a day trip to **Olympia** or out to the coast, you might stop by the **Little Creek Casino** (360/427.7711 ♿) run by the **Squaxin Island** people; it's in **Shelton,** about 66 miles from Seattle. And if you're heading for the north end of the **Olympic Peninsula,** the **Seven Cedars Casino** (360/683.7777; 800/4.LUCKY.7 ♿), operated by the S'Klallam, is near **Sequim** (pronounced Squim).

In the **Skagit Valley,** about an hour's drive north of Seattle, there are two gambling options. The **Swinomish Casino** (360/293.2691; 800/877.PLAY ♿) is located a few miles off I-5, near **Anacortes.** And at the north end of the valley is the huge **Harrah's Skagit Valley Casino** (off exit 236 of I-5; 360/724.7777, 800/427.7247 ♿), which offers nightly live entertainment, three restaurants, interactive video games, and valet parking.

Leschi to Seward Park

86 Leschi Park The name comes from an 1850s Nisqually tribal leader who liked to camp here and who was accused by Territorial Governor Isaac Stevens of leading attacks against Seattle's pioneers in the Battle of Seattle; it was a bloody uprising and resulted in death on both sides. Chief Leschi, the focus of so much hatred, was tried for the deaths of two federal peacekeeping volunteers, and then shamefully hanged despite evidence of his innocence.

At the turn of the century a trolley carried Seattleites here to an amusement park and opera house, both long gone; and a cross-lake ferry docked here before the Interstate-90 floating bridge was opened in 1940. The Olmsted-designed park across the street from the marina is styled as a classic English garden and includes an ancient stone bridge (over which the trolley once rumbled). Until the 1970s the neighborhood was decidedly blue-collar and bohemian, and ascended to its present affluent status only in the last two decades—as indicated by the modern architecture of its homes and condos. Joggers and cyclists travel frequently over the 10 tree-lined and lightly trafficked miles between this greenbelt and **Seward Park** to the south. ♦ Lakeside Ave S and S Main St

86 Leschi Lakecafe ★★$$ A busy bar (with 18 beers on tap) and a kitchen that does its best work with fresh- and saltwater fish, particularly salmon, are the main attractions. In warm weather the outdoor tables are packed with the tanned and single. Fish-and-chips from the cafe's adjacent **Koby's** take-out counter are delicious (some critics contend that they're even better than the greasefests dished up by **Spud Fish and Chips**), but they're also overpriced. ♦ Seafood ♦ Daily lunch and dinner. 102 Lakeside Ave S (south of Leschi Park). 328.2233 &

86 Daniel's Broiler ★★$$$$ As the name suggests, the emphasis is on flame-broiled prime steaks and chops, but chef Gary Warstler also makes a number of good seafood specialties. The restaurant offers a terrific perspective of Mount Rainier and Lake Washington to the east. There's a second, more chichi venue in Bellevue. ♦ American ♦ Daily dinner. 200 Lake Washington Blvd S (at the Leschi Marina) 329.4191 &. Also at: Seafirst Bldg, Bellevue Place (10500 NE Eighth St, between 106th Ave NE and Bellevue Way NE), Bellevue. 462.4662 &

87 Remo Borracchini's A lot of Seattleites wouldn't go anywhere other than this landmark Italian bakery to get cakes for special occasions. The confections are outrageous: the chocolate Bavarian cream should really be listed as a controlled substance. The bakery also makes pasta and breads, and sells Italian canned goods and wines. And, while not officially a restaurant, it has a few tables for snackers and serves sandwiches, a rich lasagna, pizza, and baked items. ♦ Daily from 6AM. 2307 Rainier Ave S (between S College and S Walker Sts). 325.1550 &

87 Mutual Fish Company Here's the best seafood store south of **Pike Place Market.** Owned and operated by the Yoshimura family since about the beginning of time, they'll pack purchases for the trip home. ♦ M-Sa. 2335 Rainier Ave S (at S College St). 322.4368

88 Evans House This is the compelling work of **Ellsworth Storey,** a Chicago native who arrived in Seattle in 1903 and set about building houses in the developing neighborhoods along the west bank of Lake Washington, especially Madrona and Mount Baker. Apparently not interested in a large-scale practice, **Storey** stuck with residential design, an eminent example of which is this wood home. Note the strong diagonal emphasis. ♦ 2306 34th Ave S (between S McLellan and S Walker Sts)

89 Stan Sayres Memorial Park On the first weekend in August this park becomes—in more ways than one—"The Pits" staging area for the annual Seafair hydroplane extravaganza. The race course is a long oval just off the park, with straightaways paralleling the shoreline. The usually quiet park becomes a circus of noise, warm beer, exposed flesh, and confusion, with attendees angling for close-up looks at the monster boats and their frenzied crews. For years, young Seattleites anxiously awaited this weekend, packing the shoreline and engaging in a variety of creative behaviors, but that tradition seems to be on the wane as Seafair swings more toward the family values crowd. Race-day attendance is noticeably slimmer, down from the half-million reported in the 1970s and 1980s. ♦ Lake Washington Blvd S and 45th Ave S

90 Seward Park According to the Olmsteds' comprehensive plan, this was intended to be a "wild" park, contrasting with more manicured garden spots like **Volunteer Park.** The peninsula's 277 acres of mainly Douglas fir trees are true old-growth forest; a 2.5-mile paved roadway circles the park's outer shoreline, offering strollers, joggers, in-line skaters, and cyclists a quiet respite. Somehow, the park never seems crowded.

A variety of pathways—some marked, some obscure—lace the woodlands, and a public fishing pier and swimming beach provide recreation on the northern end. Boaters will find a public ramp and city docks a short distance north. In addition to picnic tables, barbecue pits, and a small amphitheater atop the hill, there is a state trout hatchery out at the end of the point and Japanese gardens, which, while quite pleasant, are obviously outclassed by those at the **Washington Park Arboretum.**

A grouping of three traditional Japanese stone lanterns and an inscribed granite boulder stand sentinel at the park's entrance. These were placed here during the 1976 US bicentennial to commemorate the gift of one thousand cherry trees given by the citizens of Japan to the American people. Though shaped from Washington State granite, the lanterns were carved in Japan; the granite boulder carries an inscribed duplication of calligraphy painted by Takeo Miki, then prime minister of Japan. Translated, it reads "Congratulations on the bicentennial of the United States of America's independence."

Visitors may wish to avoid the parking lot along the southern shoreline, where local youths hang out and crank their cars' stereo equipment into the upper decibel ranges. ♦ S Juneau St and Lake Washington Blvd S

91 Kubota Gardens A Japanese immigrant to Seattle started this 20-acre garden in 1929 in the midst of a swamp which he transformed into a delight to the eye (not to mention the nose). A creek trickles through the lush greenery, feeding five ponds. Among the many rare plants are tanysho pines and weeping blue atlas cedars. ♦ Renton and 55th Aves S. 725.4400

92 El Palacio ★★$ Any restaurant that has *menudo* on its menu is at least trying to serve authentic Mexican cuisine. The kitchen here prepares delicious *menudo* sausage, which in the old country is thought to be a hangover cure and is best left undiscussed as far as its preparation goes. Seafood dishes are also exquisite: try the shrimp, either *camarones gigantes* or the *camarones al mojo de ajo* (prawns with garlic and butter sauce). The tortillas are homemade, of course. ♦ Mexican ♦ Daily lunch and dinner. 5212 Rainier Ave S (between 42nd and 39th Aves S). 725.9139

93 Pho Hòa ★★$ The menu gets no more expansive than *pho,* a Vietnamese soup, but that's actually quite enough. The broth has a wide variety of spices and textures; diners select additional ingredients from a long list of meats and veggies. The growing clientele

is no longer restricted to Vietnamese-Americans, but you may still overhear old-timers replaying the fall of Saigon. ♦ Vietnamese ♦ Daily breakfast, lunch, and dinner. 4406 Rainier Ave S (between S Oregon and S Genesee Sts). 723.1508

95 Museum of Flight Biplanes, military jets, early mail planes, and a giant B-47 dangle from the ceiling of this museum's glass-and-steel **Great Gallery.** Children especially love to wander among these relics; they can study a reproduction of Boeing's first seaplane and a real DC-13, or trace the history of flying in the adjacent **Red Barn,** which was the Boeing Company's original 1910 airplane factory.

Although the museum is often called "Boeing's Museum of Flight," it is, in fact, an independent operation adjacent to the **Boeing Development Center.** A gift shop is fully stocked with models, books, and leather bomber jackets. ♦ Admission; discounts for senior citizens and children. Daily; Th until 9PM. 9404 E Marginal Way S (at Boeing Field)

Bests

Jean Enersen
TV News Anchor, KING-TV

Sit 'n' Spin: A place where you can have micro-brews, play games from the 1970's under the light of lava lamps, and do your laundry at the same time!

Il Bistro: Perfect place to meet someone late at night. They have the best bartender in town, Murray. . . and the ambience is very Euro-hip. The only trick is to find it tucked underneath the **Pike Place Market.**

Ruby Montana's Pinto Pony in **Pioneer Square:** Everything in here has either a cowboy or Elvis Presley theme. No matter what you get, you can't go wrong. Love those cowgirl christmas lights.

First Avenue: Stroll the length of it from **Belltown** to downtown, and in the process find my favorite restaurant **(Lampreia).**

And finally, when you need to find out what makes Seattle really great, hop on a ferry to **Bainbridge Island** (from downtown Seattle), or cruise by ferry from **Anacortes** through the **San Juan Islands.** This, my friend, is paradise.

Jack W. Singer
Research Chairman, Executive VP and Founder, Cell Therapeutics, Inc.

Cool Hand Luke's—inexpensive restaurant in **Madrona.**

Lampreia—best gourmet restaurant.

Rover's—next-best gourmet restaurant.

Wild Ginger—most creative restaurant.

The **Lobby Lounge** in the **Sorrento Hotel**—best place for late night drink.

West Seattle

On balmy summer afternoons, **Alki Beach** in West Seattle is a polychromatic amalgam of people and vehicles and noise, noise, noise. Sunbathers stroll along the sand, boom boxes blare, and skaters, cyclists, runners, strollers, and families with tethered German shepherds jockey for position along the bike path. On the other hand, if you go in the late evenings, on weeknights, or even in the off-season (September through June), you might see herons and sea lions on the shore along with a few solitary, contemplative people. Along **Alki Avenue SW**, a variety of restaurants provide everything from elegant dinners to fast food. It's not exactly LA's Venice Beach, but then again it's not stereotypical Seattle either.

Today's scene is in marked contrast to that of November 1851, when a schooner dropped Arthur Denny's small cadre of pioneers at this very same spot. The settlers built their first cabins in the primitive Alki wilds and established relationships with the native Duwamish tribespeople before moving on to seek shelter on **Elliott Bay**.

Located southwest of downtown, across the **Duwamish River**, West Seattle is primarily a collection of residential areas distinguished by their views of downtown, **Harbor Island**, the **Cascade** and **Olympic Mountains**, and three **Puget Sound** islands: **Vashon, Blake,** and **Bainbridge.** Downtown West Seattle, as it is occasionally (if facetiously) called, is centered on the confluence of **California Avenue SW** and **SW Alaska Street**, and is best known simply as "The Junction." This central shopping area has had its ups and downs over the years; a number of businesses have made fleeting appearances, while others have stood almost unchanged for more than half a century. Although the growing number of high-rise condominiums on Alki Avenue SW attracts young urbanites, property values in many parts of West Seattle remain affordable, and the area retains some of its historic working-class spirit. But Alki Beach—which many residents claim is the only *real* beach in Seattle—is the area's principal attraction, boasting a wide expanse of sand, a long lane for cycling, jogging, and in-line skating, a boat launch, and grassy areas dotted with picnic tables.

1 Salty's on Alki ★$$ Owner Gerald Kingen claims no other place in the city commands as good a view as his upscale restaurant. That's debatable, but you do get a fine perspective on the downtown skyline and the ferries cruising across Puget Sound; it's especially beautiful at night. The food is a little pricier here than at most West Seattle restaurants, but it's served with more flair. Alder-smoked salmon stuffed with Dungeness crab, and clams steamed with vegetables and white wine are two favorites. Noise, however, can be a problem. ♦ Seafood ♦ M-Sa lunch and dinner; Su brunch and dinner. Reservations recommended. 1936 Harbor Ave SW (between SW Florida St and Fairmount Ave SW). 937.1600

2 Seacrest Park and Boathouse This clean park has watercraft for hire, a simple coffee shop, and a fishing pier. You can rent a wide variety of vessels, from fiberglass 13-foot-long double-hull fishing boats with six-horsepower motors to sea kayaks. Even if you never get so much as a bite on your line, views from out on the water are spectacular. ♦ W-Su 4:30AM-8PM July-Oct; 5:30AM-5PM Nov-June. 1660 Harbor Ave SW (near Fairmount Ave SW). 932.1050

3 Don Armeni Park Boat Ramp A popular place for boaters to enter Puget Sound, this ramp was named after a deputy sheriff, active in fishing derbies, who was shot and killed in the line of duty in 1954. ♦ Harbor Ave SW (north of California Way SW)

4 Duwamish Head Thanks to its views of Elliott Bay and downtown, this headland has long been a popular spot. In the late 19th and early 20th centuries the broad shoulders of beach were frequented by summer revelers and campers. In 1901 a former Klondike gold miner built the **Coney Island Baths,** which offered "a good bath and swim and use of fresh running water." Six years later, it became the site of the largest and showiest amusement park ever built in Seattle: **Luna Park.**

As with many other amusement parks of the early 20th century, this one sat on the water—actually and symbolically on the very edge of things. Created by Charles I.D. Looff, a German who had installed the first carousel at Coney Island, New York City, in 1876, **Luna Park** stretched over more than 10 acres, an imposing admixture of Atlantic City kitsch, Spanish Mission, and carnival gothic. This fantasyland wanted to be all things to all people, and that's what finally got it in trouble. Along with the arcades and thrill rides, it also boasted "the longest bar on the bay," an easy target for reform-minded West Siders shocked by tales of drunkenness. The final straw came when Looff was implicated in a scandal involving the construction of a 500-room brothel on Seattle's Beacon Hill. When the park opened for the summer of 1913, Looff was gone. The park itself closed down three years later, but the natatorium (with its huge billboard exhorting, "Let's Swim!") remained until an arsonist set fire to the one-story frame building in 1931. All that's here now is a popular beach and some apartment buildings. ◆ Alki and Harbor Aves SW

5 Hamilton Viewpoint Generations of West Seattle teenagers have come to this lookout to, uh, "watch the submarine races." They couldn't help noticing also that it offers one of the most outstanding views of downtown Seattle across Elliott Bay. It's also a stop on **Gray Line**'s Grand City Tour (call 624.5213 for more information). Two coin-operated telescopes are available for a closer look. ◆ California Ave SW and SW Donald St

6 Cherry Blossom Teriyaki $ Seafood and, naturally, teriyaki dishes are the specialties of this small restaurant across the street from the beach. ◆ Japanese ◆ Daily lunch and dinner. 2620 Alki Ave SW (at 55th Ave SW). 933.0848

7 Alki Beach Park For many years this was the spot where teenagers showed off their cars and themselves. In the 1980s laws were passed that prohibited both cruising and amplified sound on the beach, thus cutting down considerably on the summer noise and traffic that had plagued local residents, but hardly decreasing the park's popularity. Today, the park is a two-and-a-half mile stretch with a sandy strip that's the closest thing Seattle can claim to a southern California beach. Volleyball courts on the sand are usually filled with players and lined with spectators when the sun shows its face. A bike path is active with skaters and runners. Picnic tables and shelters are available, and this is one of the few city parks that allows beach fires, although only in designated concrete rings. There are no lifeguards on duty, so swim at your own risk. ◆ Alki Ave SW (between Duwamish Head and 63rd Ave SW)

8 Alki Playground Facilities at this small playground about a block from the beach include a softball field, a soccer field, children's play equipment, and two lighted tennis courts. An artistic touch is added by *Whale's Tale,* a huge sculpture shaped like a whale's tail that was created in 1982 by local artist Richard Beyer (who also did the popular *Waiting for the Interurban* sculpture in Fremont). ◆ 58th Ave SW and SW Lander St

9 Alki Community Center Local families come here to roller-skate on Friday nights, to shoot pool, or for basketball and volleyball games in the gym. ◆ Daily. 5817 SW Stevens St (at 58th Ave SW). 684.7430

10 Spud Fish and Chips ★$ Two English guys, Jack and Frank Alger, opened a summer fish-and-chips stand here in 1935. Fish-and-chips were then 10¢ per order, to go. Today, the same owners still run it, though now it's a year-round eatery that seats as many as 82 people inside. That's not the only change: These days, the food is a bit more expensive. Eating here, however, remains part of the quintessential Seattle experience. The menu includes prawns, oysters, clams, and scallops, as well as chocolate chip cookies and milk shakes. ◆ Seafood/Takeout ◆ Daily lunch and dinner. 2666 Alki Ave SW (at 59th Ave SW). 938.0606 ♿. Also at: 6860 E Green Lake Way N (at Second Ave NE). 524.0565 ♿

11 Alki Bathhouse Art Studio The old bathhouse on Alki Beach is now open to all local artists as a free studio (available on a first-come basis). It's staffed by volunteers and administered by the **Alki Community Center.** ◆ M, W 10AM-3PM. Alki and 60th Aves SW. 684.7430

12 Phoenicia at Alki ★★★$$ Since this eatery opened its doors in 1975, it has changed locations again and again, but its many loyal fans keep following it, lured by the fine cooking of owner/chef Hussein Khazal. In this casual beach setting, the restaurant's third locale, Khazal presents the ultimate pan-Mediterranean experience: Highlights include marinated lamb, pine-nut risotto with shell-fish, and Moroccan eggplant. Even if you're not a beach person normally, it's worth the trip just to eat here. ◆ Mediterranean ◆ Tu-F lunch and dinner; Sa dinner. 2716 Alki Ave SW (between 60th and 61st Aves SW). 935.6550 ♿

12 Liberty Deli ★★$ After 14 years of yearning for the deli food they were used to in Manhattan, the three Ansart brothers (Bob, Tom, and Nick) decided to open their own place here in 1995. To ensure authenticity, they import their cold cuts from New York, make their own soups (including chicken basil and Manhattan clam chowder), and feature quintessential deli staples, such as corned beef on rye and lox and bagels. But there's also a local flavor to the menu: The breads come from **The Essential Bakery,** and Thomas Kemper root beer and cream soda are available. ◆ Deli ◆ Daily lunch and dinner. 2722 Alki Ave SW (between 60th and 61st Aves SW). 935.8420 &

12 Alki Cafe ★$ A local fave for weekend breakfasts (omelettes, fresh-baked bread, and cinnamon rolls), this long, narrow cafe also serves lunch and dinner. (Try the linguine primavera or the filling cheese tortellini with chicken and rosemary.) In 1992 cafe owner Kevin Piper (who also owns the **Point Grill**— see below) moved the **Alki Bakery** (935.1352) across the street to a former drugstore space. This is where they bake all the bread and pastries served in the cafe. You can also pick up baked goods and espresso drinks to go there. ◆ Continental ◆ Daily breakfast, lunch, and dinner. 2726 Alki Ave SW (at 61st Ave SW). 935.0616

13 Statue of Liberty The Boy Scouts of America dedicated this three-foot-high replica of New York City's harbor heroine to the City of Seattle in 1952. 61st and Alki Aves SW

14 Pegasus Pizza & Pasta on Alki ★$ The pizza here has become legendary. One of the best varieties is Tom's Special, with mushrooms, green peppers, onions, olives, feta and mozzarella cheeses, spinach, pepperoni, fresh garlic, diced tomatoes, and sunflower seeds. The Greek pizza (with feta and mozzarella cheeses, spinach, onions, and ground beef), the feta bread, and the ravioli are also worth a taste. Expect a line on weekends. ◆ Italian ◆ Daily lunch and dinner. 2758 Alki Ave SW (between 61st and 62nd Aves SW). 932.4849 &

14 Point Grill ★$$ "Smoke 'em if you got 'em" is the culinary motto here. The kitchen smokes its own salmon, then serves it atop a

111

fine Caesar salad. Ribs and chicken are also smoked, then barbecued. Also on the menu: pot roast and turkey dinners. ♦ Barbecue ♦ Daily lunch and dinner. 2770 Alki Ave SW (at 62nd Ave SW). 933.0118 ♿

15 Alki Homestead ★$$ Originally a log cabin and a roadhouse for people who made the long journey by automobile from Seattle, this restaurant features a romantic ambience with lace curtains and light flickering from the crystal lamps on the tables. The food is straight out of the 1940s—the specialty is panfried chicken with mashed potatoes, gravy, and green beans (which appear to be of the canned variety). The menu also includes steak, prime rib, and seafood. Cocktails are served in a spacious glassed-in porch. ♦ American ♦ W-Su dinner. 2717 61st Ave SW (between SW Stevens St and Alki Ave SW). 935.5678 ♿

16 Sunfish Seafood ★$ You can get regular fish-and-chips here, or for a little more (and the difference is worth paying), halibut-and-chips. The influence of the Greek brothers who own this place shows up in such menu offerings as halibut shish kebab and calamari. Indoor and outdoor seating are both available. ♦ Seafood/Takeout ♦ Daily lunch and dinner. 2800 Alki Ave SW (at 62nd Ave SW). 938.4112 ♿

17 Monument to the Birthplace of Seattle A concrete pylon marks the spot where Arthur Denny's pioneering party landed in 1851. Presented to the city in 1905 by Denny's daughter, Lenora, the column was originally installed beside the old **Stockade Hotel,** just across the street. It was moved to the beachside in 1926 when a piece of Massachusetts's famed Plymouth Rock was embedded in the pylon's base and a plaque was added to commemorate the occasion. The hotel, by the way, folded in 1936; apartments now occupy its former site. ♦ 63rd and Alki Aves SW

18 Alki Point Light Station Alki Point marks the southern entrance to Seattle's harbor, Elliott Bay. It's been the site of a warning beacon for ships since the mid-1870s, when Hans Martin Hanson, who bought the land from pioneer Doc Maynard, began lighting lanterns on the point every night. In the 1880s the US Lighthouse Service erected a lens-lantern on a scaffold. The present 37-foot-high octagonal tower (pictured

below) was completed in 1913. Its light was converted to electricity five years later, and in 1984 its operation became fully automatic. Today, the lighthouse stands surrounded by apartments and condominiums. The station is maintained by the US Coast Guard. ♦ Walk-in tours Sa-Su, holidays May through August; tours by appointment W noon-4PM May through August. 3201 Alki Ave SW (at Point Pl SW). 217.6123

19 Weather Watch Park Once a dock site for Puget Sound's ferry service from Seattle, this teeny lookout, on a small knoll between the apartments and cottages lining Beach Drive, was designed by local artist Lezlie Jane in 1991 and built with the help of many local residents. The centerpiece is an interpretive column—it's got a sundial, information on cloud formation and weather prediction, and historical photographs, all topped off by a sculpture of ducks in flight. With its brick patio and benches, this makes a lovely spot from which to watch the weather over Puget Sound and the Olympic Mountains. ♦ Beach Dr SW and SW Carroll St

Alki Point Light Station

M. BLUM

20 Schmitz Park Donated to the city by wealthy West Siders Ferdinand and Emma Schmitz in 1908 on the condition that the land be forever maintained as closely as possible to its natural state, this park is now home to one of the last stands of old-growth forest—some of the trees are more than 800 years old—within the city limits. It is also a 50-acre nature preserve where narrow trails through the thick woods can be hard to follow. There are no picnic areas or playgrounds. ♦ SW Stevens St and SW Admiral Way

21 Parkside News Cafe ★$ Espresso, salads, and sandwiches are the specialties at this friendly place. Try the excellent hazelnut torte, the tiramisù, or the carrot cake. In keeping with the shop's name, a wide variety of magazines and newspapers are for sale. ♦ Cafe ♦ Daily breakfast, lunch, and dinner. 2735 California Ave SW (between SW Stevens and SW Lander Sts). 932.2279 &

22 Alki Bicycle Company This store has been outfitting local cyclists for years. (Its name reflects the shop's original location on Alki Beach.) Besides peddling bikes and all manner of accessories, it also provides repair services, sells used bikes on consignment, and offers classes in road safety. The Alki Bicycle Club operates out of this shop, with free Wednesday night rides and guided tours available to groups of five or more. ♦ Daily. 2611 California Ave SW (between SW Lander St and SW Admiral Way). 938.3322

23 Starbucks ★$ No Seattle neighborhood seems complete anymore without its own branch of this coffee chain, selling pastries, espresso drinks, coffee by the pound, and all the equipment you need to brew your own beans at home. ♦ Coffeehouse ♦ Daily. 4101 SW Admiral Way (at 41st Ave SW). 937.5010. Also at: Numerous locations throughout the city

24 Peace Cafe ★$$ According to owner Bashar Al-Nakhala, this establishment got its name because "It's about time for peace in this world." Falafel and *shawarma* (rotisserie-roasted meat) sandwiches, as well as more typical American dishes, are offered. Be sure to save room for an espresso and one of the savory cakes, pies, tortes, biscotti, and brownies that come from Capitol Hill's **B&O Espresso.** ♦ Middle Eastern ♦ Daily breakfast, lunch, and dinner. 2352 California Ave SW (between SW Admiral Way and SW College St). 935.1540 &

24 Admiral Benbow Inn $ This replica of an old English inn was modeled after the fictional hostelry where pirates planned their voyage in Robert Louis Stevenson's *Treasure Island.* The **Chart Room Lounge,** a replica of the fictional ship *Hispaniola,* is a good place to stop in for a cocktail. In the dining room, fare ranges from seafood to prime rib, but the place isn't as interesting as Stevenson's story promises. ♦ American ♦ M-Sa lunch and dinner. 4212 SW Admiral Way (between 42nd and California Aves SW). 937.8348 &

25 Angelina's Trattoria ★$ Here is yet another member of Dany Mitchell's group of Seattle trattorias. Like the others (including **Stella's** in the University District and Pioneer Square's **Trattoria Mitchelli**), this restaurant provides Italian fare at reasonable prices. Entrées range from simple pastas of the day with marinara sauce to the more elaborate *fettuccine con pollo e nocciole* (pasta in a velouté sauce with roasted hazelnuts and chicken). ♦ Italian ♦ M-F lunch and dinner; Sa-Su breakfast, lunch, and dinner. 2311 California Ave SW (between SW Admiral Way and SW College St). 932.7311 &

25 Ristorante di Ragazzi ★$ In a comfortable setting replete with murals, faux marble walls and deep-green wicker furniture, "The Boys' Restaurant" (as its name translates) serves great salads, innovative pastas, and good pizzas (try the pie with pesto and artichoke hearts). It's also a good stop for an after-movie cappuccino or a glass of wine. ♦ Italian ♦ M-F lunch and dinner; Sa-Su dinner. 2329 California Ave SW (between SW Admiral Way and SW College St). 935.1969 &

25 Admiral Theater Originally built as the **Portola Theater** in 1919, this playhouse has had a colorful history. In the 1920s the theater—along with the nearby **Olympus** and **Apollo** theaters—screened feature films, newsreels, and comedy shorts, all for a mere 20¢ per customer. An $18,000 pipe organ was added in 1924, talkies followed in 1929, and, in response to the realities of the Depression, in 1933 admission was dropped to 15¢.

In 1942 the moviehouse was expanded amid great fanfare. John Danz, the owner, held a contest for West Seattle residents to name the picture palace. The architect was **B. Marcus Priteca,** famed designer for Alexander Pantages's nationwide theater chain, whose local work may be remembered best in the **Coliseum** and **Paramount** theaters in downtown Seattle. **Priteca** used the winning moniker as a theme, adding nautical allusions to the facade (note the portholes, anchors, and a giant mast with crow's nest on the "upper deck," as well as the seahorses riding exit signs). Usherettes sported naval uniforms. A gala opening in 1942 drew 3,000 people to a showing of *Weekend in Havana,* starring Alice Faye, Carmen Miranda, and John Payne. In 1953 the theater put in "the first panoramic wide screen installed in a suburban theater."Twenty years later it was converted to a "twin" with two 430-seat viewing rooms. But the theater closed in 1989, after several years of false hopes that its Canadian owners would restore its original majesty. A campaign by the Southwest Seattle Historical Society finally led locals to purchase the theater in 1991 and open it as a second-run movie palace. There are now five to six shows per week at about $2 a seat, a bargain price these days. ♦ 2343 California Ave SW (between SW Admiral Way and SW College St). 938.3456

Painting the Town

Historical murals have become increasingly familiar sights in West Seattle. Located primarily in the **Junction** area, these paintings reflect a variety of artistic styles, ranging from a stylized folk-art look to trompe l'oeils, but most are lifelike images of West Seattle in the late 1800s and early 1900s.

After admiring murals in southwestern Washington and in Chemainus, British Columbia, where more than 25 murals serve as that town's primary tourist draw, area resident Earl Cruzen decided that his neighborhood should adopt the popular public-art theme. Most of the 11 murals painted in West Seattle have been funded by local donations, city matching funds, and contributions from building owners. Brochures are available from the **West Seattle Chamber of Commerce** (4151 California Ave SW, between SW Genesee and SW Dakota Sts, 932.5685). Here's a brief guide to the works of art:

The Junction depicts the intersection during the 1920s, when the old streetcar lines converged here. The work of Eric Grohe, this trompe l'oeil looks so realistic that local wits have suggested the city hang a traffic light in front of the painted streetcar tracks. You'll find it framed by a mock concrete arch on the south wall of the **Junction Feed & Seed Store** (4747 California Ave SW, between SW Edmunds and SW Alaska Sts).

Part of the west side of **Morton's Drugs** (4707 California Ave SW, at SW Alaska St) is covered with a montage that includes images of onetime local attraction **Luna Park,** the old **West Seattle Cable Railway,** and turn-of-the-century ferries. Artist William Garnett of Portland, Oregon, completed the mural in 1989 and dubbed it *West Seattle Ferries.*

A deep-blue nighttime scene of a horse-drawn wagon dashing away from the 1913 Junction Fire Station brightens the south side of the **Don Swanson Insurance Building** (4711 44th Ave SW, near SW Alaska St), across from where that fire station once stood. Seattleite Don Barrie painted the mural, titled *Midnight Call,* in 1990.

The First Duwamish Bridge, a panorama of the old swing bridge that crosses the **Duwamish River,** is the work of Louisiana artists Robert and Douglas Dafford. Located on the north wall of the **Jacobson Building** (44th Ave SW and SW Edmunds St), it shows a trolley crossing the river, with the Cascade Mountains in a background of dreamy sunset shades.

A colorful 1937 view of the old *Morgan Street Market* was painted in 1990 by Nova Scotian artist Bruce Rickett on the west wall of **Olsen's Drugs** (6501 California Ave SW, at Fauntleroy Way SW). The original market stood across the street.

Another artist from Nova Scotia, Susan Tooke Crichton, depicted a 1910 landing by the old steam-ships that hauled freight and passengers between **Puget Sound**'s ports. *Mosquito Boat Landing* can be seen on the east wall of the **Campbell Building** (California Ave SW and SW Alaska St).

Huling's Chevrolet dealership (4755 Fauntleroy Ave SW at SW Alaska St) is the site of another Bruce Rickett mural, this one entitled *Alki in the Twenties,* a portrait of a 1919 Chevrolet and a woman painting. In the background are Alki residences, a streetcar line, and ferry dock.

Tuesday's Bank Day is the subject of the mural on the north side of the **Washington Mutual Bank** building (California Ave SW and SW Oregon St). It commemorates a project begun in 1923 to teach school children about saving money; at the time, this was the only bank that was willing to take the pennies, nickels, and quarters that kids wanted to deposit, and they even offered interest on accounts exceeding a few dollars. British Columbian Alan Wylie was the artist.

Lany Little of Gresham, Oregon, depicted the *Wizard of Oz* float from a 1973 parade in a mural on the wall of the **West Seattle Post Office** (4412 California Ave SW, between SW Oregon and SW Genesee Sts).

The Old Mud Hole by Mike Svob of Coquitlam, British Columbia, shows the old swimming area that Laurence Colman created in what is now **Lincoln Park.** In 1940, the Colman family donated funds for a swimming pool to be built at the same site. The mural is on the side of an apartment building (44th Ave SW, between Alaska and Oregon Sts).

The days of hot metal type are revived in *Press Day,* a mural illustrating putting the *West Seattle Herald* to bed. Painted by Alan Wylie of Fort Langley, British Columbia, the mural is on the **Seawest Building** (44th Ave SW, between SW Edmunds and SW Alaska Sts).

26 Pailin Thai Cuisine ★★$ This comfortable restaurant is a neighborhood favorite. The food—especially the *pad thai* noodles—is good and the prices can't be beat. ◆ Thai ◆ M-F lunch and dinner; Sa-Su dinner. 2223 California Ave SW (between SW College and SW Walker Sts). 937.8807

27 West Seattle Library This attractive 1910 brick building was created by **W. Marbury Somervell** and **Joseph C. Cote,** who also designed three other Carnegie libraries: the **University Branch Library,** the **Green Lake Public Library,** and the **Queen Anne Library.** In addition to the usual services, free special programs are offered for children and adults. ◆ M-W, F-Su. 2306 42nd Ave SW (between SW Admiral Way and SW College St). 684.7444

28 Belvedere Viewpoint The totem pole here, carved by Boeing engineers Michael Morgan and Robert Fleishman and dedicated in 1966, is modeled after one that had been presented to the city in 1939 by J.E. "Daddy" Standley, owner of downtown's **Ye Olde Curiosity Shop.** (Standley's original, crafted by the Bella Bella tribe of British Columbia's Queen Charlotte Islands, had decayed beyond repair.) There's an excellent view over Harbor Island to downtown. Be forewarned: There are only a few parking spaces in a tiny lot nearby. ◆ SW Admiral Way and SW Olga St

29 Hainsworth House $ An 18-room 1906 Tudor mansion offers excellent views of downtown Seattle, lovely landscaped grounds, and two guest rooms with private baths. The larger room, decorated in French country style, has an antique Austrian king-size bed, a private deck, a fireplace, and a full view of the city. The second has a partial view, a deck, and an antique oak bedroom set. Guests are treated to coffee half an hour before the complimentary full breakfast served by owners Carl and Charlotte Muia. No smoking is allowed, and visitors with animal allergies beware: There are two resident dogs. ◆ 2657 37th Ave SW (at SW Olga St). 938.1020

30 Luna Park Cafe ★$ Eat 1950s-style food beneath a black-velvet Elvis painting. A neon-lit Seeburg jukebox (the remote selectors at each table actually work) spins 200 eclectic selections from Elvis to Frank Sinatra, Bob Marley, and Annette Funicello, and costs an amazing dime per play. A 1946 Wurlitzer 1015 Bubbler is a display jukebox only. Other kitschy decor includes an impressive collection of children's lunch boxes along with old business signs.

The food here is basic but good. (Try the meat loaf on whole wheat or the Cobb salad—turkey, bacon, blue cheese, egg, Swiss cheese, tomato, and olives.) The milk shakes (root beer, coffee, fresh fruit, and more) are much in demand on steamy days. The name is taken from the amusement park that once

graced Duwamish Head (see page 109). ◆ American ◆ Daily breakfast, lunch, and dinner. 2918 Avalon Way SW (near SW Charlestown St). 935.7250

31 YMCA The main branch of the West Seattle **Y** is also the most deluxe. There's a swimming pool, a weight room with free weights and exercise machines, basketball and volleyball courts, a running track, two racquetball courts, and a spa. All facilities, except regularly scheduled classes, are available on a drop-in basis for a fee. ◆ Daily. 4515 36th Ave SW (at SW Oregon St). 935.6000

32 Foreign Accents For aromatherapy and all kinds of soaps, lotions, potions, and gifts in more than 85 fragrances, this is the place. ◆ Daily. 4511 California Ave SW (between SW Alaska and SW Oregon Sts). 932.3747

CAPERS
ESPRESSO CAFÉ
GOURMET ACCESSORIES

32 Capers ★$ The kitchen here whips up terrific scones, muffins, and cobblers, as well as an estimable seafood salad and a daily quiche. It's a popular lunch spot for local office workers. A variety of Martha Stewart–ish decorator items for the kitchen and dining room, as well as **Dilettante** chocolates and coffee by the pound, are also sold. ◆ Cafe ◆ Daily breakfast and lunch. 4521 California Ave SW (between SW Alaska and SW Oregon Sts). 932.0371

33 Reflections This shop specializes in Native American crafts and artifacts, including art, incense, dream catchers, shields, medicine bags, sage, and sweetgrass. ◆ M-Sa. 4537 California Ave SW (between SW Alaska and SW Oregon Sts). 937.6032

33 West Seattle Speedway and Hobby Behind the stacks of plastic and intricate wooden model kits, this shop boasts a 135-foot, Euro hill-climb slot-car track, one of only a few left in the city. The sport owes its historical debt to auto racers of the 1920s, who, before the advent of dragsters and mud racers, gunned Duesenbergs and Millers around 24 steeply banked board tracks (none of which survived the Depression years). In addition to renting the slot cars and track time, the shop also sells the cars, parts and accessories. ◆ Daily. 4539 California Ave SW (between SW Alaska and SW Oregon Sts). 932.9620

33 Pegasus Book Exchange This bookshop buys, sells, and trades used books. Its principal stock is in paperback fiction, but the owner also has an interest in metaphysics and will help you find anything in that category that isn't already available here. ♦ Daily. 4553 California Ave SW (between SW Alaska and SW Oregon Sts). 937.5410

33 Easy Streets Records Right in the middle of The Junction is a store selling new and used records and CDs in a wide range of styles, from rap and world music to classical and jazz. ♦ M-F until 9PM; Sa until 8PM; Su until 6PM. 4559 California Ave SW (at SW Alaska St). 938.3279; fax 938.3284

34 California and Alaska Street Brewery Brewmaster Charles McElevy of this tiny brewpub trained in Germany and was formerly with the Rainier Brewing Company and Fremont's Red Hook Brewery. The beer names reflect local geography: Junction Ale, Alki Ale, Fauntleroy Stout, and the like. Alki Ale is red, with medium body. Hi-Yu Brown Ale (which means "Big Time" in Chinook jargon and also applies to an annual festival held in West Seattle since 1934) is rich and malty. Pub grub is limited, covering the short span betwixt chili and sandwiches. For entertainment, there are dart boards and board games. ♦ Tu-Th 4-10PM; F 4-11PM; Sa noon-10PM. No smoking permitted. 4720 California Ave SW (at SW Alaska St). 938.2476 ♿

35 Husky Delicatessen A local institution since 1933, this family-owned establishment grew from an ice-cream parlor specializing in large chocolate-covered cones to a full-fledged deli. It attracts customers from all over Seattle with its homemade ice cream; also available are cold cuts, salads, beers and wines, and truffles. ♦ Daily; Tu-Su until 10PM. 4721 California Ave SW (at SW Alaska St). 937.2810

35 Northwest Art & Frame One-stop shopping for graphics needs: calligraphy pens and paper, rubber stamps, fabric painting supplies, watercolors, oils, enamels, children's art supplies, stationery, gifts, and cards. Picture framing is also available—do it yourself or pay more and have it done professionally. ♦ Daily. 4733 California Ave SW (between SW Edmunds and SW Alaska Sts). 937.5507

36 ArtsWest This nonprofit organization has established a cultural center within **Jefferson Square,** a retail/residential complex named for the brick elementary school that stood at this site from 1912 to 1985. The center offers educational theater, music, dance, and other arts programs. There's also an art gallery that displays local talent. ♦ Tu-Sa. 4734 42nd Ave SW (between SW Edmunds and SW Alaska Sts). 938.0963

37 Villa Heidelberg $ A converted 1909 house (constructed and named by a German immigrant), this bed-and-breakfast inn has lead-glass windows, beamed ceilings, a finely landscaped yard (from which the owners pick their decorative flowers), and a wraparound covered porch with a stunning view of the Olympic Mountains. Four guest rooms share two baths. One of the rooms offers an Olympic-view sundeck; another has a fireplace. Popovers are a treat at breakfast. ♦ 4845 45th Ave SW (at SW Hudson St). 938.3658, 800/671.2942; fax 935.7077

38 West Seattle Nursery This is a wonderful place to find answers to your gardening dilemmas. The nursery carries a full line of seeds, bulbs, bedding plants, perennials, vines, shrubs, trees, landscaping paraphernalia, gardening videos, plus horticultural books for gardeners of all ages and stages, charming gifts, and botanical items. The staff is friendly and knowledgeable. ♦ Daily. 5275 California Ave SW (at SW Brandon St). 935.9276

39 West Seattle Golf Club Set on relatively hilly terrain, this public 18-hole course features tree-lined fairways and great views of the city skyline. ♦ Greens fees. ♦ Daily. Reservations required. 4470 35th Ave SW (between SW Snoqualmie St and Avalon Way SW). 935.5187

40 Camp Long One of the city's few parks to offer overnight facilities, this 68-acre patch is open to organized groups for camping and wilderness-skills programs. There are 10 cabins for rent (each sleeps 12), picnic shelters, and a rustic lodge which is a popular spot for weddings. There's a rock wall for climbing practice and instruction (with a minimum class size of 15). Free nature walks are scheduled on Saturdays, and there are educational programs for youngsters; call ahead for a rundown. ♦ Park ranger station Tu-Sa. 5200 35th Ave SW (at SW Dawson St). 684.7434

Crystal Mountain, one of the area's most spectacular ski slopes, is a two-hour drive southeast of downtown Seattle. There are 55 ski runs, and the 10 lifts are capable of transporting 15,060 skiers per hour.

41 Walker Rock Garden Local businessman Milton Walker designed and constructed this 100-square-foot space, which was built between 1959 and 1979. Fountains, bridges, towers, and small mountains have been fashioned from various rocks that Walker and his wife collected during their travels (including volcanic rock, pumice, colored stones, and even some semi-precious gems). The garden is still owned by the Walkers, who lead guided tours through it by appointment. ◆ Daily by appointment; closed September through late April. 5407 37th Ave SW (at SW Brandon St). 935.3036

 42 Lowman Beach Named after a former Seattle parks commissioner, this tiny park offers not only access to the sand but a swing set and one tennis court. In December, locals gather here to watch Seattle's ceremonial Christmas ships make their loop through Puget Sound. Walkers can take pleasant strolls down an access road into the lower portion of adjacent **Lincoln Park.** ◆ 48th Ave SW and Beach Dr SW

43 Cat's Eye Cafe $ Most of the sandwiches served at this deli feature cute feline names: the Kit Cat (sliced chicken, avocado, tomato, and sprouts), the Cat on a Hot Tin Roof (a classic Reuben), and the Cat in Heat (tuna melt with tomato). Other menu items include pesto lasagna, quiche, chili, and salads. The deli does a brisk business in espresso, although the richness falls far short of **Starbucks.** On sunny days sit outside at one of the picnic tables on the grass. ◆ Deli ◆ Daily breakfast, lunch, and dinner. Fauntleroy Way SW and SW Othello St. 935.2229

 44 Lincoln Park Designed by Frederick Law Olmsted Jr. and John Charles Olmsted, who developed Seattle's 1903 comprehensive greenery plan, this park comprises 130 acres of wooded and waterfront trails, with picnic areas, tennis courts, softball fields, horseshoe pits, and children's playground equipment. Access is limited to foot traffic; park roads are open only to park vehicles or for emergencies. As with most beach parks on Puget Sound, no lifeguards are on duty even during summer months. A bit of historical trivia: the park was named at the request of the local Young Men's Republican Club, which promised to erect a statue of Honest Abe at the park entrance. The promise was never kept. ◆ Fauntleroy Ave SW and SW Kenyon Pl

Within Lincoln Park:

 Colman Pool This heated, outdoor, Olympic-size pool is filled with both chlorinated freshwater and saltwater. One negative: It's open only during summer vacation for the Seattle School District. Admission; discount for senior citizens, disabled persons, and children 18 and younger. ◆ Daily noon-7PM late June-Aug. 684.7494

45 Fauntleroy Ferry Dock Washington State Ferries leave this dock to take passengers to Vashon Island, a 28-minute ride that's packed with commuters on weekday mornings and late afternoons. Vashon is a charming rural area; many residents work in town, but others have found work on the island itself in industries such as ski manufacturing (K2 Corporation), orchid growing, or food processing. ◆ 47th Ave SW and SW Henderson St. 464.6400, 800/542.0810

46 Bakery The Original A working bakery, specializing in gooey cinnamon rolls, birthday cakes, and bread, this place also has a small seating area and serves espresso. ◆ Bakery ◆ Tu-Su. 9253 45th Ave SW (at SW Wildwood Pl). 938.5088

47 Georgie Cafe ★$$ This eatery offers hummus, gyros, and a variety of other Greek and Middle Eastern specialties. Sit in the outdoor dining area above the restaurant on sunny days. ◆ Greek/Middle Eastern ◆ Daily breakfast, lunch, and dinner. 9214 45th Ave SW (near SW Wildwood Pl). 933.8413

 48 High Point The highest point in Seattle, this intersection tops off at 518 feet above sea level, higher even than lofty Queen Anne Hill. The views, from Puget Sound to the Olympic Mountains, are expansive. ◆ 35th Ave SW and SW Myrtle St

Seattle certainly has its share of local celebrities. Among the familiar faces who hail from the Emerald City are Kate Mulgrew (who plays Captain Janeway on "Star Trek: Voyager"), Josie Bissett (Jane on "Melrose Place"), Dawn Wells (Mary Ann on "Gilligan's Island"), Richard Karn (Al on "Home Improvement"), and Patrick Duffy (Bobby on "Dallas").

Restaurants/Clubs: Red	**Hotels:** Blue
Shops/ Outdoors: Green	**Sights/Culture:** Black

Queen Anne/Magnolia

In 1853 Seattle pioneer Thomas Mercer staked a claim to 320 heavily forested acres on what is now **Queen Anne Hill.** Looking out at **Puget Sound** and the **Olympic Mountains,** you will no doubt understand why Mercer called his new home "Eden." At a dizzying crest elevation of 456 feet above sea level, this is the second-highest point in the city (surpassed only by the intersection of 35th Avenue SW and SW Myrtle Street in West Seattle, which tops out at 518 feet).

To much of Seattle's old guard, Queen Anne and adjacent Magnolia *did* represent idyllic escapes from the burgeoning city. After First Hill and Capitol

Hill were developed, it was to this area that the wealthy retreated, erecting their capitalist castles as the 20th century made its debut. "The Hill," as residents called it, looked down its nose—both literally and figuratively—at the city's center. The exclusive area adopted an air of elegance; so many of the homes on its south flank were designed in an Americanized spin on classic Queen Anne architectural style that by the 1880s the district had been dubbed **Queen Anne Town.** Unfortunately, most of the towered villas that inspired this name a century ago are now gone. Many of the other older dwellings have been carved into duplexes and triplexes to make room for the neighborhood's growing population (upwards of 30,000).

For nos. 5-32, see pg. 121

Bordered by water on three sides (**Elliott Bay** to the south and west, **Lake Union** to the east, and the **Lake Washington Ship Canal** connecting them), for years Queen Anne managed to maintain the atmosphere of a place set apart. In time it was conquered by cable-car lines and then annexed to the city of Seattle in 1883. Today hideous 500-foot-tall television towers—which, ironically, disturb TV and radio reception in the immediate neighborhood—have been thrust up against the sky here. But still, Queen Anne strives to rise above it all.

Magnolia is even more luxuriously isolated. Connected to Queen Anne and the rest of the city by only three streets and a bridge, this hamlet—named in 1865 after a United States Coast Survey misidentified a stand of madrona trees as magnolias—used to be dominated by single-family houses. Along with the properties bordering **Magnolia Bluff** and the waterfront homes hugging **Perkins Lane**, the area now has many apartment and condo complexes. A clear indication of Magnolia's shifting profile is the main shopping district along **West McGraw Street** between **32nd** and **35th Avenues.** More than half the businesses in "The Village," as Magnolians call the area, have opened since the mid-1980s. Successful thirtysomething couples are moving in, drawn to Magnolia's manageable size (only about 16,000 residents so far), natural beauty, and relative calm.

Queen Anne

1 Kinnear Park This 14-acre park of majestic trees, sloping lawns, and mountain and Puget Sound views was donated to the city by Midwesterner George Kinnear, who visited Seattle in 1874 and invested his money in local real estate. Unfortunately, in addition to natural views, the park also looks down on the Port of Seattle grain terminal, which is second only to the **Kingdome** among Seattle's few real eyesores. ♦ Bounded by W Mercer St and W Olympic Pl, and Sixth and Ninth Aves W

2 Queen Anne Counterbalance The name for the steep ascent on Queen Anne Avenue north of Roy Street dates back to the late 1800s and early streetcar technology. While other Seattle cable-car lines employed conventional underground mechanical power until 1940, the car that ran through these parts was converted in 1900 to draw electricity from overhead wires. But in order to scale the 18-percent incline of Queen Anne Hill, the streetcar needed assistance from a pair of special counterweight arrangements. Here's how it worked: one streetcar could go up the hill and one could go down, each linked via cable to a 16-ton "truck," which ran on tracks through a tunnel beneath the street. As the truck went downhill, it helped pull the heavier streetcar uphill. Going the other direction, the ascending truck restrained the descending streetcar. At eight miles per hour, it was slow going.

In a race up the **Counterbalance** on 5 March 1937, a more modern trackless trolley loaded with 92 passengers "embarrassed the Queen Anne streetcar, making the 2,150-foot hill in less than half the time required by the streetcar," reported the *Seattle Times* the next morning. The **Counterbalance**'s last two cable cars were retired in 1943, but the pair of tunnels remain in place under Queen Anne Avenue. ♦ Queen Anne Ave N (between Roy and Galer Sts)

3 Adriatica Cucina Mediterranea ★★★★$$$ From this immensely popular restaurant's hillside location—you have to climb a couple of flights just to reach the front door—diners can look out over the south end of Lake Union and its twinkling lights after dark. An upstairs bar offers a second level of gorgeous views, and a more casual atmosphere than in the dining room.

The kitchen is the province of talented Katherine MacKenzie (formerly of the **Ponti Seafood Grill** in Fremont), who plans the menu with the collaboration of co-owner Connie Malevitsis. No one in Seattle makes better fried calamari, and, for entrées, the prawns served on a bed of angel hair pasta with cilantro and roasted–red-pepper cream are wonderful, as are the lamb loin chops and the fettuccine with smoked duck. Co-owner Jim Malevitsis, an engaging and gregarious host, is always happy to recommend a wine from his carefully chosen list of fine European and California labels. ♦ Mediterranean ♦ Daily dinner. Reservations recommended. 1107 Dexter Ave N (between Aloha St and Highland Dr). 285.5000

4 Latitude 47 The dance floor of this club is small, mirrored, and circled by TV sets playing rock videos. A stop here is often the opening act for an evening's cruise of wilder joints around Belltown or Pioneer Square. Latin salsa cuts in on the top-40 repertoire on Wednesday and Sunday nights. Like some other Seattle area clubs, this place operates as a restaurant during the earlier hours, serving your basic American food for lunch and dinner daily. ♦ Cover. M-Sa until 1:30AM; Su until 11PM. 1232 Westlake Ave N (at Lake Union). 284.1047 &

5 Williams House $ Doug and Sue Williams are the owners of this charming bed-and-breakfast located in a quiet residential neighborhood on the east side of the hill. Built in 1905, the small, beautifully restored Edwardian mansion has five spacious guest rooms with private baths; most offer commanding views south and west. A winning sun porch on the first floor also faces south. ♦ 1505 Fourth Ave N (at Galer St). 285.0810

6 Bhy Kracke Park Werner "Bhy" Kracke, a wealthy bank auditor, world traveler, and gardener, donated 1.5 acres of his property to the city, along with $20,000 to develop the land as a park, but he died before the deal could be closed. (Kracke got his nickname from "By cracky," one of his favorite expressions.) His heirs completed the

transaction, and the city created the park and named it in Kracke's memory. Visit here for the views, sweeping from Lake Union and the Cascade Mountains to the **Space Needle.** The park is constructed on several levels; follow the winding paved path. You'll feel you've discovered a little gem that most locals don't know exists—and you'll be right. For parking, look for the street sign signaling Comstock Place and Bigelow Avenue N, ignore the Dead End sign, and head east to the three-car parking area just ahead. ♦ Bigelow Ave N and Comstock Pl

7 Queen Anne High School Apartments A successful conversion from institution to residence, this school closed its doors in 1981 and now has 139 apartments on five floors. Many of the units have expansive views; from a top-floor apartment, for instance, you can see almost all the way to Canada. The school was designed in 1909 by **James Stephen,** the accomplished son of a Scottish cabinetmaker, who received his architectural training through a Chicago correspondence course and served as the Seattle School District's resident architect from 1899 to 1908. (He also created **Summit Grade School** on First Hill, **Latona Elementary** and **Interlake School**— now **Wallingford Center**—in Wallingford, and many other educational facilities needed to service the city's growing population during its early boom years.) The building was converted by **Bumgardner Architects** in 1988 and is still the most visible landmark on the hill, especially at night, when the windows are lit up. ♦ 201 Galer St (at Second Ave N). 285.8800

A Mini-Guide to Seattle

In a perfect world, you would have all the time you needed to explore Seattle thoroughly, visiting every corner of every neighborhood until eventually you would know more about the city than the locals did. But in reality, whether you're coming to Seattle for business or pleasure, you'll only be here for a few days and will have to pick and choose which sights to visit. What follows is our short-stay list of the outstanding attractions here, by neighborhood, to help you make the most of your time.

Pioneer Square/International District: Start with a dim sum lunch at **Linyen** (424 Seventh Ave S at S King St, 622.8181), and then walk to **Uwajimaya** (519 Sixth Ave S between S Weller and S King Sts, 624.6248), one of the best Asian supermarkets in the country. If you're up for a long stroll, continue west down **S Jackson Street** toward **Occidental Avenue S**. Take the time to look into some of the galleries and boutiques here. Finish your shopping trip with a browse through the **Elliott Bay Book Company** (101 S Main St at First Ave S, 624.6600), and then enjoy a coffee or a beer at the **Elliott Bay Cafe** (682.6664) on the premises. From there, walk two blocks north to **Doc Maynard's Public House** (610 First Ave between James and Cherry Sts, 682.4649) and take the tour of **Underground Seattle.**

Business District: Park at the **Seattle Center** (bounded by Fifth and First Aves N, and Denny Way and Mercer St) and take the **Monorail** to **Westlake Center** (Fourth Ave and Pine St). Take a peek inside **Nordstrom,** and then head north along Fifth Avenue. Stop at an espresso stand (there's one about every 50 feet in this area) and pick up a *latte* and a pastry to take to **Freeway Park** (Sixth Ave and Seneca St). Relax and enjoy the greenery, and then walk west on **Seneca Street** downhill to **Second Avenue.** Turn left and head south through the financial district, making sure to check out the fantastic terra-cotta architecture of the older buildings—especially the walruses on the **Arctic Building** (700 Third Ave between Cherry and Columbia Sts)

Pike Place Market/Waterfront: If you have only a little while, spend it all in the **Pike Place Market.** There is no area more quintessentially Seattle, not only because of its pioneer spirit and laid-back atmosphere, but also because of its history. Start your tour at the corner of **Pike Street** and **Pike Place** under the big **Market Clock.** Wander through the **Main Arcade** (Pike Pl between Pike and Pine Sts) and watch the goings-on at **Pike Place Fish** (682.7181, 800/542.7732; fax 682.4629) as the vendors fling salmon and crab back and forth over their customers' heads. At the northernmost end of the arcade, cross Pike Place and watch the street performers in front of the **Soames-Dunn Building** (Pike Pl between Stewart and Virginia Sts). The **Triangle Building** (Pike Pl and Pine St), the **Sanitary Market Building** (Pike Pl between Pine and Pike Sts), and the **Corner Market Building** (Pike Pl and Pike St) are also worth a look. Good dining choices include **Chez Shea** (in the Corner Market Building,

467.9990), **The Painted Table** (in the Alexis Hotel, 1007 First Ave at Madison St, 624.3646), **Il Bistro** (93A Pike St off Lower Post Alley, 682.3049), and **Maximilien-in-the-Market** (in the Main Arcade, 682.7270 &).

Belltown/Seattle Center: If you have tots in tow, spend your time at the **Seattle Center** (bounded by Fifth and First Aves N, and Denny Way and Mercer St), especially the **Pacific Science Center** (443.2880, recorded information 443.2001), the **Children's Museum** (441.1768), and the **Charlotte Martin Theatre** (441.3322), home of the **Seattle Children's Theatre (SCT).** Shoppers' delights include **Jet City Vintage** (2200 First Ave at Blanchard St, 728.7118), offering classic 1950s memorabilia; **Uno-Duo** (2209 First Ave between Blanchard and Bell Sts, 448.7011), with upscale men's and women's fashions; and the tiny **Sub-Pop Mega-Mart** (1928 Second Ave between Stewart and Virginia Sts, 443.0322), which always seems to carry the hippest music. The best restaurant choices here include **Flying Fish** (2234 First Ave at Bell St, 728.8595 &), **Lampreia** (2400 First Ave at Battery St, 443.3301 &), and **Panos** (2815 Alaskan Way at Broad St, 441.5073 &).

Capitol Hill to Seward Park: Start your exploration of this area in or around **Volunteer Park** (bounded by E Prospect and E Galer Sts, and 15th and 11th Aves E). While you're here, spend some time in the small but beautiful **Conservatory** (north side of the park, 684.4743) and visit the **Seattle Asian Art Museum** (1400 E Prospect St, south side of the park, 625.8900), which features one of the most comprehensive collections of Chinese and Japanese art in the country. Leave the park by the east exit and cross the street to **Louisa Boren View Park** (15th Ave E and E Garfield St) to enjoy the view of the **University of Washington,** the **Montlake Cut,** the **Arboretum,** and **Lake Washington.** Then wander through the **Lake View Cemetery** (1554 15th Ave E at E Garfield St, 322.1582); father-and-son movie stars Bruce and Brandon Lee are interred here. Walk back through **Volunteer Park,** and then turn right onto **E Prospect Street.** Take a left on **10th Avenue E,** which turns into **Broadway** after a couple of blocks. Browse through the **Broadway Market** (401 Broadway E at E Harrison St, 322.1610 &) and then grab a coffee at **B&O Espresso** (328.3290 &).

West Seattle: Exit the **West Seattle Freeway** at **SW Admiral Way** and go up the hill to **Belvedere Viewpoint** (SW Admiral Way and SW Olga St) to watch planes land at **Boeing Field** and ships unload at **Harbor Island.** Back in the car, follow SW Admiral Way through West Seattle, past **Schmitz Park.** Take a right on **63rd Avenue SW** and park near **Alki Beach.** Walk along the beach to **Duwamish Head** and stop to eat at **Spud Fish and Chips** (2666 Alki Ave SW at 59th Ave SW, 938.0606).

Queen Anne/Magnolia: Take the **Garfield Street** viaduct to **W Galer Street** in **Magnolia.** Follow W Galer to **Magnolia Park** (W Garfield St and Magnolia Blvd W), taking in the fantastic view along the way.

Turn left onto **Magnolia Boulevard** and continue to **Discovery Park** (bounded by W Emerson and W Cramer Sts, and 36th Ave W and Puget Sound). Wander through the park, stopping at the **Daybreak Star Indian Cultural Center** (285.4425) and the 19th-century **West Point Lighthouse.** Exit the park via **W Government Way,** which turns into **Fort Street** and, later, **Gilman Avenue W;** turn left and cross the bridge to **W Emerson Place.** Continue along W Emerson Place to **15th Avenue W,** passing **Fishermen's Terminal** on the way. Head south on 15th Avenue W (which eventually becomes **Elliott Avenue W**) and turn left onto **Mercer Street.** Take Mercer to the **Queen Anne Counterbalance** (Queen Anne Ave N between Roy and Galer Sts). Have lunch at the **5-Spot** (1502 Queen Anne Ave N between Galer and Garfield Sts, 285.7768 &) or dinner at the excellent **Adriatica Cucina Mediterranea** (1107 Dexter Ave N between Aloha St and Highland Dr, 285.5000) or **Canlis** (2576 Aurora Ave N at the south end of Aurora Bridge, 283.3313).

Ballard: Start out by visiting the **Hiram M. Chittenden Locks** (3015 NW 54th St between NW Market St and 32nd Ave NW, 783.7059), which is also known as the **Ballard Locks.** Leaving the locks, turn left, passing under the **Salmon Bay Bridge** and follow **Seaview Avenue NW** to the beach at **Golden Gardens** (end of Seaview Ave NW), where you can swim in icy water and watch sea lions frolic. After lunch at **Ray's Boathouse** (6049 Seaview Ave NW on Shilshole Bay, 789.3770 &) take **Ballard Avenue** to the **Ballard Bridge,** continuing across to **Fishermen's Terminal** (3919 18th Ave W off W Emerson Pl, 728.3395), where you can observe hundreds of ships moving in and out of the port.

Fremont/Wallingford: If your time is limited, spend it exploring the fascinating anachronism that is Fremont. Park your car along the canal on **N 34th Street.** Take a look at *Waiting for the Interurban,* then head north on **Fremont Avenue N,** poking into the **Daily Planet** (3416 Fremont Ave N between N 34th and N 35th Sts, 633.0895) and **Fritzi Ritz** (3425 Fremont Pl N at N 35th St, 633.0929) retro shops on your way. Stave off hunger pangs at the **Triangle Tavern** (3507 Fremont Pl N at N 35th St, 632.0880) or pick up an espresso at the funky **Still Life in Fremont** (709 N 35th St between Aurora and Fremont Aves N, 547.9850 &). Return to your car and drive east on **N 36th Street,** tipping your hat to the famed **Fremont Troll,** and cap off your time with a visit to **Archie McPhee's** madcap emporium (3510 Stone Way N between N 35th and N 36th Sts, 547.2467).

Green Lake/Greenwood/North Seattle: If you're an animal lover, spend the afternoon at the **Woodland Park Zoo** (5500 Phinney Ave N at N 55th St, 684.4800); if you're more interested in humans, the entire Green Lake area is great for people watching. In warm weather, sit on the grass at the edge of the lake and enjoy a treat from **The Urban Bakery** (7850 E Green Lake Dr N at Wallingford Ave

N, 524.7951). More substantial (and excellent) meals can be had at **Saleh al Lago** (6804 E Green Lake Way N between Second and First Aves NE, 522.7943 &), the **Santa Fe Cafe** (5901 Phinney Ave N between N 59th and N 60th Sts, 783.9755), or **Mae's Phinney Ridge Cafe** (6412 Phinney Ave N between N 64th and N 65th Sts, 782.1222 &).

University District/Ravenna: The choice here is simple: Spend your time on the **UW** campus. Go to the **Thomas Burke Memorial Washington State Museum** (NE 45th St between Memorial Way and 15th Ave NE, 543.5590), and then wander over to the **Suzzallo/Allen Library** (Central Plaza) and visit the **Graduate Reading Room.** From the library, walk southeast toward **Husky Stadium** (Montlake Blvd NE, 543.2200), passing the *Drumheller Fountain* along the way. If you feel like shopping, check out **The University Book Store** (4326 University Way NE between NE 43rd and NE 45th Sts, 634.3400), as well as the **Folk Art Gallery—La Tienda** (4138 University Way NE between NE 41st and NE 42nd Sts, 632.1796). For food, try **The Continental Restaurant** (4549 University Way NE between NE 45th and NE 47th Sts, 632.4700) or, for dinner only, **Toscana** (1312½ NE 43rd St between University Way NE and Brooklyn Ave NE, 547.7679) or **Mamma Melina Ristorante** (4759 Roosevelt Way NE at NE 50th St, 632.2271 &).

Eastside: With its village-like feel, **Kirkland** is the most walker-friendly town on the Eastside. Park your car in the downtown center, which is an easy stroll from beach parks, art galleries, restaurants, and elegant shops. Top sights include **Shamiana** (10724 NE 68th Pl at Sixth St S, 827.4902 &), a popular Indian restaurant; and the **Gunnar Nordstrom Gallery** (127 Lake St S south of Kirkland Ave, 827.2822), exhibiting noteworthy abstract art. If you're in **Bellevue,** check out the beautiful **Bellevue Botanical Gardens** (12001 Main St between 124th Ave NE and 118th Ave SE, 462.2749) or the **Bellevue Downtown Park** (10201 NE Fourth St at 102nd Ave NE); get a taste of the Christmas season at **Christmas House** (10230 Main St between 103rd and 102nd Aves NE, 455.4225); and grab a pizza at **Spazzo** (10655 NE Fourth St between 108th and 106th Aves NE, 454.8255).

123

Riddle House

M. BLUM

8 Riddle House Proving the diversity of architectural vision along Highland Drive is this 1893 Queen Anne–Shingle style residence (pictured above), with its colonial allusions and great rounded bows of windows. The designer was **E.W. Houghton,** who 15 years later would put his finishing touches on the ambitious **Moore Theater** downtown. ◆ 153 Highland Dr (at Warren Ave N)

9 Gable House This house of 14 gables was completed in 1905 by Harry Whitney Treat, an investment banker who came to Seattle in 1904. His first act—a confirmation of his wealth and stature—was to commission the firm of **Bebb & Mendel** (responsible for downtown's **Hoge Building** and the vast **University Heights Elementary School**) to design a Queen Anne residence that would accommodate his family of four, plus a domestic staff of 14, and would cost exactly $101,000.

Treat kept coaches and horses and a tallyho pulled by blooded steeds purchased from the New York Vanderbilts. Not content with his existing fortune, he bought hundreds of acres just north of Ballard, creating Loyal Heights (named after one of his two daughters) and establishing **Golden Gardens Park.** An acquaintance of Colonel William F. "Buffalo Bill" Cody, Treat had Cody's entire Wild West troupe come to Queen Anne Hill to entertain his daughter on her ninth birthday. It was also in this house that Treat and Cody planned the acclaimed Whitney Gallery of Western Art in Cody, Wyoming. Originally, 61 rooms occupied the 18,000 square feet of living space; it now has 15 private residential suites. ◆ 1 W Highland Dr (at Queen Anne Ave N)

10 Highland Drive Heading west from Queen Anne Avenue and about halfway up the hill, this elegant residential street reflects a variety of architectural styles in its mix of mansions and lovely brick apartment houses. For many years, beginning at the turn of the century, Highland Drive was *the* finest address in Seattle. One of the most prominent residents there was Alden J. Blethen, a bombastic former lawyer from Maine who'd entered journalism in the Midwest and lost a fortune there before moving to Seattle in 1896 to found the *Seattle Times.* So proud was Blethen of his pillared manse and the neighborhood in which it sat that for years he paid out of his own pocket to have Highland Drive gaslit every night.

Leisurely strolls are highly recommended along this route; at the end of Highland Drive notice the brick-in-concrete retaining walls at Seventh and Eighth Avenues, designed by W.R.B. Wilcox in 1913. The steps, railings, and lights are all part of the design. ◆ Between Queen Anne Ave N and Eighth Ave W

10 Ballard-Howe Mansion This stately white house, built in 1906, was designed in the Colonial Revival style by **August Heide,** whose larger-scale work can be seen in the **Lowman Building** at Pioneer Place. It now contains apartments. ◆ 22 W Highland Dr (between Queen Anne Ave N and First Ave W)

11 Victoria Apartments Built in 1921, this large, Tudor-style brick apartment building, enclosing a lovely, expansive courtyard, was designed by prolific architect **John Graham Sr.** It was later refurbished as Seattle's first condominium complex. ◆ 100 W Highland Dr (at First Ave W)

12 Kerry Park From this small, rectangular park, views of the **Space Needle,** downtown office spires, and Elliott Bay are stunning, day or night; the sight of Mount Rainier will take your breath away. Also worth appreciating: *Changing Form,* a steel sculpture of giant framed holes created by local artist Doris

Chase in 1969, and a seemingly out-of-place totem pole across from Kerry Park at W Highland Drive. ♦ 211 W Highland Dr (between Second and Third Aves W)

13 Black House Architect **Andrew Willatsen,** who worked in **Frank Lloyd Wright**'s Chicago office, designed this precisely lined residence (illustrated below), which was built around 1914. According to Sally B. Woodbridge and Roger Montgomery in *A Guide to Architecture in Washington State,* the home's "strong Prairie School character is revealed by the low-pitched, broadly overhanging gable roof, the band of second-story windows tied to a belt course, and the large, boldly framed ground-floor windows." ♦ 220 W Highland Dr (at Third Ave W)

14 Betty Bowen Viewpoint Tony Bennett would be the ideal musical accompaniment on a visit to this romantic spot at the end of Highland Drive. From here the views of Puget Sound, the Olympic Mountains, and the dying blaze of sunsets are unrivaled. The overlook was designed in 1977 by **Victor Steinbrueck,** the architect and preservationist who brought the **Space Needle** to concrete reality and fought successfully to save **Pike Place Market.** ♦ Seventh Ave W and W Highland Dr

15 West Queen Anne Elementary School This historic brick structure, with its whimsical medieval hints, was created in 1896 by the Seattle architectural firm of **Skillings and Corner** (responsible also for the **Old Main Building** at Bellingham's **Western Washington University**). It was used as a school until the 1980s, when it was converted into condominiums by local architect **Val Thomas** (who reserved the former gymnasium for himself). The building rests on lovely landscaped grounds in a neighborhood of residential grandeur. ♦ 515 W Galer St (at Fifth Ave W)

16 Queen Anne Branch Library On New Year's Day 1914, this library was opened in a festive celebration attended by more than a thousand people. *Seattle Times* owner Alden J. Blethen had contributed $500 to help buy the land, and the city kicked in the remaining $6,500. Pennsylvania steel-and-iron magnate Andrew Carnegie had donated the money for the building: $32,667. And a couple of prominent architects had been brought out to develop the handsome library in a style that might best be labeled English Scholastic Gothic: **W. Marbury Somervell,** who, along with partner **Joseph C. Cote,** already had the **Providence Hospital** in the Central District and the **West Seattle Public Library** on his curriculum vitae; and **Harlan Thomas,** best remembered for downtown's 1924 **Chamber of Commerce** building on Columbia Street.

During the library's first year, it circulated 71,623 books and became an active community center. Interior highlights include small-pane, leaded-glass windows, oak-panel doors with bronze mortise handles and locks, and stained-glass entry windows. *Quintet in D,* a vividly colored art-glass mural created by Seattle artist Richard Spaulding in 1978, hangs on the north wall. ♦ M-Th; Sa. 400 W Garfield St (at Fourth Ave W). 386.4227

17 Westside Stories This charming small bookstore sells new, used, and rare books on a wide range of subjects. While there is a large stock of books about art, history, travel, and biography, the fiction selection is especially good. ♦ Daily. 314 W Galer St (between Third and Fifth Aves W). 285.2665

18 Be Bop-A-Latte ★$ Coffee imported from Italy and unusually well-brewed *lattes* pack the patrons in at this handsome coffee bar (formerly **La Tazza di Caffè**), which also serves five kinds of *panini* (sandwiches), including the tasty *Fresca:* fresh mozzarella,

Black House

M. BLUM

tomatoes, and fresh basil on focaccia. Several malt-shop specialties, such as chili dogs, banana splits, and ice cream sundaes, have been added to the menu as well. ♦ Coffeehouse/Ice Cream ♦ Daily. 1503 Queen Anne Ave N (at W Galer St). 284.8984 &

19 Olympia Pizza & Spaghetti House ★$$ Perched at the top of the **Counterbalance,** this eatery offers 30 varieties of pizza, including the three house specialties: the Spiro (pepperoni, Canadian bacon, shrimp, mushrooms, olives, green peppers, cheese, and tomato sauce); the Olympia (sausage, Canadian bacon, fresh garlic, mushrooms, olives, onions, and fresh or cooked tomatoes); and the House Special (salami, pepperoni, sausage, Canadian bacon, green peppers, olives, cheese, mushrooms, and tomato sauce). Delivery is available, of course. ♦ Pizza/Takeout ♦ Daily lunch and dinner. 1500 Queen Anne Ave N (at Galer St). 285.5550 &

19 The 5-Spot ★★$
Local restaurateur Peter Levy has stretched himself here, developing a menu strong on regional American cooking. Some representative dishes: salmon linguine from the Northwest; shrimp enchiladas *con queso* (with cheese) from the Southwest; steaming bowls of smoked chicken and corn chowder à la New England; and, from the heart of Dixie, Hoppin' John (seasoned black-eyed-pea pancakes topped with sour cream and salsa). There's also a dynamite red-flannel hash served for breakfast and a different dinner special every day, dished up from 5PM "till it's gone." Portions are plentiful and the **Counterbalance Room** bar, set off near the kitchen, is a surprisingly peaceful place, rarely crowded. Weekend mornings, there's a line out the door for the dining room. ♦ American ♦ Daily breakfast, lunch, and dinner. 1502 Queen Anne Ave N (between Galer and Garfield Sts). 285.7768 &

20 Pasta Bella ★$$ Owner David Rasti has created a cozy decor in this restaurant, where deep, rich green predominates. A very pleasant deck enhances warm-weather meals (try to ignore the monstrous TV tower next door). *Linguine amatriciana* (fresh tomatoes, pancetta, chili, garlic, and wine), *linguine con vongole* (clams, garlic, wine, butter, and cheese), and *pollo piccata* (breast of chicken with capers, garlic, butter, and wine in a lemon-cream sauce) are highly recommended. The selective wine list is 80 percent Italian. ♦ Italian ♦ Daily lunch and dinner. Reservations recommended. 1530

Queen Anne Ave N (at Garfield St). 284.9827. Also at: 5909 15th Ave NW (at NW 59th St). 789.4933

21 Nelly Stallion If you are interested in wonderful unconstructed casual garments or designer suits and dresses, visit this specialty womenswear shop. ♦ Daily. 1622 Queen Anne Ave N (between Garfield and Blaine Sts). 285.2150

22 Queen Anne Avenue Books Alice Osborne and Randy Brownlee are the founders and owners of this fine small bookstore. It's a general interest store, especially strong on fiction, with a good selection of travel books, magazines, and children's literature as well. ♦ Daily. 1629 Queen Anne Ave N (between W Garfield and W Blaine Sts), Suite 101. 283.5624

23 Queen Anne Thriftway Seattle's first—and many would say its best—upscale supermarket boasts everything from an exceptionally good wine department, with depth in European, California, and Northwest labels, to an organic gourmet salad bar. The bakery section features French breads, croissants, and other fresh comestibles from the justly celebrated **Boulangerie** in Wallingford. The seafood department is likewise estimable, and the staff is helpful and friendly, even at 3AM. ♦ Daily 24 hours. 1908 Queen Anne Ave N (between Howe and Crockett Sts). 284.2530

24 Paragon ★★★$$ Talented chef Nancy Flume, a graduate of Seattle Central Community College's acclaimed culinary arts program and previously in charge of the kitchen at **Adriatica Cucina Mediterranea,** does the honors at this newly opened restaurant. Her style is to serve simple and traditional food with elegant, innovative touches. In a very short time, the place has become a local favorite, and the lively dining room can get crowded (and no reservations are taken, so the wait for a table can be long unless you come in the early evening). The menu changes frequently, depending on what seasonal ingredients Flume can find; popular dishes include grilled lemon chicken on a rosemary skewer and marinated flank steak. Decorated in fine woods and leathers, the room has a faded elegance that is completely charming. ♦ American ♦ Daily dinner. No reservations. 2125 Queen Anne Ave N (between W Crockett and W Boston Sts). 283.4548 &

24 Starbucks ★$ Here's yet another outpost of this granddaddy of the Northwest coffee revolution. Limited, uncomfortable seating discourages lingering, so order your *caffè latte*—make it a *grande*—to go. ♦ Coffeehouse ♦ Daily. 2135 Queen Anne Ave N (at W Boston St). 301.9477 &. Also at: Numerous locations throughout the city

TEACUP

25 Teacup Order a cup of tea from the counter at Mary Noe's charming shop, then place your bulk-tea order from a list of more than a hundred selections. She sells fine English marmalades and other imported goodies, too. ♦ Daily. 2207 Queen Anne Ave N (between W Boston and W McGraw Sts). 283.5931

25 McCarthy & Schiering Wine Merchants This is the second location for the friendly and knowledgeable team (the original shop is in Ravenna) who are as attentive to your request for a $10 Chardonnay as they are to someone else's interest in a case of Bâtard-Montrachet. The owners have built a state-of-the-art wine-cooling room, so you can order a case of Taittinger Blanc de blancs in the morning and pick it up chilled for the evening's dinner party. ♦ Tu-Sa. 2209 Queen Anne Ave N (between W Boston and W McGraw Sts). 282.8500. Also at: 6500 Ravenna Ave NE (at NE 65th St). 524.0999

26 Broadway Clock Shop Certified master clockmaker Roger Hewat moved his business from Capitol Hill some years ago but kept the original store's name. Browsing among the antique wall clocks and wonderful grandfather timepieces is like stepping back in, well, time. ♦ W-F 2-6PM; Sa 10AM-3PM; or by appointment. 2214 Queen Anne Ave N (between Boston and McGraw Sts). 285.3130

26 Pirosmani ★★★$$$ A cozy restaurant in a converted house, the kitchen dishes up Mediterranean-influenced cuisine ranging from the south of France to Tunisia. Food from the Republic of Georgia, a former state of the USSR, is also featured. Located on the Black Sea, Georgia is a southern clime, which is reflected in its cooking—recipes emphasize fresh herbs, as well as plentiful fruits and vegetables. One good example is the *badrijani* appetizer (slivered eggplant wrapped around a puree of walnuts, coriander, and garlic). Combination Georgian/Mediterranean plates are also served. ♦ Georgian/Mediterranean ♦ Tu-Sa dinner. 2220 Queen Anne Ave N (between Boston and McGraw Sts). 285.3360

27 Nancy's Sewing Basket Amateur and professional tailors alike will enjoy all the exotic silks, imported cottons, and designer fabrics for sale. There's even a separate **Ribbon Room,** with a sumptuous selection of brocade, embroidered, silk, cotton, and rayon ribbons from whisper-thin to six inches wide. ♦ Daily. 2221 Queen Anne Ave N (between W Boston and W McGraw Sts). 282.9112

28 Ristorante Buongusto ★★$$ Hailing from Naples, the Varchetta brothers, Salvio and Roberto, and Anna, Salvio's wife, operate one of Seattle's favorite Italian restaurants. The space, a former house, is warm and inviting. Dinner highlights include the superb *gamberoni alla brace* (grilled jumbo prawns with garlic, olive oil, parsley, and red pepper), *agnello alla griglia* (grilled lamb chops), and *linguine alla pescatora* (with shellfish and calamari in a fresh tomato sauce). Eggplant parmigiana and panfried calamari lead the list of appetizers. Choose from a strong selection of fine Italian wines. ♦ Italian ♦ Daily lunch and dinner. Reservations recommended. 2232 Queen Anne Ave N (at W McGraw St). 284.9040

29 A&J Meats In addition to the usual meat market offerings, this shop purveys convenient prepared specialties: Bavarian Rouladen (rolled beefsteak stuffed with onion, bacon, mustard, dill pickles, and sliced carrots), chicken Cordon Bleu, meatballs, chicken puff pastries, and more. There's a variety of fine sausages, too. ♦ Tu-Sa. 2401 Queen Anne Ave N (at W McGraw St). 284.3885

30 McGraw Street Bakery Bakers Mark and Debra Dubief turn out pastries, European-style desserts such as raspberry truffle brownies and fruit Danish, and bread from the brick oven in this storefront. Regular clients include **Nordstrom** espresso carts, some of the city's better supermarkets, and the Eastside's natural-food stores. It's a popular neighborhood hangout where regulars linger over a pastry, a cup of good coffee, and the house copy of *The New York Times.* ♦ Daily. 615 W McGraw St (between Sixth and Seventh Aves W). 284.6327

31 Queen Anne Hill Bed & Breakfast $ Mary and Chuck McGrew own this charming B&B situated at the top west side of Queen Anne Hill. There are three guest rooms upstairs, including one with a private deck which affords glorious views of the Olympic Mountains and the sunsets, and another that boasts the place's sole private bath. (The shared bath, however, is big and airy, and has a claw-foot tub.) There are two more bright and cheerful bedrooms downstairs. Common areas include a deck facing west, a cozy living room, and a small sun porch. The lovely English garden is a good place to relax. The full breakfast often includes croissants and quiche. The house is decorated with attractive artwork—from original works to posters. ♦ 1835 Seventh Ave W (at W Howe St). 284.9779

32 Cadiz Espresso ★$ The wall hangings and other art decorating the walls of this intimate coffeehouse are the legacy of owner Jean Villagas's extensive world travels. She believes in expressive art and real espresso; no coffee milk shakes here. The delectable pastries come from the **Uppercrust Bakery** in Magnolia. ◆ Coffeehouse ◆ M-F until 1PM; Sa until 3PM. 1905½ 10th Ave W (between W Howe and W Crockett Sts). 282.0779 ⓖ

33 Canlis ★★★★$$$$ Since 1950, Peter Canlis's restaurant—now in the capable hands of his son, Chris—has occupied a commanding position high above Lake Union at the south end of the George Washington Memorial (better known as the Aurora) Bridge. And the service is impeccable—from the moment you walk in, you'll be pampered by the kimono-clad waitresses (a **Canlis** tradition).

For an appetizer, try the Dungeness crab legs with mustard sauce and the lobster bisque. The place made its rep as a steak house, and many people think the cuts of beef here are the very best in town. The mahimahi broiled over Kiawe wood and the butterfly prawns with pork are other highly recommended main courses. And the ever-popular **Canlis** salad ("with no apologies to Caesar," as the menu says) is prepared at your table; pick up the recipe at the reception desk on your way out. ◆ Steak house ◆ M-Sa dinner. 2576 Aurora Ave N (at the south end of George Washington Memorial Bridge). 283.3313

34 Turret House This arresting residence is a multigabled, cedar-shake structure, complete with solarium, turret, and a widow's walk. In the 1970s this was the home of the commune of the controversial Love Israel Family. It's since been carved up into apartments. ◆ W Halladay St and Sixth Ave W

35 Seventh Church of Christ, Scientist Built in 1926, this impressive, if somewhat squat looking, red tile-roofed structure anchors the northwest corner of Eighth Avenue W and Halladay Street. It was designed in Neo-Byzantine/Early Christian Revival church style by the firm of **Thomas, Grainger & Thomas,** which a few years later created **Harborview Hospital** on First Hill. ◆ 2555 Eighth Ave W (at W Halladay St)

Contrary to popular opinion, the Queen Anne Counterbalance is not the steepest street in Seattle. According to the Seattle Engineering Department, the section of E Roy Street between 26th and 25th Avenues E has a 26 percent grade, while the Counterbalance's grade is only 18 percent.

Restaurants/Clubs: Red   **Hotels:** Blue

Shops/♥ Outdoors: Green   **Sights/Culture:** Black

Magnolia

36 Pandasia ★★$ Like its much-praised older sibling in northeast Seattle, this restaurant is known for relatively inexpensive, high-quality food, and fast, friendly service. Soup noodles, dumplings, buns, and sauces are made fresh daily. The Orange Beef (tender beef slices with an orange sauce) and Happy Family (stir-fried scallops, shrimp, and breast of chicken) specials are outstanding. Sit at the counter and observe firsthand the kitchen staff's skill. ◆ Chinese/Takeout ◆ Daily lunch and dinner. 1625 W Dravus St (between 16th and 17th Aves W). 283.9030; fax 283.2126 ⓖ. Also at: 7347 35th Ave NE (between NE 73rd and NE 75th Sts). 526.5115 ⓖ

37 Romio's Pizza ★$$ One of this chain's four Seattle locations, this joint is just west of **Burlington Northern**'s main railroad yard. It's a popular, busy stop, with a constant stream of deliveries going out the door. While all the pizzas are good, the Zorba (onions, tomatoes, Greek feta cheese, olives, and gyro meat with a housemade yogurt-cucumber sauce), and the GASP (an acronym for garlic, artichoke hearts, sun-dried tomatoes, and pesto) are the most memorable. ◆ Pizza/Takeout ◆ M-Th until 11PM; F-Sa until midnight. 2001 W Dravus St (between 20th and 21st Aves W). 284.5420. Also at: 8523 Greenwood Ave N (between N 85th and N 86th Sts). 782.9005; 3242 Eastlake Ave E (at Fuhrman Ave E). 322.4453; 917 Howell St (between Terry and Ninth Aves). 622.6878

38 Runions House Built in 1972 on a triangular site, this striking home was designed by Seattle architect **Ralph Anderson.** With its expanse of glass, wide eaves, decks, and fine integration with the natural environment, it represents a late flourishing of what's come to be known as Northwest Style architecture—a regional, mostly residential style that took root in the 1930s. Northwest Style was organic in nature and functional in form, drawing from modernism, common barn design, the early 20th-century Western Stick Style (itself a derivative of florid Victorian architecture), and even Japanese design. It was created by **Anderson,** along with Seattleite **Paul Thiry** and Oregon architects **Pietro Belluschi** and **Van Evra Bailey.** ◆ 2587 W Galer St (near 26th Ave W)

39 Elliott Bay Marina This privately owned state-of-the-art marina, located at the base of Magnolia Bluff, can accommodate 1,200 boats. An interesting mix of graceful old boats and sleek new yachts are moored here, some of them one hundred feet long. This is a select sight-seeing spot for all recreational sailors. ◆ 2601 W Marina Pl (at Elliott Bay). 285.4817

At the Elliott Bay Marina:

Palisade ★★$$$ Rich Komen, the man behind Restaurants Unlimited (**Triples, Palomino, Cutters Bayhouse**) never does anything without a splash. And this huge, high-concept, $4-million Polynesian restaurant is no exception. The main dining room, designed by interiors architect **Gary Dethlefs,** is a soaring space, complete with an elevated piano trellis and player piano. To get to it, you cross a 60-foot-long bridge over a 1,000-square-foot pool of seawater filled with Pacific Northwest finfish and shellfish. The 180-degree view spans the Port of Seattle grain terminal, past downtown, across Elliott Bay to West Seattle and Alki Point, and out to Puget Sound and the Olympic Mountains.

Fish, poultry, and meat dishes are prepared here in a variety of ways: from the wood-fired oven, searing grill, wood-fired rotisserie, or apple-wood broiler. Menu highlights include a shellfish chowder, Dungeness crab cakes, wood-oven roasted black tiger prawns, and applewood-grilled salmon (king or silver). ♦ Northwestern ♦ Daily lunch and dinner. Reservations recommended. 285.1000 ♿

Maggie Bluffs $ This cafeteria-style restaurant below **Palisade** specializes in grilled seafood, burgers, and breakfasts. Unfortunately, it is almost impossible to escape the TV, but those who want to catch the latest sports scores with their burgers will do well here. ♦ American ♦ M-F lunch and dinner; Sa-Su breakfast, lunch, and dinner. 283.8322 ♿

Elliott Bay Yachting Center If you've always wanted to lease a yacht—sail or power, 27 feet to 50 feet—you've come to the right place. Various options are available, and expert instruction is provided when you sign up. ♦ Daily. 285.9499, 800/422.2019 in Washington and Oregon

40 Smith Cove Park On the Elliott Bay waterfront between **Pier 91** and the **Elliott Bay Marina,** this small spot of greenery is a fine place to catch sea-level views of the harbor and watch the car-carrying ships docked at **Pier 91.** Two men played key roles in establishing this place, the more powerful being James J. Hill, of the **Great Northern Railroad.** After Hill muscled his tracks to Seattle in 1893, he constructed giant double docks at Smith Cove to service the steamers *Minnesota* and *Dakota,* which carried silk

from the Orient to be loaded onto trains in Seattle and shipped to East Coast markets. It was a lucrative trade until about 1940, when nylon replaced the demand for silk.

Smith Cove was taken over for a time by the US Navy, but the Port of Seattle bought it back in the 1970s and created this park, named for Dr. Henry A. Smith, who arrived from Ohio and built a log cabin here in 1853. A well-liked gentleman farmer, poet, and surgeon, known for anesthetizing patients through hypnotism and promoting the therapeutic use of dream analysis, Smith was King County's first school superintendent and a territorial legislator. He also supposedly translated Duwamish Indian Chief Sealth's famous 1854 caution to invading white men that their day of decline would come as surely as had the Native Americans'—a translation that became controversial in the early 1990s when questions were raised about its authenticity. The argument has not yet been resolved. ♦ 21st Ave W and W Marina Pl

41 Magnolia Park Take a break, enjoy the breeze and the quiet, and gaze up at the trees or out to the water—this is one of the most spectacular viewpoints in the city. It's also a great picnic site. Look for a small parking area on the boulevard's west side. ♦ W Garfield St and Magnolia Blvd W

42 Magnolia Boulevard This scenic route west of the Magnolia Bridge (it's called West Galer Street until **Magnolia Park**) is noteworthy for its distinctive madrona trees and views of Puget Sound and the Olympic Mountains. Heading west on the boulevard leads to Seattle's largest park, **Discovery Park.** ♦ Between 32nd Ave W and W Emerson St

43 Magnolia's Bookstore Thanks to owner Molly Cook, this neighborhood has a bookstore to call its own. There's a good selection of general fiction and mysteries, along with travel, self-help, cooking, reference, and other categories. A surprising variety of alternative magazines greets you up front, and more conventional magazines are found in the back of the store. ♦ Daily. 3206 W McGraw St (between 32nd and 33rd Aves W). 283.1062

When they were built by the Port of Seattle in 1915, Piers 90 and 91 below Magnolia were the longest earth-filled piers in the world.

44 Caffè Appassionato ★$ At this unusually handsome coffeehouse, the namesake beans are roasted on site, so the coffee could hardly be fresher. *Caffè latti* are consistently tasty, and the pastries, made off-premises by a "cottage-industry" baker, are also delicious. Lightly grilled *panini* (sandwiches)—including a variety with prosciutto, provolone, tomato, and fresh basil served on *schiaciatta* (Tuscany's version of focaccia)—make a satisfying lunch. A second, slightly larger store operates in Bellevue. ♦ Coffeehouse ♦ Daily; F-Sa until 11PM. 3217 W McGraw St (between 32nd and 33rd Aves W). 281.8040. Also at: Bellevue Square (NE Eighth St, between Bellevue Way NE and 100th Ave NE), Bellevue. 450.0886

45 Szmania's ★★★★$$$ Thanks to owners Ludger and Julie Szmania, Magnolia finally has a restaurant of the first order. Chef Ludger uses regional ingredients but reveals his German roots in the signature sauerkraut "à la Szmania," with smoked pork loin and homemade sausages. The imaginative dinner menu includes potato-crusted king salmon in black and green olive and pesto sauce, and roast duckling with balsamic onion confit and gorgonzola polenta. Some regulars opt to sit at the bar with a glass of wine and appetizers (try the blackened scallops and the risotto with mushrooms and asiago cheese). There's also a large outside deck, an unusual touch in these wet parts. ♦ German/Northwestern ♦ Tu-F lunch and dinner; Sa-Su dinner. Reservations recommended. 3321 W McGraw St (at 34th Ave W). 284.7305 &

46 Starbucks ★$ The tentacles of this company reach into every neighborhood. But the *lattes* are dependable. ♦ Coffeehouse ♦ Daily. 3320 W McGraw St (at 34th Ave W). 298.3390 &. Also at: Numerous locations throughout the city

46 Hot Cha Cha Interactive art reaches a boisterous high in this kinetic sculpture, created in 1987 by artist Kenny Schneider and located beside Fire Station No. 41. Seventy-seven identical stainless-steel firefighters, arranged in 11 rows, dance at a speed determined by turning a wheel on the sculpture's side, a peculiar ode to hand-cranked motion pictures of the early 20th century. The piece's name is a humorous allusion both to the movement of the figures and to the working environment of firefighters everywhere. ♦ 34th Ave W and W McGraw St

47 Catherine Blaine Elementary School Built in 1952, this school was designed by Seattle architects **J. Lister Holmes and Associates,** with **Robert Dietz** and **Charles MacDonald.** "An outstanding example of the large public school in the full-fledged post-war Modern idiom," enthuses *A Guide to Architecture in Washington State,* "with natural lighting through sawtooth skylights, antiglare ceiling baffles, window walls, and modular construction." ♦ 2550 34th Ave W (between W Smith and W Raye Sts)

48 Eleganza Ltd. Despite its obscure location on an alleylike street, this nationally known importer of fine statuary and museum reproductions is worth a visit. ♦ Daily; irregular hours on Saturday, call ahead. 3217 W Smith St (between 32nd and 33rd Aves W). 283.0609

49 Village Pub ★$ Popular for lunch, this friendly public house draws all segments of the Magnolia community: long- and short-termers, old and young, well-to-do and just barely squeaking by. Though it is known for its juicy hamburgers and "snowshoe fries" (huge, wide, and flat), the kitchen also turns out good fish-and-chips. ♦ American ♦ Daily lunch and dinner; bar until midnight. 2410 32nd Ave W (at W McGraw St). 285.9756 &

50 Magnolia Library Designed by Seattle architect **Paul Kirk,** this handsome modern institution occupies three lots that were acquired from the Catholic Diocese. **Kirk** used weathered cedar shingles and large plate-glass windows which would "bring the beauty of the outside inside." Clerestory windows face north to admit the best light for reading. Even the furniture is noteworthy: hand-crafted solid walnut chairs and tables that were made by Pennsylvania artist George Nakashima. Outside, a bronze sculpture by Glen Alps graces the courtyard wall; inside, you'll find a fused-glass screen by Steven Fuller, and two ceramic sculptures by Ebba Rapp McLauchlan.

The building was dedicated in 1964, and two years later won awards from the American Institute of Architecture, the National Book Committee, and the American Library Association. Despite those laurels, the library has not won unanimous neighborhood approval; occasional complaints about the "raw shingles" and "big, bare windows" can still be heard. ♦ M-Th; Sa. 2801 34th Ave W (at W Armour St). 386.4225

51 Discovery Park When Captain George Vancouver was exploring Puget Sound in 1792, he reportedly anchored nearby; the park is named after his ship, the *Discovery*. This is the largest park in Seattle, comprising 527 acres of richly varied terrain—woods, bluffs, beach, meadows, and trails. The farthest link in the 20-mile string of Frederick L. Olmsted's planned parklands built north and west from **Seward Park** on Lake Washington during the early 20th century, it is a haven for Seattleites desperate to escape urban forests of concrete and steel.

Walking or jogging along the 2.5-mile loop trail will take you through a quiet forest, across colorful meadows, and up to windy bluffs with panoramic views west to the sound and mountains. Follow signs for trails to the beach and to the **West Point Lighthouse,** a still-functioning lighthouse built in 1881. Bald eagles are a common sight here (you'll know where they are by the crowds of people milling about with their faces craned to the sky). In 1982 a cougar also turned up in the park; mercifully, restraint and sensitivity prevailed, and the creature was captured without harm. Picnic possibilities are endless and playing fields abound. ♦ Bounded by W Emerson and W Cramer Sts, and 36th Ave W and Puget Sound. 386.4236

Within Discovery Park:

Daybreak Star Indian Cultural Center
Built in 1977 on a piece of parkland leased for 99 years to the United Indians of All Tribes Foundation, this dramatic timbered building was designed by **Arai Jackson** in collaboration with **Lawney Reyes.** The place is filled with interesting works of art by Native American artists, including John J. Hoover's carved polychromed cedar panel, *Ancestor Spirit Boards; Buffalo Hunt,* a ceramic-tile mural by Glenn LaFontaine; and Marvin Oliver's painted and carved fir tree, *Bear and Raven.* There's also a small gallery of rotating Native American art, and the center sponsors a variety of Native American activities. Energetic children will delight in the well-equipped playground, and everyone will enjoy relaxing at the picnic tables and savoring the spectacular view. ♦ W-Su. 285.4425

Pining for Nature: Seattle's Lush Evergreens

Nature lovers who visit Seattle don't have to drive out to the nearby **Olympic Peninsula** or the foothills of the **Cascade Mountains** when they want to get their fill of forests; trees can be found all over the city. They fill the parks, line streets and freeways, and decorate the yards of private homes. And since most of them are of the evergreen variety, they can be enjoyed throughout the year. Below are several of the more common evergreens you'll see in and around Seattle.

Western Red Cedar
This tree has fibrous reddish-gray bark, scaly leaves, and drooping branches that overlap each other. The Salish carved the trees into totem poles, used the inner bark to weave clothing, and hollowed out the trunks to make seafaring canoes. Because the heartwood is rot-resistant, the western red cedar is used to make roofing material, fence posts, house siding, and outdoor furniture and decks.

Western Hemlock
Designated the state tree in 1947, the western hemlock has short, rounded needles and small cones. The graceful, lacy branches and drooping top make it easy to identify. Because it requires little maintenance, is drought resistant, and grows well in the shade, the tree is an especially popular choice to plant on parkland, and it's also used for lumber and pulp.

Douglas Fir
The cones of this tree, which range from three to four inches long, feature distinctive, leaflike brachts (protrusions). The needles are a little over an inch long. The Douglas fir's strong, durable wood is a mainstay of the region's timber industry, and the tree itself is frequently planted alongside freeways. It's also used as a Christmas tree.

Lodgepole Pine
Another popular choice for Christmas trees, the lodgepole pine sports one- to three-inch needles that grow in bunches of two. In this coastal area, the tree can grow as tall as 25 to 30 feet. As its name suggests, it has been used for poles; it's also good for lumber and pulp.

Western Larch
Unlike most evergreens, the clustered needles of the western larch turn golden as they get old and drop off in the fall. It is easily identifiable in the spring because of its bright green color, in contrast to the darker green of other conifers (cone bearers) around it.

Pacific Madrona
Even though it has neither cones nor needles, the Pacific madrona qualifies as an evergreen because its dark green, leathery leaves do not change color in autumn or fall off in winter. Technically, it belongs to the "broadleaf evergreen" category. The tree's unusual, smooth, reddish bark curls and peels periodically to reveal an avocado green underskin. Madronas often can be seen clinging to rocky outcroppings along **Puget Sound,** growing twisted and contorted like giant bonsai.

Ballard

Located north of the **Lake Washington Ship Canal** and extending west to **Puget Sound**, Ballard was once home to a settlement of Shilshole Indians. (*Shilshole*, meaning "tuck away a bit" in the Salish dialect, aptly describes old Ballard's protected position on **Salmon Bay**.) Concealed from raiding parties, the village's location served the natives well, and their population grew to about 1,000. But Ballard was eventually discovered and repeatedly attacked by northern tribes. By the beginning of the 19th century, the population of the village had dwindled to a mere dozen families. Enter Ira Wilcox Utter, who in 1852 filed a claim to become the first white settler at Salmon Bay, then an area of pristine beauty, with a virgin forest of giant thousand-year-old cedars. By 1870, 50 to 100 white settlers had staked claims in the area; before the decade was over, the logging of the bay's shore—which was to change this place forever—had begun.

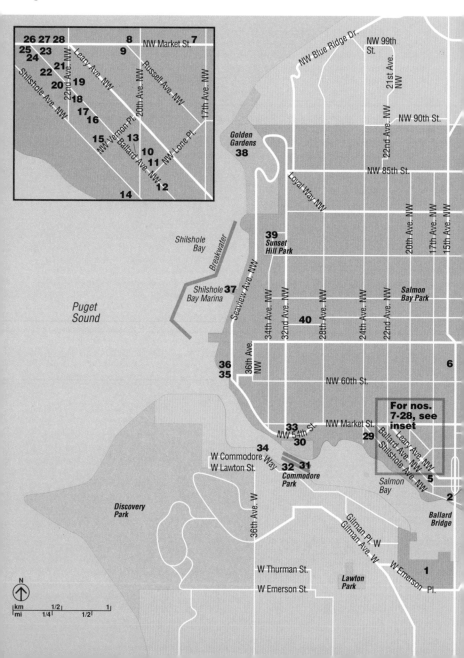

In 1890, with a population of 1,636, Ballard was the first community to incorporate as a city after Washington became the 42nd state. It started out as an industrial city with a predominantly Scandinavian population, boasting five shingle mills, three sawmills, a sash-and-door factory, a steel-and iron-works, a boiler works, three shipyards, a blacksmith shop, and a booming saloon district to service all of the workers. The sawmills provided much of the wood used to rebuild Seattle after the devastating fire of 1889. The mills clouded the skies with a blizzard of what was termed "Ballard snow"—air pollution dense enough to produce a "vast wall of smoke which makes an impenetrable barrier between the city and Salmon Bay," in the words of one frustrated photographer.

The waterfront was equally bustling: Salmon Bay had become a harbor for log shipping, the commercial fishing fleet brought in tons of halibut, salmon, and cod, and oceangoing ships docked at nearby shipyards for hull repairs. (Today it's still home to one of the largest fishing fleets in the world.)

By 1906 Ballard had more than 10,000 residents and was the seventh-largest town in the state. Such rapid growth brought inevitable problems, none more urgent than finding an adequate water supply. Annexation to the city of Seattle, which was eager to expand northward, became a hot topic. After a bitter, divisive battle, the citizens of Ballard narrowly approved the merger.

Separated geographically from the main body of Seattle, Ballard continues to exist very much as a small town within larger metropolitan boundaries. The community has managed to preserve its historic character while gentrifying its older sections. Young professionals are moving in, attracted to the abbreviated skyline, classic main street, unpretentious style, and reasonably priced housing. They describe their neighbors in the most generous of terms. "A typical native Ballardite," says one, "is a down-to-earth sort of person, careful with money but generous with friendship."

1 Fishermen's Terminal Owned and operated by the Port of Seattle since 1913, this terminal, located at the south end of the Ballard Bridge on Salmon Bay, is home base to more than 700 commercial fishing vessels, ranging in length from 30 to 300 feet. Here are the trollers, gillnetters, seiners, longliners, crabbers, and trawlers that make up the North Pacific fleet, one of the largest commercial fishing fleets in the world. Every year, Washington fishers harvest 2.3 billion pounds of fish and other seafood, more than half the total edible catch in the United States. The huge factory trawlers that moor at the terminal—some as long as a football field—catch 85 percent of the bottom fish taken in US waters. The moorage provides not only a good location for sightseers and photographers but opportunities to buy whole fish right off the boat. Take a peek at the bulletin board inside, advertising everything from Puget Sound seine permits to all manner of ships for sale, for a glimpse into the world of commercial fishing. ◆ 3919 18th Ave W (off W Emerson Pl). 728.3395

At Fishermen's Terminal:

Chinook's ★★$$ As you might expect, fresh Northwest seafood is featured—as is a wall-to-wall view of the fishing boats—at this popular addition to the **Anthony's Homeport** restaurant fleet. The grilled Copper River salmon (seasonal) is superb, and the mussels are fresh and flavorful. Right next door is **Little Chinook's,** an informal and inexpensive fish-and-chips bar under the same ownership. ◆ Seafood ◆ M-F lunch and dinner; Sa-Su breakfast, lunch, and dinner. 283.4665 ⅙

Bay Cafe $ Specialties of the house include a three-egg omelette of havarti cheese, bacon, fresh mushrooms, onion, and green pepper; and the grilled Alaskan halibut. If you're seated at a window booth, you'll be close enough to the fishing boats to read their registration numbers. ◆ American ◆ Daily breakfast and lunch. 282.3435 ⅙

Wild Salmon From Alaskan king salmon to Dungeness crab, the catch is always the freshest at David Leong's superb seafood market. One of the best in Seattle, this place will also ship anywhere in the US. The canned tuna here will make

you forget all about the stuff you buy in the supermarket. ◆ Daily. 283.3366

E.F. Kirsten Tobacconist Get a world-renowned Kirsten pipe and choose from a broad selection of pipe tobaccos, including the unusual Mariner's Mixture and Dutch Harbor Blend. The cigar humidor is as big as a walk-in closet. You'll also find a serious selection of knives, card decks, and flasks. ◆ M-Sa. 286.0851

Seattle Ship Clothing The heavy-duty outdoor gear sold here is designed for professional fishers. The Stormy Seas Clothing line was developed by commercial fisherman Michael Jackson after he had been swept overboard in Alaska's Bering Sea. ◆ M-Sa. 283.0830

Seattle Fishermen's Memorial The gathering point for the ceremonial blessing of the fleet, held annually in May, this memorial (pictured at left) was created by Seattle sculptor Ron Petty in honor of the 400 Seattle fishers lost at sea during this century; their names are inscribed on a plaque at the base. Dedicated 8 October 1988, the memorial is a bronze-and-concrete sculpture, with a variety of North Pacific marine life sculpted at the base and a lone bronze fisherman perched at the top.

2 **Mike's Chili Parlor** ★$ This little, red-brick place looks like a diner you'd see somewhere along Route 66. Mike Semandaris started out here in 1933 with a sidewalk stand, and the popular tavern is still owned by his family. The chili—beans on the side for nonpurists—is still good. The eatery was a featured location in filmmaker Bud Yorkin's 1985 movie *Twice in a Lifetime.* ◆ American ◆ M-Sa lunch and dinner. 1447 NW Ballard Way (at 15th Ave NW). 782.2808

3 **Bardahl Manufacturing Corp.** Manufacturers of the best-selling motor-oil additive Bardahl, this company was founded in 1939 by Ole Bardahl, a native of Norway. By 1952 the company was an industry leader in automotive and industrial additives. Today, it produces more than 100 oil and fuel additives, which are sold in 80 countries. The company's hydroplane, *Miss Bardahl,* has won five gold cups and six national championships, and has set numerous world records. The gigantic sign—"ADD BARDAHL OIL"—clearly visible from the Ballard Bridge, announces the company's location (and stature). ◆ 1400 NW 52nd St (at 14th Ave NW). 783.4851

4 **Le Gourmand** ★★★$$$ One of the city's finest French restaurants, this intimate dining spot is located in a nondescript building at the eastern edge of Ballard. Ingredients are fresh and the menu is limited so owner/chef Bruce Naftaly's kitchen can concentrate on—and unfailingly deliver—excellence. Roast duckling with black currant sauce and sautéed rabbit with chanterelles are a pair of aces in a

Seattle Fishermen's Memorial

M. BLUM

deck full of kings. The wine list is as selective as the menu items—and just as good. ◆ French ◆ W-Sa dinner. Reservations recommended. 425 NW Market St (between Fourth and Fifth Aves NW). 784.3463. &

5 St. Charles Hotel When it was built in 1902, this place, with its projecting bays and 100 feet of building frontage, was an imposing presence in early Ballard. Now painted an appalling lavender, the building is home to Ballard Mini Storage. ◆ 4714 Ballard Ave NW (between 17th Ave NW and NW 48th St)

6 Secret Garden Bookshop Named for the well-known story by Frances Burnett Hodgson, the oldest and best children's bookstore in the Seattle area carries hundreds of titles, many at bargain prices. There's a table piled high with toys, an inviting reading area, and a helpful staff. The shop sponsors weekly storytimes and regular book signings. ◆ M-W, F-Sa; Th until 8PM; Su 1-5PM. 6115 15th Ave NW (at NW 62nd St). 789.5006

7 The Old Pequliar Ale House The only thing peculiar about this place is the spelling of its moniker. Before it went *veddy veddy* British, it was known as the **Valhalla Tavern**—a tad more in keeping with Ballard's Scandinavian heritage. There is a good selection of Northwest brews on tap. ◆ Daily. 1722 NW Market St (between 17th and 20th Aves NW). 782.8886

8 Carnegie Library Raised in 1904 with a $15,000 grant from the Andrew Carnegie Foundation, this was the first Carnegie library built in King County. (A total of 10 were eventually erected in the Seattle area.) The structure was designed by local architect **Henderson Ryan,** and it served bookish Ballardites for nearly 60 years, until it was replaced by a new and much less interesting facility in 1963. Today, it hosts a nondescript mall filled with antiques vendors and a law firm. ◆ 2026 NW Market St (between 20th and 22nd Aves NW)

9 Ballard Firehouse Built in 1908, **Firehouse No. 18** was designed by the successful Seattle architectural firm of **Bebb & Mendel.** It served Ballard for 62 years before being replaced in the early 1970s by a new station just a few blocks away. Now a hot spot on the Ballard nightclub scene, this is a big space, with lots of room for dancing to the blues, country, reggae, and rock bands that play here nightly. You can also grab lunch or dinner; the kitchen features Italian fare. ◆ Cover. Daily until midnight. 5429 Russell Ave NW (at NW Market St). 784.3516

10 Cors and Wegener Building Once the grandest edifice in town, it had an elegant wine room on the ground floor in the 1890s and early 1900s, and the *Ballard News* occupied the second floor for years. One of the first of the city's old buildings to be renovated, it now has apartments on the top floor and offices along the street level. ◆ 5000-5004 20th Ave NW (at Ballard Ave NW)

11 Conor Byrne's Soccer Stadium This traditional Irish pub features the requisite dark-wood bar, stained-glass lamps, and brick walls. There's live Irish music on Wednesdays, Fridays, Saturdays, and Sundays beginning at 9PM. ◆ Cover. Daily until 2AM. 5140 Ballard Ave NW (off 20th Ave NW). 784.3640

Fowl Play

Northwesterners seem generally fascinated by the peregrinations of birds, and Seattle residents are no exception. On almost any weekend you'll see clutches of watchers bouncing high-tech binoculars on their chests or toting cameras mounted with lenses big enough to subdue a charging elk. Bird watching is best here in winter, when migrating species make the long flap down from the north in pursuit of warmer climes. But early and late summer aren't without their viewing opportunities.

The local Audubon Society recommends that bird watchers scope out **Lincoln Park** in **West Seattle, Magnolia**'s **Discovery Park** (where more than 150 bird species have been sighted, including red-tailed hawks, goldfinches, and ospreys), the **University of Washington** campus, and the **Washington Park Arboretum** (a stopping point—by last count—for some 200 species). Endangered peregrine falcons have been spotted in north **Ballard,** and another threatened species—purple martins—have been known to nest downtown, amazingly enough on the skybridge of **The Bon Marché** department store. Green Lake, in summer one of the best locations to espy the "red-breasted Coppertone slatherer" and the "oggle-eyed people peeper," is most attractive for birders in the winter. Mergansers, mallards, and other ducks swoop down from November through January to grab bread crumbs, as do the visiting Canadian geese on their migration southward. Bald eagles are also known to perch in trees above **Green Lake,** but they actually nest in **Discovery Park** and **Seward Park** on the west bank of **Lake Washington.** And, as is common with other port cities, sea gulls are ubiquitous in Seattle. Their screeches are as memorable as the blast of a ferry horn, and their flight patterns as familiar as the march of rain clouds.

If you have time for a day trip, about an hour's drive to the south, amidst the docklands near **Tacoma**'s **Lincoln Avenue Bridge,** is the **Gog-le-hi-te Wetland,** an artificial estuary inhabited by more than a hundred varieties of birds.

12 Ballard Avenue Named a Historic Landmark District in 1976, this seven-block stretch—slanting southeast off Market Street toward Salmon Bay—represents the heart, if not also the soul, of Ballard. It contains many of the community's oldest buildings (and newest businesses). The majority went up between 1890 and 1930: brick, stone, and stucco constructions of no more than two or three stories in height. Thanks to a shift of commercial development north to Market Street in the 1930s, these buildings were still sitting here, just waiting to be revitalized, in the 1970s. Pick up a "Historic Ballard Avenue Walking Tour" brochure, available from most avenue merchants. The **Ballard Historical Society** (782.6844) also conducts guided excursions, sometimes with docents in 1890s attire; call for schedules and reservations; donation requested. ♦ Between 17th and 24th Aves NW

13 The Junction Block Built in the late 1890s, this was once a three-story structure (now it's two), complete with elaborate turret, and one of the largest brick buildings on Ballard Avenue. It was a gathering place for locals, who held meetings and dances here. Today, the edifice is home to a community arts center which offers classes in printmaking, painting, and watercolor. ♦ 5202-5210 Ballard Ave NW (at 20th Ave NW)

14 Salmon Bay Cafe ★$ Hearty breakfasts draw a devoted clientele every morning and a lined-up-out-the-door crowd on weekends. Among the many egg dishes, the Ballard omelette—with bacon, cream cheese, green onion, and tomato—and the crab, shrimp, and green onion omelette topped with hollandaise stand out. You can also get eggs with steak or with Polish or Italian sausage. A side order of the huge french fries makes a satisfying meal in itself. ♦ American ♦ Daily breakfast and lunch. 5109 Shilshole Ave NW (at 20th Ave NW). 782.5539 &

15 C.D. Stimson Company Charles D. Stimson, the one-armed scion of a wealthy Michigan lumber family, arrived in Seattle just in time to help fight the Great Fire of 1889. When the nascent milling industry moved from what's now Pioneer Square north to Lake Union and Ballard, Stimson went with it and founded the huge Stimson Mill Company. This surprisingly modest single-story dark brick building was designed in 1913 in a modern English style by noted Spokane architect **Kirtland K. Cutter** (who also created the **Rainier Club** in downtown). It still houses the Stimson offices, although that company is no longer in the lumber business. The combination of declining markets and escalating tariffs sent Ballard's shinglemaking industry into a tailspin in the early 20th century and eventually forced the mill to close. The Stimson operation now leases commercial real estate in the Seattle metropolitan area and operates a pleasure-boat marina on Salmon Bay. ♦ 2116 NW Vernon Pl (at Shilshole Ave NW)

16 Cafe Illiterati ★$ Bobby Beeman's refreshingly idiosyncratic restaurant serves such specialties as grilled pork sandwiches with provolone cheese, red onions, and roasted peppers; hearty beef and chicken dishes; baked tomatoes stuffed with ricotta and spinach; bread pudding French toast; and cappuccino eggs—three eggs steamed using the steam wand on an espresso machine, with fresh herbs and cheese. The deck out back, cats and all, is a most inviting setting for weekend brunch. ♦ American ♦ M-F breakfast and lunch; Sa-Su brunch. 5327 Ballard Ave NW (between NW Vernon Pl and 22nd Ave NW). 782.0191

17 Jay White Law Offices This wood-frame structure is a combination of two pre-1890 houses, looking much like those that lined Ballard Avenue around 1900. In 1976 the Historic Seattle Society rescued the buildings from development in the International District and moved them to their present location. A bordello reportedly occupied the houses in their first lives. ♦ 5341 Ballard Ave NW (near 22nd Ave NW)

18 Guitar Emporium Owner Robb Eagle's merchandise ranges from fine inexpensive imported instruments to handmade acoustic masterpieces. He'll also recommend instructors—and offer encouragement—to would-be Segovias. ♦ Tu-Sa. 5349 Ballard Ave NW (at 22nd Ave NW). 783.7607

19 Sunset Building This three-story brick-veneer construction, with arched windows and decorative cornice work, was built in 1901. In the 1940s a local public market occupied the street level. The residential **Sunset Hotel** still takes up the upper floors. ♦ 5400-5404 22nd Ave NW (at Ballard Ave NW)

Within the Sunset Building:

Jones Brothers Meats Carnivores can buy everything from a 35-pound "pork package" (pork chops, ham, bacon, sausage, spareribs) to a side of beef—anywhere from 250 to 400 pounds—at this butcher shop. ♦ M-F. 5404 22nd Ave NW (at Ballard Ave NW). 783.1258

Seattle's contributions to the national music scene reach much farther back than Kurt Cobain. In addition to the notorious Nirvana lead singer, other famous local musicians include Quincy Jones, Kenny G, and Jimi Hendrix. Residents also point out that Ray Charles played several Seattle clubs as a teenager before moving on to LA and eventual stardom.

20 Portland Building Erected in 1901, this two-story brick pile was home to various well-established businesses—**Cascade Drug** and **J.C. Penney** among them—before Ballard's commercial district moved to Market Street. Taverns anchored the corner storefront for 40 years until its renovation in 1985. Now, a seafood trading company, picture frame shop, and hair salon occupy the ground floor; there are studio apartments upstairs. ♦ 5403 Ballard Ave NW (at 22nd Ave NW)

21 Ballard Centennial Bell Tower Ballard City Hall, built in 1899, stood proudly on this corner for more than 60 years. The three-story structure, one of the first on Ballard Avenue, included the usual administrative warrens and a jail, community meeting rooms and, on the top floor, a dance hall. There was also a bell tower, whose occupant—a 1,000-pound brass noisemaker—was saved when the building was torn down in 1965 after extensive earthquake damage. Thanks to efforts by former state senator Ted Peterson, who grew up hearing the bell, it has been returned to its original site and is now housed in a copper-capped cylindrical obelisk designed by architect **Thom Graham.** ♦ 22nd and Ballard Aves NW

22 Burk's Cafe ★★$$ The joys of gumbo and crayfish (in season) await at Terry Burkhardt's lively cafe. Spicy sausages, catfish, and exceptional pecan pie are likewise memorable draws. Try the mild pickled okra—there's a jar of it on every table. The building, erected in 1891 to house a tavern, was remodeled in 1968 to revive its wooden-frame origins. A serene fenced courtyard buffers the dining room from the sidewalk. ♦ Creole/Cajun ♦ Tu-Sa lunch and dinner. 5411 Ballard Ave NW (between 22nd Ave NW and NW Market St). 782.0091 &

23 Ballard Computer One of the largest computer retailers on the West Coast, this store sells laptops, PCs, notebooks, printers, software, books, cables and switch boxes, memory boards, templates, dust covers, and. . . well, you get the idea—the price list is 36 pages long. The knowledgeable salespeople welcome questions, even over the phone. The service department is in a separate building. ♦ Daily. 5424 Ballard Ave NW (between 22nd Ave NW and NW Market St). 781.7000

24 Ballard Smoke Shop $ It's not a smoke shop at all (although it is smoky inside) but a simple, old-fashioned restaurant (with a separate entrance to the bar), where you can still get an eight-ounce New York steak for $10. Built in 1903, this is one of the last frame structures left from Ballard's early days. Remodeled in the 1920s, it is now Spanish-style white stucco with a red-tile roof. ♦ American ♦ Daily breakfast, lunch, and dinner. 5443 Ballard Ave NW (between 22nd Ave NW and NW Market St). 784.6611

25 Scandie's at Ballard $$ This may be the only restaurant left in Ballard that specializes in Scandinavian cuisine. Look for such delicacies as *kokt torsk* (poached cod) and *friskadeller* (Swedish meatballs). ♦ Scandinavian ♦ M-W lunch; Th-Su lunch and dinner; Sa-Su breakfast, lunch, and dinner. 2301 NW Market St (at Ballard Ave NW). 783.5080 &

26 Olsen's Scandinavian Foods Everything from *rullepølse* (lamb sandwich meat) to *kransekake* (marzipan cake) can be found here. Erik Olsen took over from his parents Reidar and Ebba, who ran the shop for more than 20 years, and continues a line of homemade specialties, including outstanding lamb sausage, fish cakes, fish loaf, and smoked salmon. There are also imported foods, such as dry soups from Norway, Swedish peas, and cloudberries. ♦ Daily. 2248 NW Market St (between 22nd and 24th Aves NW). 783.8288

27 American Eagles Inc. A paradise for serious hobbyists, this store packs in precisely detailed train sets and models of virtually every airplane that's ever caught an updraft. ♦ M-Sa. 2220 NW Market St (between 22nd and 24th Aves NW). 782.8448

28 Ballard Building This four-story Second Renaissance Revival edifice—representing the only large-scale use of terra-cotta in Ballard—was erected in the early 1920s by the Fraternal Order of Eagles. Ballard's community hospital occupied the second floor from 1928 to 1954, with doctors' offices on the third floor. The second level now contains offices of the *Ballard News-Tribune.* ♦ 2208 NW Market St (at 22nd Ave NW)

Within the Ballard Building:

The Backstage A showcase venue for national acts, this basement club features live blues, rock, jazz, and folk. Get here early for a good seat. ♦ Cover. Th-Sa (call ahead for other nights); box office: M-F. 781.2805, box office 789.1184

Seattle gets 16 hours of daylight in summer, but only nine in winter.

Lombardi's Cucina ★$$ The former home of **Lafferty's Drugstore and Soda Fountain** (which moved—sans soda fountain, alas—to 5312 17th Avenue NW), this place serves such honest Italian cuisine as *gamberoni di scampi* (shrimp sautéed with garlic, capers, red pepper, white wine, and lemon juice). There's a select list of good Italian wines, moderately priced, and pleasant outdoor seating in warm weather. ♦ Italian ♦ M-F lunch and dinner; Sa lunch and dinner; Su brunch and dinner. 783.0055 ♿

29 Yankee Diner ★$$ This location on the Lake Washington Ship Canal is the third Seattle venue for the chain. The dinner menu features meat loaf, breaded veal cutlets, chicken-fried steak, Yankee pot roast, and roast turkey. Fresh seafood and daily breakfast specials are available, too. ♦ American ♦ M-Sa breakfast, lunch, and dinner; Su breakfast and dinner. 5300 24th Ave NW (off NW Market St). 783.1964. Also at: 1645 140th Ave NE (at Bellevue-Redmond Rd), Bellevue. 643.1558; 4010 196th Ave (at 40th Ave), Lynnwood. 775.5485 ♿

30 LockSpot Cafe & Tavern ★$ You can't miss this place, sitting at the northern edge of the **Chittenden Locks,** with its sign boasting the "World's Best Fish and Chips." The claim is open to debate, but the restaurant does have a long history here; it opened in the early 1930s to take advantage of traffic at the locks and along Seaview Avenue. There's a convenient take-out window. ♦ Seafood/Takeout ♦ Daily breakfast, lunch, and dinner. 3005 NW 54th St (off NW Market St and 32nd Ave NW). 789.4865 ♿

31 Hiram M. Chittenden Locks Completed in 1917, after decades of indecisiveness, legal delays, and government red tape, the eight-mile long Lake Washington Ship Canal—winding through the Ballard, Fremont, Wallingford, University, and Montlake districts—is a protected route connecting the saltwater of Puget Sound and Shilshole Bay with the higher-elevation freshwater of Salmon Bay, Lake Union, and Lake Washington. Attended by much fanfare, the locks were officially opened two months after completion of the canal, on 4 July, when the *Roosevelt,* flagship of Admiral Robert Edwin Peary's North Pole expedition, led a

procession of ships through the canal. In 1956 the locks were named for Major Hiram M. Chittenden, who, as Seattle's district engineer of the Army Corps of Engineers from 1906 to 1908, had chosen and designed the site for this project; locals also call them the **Ballard Locks.** The buildings were created by renowned Seattle architect **Carl Gould.**

In an average year, 100,000 commercial and pleasure craft, and two million tons of cargo and logs pass through the locks. People line up on weekend afternoons to watch the regatta rise and fall. The shorter of the two locks—150 feet long and 28 feet wide, with a wall 42 feet high—is used for small pleasure boats; larger vessels are "locked" through the bigger portal: 825 feet by 80 feet, with a 55-foot-high wall. Depending on tides and lake levels, the lift varies from 6 feet to 26 feet. ♦ Visitors' Center: daily; guided tours: daily 1PM and 3:30PM. 3015 NW 54th St (off NW Market St and 32nd Ave NW). 783.7059

At the Hiram M. Chittenden Locks:

Fish Ladder In 1976 this $2.3-million, 21-level fish ladder—connected by walkways to the locks—was opened on the south shore of the canal adjacent to **Commodore Park.** More than a half-million salmon, steelhead, and trout scale the ladder annually, bound for spawning areas in the Cascade range. You can watch (and even cheer on) their progress from an interior viewing port. In the mid-1980s sea lions, recognizing a feast when they smelled one, caused quite a stir with their extended stay near the fish ladder. Officials were determined to send them packing, and locals were equally determined that the creatures—known collectively as Herschel—not be harmed. After defeating a number of human (and humane) efforts to discourage them, Herschel was sent to California; undaunted, some of the sea lions turned right around and swam back home to Seattle. ♦ South shore

 Carl S. English Jr. Ornamental Gardens These lovely seven acres of lawn, trees, shrubs, and flowers—a thousand plant species in all, including palm trees—were developed from a handful of plantings in 1916. A fine spot for picnicking, the gardens are named for the man who, as head of the Corps of Engineers' gardening staff, spent 34 years cultivating them. ♦ South shore

32 **Commodore Park** Across the locks in the Magnolia neighborhood, this aptly named park is a secluded spot for picnicking underneath the trees while watching boats cruise by. ♦ Along W Commodore Way

The first live concert on the Internet was performed on 10 November 1994 by a Seattle-based rock band called Sky Cries Mary.

Hiram M. Chittenden Locks

33 Totem House $ Originally opened in 1937 as an Indian artifact shop, the building that houses this restaurant is a replica of an Indian *haiat* house (resting place). It became a fish-and-chips place during World War II, and that dish is still a specialty here, as is the homemade clam chowder. ◆ Seafood ◆ Daily lunch and dinner. No credit cards accepted. 3058 NW 54th St (at 32nd Ave NW). 784.2300

34 Salmon Bay Bridge Built in 1914 by the Great Northern Railroad (now Burlington Northern) to limit congestion along the Ballard waterfront and to handle the boat traffic from the locks, this imposing bascule bridge can be raised quickly to allow passage for big ships (and high-masted sailboats). Normally suspended, the bridge is lowered only for approaching trains. ◆ Just west of Hiram M. Chittenden Locks and Commodore Park

35 Ray's Boathouse ★★★$$$ Begun in 1946 as a coffee shop at a charter-fishing boat dock, this place has passed through several incarnations on its way to becoming one of Seattle's best seafood restaurants—and some say it's *the* best. The kitchen, run by executive chef Charles Ramseyer, makes good use of fresh regional ingredients, and both the steamed clams and the pasta with smoked salmon have won raves from food critics. So popular is the main-floor restaurant that you may want to head upstairs to the blond wood-and-glass cafe with a similar, but smaller, menu. Both floors have views of the water, the Olympic Mountains, and spectacular sunsets. ◆ Seafood ◆ Daily lunch and dinner. Reservations recommended at the restaurant; no reservations at the cafe. 6049 Seaview Ave NW (on Shilshole Bay). 789.3770 &

36 Anthony's Homeport ★★$$ With its waterfront location and plentiful outdoor seating, this restaurant is a great place for views of Puget Sound and the Olympic Mountains, especially at sunset. Fresh seafood is the order of the day, with cioppino a particular palate-pleaser. ◆ Seafood ◆ M-Sa lunch and dinner; Su brunch and dinner. Reservations recommended. 6135 Seaview Ave NW (on Shilshole Bay). 783.0780 &. Also at: Moss Bay Marina, 135 Lake St S (at Second Ave S), Kirkland. 822.0225 &; Des Moines Marina (Dock St between S 227th and S 222nd Sts), Des Moines. 824.1947; Edmonds Marina (Dayton St and Admiral Way), Edmonds. 771.4400; Everett Marina, Everett. 252.3333

37 Shilshole Bay Marina In 1950 the waterfront at Shilshole was not a pretty sight, what with its derelict ferry dock, scattered boathouses, vacant, untended land, a shipyard in decline, and what one writer derisively described as an "expanse of beach with a perimeter road that kept slipping off into the water." Today, after a 30-year effort to build a breakwater (completed in the early 1980s), the marina is the preferred moorage of Seattle's sailboat fleet; the waiting list to win berth space there is a mile long. The boat ramp is a terrific place to waste an afternoon watching boat owners curse their craft onto or off of trailers. ◆ 7001 Seaview Ave NW (on Shilshole Bay). 728.3385

Within the Shilshole Bay Marina:

Charlie's Bar & Grill $ Come early for a quiet waterfront breakfast, or enjoy a late afternoon drink while gazing at the sailboats and the sunset. ♦ American ♦ M-F lunch and dinner; Sa-Su dinner. 783.8338 &

Sharky's Beach Bar Dancing is the main attraction here, with traditional rock 'n' roll bands mounting the stage five nights a week. ♦ Cover. Tu-Sa 3PM-2AM; live music starts at 9:30PM. 784.5850 &

Wind Works Take a basic sailing course or (if you've passed the official qualifying course) rent a sailboat from this enterprise, one of Seattle's leading big-boat sailing schools. The friendly and helpful instructors, all US Coast Guard–licensed captains, teach on 28- to 40-foot crafts. ♦ Daily, but hours vary; call ahead. 784.9386

38 Golden Gardens Harry Whitney Treat, a New York investments mogul and real-estate mover, established this park soon after he moved to Seattle in 1904. Treat even built a special trolley line (the fare: 3¢) from downtown Ballard, which was later incorporated into the Seattle transit system. Much of this 95-acre reserve is covered in woods and crisscrossed with trails, but it is always the expanse of beach north of the marina—where Ballard families used to camp for weeks at a time during the summer—that receives the most attention. It's perfect for beachcombing, walking, or just looking out to Puget Sound

and breathing in what is arguably this city's freshest air. Windsurfers test their mettle nearby, in part because the sound is warmer than Lake Washington during the wintertime (but that doesn't mean it's comfortable—the water here is only for the hardy). Lawrence Beck's enamel and welded-steel sculpture, *Atala Kivlicktwok Okitun Dukik (The Golden Money Moon),* is at the park's south end. ♦ End of Seaview Ave NW

39 Sunset Hill Park From here, high above **Golden Gardens,** the unobstructed view is, in a word, spectacular. ♦ NW 75th St and 34th Ave NW

40 Nordic Heritage Museum Founded in 1979, this is the only museum in the United States that covers all five Scandinavian countries: Denmark, Finland, Iceland, Norway, and Sweden. Its emphasis is on the Nordic people who settled in the Pacific Northwest. Permanent exhibits include *Promise of the Northwest,* which describes life in early Washington, and *Ballard Story,* a richly detailed history of the community. The museum also offers Scandinavian language classes, lectures and films, and sponsors ethnic festivals. ♦ Free for children under six and on the first Tuesday of the month. Tu-Su. 3014 NW 67th St (between 30th and 32nd Aves NW). 789.5707

Lights, Camera, Action: Seattle on Film

New York and Los Angeles are both overused (and increasingly expensive) backdrops for films, so many directors have chosen to set their stories in the Northwest instead. And Seattle—with its unusual combination of gritty urban reality and beautiful natural settings—has been cashing in on this trend. In recent years, the city's multifaceted character has been highlighted in movies ranging from romantic *(Sleepless in Seattle)* to suspenseful *(Disclosure)* to family-oriented *(Free Willy).* Here are a few of the better-known theatrical and TV flicks shot in the Seattle area:

American Heart (1993) tells the story of ex-con Jeff Bridges, whose life changes irrevocably when his son comes to live with him. The two of them try to make a life together on Seattle's rough **Waterfront,** but Jack's dark past catches up with him.

Black Widow (1987) pits determined investigator Debra Winger against seductress Theresa Russell, who has murdered two previous husbands and is now in hot pursuit of a rich Seattle businessman.

The **Elliot Bay Book Company** and the **Olympic Hotel** can be seen, and the **P-I Building** stands in for FBI headquarters in Washington, DC.

In *The Changeling* (1980), a man (George C. Scott), whose family is killed in a car accident, moves to a lonely Seattle mansion that is haunted by a dead child.

Cinderella Liberty (1973) shows a shabby Seattle, a perfect backdrop for the troubled relationship between sailor James Caan and hooker Marsha Mason.

Disclosure (1994) In this film adaptation of the best-selling novel by Michael Crichton (author of such blockbusters as *Jurassic Park* and *Rising Sun*), a ruthless executive (Demi Moore) falsely accuses a colleague (Michael Douglas) of sexual harassment. Although somewhat implausible and a bit too jargony for its own good, this tale of corporate intrigue did stimulate debate about the controversial issue of sexual harassment. Some scenes take place in **Pioneer Square,** the **Four Seasons Hotel,** and the **Washington Park Arboretum.**

The Fabulous Baker Boys (1989) takes place in a jazzy Seattle, home o two piano-tickling brothers (Jeff and Beau Bridges) and the singer Michelle Pfeiffer) who joins heir act and changes both heir lives. It's worth seeing, f only for the spectacle of he seductive Pfeiffer, clad n a tight red dress, crooning "Making Whoopee" on top of Jeff Bridges's piano.

Frances (1983) is a aunting portrayal of 1930s lm star and Seattle native Frances Farmer (played by Jessica Lange, who got a Best Actress Oscar nomination). n a powerful performance, Kim Stanley portrays Farmer's unstable, domineering mother.

Free Willy (1994) This heartwarming hit is about a young boy who befriends a killer whale in an aquarium and helps him escape and return to his family.

The Hand That Rocks the Cradle (1992) tells the story of an embittered childless widow (Rebecca DeMornay) who seeks revenge against the woman who ruined her life (Annabella Sciorra).

House of Games (1987) stars Joe Mantegna as a gambler who fears he'll be murdered over a bad debt and Lindsay Crouse as a psychiatrist who becomes intrigued with his high-stakes world in playwright David Mamet's directorial debut.

It Happened at the World's Fair (1963) shows Elvis Presley eating dinner at the **Space Needle** and singing on the **monorail**. The plot is inconsequential a young cropduster wanders around the fair, woos a nurse, and breaks up a smuggling ring, but Presley sings some pleasant songs, including "A World of Our Own" and "Happy Ending."

Hype! (1996) is a documentary chronicling the rise of grunge rock in Seattle and its growing national popularity. It includes live performances by Pearl Jam and Nirvana, among other groups.

McQ (1974) stars John Wayne in a chasefest about a Dirty Harry–like cop who lives on a boat at the docks n **Fremont**. The seamier side of the downtown area s featured, as well as some lovely Washington Coast scenery.

The Night Strangler (1973) was a TV film that featured Darren McGavin as a rumpled reporter hot on the trail of a murderous member of the "living dead" beneath the streets of Pioneer Square.

An Officer and a Gentleman (1982) was shot in Seattle and **Port Townsend.** Richard Gere plays a loner and aspiring Navy pilot who tries not to fall in love with local factory worker Debra Winger, who in turn refuses to become pregnant to trap Gere into marriage. The second intense relationship in this story is between Gere and a strict sergeant played by Lou Gossett Jr.

The Parallax View (1974) tells the tale of a senator's assassination. Warren Beatty portrays a local reporter determined to get to the truth in Alan Pakula's **Space Needle**–hanger.

Say Anything (1989) is a touching coming-of-age story about a beautiful straight-A student (Ione Skye) caught in an uncertain world inhabited by an unlikely but supportive swain (John Cusack) and a benevolent but ultimately untrustworthy father (John Mahoney). The movie (directed by Cameron Crowe) is unusual in its three-dimensional portrayal of teenagers.

Singles (1992) stars Campbell Scott, Bridget Fonda, and Matt Dillon. Director Cameron Crowe's second film, this disarmingly sweet-spirited tale of twentysomething love is set amidst Seattle's grunge-rock scene, with appearances by members of Pearl Jam and Soundgarden. Matt Dillon's character works at the **OK Hotel Cafe/Gallery.**

Sleepless in Seattle (1993) A paean to the classic weeper *An Affair to Remember,* this mega-hit romance (written and directed by Nora Ephron) features Tom Hanks as a lonely man who moves to Seattle in an attempt to recover from the death of his wife. Meg Ryan also stars as a woman who hears Hanks on a nationally syndicated radio show and decides to travel across the country to meet him. Hanks and his young son live on a houseboat on **Lake Union.**

The Slender Thread (1965) A **University of Washington** psychology student (Sidney Poitier) working at a suicide hotline fields a call from a desperate woman (Anne Bancroft). Director Sydney Pollack's first movie, it was filmed at the university, **Capitol Hill, Ballard,** and the downtown area.

Trouble in Mind (1985) is a not-quite-futuristic yarn with Kris Kristofferson as an ex-cop and ex-con trying to remake his life in "Rain City," a Seattle of the imagination, in which the former **Seattle Art Museum** building on Capitol Hill becomes the mansion of an arch-gangster. Much of the action is set in the **Kingdome.**

Tugboat Annie (1933) stars Marie Dressler and Wallace Beery. The film was inspired by Norman Reilly Raine's popular "Tugboat Annie" stories of the 1930s, which were in turn inspired by the tale of Thea Foss, who, operating from **Tacoma** in the late 19th century, began one of the country's largest tugboat empires.

Twice in a Lifetime (1985) is one of the few movies to accurately portray Seattle's blue-collar community. Gene Hackman plays a middle-aged husband who creates a family crisis when he falls in love with a young barmaid (Ann-Margret). Ellen Burstyn, Amy Madigan, and Ally Sheedy also star. **Mike's Chili Parlor** in Ballard is prominently featured.

Fremont/Wallingford

The two neighborhoods to the north and west of **Lake Union** were once suburban, but today Fremont and Wallingford are about as citified as they can get without actually having highrises in their midst. In fact, Fremont is home to one of the city's most popular public works of art, *Waiting for the Interurban,* a sculpture reflecting that ultimate urban experience—public transportation. Both areas are filled with funky shops, friendly taverns, and inexpensive restaurants, and teem with traffic. (In a tizzy over parking congestion caused by Wallingford's popularity, residents have won restrictions that make it near impossible to park within a quarter-mile of a given destination on a Friday or Saturday night.)

Fremont was originally a mill town, plotted first as the **Denny-Hoyt Addition** in 1888, where sawmills operated until 1932. Wallingford was stitched together from the rural communities of **Latona** and **Edgewater**—an area that once supported dairies, a furrier, and a candy store that made Easter eggs to order. In 1907 the Seattle Gas Company plant opened on Lake Union and transformed Wallingford into a working-class district showered with sparks and soot from the burning of coal. The gasworks shut down in 1956, and 25 years later were transformed in the high-tech **Gas Works Park.**

Today both neighborhoods come across as confident and cool, with a long history of protest and civic activism, although Fremont is by far the more adical of the two. In the late 1970s, Fremont declared itself one of the city's earliest Nuclear-Free Zones—no nuclear waste or power plants here. More recently, on 18 June 1994, it also "seceded" from Seattle, Washington State, and the rest of the country, calling itself "The Republic of Fremont, Center of the Known Universe." Wallingford, which plays the civil, quiet sibling to the rebellious republic, has defended itself successfully against urban blight and low-flying seaplanes, in addition to blocking the assembly of an enormous set of Golden Arches on the local **McDonald's.** It's clear that both districts have a strong sense of their own identities and are determined to protect themselves from the ravages of unnecessary "progress."

Fremont

1 Ponti Seafood Grill ★★$$ The location—right on the south lip of the Lake Washington Ship Canal, with a direct watch on the tiny blue-and-orange Fremont Bridge—cries out for a restaurant with big windows. And that's exactly what owners Jim Malevitsis (of **Adriatica Cucina Mediterranea**) and Richard and Sharon Malia created in this upscale establishment. Chef Alvin Binuya offers wonderfully fresh seafood salads, and the dishes are often influenced by Mediterranean or Asian cooking styles. One gripe is the stingy portion sizes of the appetizers; a serving of peppered tuna, for instance, could hardly satisfy a squirrel, much less a hungry human. The wine list is on the expensive side, and service can be slow when the house is packed. In summer ask for seating on the porch, where the views compensate for the restaurant's few deficiencies. ♦ Northwestern/Seafood ♦ M-Sa lunch and dinner; Su brunch and dinner. Reservations recommended. 3014 Third Ave N (at Nickerson St). 284.3000 ♿

2 Vertical World Practice your mountaineering technique on this gym's 11,000 feet of indoor climbing walls. Established in 1987, the facility, which is regarded by knowledgeable locals as the top indoor rock gym in America, gives participants the opportunity to lead, top rope, and boulder via 100 different routes on the 35-foot-high walls. Day passes are available, and instruction is extra. A complete line of climbing gear is also sold here. ♦ 755 N Northlake Way, Suite 100 (under the Fremont Bridge). 632.3031

3 Waiting for the Interurban The first work created by local artist Richard Beyer, this sculpture portrays a motley clutch of people anticipating the approach of a bus or train.

Installed in 1978, the popular cast-aluminum tableau is decorated appreciatively through the seasons, making it one of the most interactive pieces of art in the country. Beyer, who has lived in Seattle since 1957, is also responsible for a number of other works around town, including the wooden *Sasquatch* at **Pike Place Market;** *The Itinerant,* which portrays a newspaper-draped man sleeping on a bench in Capitol Hill's Broadway district; and the *Kingstones,* a takeoff on the cartoon Flintstone family, with a mom, dad, and kids sitting around the television set in front of the **KING-TV** studios on Dexter Avenue N. ♦ Fremont Ave N and N 34th St

4 Frank and Dunya Here's the place to shop for colorful and sometimes outrageous home furnishings and accessories made by local artists. Canines are popular motifs in the statuary, jewelry, and hangings, but so are other members of the wild kingdom—a two-legged drinking cup painted like a cow, or a huge green frog perfect for mounting on your dining room wall. ♦ Daily. 3418 Fremont Ave N (between N 34th and N 35th Sts). 547.6760

4 The Daily Planet Fremont has a rep as the North End's vintage and retro capital, thanks to places such as this one, dense with old lamps, fans, hats, clocks, mirrors, globes, and even a motorbike or two. Daily. 3416 Fremont Ave N (between N 34th and N 35th Sts). 633.0895

5 Red Door Ale House One of several upscale groggeries in Fremont, this is the neighborhood's best-known and most crowded after-work hangout. (Don't even *try* to get in on a Friday night.) The least claustrophobic seating can be found on a small back deck. Inside, try for a bar seat—no easy task. Twenty-one beers are on tap, and there's a small menu which is strongest on steamed mussels, burgers, and french fries. ♦ Daily until 2AM. 3401 Fremont Ave N (at N 34th St). 547.7521 &

5 Fremont Sunday Market On Sundays a parking lot behind the **Red Door Ale House** fills up with vendors of jewelry, pottery, produce, and hot dogs. In classically lowbrow Fremont fashion, there are also people here selling recycled castoffs—old radios and books, used videotapes, clothes, shoes, and lamps. Musicians provide entertainment, as do the shoppers themselves, a cross section of hippie holdouts and slumming stockbrokers. ♦ Su May-Dec. 670 N 34th St (between Fremont and Evanston Aves N)

6 Fremont Antiques Mall The entrance is at street level, but the goods—collectible toys and appliances, along with some larger antique furniture—are in the basement of this mall, built in 1901. Take a nostalgic browse. ♦ Daily. 3419 Fremont Pl N (between Fremont Ave N and N 35th St). 548.9140

6 Fritzi Ritz A Marlene Dietrich fantasy of a vintage store where you'll find feathered boas and sequined dresses on display. Well-preserved wing-tip shoes and fedoras wait for Fred Astaire to waltz through the door. ♦ Daily. 3425 Fremont Pl N (at N 35th St). 633.0929

6 Simply Desserts Some of the baked delights you've enjoyed at several of the more upscale movie theaters around town can now be savored with a cup of espresso from this dinky outlet store. The white-chocolate strawberry cake is outstanding. ♦ Daily; F-Sa until 11:30PM. 3421 Fremont Ave N (at N 35th St). 633.2671

6 Fremont Place Book Company For a small shop, this general bookstore carries a lot of feminist and ecological titles, as well as a good selection of regional literature. ♦ Daily. 621 N 35th St (at Fremont Pl N). 547.5970 &

7 Still Life in Fremont ★$ This unpretentious coffeehouse once epitomized the hippie attitude of Fremont. Well, the 1960s may be long gone, but this anachronism continues to serve some of the better cafe grub in town: Pasta specials are usually terrific, soups are chunky, and sandwiches are thick and savory. The sidewalk seating is pleasant—much better than enduring the interior stagnation in summer. And it's a quiet spot for coffee drinking. There is jazz or folk music some Thursday nights from 8 to 10PM; call ahead for the schedule. ♦ Vegetarian ♦ Daily breakfast, lunch, and dinner. 709 N 35th St (between Aurora and Fremont Aves N). 547.9850 &

8 Guess Where There's something classy about this retro resource—from the winged cherubs in the front windows to the statuary that looks as if it's waiting to decorate some dear departed's grave. Take a look at the wide array of vintage men's shoes and suits, now back in style. ♦ M, Th-Su; Tu-W noon-6PM. 615 N 35th St (between Fremont and Evanston Aves N). 547.3793

9 Triangle Tavern ★★$ Some of the ancient pensioners who knew this place as the **Classic** may have trouble getting used to its new 1990s look. Odd-shaped tiles crawl up the support pillars; old phones dangle from the walls; the dining room ceiling has an earthquake-distressed look. It's a hip spin on the traditional tavern—"Cheers" by way of MTV. Lots of bar-type grub is offered on the menu, from mediocre burgers to spinach lasagna to pizzas big enough for two. The broad pick of beers specializes in West Coast craft varieties. ♦ American ♦ Restaurant: daily lunch and dinner. Bar: until 2AM. 3507 Fremont Pl N (at N 35th St). 632.0880

10 Deluxe Junk A stock of mid-20th century clothing (which rotates seasonally), furniture, housewares, and stacks of kitschy doodads are all on display in a onetime funeral parlor. ♦ Daily. 3518 Fremont Pl N (between N 35th and N 36th Sts). 634.2733

11 Redhook Ale Brewery Seattle's first microbrewery has an unusual setting: Fremont's 1905 Seattle Electric Company streetcar barn. Trolleys used to roll out of this building on their various routes, but when the city converted to trackless trolleys in 1940, the barn went first to the US Army for use as a wartime warehouse and later to a garbage company. Paul Shipman and Gordon Bowker, owners of the Redhook beer company, ultimately bought the barn and commissioned architect **Skip Satterwhite** to turn it into a brewery, which opened in 1988. ♦ Fee. Daily one-hour tours; call for times. 3400 Phinney Ave N (at N 34th St). 548.8000

Within the Redhook Ale Brewery:

Trolleyman Pub As expected, all Redhook brews are on tap at this tavern, from the ESB (extra special bitter) to the Blackhook porter and the seasonal Winterhook Christmas Ale. It's a bit harshly decorated for a pub—all white walls and neatly arranged tables—but it has cozy elements too, like a good-sized fireplace and a piano. Live jazz and blues music is performed on Monday and Saturday nights. The snack menu is small, highlighted by black-bean burritos served with two cheeses, sour cream, and salsa. ♦ M-Sa until midnight; Su. 548.8000 &

It's About Time

Seattle is laid-back by reputation, a major city with the easygoing attitude of a small town. Its residents are hardly clock watchers, and many people visit (for short and long stays alike) precisely because the city is so free of the stress and pressures of large metropolises. So why are there so many street clocks here? Seattle proper boasts 13 of them—more than any other city in the country. These cast-iron timepieces weigh an average of a ton apiece, and some of them are as tall as 20 feet. People bump into them, lean against them to tie their shoes, use them as handy meeting spots, and sometimes even check their watches by them.

Originally these clocks were to jewelers what red-and-white-striped poles were to barbershops. Most of them were made by **Mayer and Co.**, whose factory was on **Dexter Avenue N.** They became popular in 1913, when **Carroll's Fine Jewelry** set one up on the sidewalk outside its shop on **Fourth Avenue** (where it still stands today). Other jewelers followed suit, and eventually shopping plazas, bookstores, and restaurants got into the act as well.

Though Seattleites are now passionately fond of their street clocks, they have not always felt that way. In 1953, convinced that the 28 clocks in the downtown area were a nuisance and a public hazard, the Board of Public Works proposed a measure to abolish them. Clock lovers and historians fought back, and finally a compromise was reached: The clocks could remain, provided they were kept to the proper time. The task of checking the clocks' time each morning fell to the jewelers, who were less than pleased with this new responsibility. Many of the clocks ended up being moved to the backyards of

private homes or banished to scrap heaps. Their number dwindled to 11 by 1980, when the city council suddenly woke up to the historical value of the clocks and began the process of registering them as official landmarks. Ten of them eventually were so designated, and in the ensuing years two new ones were built and a third was moved to downtown Seattle from the nearby suburb of **Kirkland.**

The designs range from whimsical to kitschy to elegant. The **Hickory Dickory Clock** in front of the **1201 Third Avenue Building** (between Seneca and University Sts) has two small mice running up a column that leans crazily to one side. The modern clock that stands in front of **Jay Jacobs** (1530 Fifth Ave at Pine St) looks as if its face is being yanked around by the giant crescent wrench that makes up its column. The clock in front of the **West Earth Company** (406 Dexter Ave N between Harrison and Republican Sts) near **Seattle Center** is painted a rather garish red, and the clock in front of **Carroll's Fine Jewelry** (1427 Fourth Ave at Pike St) sports lamp fixtures that look like antlers.

Other noteworthy timepieces in the downtown area are at **Ben Bridge Jewelers** (Fourth Ave and Pine St) and **Century Square** (1529 Fourth Ave between Pike and Pine Sts). In **Pioneer Square,** there are clocks at **F.X. McRory's** (419 Occidental Ave S at S King St) and the **Elliott Bay Book Company** (101 S Main St at First Ave S). Other examples in the area include clocks outside **Greenwood Jewelers** (129 N 85th St between Greenwood Ave N and First Ave NW, Greenwood), the **Lake Union Cafe** (3119 Eastlake Ave E at E Allison St, Capitol Hill), and **Menashe & Sons Jewelers** (4532 California Ave SW between SW Alaska and SW Oregon Sts, West Seattle).

MICHAEL STORRINGS

12 Fremont Public Library This was the last of 10 Carnegie-financed libraries raised in the Seattle area during the early 20th century. Money for construction—$35,000—had been promised from the Carnegie Corporation in 1917, but work didn't get underway until after World War I, and the library didn't open until 1921. **Daniel R. Huntington,** for many years Seattle's city architect, designed this excellent neighborhood library in an echo of California Mission style. ♦ M-Sa. 731 N 35th St (between Aurora and Fremont Aves N). 684.4084

13 Fremont Troll Come face to face with a Brothers Grimm nightmare: the crook-nosed, long-haired, malevolent looking troll that hides beneath the north end of the Aurora Bridge (waiting for the Three Billy Goats Gruff?). Constructed in 1990 of ferroconcrete, with a real Volkswagen Bug squeezed in its left hand, the 18-foot-high sculpture was a whimsical

community project from the Fremont Arts Council, built with money from the Seattle Neighborhood Matching Funds Program. Adults and children seem equally ready to climb all over it. ♦ Heading east on N 34th St, turn left up the hill under the Aurora Bridge

14 Aurora Bridge Nobody uses its proper name—George Washington Memorial Bridge—and most don't even know it. (The bridge's 1932 dedication to the first US President can only be found on a plaque at its south end, not on regular city maps.) And sometimes this span is referred to as Suicide Bridge because of the number of people (an average of three per year) who leap from its 135-foot height into Lake Union below. The sidewalk across is narrow; walk at your own risk and never on rainy days, when taking a bath in your clothes would leave you less soaked than the speeding traffic does. ♦ Aurora Ave N (over Lake Union)

The Word Out West

Seattle is a bibliophilic town. Nationally, the average per-household expenditure for books is $50 a year. Here, it's about double that. Meanwhile, Seattle public libraries loan out more volumes per capita than any other system in the country. Noteworthy authors—including the likes of Norman Mailer, Terry McMillan, Carlos Fuentes, Philip Roth, Jill Eisenstadt, and Robert B. Parker—cycle through town for readings or book signings, and the **Seattle Arts and Lectures Series** schedules about half a dozen famous writers annually for lectures and special events (call 621.2230 for schedule and registration). In addition, a number of nationally recognized authors—including Mark Helprin, Jonathan Raban, and Pete Dexter—have relocated to Puget Sound country.

Is Seattle's bookwormish tendency attributable to high standards in local education? Or can it be traced simply to the number of inclement days that send waterlogged residents inside to the comfort of their reading lamps? Whatever the reason, the publishing industry has benefited. Counting the number of bookstores per person, Seattle ranks seventh in the nation (San Francisco tops the list).

A number of useful guidebooks and historical studies have evolved with Seattle's increasing popularity. The city has also become a popular setting for detective novels. However, there is still nothing that can be pointed to as the quintessential Seattle Novel—nothing that acutely captures the spirit and essence of the city. The local literati await. For the time being, however, here are some must-reads on the city of Seattle.

Nonfiction

Bertha Knight Landes of Seattle: Big City Mayor, by Sandra Haarsagen (1994, University of Oklahoma Press). A biography of Seattle's—and America's—first woman mayor, elected in the 1920s.

Calabash: A Guide to the History, Culture, and Art of African-Americans in Seattle and King County, Washington, by Esther Hall Mumford (1993, Ananse Press). Informative and well-written, this book offers a perspective of the African-American community in this area.

The Good Rain: Across Time and Terrain in the Pacific Northwest, by Timothy Egan (1990, Alfred A. Knopf). Prepare to enjoy an eminently readable and not-too-egregiously romanticized take on the Northwest's beauty and blemishes by *The New York Times*'s local bureau chief.

Jackson Street After Hours: The Roots of Jazz in Seattle, by Paul De Barros (1993, Sasquatch Books). A fascinating, often humorous take on the rise of jazz music in the city, with plenty of photographs.

Impressions of Imagination: Terra-Cotta Seattle, edited by Lydia S. Aldredge (1986, Allied Arts of Seattle). Spend a few hours flipping through this handsome, essay-filled encomium to Seattle's days as a white city on the **Sound.** It offers a wonderful architectural history.

Meet Me at the Center, by Don Duncan (1992, Seattle Center Foundation). An entertaining former *Seattle Times* writer looks back at the 1962 World's Fair and forward to the future of the site that has become the **Seattle Center.**

Out Here, by Andrew Ward (1991, Penguin). A Bainbridge Islander and lighthearted commentator with National Public Radio draws his sights on beggars, road-kill dogs, and other local exotica.

The Natural History of Puget Sound Country, by Arthur Kruckeberg (1995, University of Washington Press). Beginning with the shaping of the land by glacial activity in the ice age and volcanic eruptions later on, this book discusses the natural attributes of the region, including flora and fauna, climate, and the current ecosystem. Lavishly illustrated and clearly written, it's a fascinating read.

Seattle in the Twentieth Century, Volumes I and II, by Richard C. Berner (1991, 1992; Charles Press). If you want to find out the city's population in any year from 1900 to 1940 or brush up on political machinations in early Seattle, these are the pages to start scanning. *Volume I,* "From Boomtown, Urban Turbulence, to Restoration," covers 1900 to 1920; *Volume 2,* "From Boom to Bust," dissects 1921 to 1940.

Seattle Emergency Espresso, by Heather Doran Barbieri (1992, Alaska Northwest). A handy drinking companion in a town that cares beans about coffee, this guide designates the best and most convenient neighborhood java stops, plus the meaning of such local terminology as the "double tall skinny billiard ball" (a tall *latte* made with one percent or nonfat milk, without foamed milk on top).

Skid Road, by Murray Morgan (1978, Comstock). Morgan's book is an irreverent, insightful, often embarrassingly candid parsing of Seattle history. No one who wants to know about this area's past should be without this book.

Fiction

Fish Story, by Richard Hoyt (1985, Viking). Private eye John Denson, connoisseur of screw-top wine and raw cauliflower, gets mixed up in a Native American fishing rights case that leads to the disappearance of a federal judge and the grisly discovery of various human body parts in **Pioneer Place Park.**

Half Asleep in Frog Pajamas, by Tom Robbins (1994, Bantam Books). Frog gods from Sirius and thieving monkeys travel from the rainy climes of Seattle to Timbuktu, taking in the **Queen Anne Thriftway** and a **Ballard** bowling alley.

Picture Postcard, by Fredrick D. Huebner (1990, Random House). Lawyer Matt Riordan's efforts to locate a famous but long-missing Northwest painter take him back 50 years to a fateful houseboat party on **Portage Bay** and embroil him with more than a sufficient share of dangerous characters.

15 Pacific Inn Although this pub is pocket-sized, it has disproportionately large windows; it also serves assertively spiced fish-and-chips. Wash it down with one of the 10 microbrews on tap; espresso drinks are served as well. ♦ Daily until 2AM. 3501 Stone Way N (at N 35th St). 547.2967 &

16 Archie McPhee's This is *the* place to shop for Halloween creepy crawlies or wacko party favors—there are hundreds of spiders, fish, rubber slugs, and similar creatures here. The owner, Mark Pahlow, is a natural-history buff and a stickler for anatomical correctness in his plastic wildlife. Apparently he's had some trouble convincing manufacturers to produce cockroaches that look exactly like they do in real life! ♦ Daily. 3510 Stone Way N (between N 35th and N 36th Sts). 547.2467

17 Stone Way Cafe ★$ Don't expect any "heart smart" entrées at this restaurant. Do, however, anticipate outstanding plates of biscuits and gravy or corned-beef hash, not to mention weighty, onion-slathered hamburgers and omelettes stuffed shamelessly with meats and cheeses. Owner Charlene Iverson usually has a few healthful soups cooking (don't miss the vegetable or navy-bean varieties), and there are always muffins on hand. Expect to wait in line on weekends. ♦ American ♦ Daily breakfast and lunch. No credit cards accepted. 3620 Stone Way N (between N 36th and N 38th Sts). 547.9958

18 B.F. Day Elementary School While other classic Seattle schools have been torn down or closed, this brick structure was restored to return to the grandeur it enjoyed at its 1892 dedication. Designed by **John Parkinson,** this is the city's oldest school in continuous operation. Its history predates the building: Classes were held in private homes for some years before this edifice was built. ♦ 3921 Linden Ave N (between N 39th and N 41st Sts)

19 Buckaroo Tavern Most of the motorcycles have disappeared from out front, and there are more young white-collar businesspeople in the crowd, but the "Fabulous Buckaroo" has hardly lapsed into respectability. Billiard balls still crack against one another, voices rise in cursing contraltos, and nimbuses of cigarette and cigar smoke loom over the knife-scarred booths in the back. It is still possible to disappear here, to sink your elbows into the bar and drink beer for hours without anyone disturbing you.

Founded in 1938, the establishment has so far warded off the forces of civil gentrification that prey so merrily on Fremont. The food—burgers, thick potato wedges, steaming bowls of chili mountained with cheddar and onions—hasn't yet become "cuisine." Distinctly nongourmet hot dogs go for 25¢ apiece on Monday nights from 6PM until they run out. Twenty tap beers, many of them microbrews, can be had, too. ♦ Daily until 2AM. No credit cards accepted. 4201 Fremont Ave N (at N 42nd St). 634.3161

20 Swingside Cafe ★★$ The small, divided, and low-ceilinged dining room, fielded with baseball paraphernalia, is best enjoyed with one close friend (who isn't averse to shouting or repeating sentences several times to be heard above the din). Lunch features barbecued chicken and sandwiches, and dinners are built around pastas (they're especially proud of their ravioli). The *Seattle Weekly* recently wrote that the Louisiana gumbo here "positively sings with Northwest seafood treasures." Expect a line at the door (there are no reservations), but the wait is worth it. ♦ Mediterranean ♦ Tu-F lunch and dinner; Sa dinner. No reservations. 4262 Fremont Ave N (between N 42nd and N 43rd Sts). 633.4057 &

21 City Cafe ★$ Situated in a corner of a modern apartment building, this cafe is a handsome and convivial spot. Expect generously sized coffee drinks, muffins, and sandwiches or soup at lunch. Dawdling is encouraged, and there are copies of *Vanity Fair* and the local dailies conveniently strewn around. ♦ Coffeehouse ♦ M-Sa. 4459 Fremont Ave N (between N 44th and N 45th Sts). 633.2139 &

Wallingford

22 Bizzarro Italian Cafe ★★★$ With its funky decor (brightly painted cellos, a grand piano hanging from the ceiling, a dinosaur motif) and surprising food combinations, this neighborhood cafe offers an unusual dining experience at a reasonable price. Among the more creative entrées are spearfish with a pecan-orange-cilantro salsa, salmon ravioli, prosciutto and squash served with walnut-marsala cream, and "sordid" (a pun on assorted) marinated vegetables. No reservations are taken, so there's sometimes a wait, but take the trouble anyway. ♦ Italian ♦ Daily dinner. No reservations. 1307 N 46th St (between Interlake Ave N and Stone Way N). 545.7327 &

On the first Wednesday evening of each month, the Vintage Motorcycle Enthusiasts (VME) meet at Teddy's Tavern (on 65th NE St at Roosevelt Way NE). The event also attracts hordes of people who aren't part of the club—but come to stand outside and look at the rows of gorgeous, impeccably preserved cycles parked in front of the building.

Restaurants/Clubs: Red   Hotels: Blue
Shops/♥ Outdoors: Green   Sights/Culture: Black

23 Sorel's ★$ This place is one of the neighborhood's friendliest coffee stops. Espresso drinks are rich and poured large, perhaps to match the size of the danishes and scrumptious apple fritters sold here. Several types of sandwiches can be ordered at lunch, but try the thick chili and the soups instead. In warm weather take your coffee and the paper to the outside deck. The service is excellent. ♦ Coffeehouse ♦ Daily. 4613 Stone Way N (between N 46th and N 47th Sts). 547.7835 ᏹ

24 Musashi's ★$ This place has lots of fans, and they may all be trying to get one of the few tables on the night you visit. (Thankfully, takeout is available.) A wide variety of excellent sushi is offered, and there are a few other choices—try the teriyaki chicken. *Bento* box meals, including rice, a crab cake, sashimi, and a teriyaki chicken skewer, are available at lunchtime. Cooks tend to throw extra items in for regular customers. ♦ Japanese/Takeout ♦ Tu-F lunch and dinner; Sa dinner. 1400 N 45th St (at Interlake Ave N). 633.0212

25 Firehouse No. 11 Erected in 1913, this building is surprisingly unimposing, even given its tower (where they dry out the hoses), which was long ago blocked on the skyline behind taller structures. Architect **Daniel R. Huntington** covered the building with cedar shakes, shutters, and trellises surrounding the accordion-style doors through which horse-drawn fire wagons once charged. The design was meant to blend in with Wallingford's growing predominance of bungalow homes. At one time both police and firefighters occupied this building, but since 1984 it has been home to a community health clinic. The Wallingford-Wilmot branch of the **Seattle Public Library** shares part of the ground floor, as well. ♦ N 45th St and Densmore Ave N

26 Guadalajara ★$ This unassuming Mexican outpost can be easily (and unjustly) over-looked amid the proliferation of chic restau-rants. Although service can be curt, the kitchen turns out fine and filling burritos and enchiladas. The tacos are so-so, but the Guadalajara nachos (chicken or beef), topped with guacamole and sour cream, are excellent. A chunky salsa of veggies marinated in pepper juice is some of the hottest around. And the bartenders usually have a heavy hand on the tequila bottle when mixing margaritas. ♦ Mexican ♦ M-Sa lunch and dinner; Su dinner. 1715 N 45th St (between Wallingford and Densmore Aves N). 632.7858 ᏹ

26 Alfi News Domestic and international newspapers, and a wide array of magazines—particularly bounteous in nature, sports, and home or craft publications—are available here. Clerks sometimes are slow to get new issues racked and allow back issues of some magazines to hang around long after their usefulness has expired. ♦ M-Th, Su until 10PM; F-Sa until 11PM. 1717 N 45th St (at Wallingford Ave N). 632.9390.

27 The Store Next Door Serving fresh baked goods—breads, cinnamon rolls, and other pastries—it's a great early-morning coffee stop, but it has only three tables for lingerers. ♦ M-Sa until 9PM; Su. No credit cards accepted. 4405 Wallingford Ave N (at N 44th St). 547.3203

28 Wallingford Center There were plans in the 1950s to condemn or relocate this three-story, Neo-Classical wooden behemoth that was then the **Interlake Public School.** The neighborhood's population of children was in decline, and business leaders argued that soon there would simply not be enough of them left to justify continued operation. The school had originally been the community's pride and joy, one of Wallingford's first public buildings, created by the prolific architect **James Stephen,** who also designed the **West Queen Anne Elementary** and **Latona Elementary Schools.** It was finally closed in 1981, but before commercial interests could even aim a wrecking ball at the building, preservationists joined forces with community officials to gentrify the structure. The edifice became a warren of stores and restaurants. Outside, on the corner of N 45th Street and Wallingford Avenue N, look for *Wallingford Animal Storm,* a 1984 bronze and aluminum totem created by local resident Ronald W. Petty. A tribute to local wildlife, the installation features raccoons, Canadian geese, cats, pigeons, and even slugs. ♦ 4400 Wallingford Ave N (between N 44th and 45th Sts). 632.2781

Within the Wallingford Center:

Capons Rotisserie Chicken ★$ You'd better like chicken, because that's about all there is here—whole marinated rotisserie chickens, half chickens, chicken sandwiches, and chicken soup. The fowl is fresh and juicy. Some customers' feathers have been ruffled by scant servings, but for the most part, both the vegetables and the salads make for satisfying, if only second-fiddle, accompaniments to the birds. Service is cafeteria style, with an atmosphere that's pleasant and casual. ♦ Chicken/Takeout ᏹ Daily lunch and dinner. Main level. 547.3949

28 Garden Spot Plentiful supplies of potted flowers and hanging plants, as well as a wide range of pots, can be found here. In summer the outside courtyard is an excellent place to browse and sniff, but even the interior space seems warm and earthy. The staff is knowledgeable and helpful. ◆ Daily; M-F until 8PM. Main level. 547.5137 ♿

28 Simpatico ★$ There's a secluded, brick-walled wine bar in the back and lots of white-draped tables out front where flavorful pasta dishes are served. But when the weather allows, head for the expansive sunken patio. Order a pizza (versions with chicken and pesto top the list) and a cold microbrew, then sit in the shade provided by umbrellas, listen to the burbling fountain, and chill out in the peaceful setting. There's live jazz on weekends.
◆ Italian ◆ Daily dinner. Main level. 632.1000 ♿

28 Second Story Bookstore Along with broad offerings in new general fiction and children's lit, this bookstore provides a rental service that makes it possible to read the latest best-sellers or listen to recent books on tape. Armchairs in the back provide the proper setting for thinking over any purchases.
◆ Daily until 8PM. Second level. 547.4605 ♿

28 Zanadia Among the many nicely designed accessories for the kitchen and home are a wide array of glassware and some intriguing candlesticks. ◆ Daily; M-F until 8PM. Second level. 547.0884 ♿

29 Teahouse Kuan Yin ★$ Running distinctly against the grain in a coffee-lover's town is this quiet teahouse owned by Miranda Pirzada, who traveled throughout Asia tasting teas before selecting the blacks, oolongs, and greens served here. Quiche, pot stickers, and other light edibles provide nice supplements to the tea. In a brilliant synergistic move, the teahouse has a doorway connecting it to neighboring **Wide World Books** (see below). Readers can dive right into their newly purchased pages while sipping an aromatic brew. Staffers are always willing to educate customers about the characteristics of the different teas. ◆ Teahouse ◆ M-Th until 11PM; F-Sa until midnight. $20 minimum required for credit-card purchases. 1911 N 45th St (between Meridian and Burke Aves N). 632.2055

29 Wide World Books Here are shelf upon shelf of guidebooks and travel literature, plus staff members who have probably already been where you want to go and can help you

make the most of your visit. The shop also features maps, some luggage, and a passport-photo service. ◆ Daily. 1911 N 45th St (between Meridian and Burke Aves N). 634.3453 ♿

30 Tweedy & Popp/Ace Hardware Very organized, very well stocked, and very old-fashioned, this is the sort of small store your parents knew as kids. ◆ Daily. 1916 N 45th St (between Meridian and Burke Aves N). 632.2290

30 Murphy's Pub This Irish pub (shown above) has a facade displaying Old World charm, and dark furnishings that give the interior the almost reverential atmosphere familiar to so many historied taverns. Fifteen tap beers (primarily substantive microbrews and imports) and a trio of alcoholic ciders are on hand, accompanied by a limited menu that makes its biggest splashes with the enormous nacho platter and the cider stew. There are the requisite dart boards to one side of the bar. Wednesday is open-mike entertainment night, with live Irish music played (usually too loudly) on Friday and Saturday. ◆ Cover. Daily until 2AM. 1928 N 45th St (at Meridian Ave N). 634.2110 ♿

31 Starbucks ★$ Local resentment ran high when this ubiquitous chain took over the old premises of **Murphy's Pub.** People worried about the coffeehouse's close commercial proximity to the much-loved **Boulangerie** bakery. But so far, this venue—large, compared with some of its brethren around town—has had no negative effects on the neighborhood. In fact, it's a pleasant hangout before and after films at the **Guild 45th Movie Theater** across the street. ◆ Coffeehouse ◆ Daily; F-Sa until 11PM. 2110 N 45th St (between Bagley and Meridian Aves N). 548.9507 ♿. Also at: Numerous locations throughout the city

32 Boulangerie Repeatedly chosen by Seattleites as their favorite bakery, this place specializes in crusty baguettes and other French loaves, as well as such memorable sweets as the Tarte Normande, made of Granny Smith apple slices arranged within a nutty pastry. It's also a very popular take-out coffee and pastry stop. Try the *pain au chocolat* (croissant filled with chocolate).
◆ Daily. 2200 N 45th St (at Bagley Ave N). 634.2211

Café VIZCAYA

32 Café Vizcaya ★★$$ While some diners are put off by the laissez-faire demeanor of the servers here, others say that it lends further authenticity to this dimly lit Spanish restaurant. It's best to just forget about the time and order several different small plates of tapas to share, and toast the experience with a fine Spanish wine. In Spain, diners make whole dinners of these often heavily spiced finger foods; Seattleites tend to use the tasty morsels as appetizers. Favorites include the *gambas brava al ajillo* (prawns sautéed in a marinade of onion, garlic, paprika, cayenne, and olive oil); the more basic *crostini* (rounds of toasted bread with a variety of toppings) are accompanied by a cilantro pesto.

The entrées are a balance of Spanish and citrus-accented Cuban dishes (the owner, Barbara Soltero, is a native Cuban who lived in Spain before coming to Seattle). One specialty is marinated fillet of red snapper baked on a bed of potato slices and served with a white sauce with peppers, capers, olives, and plenty of onions. Or try the roasted pork smothered in onions. Unfortunately, salads here are less inventive, and the bread served before your meal is cold and tends to be dry. But don't let such things dissuade you from what can be a thoroughly novel and romantic experience. ♦ Spanish/Cuban ♦ Daily dinner. Reservations recommended. 2202 N 45th St (between Corliss and Bagley Aves N). 547.7772

32 Twice Sold Tales Spun off a popular used-books outlet on Capitol Hill, this shop is densely packed with general fiction, science fiction, and mystery novels. Former best-sellers crowd an extra-cheapo cart on the sidewalk outside. The owners' political leanings are reflected in newspaper clippings hanging on the front windows and walls. ♦ Daily; F-Sa until 10PM. 2210 N 45th St (between Corliss and Bagley Aves N). 545.4226. Also at: 905 E John St (at Broadway Ave E). 324.2421

33 Kabul ★★$$ Chef Sultan Mahmoud Malikyar has introduced the rich pleasures of Afghan cuisine into Wallingford's culinary melting pot. Kabobs are a good introduction, especially the tender fillets of chicken marinated in turmeric, garlic, and cayenne. A hands-down favorite is the *qorma-i tarkari* (fresh vegetables and lamb tossed with dill, saffron, turmeric, and cumin). The *ashak* (flat dumplings stuffed with scallions, leeks, and cilantro and covered in a sauce of yogurt, garlic, and ground beef) is also popular. For an appetizer, try the *burta* (crushed eggplant blended with yogurt, sour cream, garlic, cilantro, and mint); it's served with a somewhat dry but satisfying pita bread. The room is filled with small tables and pleasant sconce lighting. Service is friendly and efficient. ♦ Afghan ♦ M-Sa dinner. 2301 N 45th St (at Corliss Ave N). 545.9000

33 Erotic Bakery As you might expect, this bakery specializes in creating party cakes designed to look like male or female sex organs. It's all done with good humor and not really as ribald as it sounds. ♦ Daily. 2323 N 45th St (at Sunnyside Ave N). 545.6969 &

34 Good Shepherd Center Built in 1906 from a plan by architect **C. Alfred Breitung** (who designed other Seattle edifices such as the **Triangle Hotel Building** in the International District), this was originally a Catholic convent and residence for unwed mothers called the **Home of the Good Shepherd.** In more recent years it has become something

Gas Works Park

of a political football, fought over by historic restoration forces and Wallingforders, who can't agree on its appropriate use. Presently, Greenpeace, private art and elementary schools, and the Seattle Tilth Association all occupy some portion of the building and grounds. The grounds and the Tilth gardens are a good place for a stroll. ◆ 4649 Sunnyside Ave N (between N 46th and N 50th Sts). 547.8127

35 Dick's Drive-In $ The long, pencil-thin fries here are best consumed from the grease-spotted bag in great gangly handfuls. Complete your feast with a thick chocolate milk shake. You might be able to find better fast food in this town, but there are few more interesting human-study environments than the parking lot here. The scene is especially entertaining just before closing time on Friday and Saturday nights. ◆ Fast food ◆ Daily lunch and dinner until 2AM. 111 NE 45th St (at First Ave NE). 632.5125. Also at: 115 Broadway E (between E Denny Way and E John St). 323.1300; 9208 Holman Rd NW (at 12th Ave NW). 783.5233

36 Latona Elementary School You may see this great wooden building from Interstate 5, just north of the NE 45th Street overpass. If you have a chance, get closer for a better view. Dating back to 1906, this is the only one of architect **James Stephen**'s many Seattle schools to feature Queen Anne–style towers. ◆ NE 42nd St and Fifth Ave NE

37 Gas Works Park Twenty-five years after the Seattle Gas Company plant belched its last coal dust in 1956, the gasworks at the north end of Lake Union reopened as a park for picnickers and kite fliers, its industrial towers retained as totems of the industrial age. It's like that scene from *Planet of the Apes* where Charlton Heston rides his horse past the submerged Statue of Liberty and realizes just how much the world has changed.

Children now scamper over ground that was once so polluted it demanded intensive purifying before it was safe to walk upon. Landscape architect Richard Haag (who had earlier remodeled the Century 21 fairgrounds into Seattle Center) was responsible for seeing aesthetic value in this industrial wasteland and saving the plant as a bizarre relic. His modifications were relatively minor—bright primary colors in some covered areas, a huge symbolic sundial (created by artist Charles Greening in 1979) that's mounted atop a knoll to the west, and outdoor dining tables on the beautified grounds. Visitors have an unobstructed view of boats chopping over the lake. The park marks the beginning of the 12.5-mile Burke-Gilman Trail (see the "University District" chapter on page 169.) ◆ Lake Union (at N Northlake Pl)

Bests

Jean Godden
City Columnist, *Seattle Times*

Seattle owes its existence to a picturesque deep water harbor, the natural wonder that first drew settlers to its shores. The harbor is one of the best places to start exploring the Northwest's largest city.

A walk along the **Elliott Bay** waterfront is exciting even on blustery days. You can see freighters from afar, visit the **Seattle Aquarium,** browse through import shops, take a waterfront tour on the **Argosy** sightseeing ships, and—when hunger strikes—buy a steaming cup of clam chowder from a sidewalk cafe.

From the waterfront, take the **Hillclimb** (a public stairway across from the **Aquarium**) to the **Pike Place Market.** Founded in 1907, the colorful farmers' market houses truck farmers, greengrocers, artisans, street musicians, specialty shops, and restaurants. Fishmongers toss king salmon to one another, warning visitors to "beware of flying fish."

Three blocks east of the market lies **Westlake Park,** an urban triangle where civic events and political rallies are staged. Don't miss **The Bon Marché,** the city's glitzy department store, or **Nordstrom,** the apparel chain's flagship. A monorail station on the third floor of **Westlake Center,** a nearby shopping complex, will speed you to the **Seattle Center,** home of the highly educational **Pacific Science Center** and the **Space Needle,** the kitschy observation tower that is a city symbol.

The **US Bank Centre** at **Fifth Avenue** and **Pike Street** is Seattle's downtown living room. Arrange to meet a friend in the second floor lobby with its cushy leather chairs and world-class display of Pilchuck art glass. Near the Fifth Avenue entry, there's a **Starbucks** kiosk where you can order the city's favorite drink: a double tall latte with half an inch of foam.

Not to be missed is the **Seattle Art Museum.** A 48-foot-tall statue titled *Hammering Man* guards the building, soundlessly pounding the back of his hand two-and-a-half times a minute. Permanent exhibitions include North Coast Indian art and priceless works from African and Pacific Rim countries.

Make time to explore the **Hiram M. Chittenden Locks,** north of the city center. The locks, second in size only to the Panama Canal in the Western Hemisphere, work like a marine elevator, boosting ships from the saltwater of **Shilshole Bay** to the freshwater of the **Lake Washington Ship Canal.** Stroll across the locks for a view of salmon swimming past a glass-sided fish ladder.

Finally, go to dinner at a restaurant on Shilshole Bay (**Ray's Boathouse** or **Anthony's Homeport**). Here you can dine on seafood, sip the Northwest's prize-winning wines, and watch as tiny tugs sail past pulling giant barges and the sun sets slowly behind the snow-capped **Olympic Mountains.** It doesn't get any better than this.

For nos. 34-43, see pg. 160

NE 85th St.

NE 82nd St.

NE 80th St.

NE 77th St.

Roosevelt Way NE

NE 75th St.

NE 73rd St.

NE 70th St.

NE 65th St.

NE 62nd St.

E 62nd St.

E 60th St.

NE 56th St.

NE 55th St.

NE 50th St.

Green Lake/ Greenwood/ North Seattle

A quiet residential district, the Green Lake/Greenwood area is bordered by Ballard to the west, Wallingford and Fremont to the south, and Ravenna and the University District on the east. Its houses range from modest bungalows to some of the most desirable homes in Seattle—the large turn-of-the-century residences and modern dream houses atop **Phinney Ridge**, for instance, command views of both the **Olympic** and the **Cascade Mountains.**

The centerpiece of the area is **Woodland Park,** located at the south end of Phinney Ridge, where the **Woodland Park Zoo,** playgrounds, tennis courts, a rose garden, and acres of wooded trails and picnic areas can be found. Bisecting the park is **Aurora Avenue (Highway 99),** which in the early 1930s—following bitter public debate—was extended north from downtown Seattle. The benefits of this bit of progress are dubious: The highway created what Washington writer Ivan Doig called "a concrete gorge" in the park—the western half contains the zoo, while most of the rest of its attractions, including Green Lake, are in the eastern half.

Green Lake, with two paths circling it, is "Jogging Central" and *the* center of summertime fun in Seattle. Aside from running, there's plenty of kayaking, bicycling, in-line skating, windsurfing, pram-pushing, golfing, baseball playing, fishing, and just plain people watching here. A couple of small commercial areas on the east and north sides of the lake service the area year-round, and seasonal businesses (such as in-line skate and Windsurfer rentals) pop up in the summer. And, of course, this is Seattle, so you won't need to travel far before encountering an espresso stand.

Parallel to Aurora Avenue on the park's western edge—along the spine

153

of Phinney Ridge—runs **Phinney Avenue**, which becomes **Greenwood Avenue** farther north. With its secondhand stores spanning the gamut from junky to sublime, the avenue is ripe territory for antiques lovers. The Greenwood district, centered at the intersection of **N 85th Street** and **Greenwood Avenue N**, retains a funky charm that has endured nobly against encroaching gentrification.

A little farther afield is North Seattle. The city limits used to end at North 85th Street, but as Seattle has grown (the line now stands at **North 145th Street**), the various smaller communities embraced by the North Seattle rubric—**Lake Forest Park**, **Northgate**, **Broadview**, **Maple Leaf**, and **Wedgewood** among them—have developed. North Seattle is primarily home to auto dealerships, budget motels, strip malls, modest housing, and the world's first shopping mall, the **Northgate Shopping Center**.

Green Lake/Greenwood

1 Green Lake Small Craft Center Located at the southwest corner of the lake, this concession offers year-round canoe and kayak instruction as well as rentals. The lake is active on weekday mornings when rowers embark on their journeys. ♦ M-F 3-6PM; Sa 9AM-2PM. 5900 W Green Lake Way N (on Green Lake). 684.4074

2 Honey Bear Bakery ★$ Dropping by this place for a cup of joe and a sourdough cinnamon roll is a morning ritual for many folks. Crowded and convivial, this nonsmoking bakery has become a neighborhood institution where you can linger over conversation or grab a quick bite. The breads are locally famous, and the enormous chocolate-chip cookies or the white-chocolate brownies are excellent. Dinner is a dicier matter, although the black-bean chili is a safe bet. On some evenings, there's a wide variety of live music, including blues, acoustic guitar, folk, and jazz; call ahead. ♦ Bakery ♦ Daily breakfast, lunch, and dinner. No credit cards accepted. 2106 N 55th St (at Kenwood Pl N). 545.7296 &

3 Cafe Los Gatos ★★$ The subtle flavors of Central and South America, redolent with such herbs as cilantro and cardamom, are featured at this tiny restaurant. Fish, meat, chicken, and vegetarian specials are available nightly. Or try the pork stew, a rich sargas so of fruit and nuts with pork. Friendly service makes up for the dimly lit decor. ♦ Central/South American ♦ Tu-Su dinner. Reservations recommended. 6411 Latona Ave NE (between NE 64th and NE 65th Sts). 527.9765 &

4 Latona Pub This funky, friendly neighborhood tavern offers a good selection of wines and a frequently changing assortment of microbrews, including products from the Rogue Brewery in Newport, Oregon, and the Maritime Pacific Brewing Company in Seattle. Bartenders will give recommendations. The menu is limited, but the salads are good. There's also something called the Haystack—chips and bean dip smothered in cheese.

Sit at the bar; avoid the balcony overlooking the main floor, where the service is glacially slow and you'll feel cut off from the action. A variety of local musicians, usually of the folk or jazz persuasion, play Thursday through Sunday evenings. A small cover is sometimes charged, but if you're inside when the music starts, you can usually slide. ♦ M-Sa until 12:30AM; Su until midnight. 6423 Latona Ave NE (at NE 65th St). 525.2238

5 Boehm's on Ravenna It's somewhat off the beaten path, but this shop is worth a visit. Old man Boehm, a Swiss immigrant, was a master candymaker and a legendary mountain climber and skier; for years his factory in the town of Issaquah has been a regular stop for travelers headed east across Snoqualmie Pass. This small retail outlet caters mostly to fans of its splendid handmade chocolates, oversize muffins, buttercream-filled chocolates, and espresso drinks. ♦ Daily. 559 Ravenna Blvd NE (at NE 65th St). 523.9380 &

According to the National Association of Realtors, real estate prices in Seattle have been rising 8.5 percent per year since 1987—the fastest growth rate of any US city over that period. The median price of a house in Seattle in 1995 was $158,500.

Seattle is truly a cyclist's city. There are more than 30 miles of well-maintained (and much-used) bicycle paths in town, most of them connecting area parks.

Saleh al Lago~

6 Saleh al Lago ★★★$$ You wouldn't think this sleek restaurant with its modern and minimal pastel decor, set in an ordinary block of shops, would be one of Seattle's top Italian *ristoranti*. And the owner/chef, Saleh Joudeh, is not even Italian (he's Syrian); however, he did study cooking (as well as medicine) in Italy. His imaginative blendings of various Mediterranean influences can make even plain fare remarkable. Fresh pasta and veal dishes are consistently delicious. Special praise goes to the garlicky calamari antipasto and the chef's *ravioli al modo mio* (sauces and fillings change daily). Seafood dishes are prepared simply and excellently. ♦ Italian/Mediterranean ♦ Tu-F lunch and dinner; Sa dinner. Reservations recommended. 6804 E Green Lake Way N (between First and Second Aves NE). 522.7943 ੬

6 Spud Fish and Chips ★$ Yes, the ambience is a big zero, but this is a choice spot on sunny days when all you want is to grab a quick lunch and burn off a few skin cells beside the lake. The fish is remarkably flaky and the fries are filling and salty, but everything's a bit greasy. ♦ Seafood/Takeout ♦ Daily lunch and dinner. 6860 E Green Lake Way N (at Second Ave NE). 524.0565 ੬. Also at: 2666 Alki Ave SW (at 59th Ave SW). 938.0606 ੬

Gregg's Greenlake Cycle

7 Gregg's Greenlake Cycle This is the biggest and busiest of several shops around Green Lake that rent bicycles, in-line skates, and skateboards for a nominal fee. All these types of wheels are also for sale here, and there's a helpful service department for when things go bewilderingly wrong. ♦ Daily; M-F until 9PM. 7007 Woodlawn Ave NE (at Ravenna Blvd NE and NE 70th St). 523.1822

8 Kyllo's Lakeside Deli ★$ A bustling cafe with good sandwiches and home-baked items provides a nice break before, during, or after a rousing walk around the lake. ♦ Deli ♦ M-F breakfast and lunch until 4:30PM. 315 NE 71st St (between Woodlawn Ave NE and E Green Lake Way N). 522.9088 ੬

9 My Friends Cafe ★$ Fresh fruit and other healthy ingredients whipped up into good

breakfasts and tasty sandwiches are the offerings here. ♦ American ♦ Daily breakfast and lunch. 310 NE 72nd St (between Woodland Ave NE and E Green Lake Dr N). 523.8929 ੬

10 Rosita's ★$ Just a couple blocks off the lake, this place is commonly crowded and uncommonly efficient. Try any of the combination plates or the *chiles rellenos*. The super nachos platter is a winning appetizer. ♦ Mexican ♦ M-Sa lunch and dinner; Su dinner. 7210 Woodlawn Ave NE (between NE 72nd St and NE Maple Leaf Pl). 523.3031 ੬

11 Rasa Malaysia ★★$ The emphasis at this popular dining spot is on noodles, usually served sautéed with very fresh vegetables and a variety of fish, shrimp, or meat, and such mildly spicy sauces as a peanut topping. Fruit smoothies and not-too-sweet lemonade are the drinks of choice. ♦ Malaysian ♦ Daily dinner. 7208 E Green Lake Dr N (between NE 72nd St and NE Maple Leaf Pl). 523.8888. Also at: Broadway Market (401 Broadway E at E Harrison St), 328.8882; Pike Place Market (Sanitary Market Bldg). 624.8388 ੬

12 Green Lake Public Library Perched on a grassy knoll, this well-maintained building shows Mediterranean and Chicago School influences. Opened in 1910, it is one of eight libraries still standing in the Seattle area (two were lost to wrecking balls) that were built thanks to the largess of iron-and-steel-magnate Andrew Carnegie. Designers were **W. Marbury Somervell** and **Joseph C. Cote,** who in the year of its opening would also see two of their other library projects inaugurated: the **University Branch Library** on Roosevelt Way N and the **West Seattle Public Library** on 42nd Avenue SW. Not surprisingly, these three structures bear some resemblance to one another. ♦ M-W; F-Sa. 7364 E Green Lake Dr N (at Fourth Ave NE). 684.7547

13 Green Lake Boat Rentals Rent a canoe, small boat, or paddle-wheel craft at this Parks Department concession. Windsurfing equipment and lessons are also available. ♦ Daily May-Sept. 7351 E Green Lake Dr N (near NE Maple Leaf Pl). 527.0171

14 Urban Bakery ★$ Early morning and late-night hours (in spring and summer only) make this a convenient spot for runners and walkers to pick up an espresso or iced *latte*. Hearty sandwiches, soups, fresh pastries, and a full line of juices are also on hand. ♦ Coffeehouse/Bakery ♦ Daily breakfast, lunch, and dinner. 7850 E Green Lake Dr N (at Wallingford Ave N). 524.7951

15 Ed's Juice and Java ★$ Tiny but convivial, this joint features just what the name advertises. A variety of unusual concoctions are available in the juice department, such as carrot and wheat-grass; the coffee-based drinks are more

155

conventional. Vegetarian fast food is also offered, including wheat-free, dairy-free, and sugar-free pastries. ♦ Coffeehouse ♦ Daily. 7900 E Green Lake Dr N (at Wallingford Ave N). 524.7570

15 Guido's Pizzeria ★$ Buy it by the slice or by the pie, thin crust or thick, with the usual toppings or more uncommon choices like fresh basil and sun-dried tomatoes at this minuscule and crowded place (most of the business here is takeout). Calzones, salads, a variety of juices and mineral waters, and—as you might expect—espressos and *lattes* are also available. Several picnic tables beckon from just across the street in **Green Lake Park.** The cheerfully brash New York–style attitude of the employees is free. ♦ Pizza ♦ Daily lunch and dinner. 7900 E Green Lake Dr N (at Wallingford Ave N). 522.5553 &

16 Bathhouse Theatre Under the auspices of its irrepressible artistic director, Arne Zaslove, this theater mounts six productions annually on a year-round schedule, specializing in innovative updates of classics. The building was originally erected in 1927 as—you guessed it—a brick bathhouse; it became a theater in 1970. ♦ Box office: Tu-Su noon-7PM. 7312 W Green Lake Dr N (between N 76th St and Aurora Ave N). 524.9108

17 Beth's Cafe $ Located next to **Twin Teepees** restaurant, this greasiest of spoons attracts plenty of college students who finish up their all-nighters with a stop here to wolf down inexpensive 12-egg omelettes (be prepared to share!), layered over a two-inch bed of hash browns with toast on the side. Half orders can be had by the less gluttonous. Breakfast is served all day. Burgers and enormous french fries carry on the stomach-busting tradition. It's a real scene. ♦ American ♦ Daily 24 hours. 7311 Aurora Ave N (at Winona Ave N). 782.5588

18 Twin Teepees Restaurant ★$ A classic of roadside kitsch on the west side of Green Lake, this place is a mishmash of Native American motifs. The structure was apparently prefabricated in California and then trucked up Highway 99 to this site. Inside, you'll find substantial breakfasts and other forms of good, solid American food. ♦ American ♦ Daily breakfast, lunch, and dinner. 7201 Aurora Ave N (at N 72nd St). 783.9740

Green Lake, which has an average depth of only 15 feet, is what's left of a huge Ice Age lake that once stretched between the present cities of Everett and Olympia. Haller and Bitter Lakes, in the northern part of Seattle, are also remnants of that ancient body of water.

Restaurants/Clubs: Red   Hotels: Blue
Shops/♦ Outdoors: Green   Sights/Culture: Black

19 Woodland Park Zoo Origins of this zoo and the surrounding park go back to Guy Phinney, a flamboyant Englishman who made his fortune in Canadian real estate before moving to Seattle at the end of the 19th century. Phinney built a private park on his estate, at the southern end of the ridge that bears his name. He included—among other amenities—a trolley line, flower garden, conservatory, picnic grounds, a zoo, bathing beach, and music pavilion. The city bought the park from him in 1900 for the then-extravagant sum of $100,000.

Today, Seattle's zoo is one of the nation's best. Its most recent improvements include a $9-million re-creation of a tropical rain forest (see the map below right), complete with artificial vegetation (created by a technique pioneered in Hollywood) and digitally recorded sounds from a real rain forest; a rejuvenated version of the popular family farm petting zoo; *Northern Trail,* an exhibit that replicates the cold, rugged regions of Alaska, with brown bears, bald eagles, mountain goats, and wolves; and *Trail of Vines,* which leads visitors on a boardwalk past tufted deer, tapirs, pythons, and tropical primates.

In many of the exhibits animals are free to wander in near-natural settings: There's an African savanna (where you can peer from afar at giraffes and gazelles); an Asian elephant forest, including a replica of a Thai logging camp; and a lush, lowland gorilla enclosure, the largest of its kind in the world, in which you can get up close and personal (behind glass) with these fascinating creatures.

The zoo offers lectures, summer musical performances, and educational series for youngsters. Older children will love the periodic exhibits of raptors in flight. ♦ Admission; children under two free; discount for senior citizens, disabled persons, and children ages three to five. Daily. 5500 Phinney Ave N (at N 55th St). 684.4800

20 Santa Fe Cafe ★★★$$ Sparse but elegant decor combines with consistently high-quality, innovative cuisine to create Phinney Ridge's classiest restaurant. A couple of the appetizers alone—an order of garlic custard, say, and a luscious artichoke ramekin—could make a meal. And the green-chili stew, enchiladas, and green-chili burritos made with blue-corn tortillas are all delicious entrées.

The owners, both from Albuquerque, New Mexico, import tons of red and green chilies from their home state. If your server warns you that something like the red-chili burrito may be too hot for most palates, take his or her word for it. There's another branch in Ravenna. ♦ Southwestern ♦ M-F lunch and dinner; Sa-Su lunch. Reservations recommended. 5901 Phinney Ave N (between N 59th and N 60th Sts). 783.9755 &. Also at: 2255 NE 65th St (between Ravena and 22nd Aves NE). 524.7736 &

21 12-Step Bookstore and Gift Shop For books on a multiplicity of dysfunctions, lists of various meetings, gifts for fellow 12-steppers, bumper stickers for those who want to be less than anonymous, and notices of upcoming workshops and speakers, check out this store. ♦ Daily. 6300 Phinney Ave N (at N 63rd St). 789.6300

22 Mae's Phinney Ridge Cafe ★★$ Mae is the shared *nom de cuisine* of three women owners who have created this congenial nook for breakfast and lunch. The sandwiches, burgers, and cinnamon rolls are all wonderful. Omelettes are the top pick at breakfast, but for the truly famished, a cheese-covered mountain of hash browns is served as a main course. The **Moo Room** features a soda fountain, great milk shakes, a jukebox, and more cow-related art than you can shake a hoof at. Service can be slow, and the lines form quickly on

weekends, but the wait isn't usually too long. ♦ American ♦ Daily breakfast and lunch. No reservations. 6412 Phinney Ave N (between N 64th and N 65th Sts). 782.1222 &

23 Terra Mar This shop features an eclectic assortment of handmade items—including masks, clothes, and artwork—by a wide variety of local and international artists. The emphasis is on unusual folk art and primitive designs. ♦ Daily. 7200 Greenwood Ave N (at N 72nd St). 784.5350

24 2nd Hand Hube Furniture and kitschy stuff from the 1930s to the 1950s, some of it high-quality collectibles and some of it near junk, is featured in this browser's delight of a shop. ♦ Daily noon-5:30PM. 7217 Greenwood Ave N (between N 72nd and N 73rd Sts). 782.1335

24 The Couth Buzzard This dusty bookstore with the peculiar moniker contains a treasure trove of unlikely and sometimes unheard-of finds in used hardcovers and paperbacks. Mainstream fiction is the strongest section

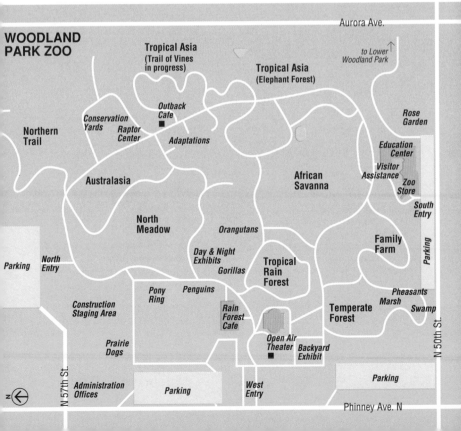

WOODLAND PARK ZOO

Aurora Ave.

to Lower Woodland Park

Tropical Asia (Trail of Vines in progress)

Tropical Asia (Elephant Forest)

Rose Garden

Northern Trail

Conservation Yards

Outback Cafe

Raptor Center

Adaptations

Education Center

Visitor Assistance

Zoo Store

Australasia

African Savanna

South Entry

North Meadow

Orangutans

Family Farm

Parking

Day & Night Exhibits

Gorillas

Tropical Rain Forest

Pheasants Marsh

Parking

North Entry

Pony Ring

Penguins

Temperate Forest

Swamp

Construction Staging Area

Rain Forest Cafe

Prairie Dogs

Open Air Theater

Backyard Exhibit

N 50th St.

Administration Offices

Parking

West Entry

Parking

N 57th St.

Phinney Ave. N

here. Look for sidewalk sales. ♦ Daily. 7221 Greenwood Ave N (between N 72nd and N 73rd Sts). 789.8965

24 Greenwood Bakery The excellent pastries, breads, cookies, and other delectables made here are complemented by the good espresso drinks. ♦ Daily. 7227 Greenwood Ave N (between N 72nd and N 73rd Sts). 783.7181

24 Ken's Market This better-than-average grocery store caters to an upscale crowd with its wealth of coffee beans, delicious deli sandwiches (try the meat loaf), and fresh pasta. The espresso drinks served here are just as good as those sold next door at **Greenwood Bakery,** and the service is faster. ♦ Daily 6AM-11PM. 7231 Greenwood Ave N (between N 72nd and N 73rd Sts). 784.3470

25 Kismet ★$ Tea is king at this Turkish-flavored spot. Co-owners Torabi Topal (who is originally from Turkey) and Mary Anne Mullin offer a menu of tasty and unusual (for Seattle, anyway) specialties such as apple tea, *borek* (a spinach pastry), and baklava. It's a wonderful place to stop while shopping on Greenwood Avenue. ♦ Turkish coffeehouse ♦ Tu-Su. No credit cards accepted. 7311 Greenwood Ave N (at N 73rd St). 783.1797 &

26 George's Corner A charmingly eccentric shop full of goofy collectibles showcases an impressive selection of cowboy paraphernalia. Indulge your inner John Wayne. ♦ M, Th-Su. 7400 Greenwood Ave N (at N 74th St). 781.0973

27 74th Street Ale House ★★$ This former hard-drinker's dive has been reincarnated as an airy neighborhood tavern serving an excellent array of Northwest microbrews and standard-issue beer (16 taps in all), along with wine. The brains behind this operation are Jeff Eagan, formerly of **Roanoke Park Place Tavern** on Capitol Hill and the **Mark Tobey** restaurant in downtown, and Jeff Reich, who runs the kitchen. The menu is brief but thoughtful. Try the big burgers (decked with grilled onions and peppers), the sausage sandwich, or the Reuben. The vegetarian sandwich, a neat orchestration of Montrachet and cream cheese, sun-dried tomatoes, artichoke hearts, and heaps of roasted garlic on country bread, is another fine choice. Some fans claim this alehouse serves Seattle's best chicken sandwich, but critics have found it to be rather dry and unexciting

compared with other offerings here. Try the white clam chowder served on Fridays. ♦ American ♦ Daily lunch and dinner. 7401 Greenwood Ave N (at N 74th St). 784.2955

27 Yanni's Lakeside Cafe ★★$ Huge portions of good Greek cooking are offered at this congenial neighborhood hangout (which, despite its name, is actually about five blocks from Green Lake). Try the gyro platter, any of the lamb dishes, roasted chicken, or moussaka. The appetizer plate of calamari can make a whole meal. Desserts are less interesting. There's a simple, no-nonsense wine list. ♦ Greek ♦ M-Sa dinner. 7419 Greenwood Ave N (between N 74th and N 75th Sts). 783.6945 &

28 Pelayo's Antiques This large, well-stocked store is at the upper end of the price continuum. Specialties are pine furniture, toys (such as elegant hobbyhorses), and crockery. ♦ Daily. 7601 Greenwood Ave N (at N 76th St). 789.1999. Also at: 8421 Greenwood Ave N (at N 85th St). 789.1333

29 Pete's Eggnest ★$ It's all about comfort foods like Denver omelettes, blueberry pancakes, liver and onions, and gyro sandwiches. The decor is nothing to write home about: checkered tablecloths and walls covered with black-and-white photos of local TV personalities. The breakfast menu is served all day. ♦ American ♦ Tu-Su breakfast and lunch. 7717 Greenwood Ave N (between N 77th and N 78th Sts). 784.5348 &

30 Bizango Within these flamingo pink walls are all manner of gift items—jewelry, posters, flying angels, candles, clocks, you name it—all hand-crafted and imported. ♦ M-Sa. 759 N 80th St (at Linden Ave N). 784.7455

31 Arita Japanese Restaurant ★★$ This very pleasant family-run restaurant serves Japanese dishes, slightly altered for the American palate. The atmosphere is calm and cool, with gentle music in the back-ground and simple furnishings. There's no sushi bar, but the sashimi and sushi dinners are fresh and reasonably priced. ♦ Japanese ♦ M-F lunch and dinner; Sa dinner. 8202 Greenwood Ave N (at N 82nd St). 784.2625 &

Quite a Road Show:
The Campy Flair of Aurora Avenue North

Aurora Avenue North, also known as **Highway 99,** used to be the main north-south highway running through Seattle. Today, it's a comparatively minor thoroughfare. At the city's heart, Aurora is an elevated highway (the **Alaskan Way Viaduct**) running along the **Waterfront;** south of the city, it's known as **Pacific Highway South.** But north of Seattle, rolling out into the suburban hinterlands of **Lynnwood,** now, that's a different kettle of kitsch. There, this road becomes the car culture equivalent of a Marrakech bazaar, bordered by blinding neon, strip malls and strip joints, questionable motels, taverns, used-car lots, and assorted other businesses—alternately cheerful and new or grim and shopworn, but always unique. Aurora Avenue's style evokes three essential aspects of American life: fast cars, quick bucks, and a high tolerance for personal weirdness.

"Aurora is the homely and affordable face of American capitalism. ..." writes Jonathan Raban, a British author expatriated to Seattle. "Driving Aurora is like riffling at speed through the text of an eccentric illustrated encyclopedia. The entries rush past too rapidly to follow, and they couple promiscuously with each other: Something about pest control gets tangled up with something about foam rubber and chiropractors and The Love Pantry."

For example, the **Twin Teepees Restaurant** (7201 Aurora Ave N at N 72nd St) is a loony tribute to Native American culture. Built in 1937, it cheerfully mixes Northwest Coast and Plains Indian clichés with no particular regard for accuracy; a case in point are the paintings that flank the entrance to the "teepees"—they look like bears (or is it whales?).

Another classic is an extremely ratty-looking life-size elephant that advertises the **Aurora Flower Shop** (8808 Aurora Ave N between N 88th and N 90th Sts). It was also built during the Depression, as were so many of these highway come-ons. Legend has it that a florist who once owned this shop kept the paunchy probos-cidean in his backyard for years before hoisting it onto a pole above busy Highway 99. **Seal's Motel** (12035 Aurora Ave N between N 109th and N 125th Sts) displays a seal balancing a ball on its nose.

And, all along the way the signs reel by, each more outlandish than the last until you reach some true showstoppers such as "Do bugs, not drugs," which promotes an exterminator.

32 Phad Thai ★$ There's been an explosion of Thai restaurants in Seattle over the past several years. This eatery is informal in decor and cheerful in service; employees have been known to take fussy children in hand for a kitchen tour, giving parents a chance to eat. The food is fresh, well-presented, and cooked without MSG. Try the vegetable curry or the chicken in peanut sauce. ♦ Thai ♦ Daily dinner; M-Tu, Th-F lunch. 8530 Greenwood Ave N (between N 85th and N 86th Sts). 784.1830

33 El Tapatio ★$ A venerable Greenwood institution, this Mexican restaurant offers few culinary surprises, but it's cheerful, inexpensive, and informal. The standards are all available—taco combination plates, burritos, enchiladas—with heaping sides of rice and beans. Kids are welcome, too; they receive helium balloons and lots of attention. ♦ Mexican ♦ Daily lunch and dinner. 8564 Greenwood Ave N (between N 85th and N 86th St). 782.7545 &

Mail carriers don't hesitate to identify Seattle's most exclusive neighborhood: The Highlands. The houses in this area west of Aurora Avenue on the bluff above the Shilshole Bay Marina don't even have addresses. Letters and packages to residents are simply addressed, "The Highlands, Seattle, WA 98177."

North Seattle

34 Carkeek Park This 198-acre greensward bordering Puget Sound has been left mostly to wilderness, though there are a number of forest trails and picnic areas for nature lovers. Crews of Camp Fire Girls conduct weeklong summer camps out here, and folks run their dogs or enjoy lunch by the water. ♦ NW Carkeek Park Rd and Ninth Ave NW

35 Tan Duc ★$ This quiet restaurant specializes in Chinese and Vietnamese food. Especially recommended are the Vietnamese box dinners—huge platters of barbecued shrimp, bean sprouts, cooked meats, vegetables, and other savories. Wrap a selection all up in a delicate rice-flour pancake, dip it in the sweet sauce, and enjoy! Friendly advice from the staff is available for novices. ♦ Chinese/ Vietnamese ♦ Daily lunch and dinner. 10007 Aurora Ave N (at N 100th St). 525.0511

36 Doong Kong Lau ★★$ Hot and spicy Hakka regional cuisine is served in this usually busy Chinese restaurant. The hot pots—the name is quite literal—are prepared in an assortment of styles (vegetarian, seafood, pork, etc.), and the garlic eggplant should not be missed. ♦ Chinese ♦ Daily lunch and dinner. 9710 Aurora Ave N (between N 97th and N 98th Sts). 526.8828

37 Larry's Market Welcome to Grocery Land USA, a pop-culture spin on the classic American supermarket. Larry McKinney was a grocer's son who inherited his first store in the 1960s and has since expanded the family business into a chain of fine food emporiums in the suburbs. The stores have a faux-industrial appearance—exposed ventilation pipes and rafters and metal racks supporting boxes of unpacked supplies. But interior design is theater, so enjoy the show. The sheer quantity and quality—of everything from fresh flowers to fresh sushi—is mind-boggling, and the especially long hours the shop keeps are convenient. ♦ Daily 6AM-1AM. 10008 Aurora Ave N (at N 100th St). 527.5333. Also at: 100 Mercer St (between Warren and First Aves N). 213.0778

38 Northgate Shopping Center Holding the dubious distinction of being the world's first shopping mall, this structure was designed in the 1950s by architect **John Graham Sr.,** who also invented the revolving restaurant and helped develop the **Space Needle** for the 1962 World's Fair. Oddly enough, considering Seattle's prevailing weather, it was originally uncovered; only later was a roof added. All the usual suspects can be found here: **Nordstrom, The Bon, B. Dalton Bookseller, Lamonts,** and **The Tux Shop.** ♦ Daily; M-Sa until 9:30PM. NE Northgate Way (off I-5). 362.4777

39 Maple Leaf Grill ★★$ Here's a true neighborhood hangout, serving an excellent assortment of beers and wines. The decor has lots of old wood and open space. Lunch and dinner choices include one of the most succulent burgers in town and a changing array of imaginative specials featuring fish, chicken, and pasta. ♦ American ♦ M-F lunch and dinner; Sa-Su dinner. 8909 Roosevelt Way NE (at NE 89th St). 523.8449 ⚲

40 Cooper's Northwest Alehouse It's technically not a brewpub (no beers are prepared on the premises), but this crowded and cheery tavern is a mecca for Northwest microbrews: 23 of its 25 tap brews are West Coast specialties. The staff is knowledgeable about the subtle distinctions of each type, and sipping samples of new brews are accompanied by enthusiastic debate over their relative merits and flaws. Wine and some bar food (like fish-and-chips) is served, but beer is the draw. Darts tournaments are held on a regular basis. ◆ M-Sa until 2AM; Su until midnight. 8065 Lake City Way NE (near 15th Ave NE). 522.2923 &

41 Pandasia ★$ Known for inexpensive high-quality food and fast, friendly service, the kitchen staff here makes its soup noodles, dumplings, buns, and sauces fresh daily. The orange beef, Happy Family (stir-fried scallops, shrimp, and breast of chicken), and *moo shu* pork (stir-fried vegetables and pork wrapped in crepes) are all outstanding. Delivery is free within the North End. ◆ Chinese/Takeout ◆ M-Sa lunch and dinner; Su dinner. 7347

35th Ave NE (between NE 73rd and NE 75th Sts). 526.5115 &. Also at: 1625 W Dravus St (between 16th and 17th Aves W). 283.9030; fax 283.2126 &

42 Wurdemann Mansion Situated in **Lake Forest Park,** this two-story Georgian manse was built in 1914 for eye surgeon Harry Wurdemann. The mansion stood on five acres of land at the entrance to the park, just off Victory Way (later rechristened Bothell Way). The grounds were planted with rose bushes, apple trees, and a cherry orchard that gave the estate its name: Cherry Acres.

Ten years later local banker (and later, embezzler) Adolph Linden bought the house and sank as much as $100,000 into improvements: a wading pool in the side yard; a fence encircling the property, made partly of white-wood latticework, partly of brick and iron; a gate from Victory Way onto a driveway that curved up to the white, pillared mansion, then swept around to a porte cochere at the rear. (This grand entrance eventually had to be locked because travelers continually mistook the mansion for a roadhouse and would come at all hours in search of lodging). The mansion fell into disuse but, after decades of decrepitude, it has been restored as the centerpiece of a small, upscale housing community, and is now privately owned. ◆ Bothell Way NE and NE Ballinger Way

43 Charlie Mac's Sports Club This sports bar replaced **Parker's,** a legendary North Seattle teen hangout of the 1950s and 1960s, and later a more sophisticated music venue. There's still dancing Wednesday through Saturday nights, but the dance floor can be converted to a basketball or volleyball court at will. There are dart boards, pool and Foosball tables, and 30—that's right, 30—color monitors and three giant screens for watching televised sports. ◆ Daily until 2AM. 17001 Aurora Ave N (at N 170th St). 542.9491

The Seattle band Soundgarden took its name from *Sound Garden,* a 1983 sculpture by California artist Douglas Hollis. The work, which stands outside the National Oceanic and Atmospheric Administration's Western Regional Center on the shores of Lake Washington, consists of twelve steel towers topped with structures resembling weather vanes. On one end of each tower is a vertical organ pipe; on the other is a wind vane that rotates the pipe. When the wind blows, a musical sound is created.

The 39 inches of rain that Seattle receives in a year is in fact less than what falls on New York or Boston or Atlanta. Miami actually puts up with a whopping 60 inches annually.

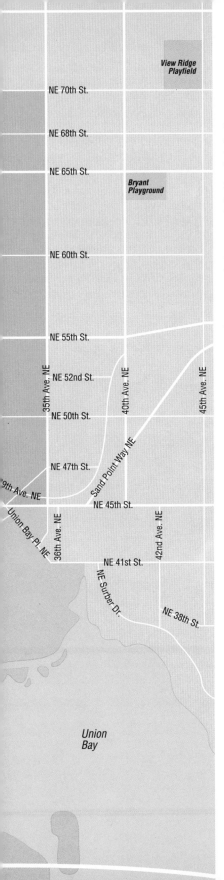

NE 70th St.

View Ridge
Playfield

NE 68th St.

NE 65th St.

Bryant
Playground

NE 60th St.

NE 55th St.

35th Ave. NE

40th Ave. NE

45th Ave. NE

NE 52nd St.

NE 50th St.

NE 47th St.

Sand Point Way NE

9th Ave. NE

NE 45th St.

Union Bay Pl. NE

36th Ave. NE

42nd Ave. NE

NE 41st St.

NE Surber Dr.

NE 38th St.

Union
Bay

University District/ Ravenna

Centered around the **University of Washington** (**UW**, which is pronounced "U Dub" by locals), the University District has grown with the institution, which opened its doors downtown in 1861, then relocated to this area just north of **Lake Union** in 1895. Around the beginning of the 20th century the "U District," as it's called, was sparsely populated, without paved streets, sewers, lights, or sidewalks. It could take half a day just to journey downtown by street-car. Residents called it "Brooklyn" back then, trusting that this neighbor-hood, like its namesake in New York, would thrive because it was adjacent to a big city.

In 1909 their faith was rewarded when Seattle held the Alaska-Yukon-Pacific Exposition (AYP) on the **UW** campus. This, the city's first World's Fair, was heavily promoted by business burghers who wished to attract East Coast attention and stimulate regional growth. University officials eagerly volunteered their land for the fair's site, hoping to reap a legacy of buildings and development for what was then a backwoods campus.

The AYP was a stunning success. It took two years to build, cost $10 million, drew 3.7 million visitors, turned a small profit ($62,676) despite the fact that liquor was banned in the district at the time, and stamped Seattle as a young city on the rise. Exhibits showcased 26 countries and featured dozens of Classical-style buildings set amid stately grounds laid out by the Olmsted Brothers of Massachusetts, the nation's foremost landscape architecture firm and principal players in Seattle's early planning. The AYP opened when President William Howard Taft pressed a golden telegraph key in Washington, DC, and switched on the fair's opening lights. (That same key would be used by President John F. Kennedy 53 years later to kick off the 1962 Century 21 Exposition.) It lasted more than four months, drawing visitors to hundreds of industrial, educational, and carnival exhibits. When the exposition was over, the neighborhood was left with sewers, water mains, and other modern amenities, and the university had been given a parklike campus and about 20 buildings. With the Olmsteds' help, the fairgrounds were adapted to university use.

Today the **University of Washington** is one of the largest single-campus universities on the West Coast. Its 694-acre tract, hosting nearly 34,000 students in 16 schools and colleges, occupies nearly half the neighborhood. A number of its component schools—including health sciences, engineering, and computer science—are counted among the nation's top 10. The neighborhood mirrors the school's diversity and energy. Streets are filled with bookstores, clothing shops, coffeehouses, and informal, inexpensive cafes. This area is a big reason why Seattle consistently ranks so high in per-capita movie attendance, book purchases, and espresso consumption. The district's spine, as well as its heart, is represented by **University Way** (better known as "The Ave"), which hosts the annual University Street Fair. Held in May, this popular arts and crafts fest brings long-haired vendors, street musicians, and the scent of patchouli oil back to these streets.

Colorful as it is, the U District isn't as interesting as it could be. Outside of the campus, it's dominated by dull, modern apartment buildings and loaded with bargain-filled restaurants, few of which are among the city's finest. And there is a dearth of places that have good music or dancing. More seriously, the Ave is frequently besieged by panhandlers and drug dealers. In general, however, this and other streets are safe to stroll after dark, which is a relief, because the district's flat topography invites walking.

Named for the large, lovely park that graces its center, Ravenna lies just north of the University District. It is a safe, well-tended, middle-class enclave where many **UW** professors and other staff members reside in 1920s and 1930s "bungaloids"—remodeled two-bedroom houses that have retained the neighborhood's original character. Only a few decades ago mainly middle-aged and older people dwelt here, but many families with young children have moved in and the playgrounds are full again. Nightlife in this neighborhood is practically nonexistent, but several good restaurants have popped up.

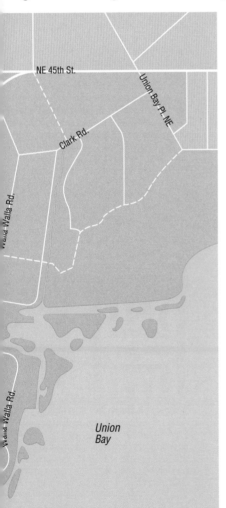

University District

1 Visitors' Information Center An ideal starting point for a tour of the neighborhood, the center offers campus maps, restaurant, lodging and bus info, and local events schedules. ♦ M-F. 4014 University Way NE (at NE Campus Pkwy). 543.9198

2 University of Washington The upper campus is the classic evocation of academia: ivy-covered Gothic buildings grouped around formal, brick-paved quadrangles; majestic sycamores, maples, and oaks; and curved walkways leading through nicely landscaped grounds. There's no denying that this is a lovely place to stroll, whether you're dazzled by the architecture, the cherry trees in bloom, or the million-dollar views of Lake Washington and the Cascade peaks from the student dorms. The lower campus, marked by newer, 1950s concrete edifices, also deserves attention for its beautiful gardens of medicinal herbs and its striking architecture (particularly the *Drumheller Fountain*, the four freestanding columns in a small grove on the southern part of campus, and even the parking garage, crowned with a small forest of evergreens and ivies). Today, the university has an enrollment of about 34,000; its most popular graduate schools are arts and sciences, engineering, medicine, law, and dentistry.

The main entrance is at the intersection of 17th Avenue NE and NE 45th Street, from which you travel along Memorial Way beneath a dramatic archway of sycamores to arrive on campus. At NE 41st Street, a pedestrian overpass crosses 15th Avenue NE to reach the university via Central Plaza. The entrance to the large parking garage (located below the plaza) is here, too. A third point of entry is on the eastern backside of campus, at 25th Avenue NE, about three-quarters of a mile north of **Husky Stadium.** ♦ 17th Ave NE and NE 45th St

In the University of Washington campus:

Central Plaza Commonly referred to as "Red Square" (attributable to its expanse of red bricks, not to any Bolshevik incidents), this campus crossroads was designed in 1972. The vast, almost treeless plaza is surrounded by stark, hard-surfaced buildings constructed in a mishmash arrangement of architectural styles. It's overpowering and strikes many people as depressing and inhuman, but on sunny days this spot resembles an Italian piazza, alive with students strumming guitars, throwing Frisbees, and enjoying brown-bag lunches. ♦ 15th Ave NE and NE 41st St

Suzzallo/Allen Library Certainly the most impressive building on campus, this ornate Tudor Gothic library was designed by **Carl Gould** and dates from about 1926. Founder of the university's architecture department, **Gould** laid out plans for 18 campus buildings (as well as **Volunteer Park**'s old **Seattle Art Museum** and, with partner **Charles Bebb,** the **Times Square Building** downtown).

The library was the crowning achievement—and, ironically, the downfall—of Henry Suzzallo, former university president (1915-26), who is often recalled as **UW**'s "modern father." Suzzallo wanted an ambitious, cathedral-like building, believing that "the library is the soul of the university." Washington Governor Roland Hartley didn't agree: He looked at the $900,000 invoice, dubbed it "Suzzallo's extravagance," and fired the respected educator, who went on to head the philanthropic Carnegie Foundation.

Outside, observe three sculptures perched over the entrance: *Thought, Inspiration,* and *Mastery,* created by Tacoma artist Allan Clark (see **Art Around the Plaza,** below). Inside, follow the curved staircase from the building's entrance to the mezzanine-level **Graduate Reading Room,** where vaulting and 36-foot-high stained-glass windows tower above. ♦ Daily; M-Th, Su until midnight (hours are more restricted during school breaks). Central Plaza

Smith Hall Twenty-eight gargoyles decorate the exterior of this 1940 building, which houses the history and geography departments. Designed by faculty member Dudley Pratt, each gargoyle symbolizes something different. Six figures at the east

entrance signify humankind's primitive needs, while those on the southeast corner depict concepts of weather. Those on the northeast corner stand for the power and war of Europe, the magic of Africa, and the knowledge of the Orient. A book-laden egghead in the grouping stands for the intelligent democracy of America. Groups on the north side depict Seattle's history. ♦ Adjacent to the Suzzallo/Allen Library

Meany Hall Named in honor of a popular and longtime history professor, Edmond S. Meany, this performing arts center contains a 1,200-seat theater, a 200-seat studio, and dance facilities. Excellent acoustics and intimate seating make it one of the city's premier venues for chamber music series, dance recitals, and concerts. ♦ Central Plaza. 543.4880

Art around the Plaza The west facade of the **Suzzallo/Allen Library** hosts 18 terra-cotta figures of famous people, including Shakespeare, Beethoven, and Plato. The original design for Darwin featured a small ape thumbing its nose at the humans below, but the university president vetoed that concept. (Look closely at Darwin, and you'll see a hole at the bottom of the figure where the ape was supposed to be.) Hidden behind oak trees, the Gothic **Administration Building** on the south side of the plaza is ringed by 24 gargoyles and other figures, each one representing an academic discipline. The square contains *Broken Obelisk,* a two-ton, 26-foot steel work that resembles an upside-down pencil and is a rare sculpture by Barnett Newman, a New York painter known mostly for abstract color fields. The three faux-campaniles that soar into the sky are visually striking but have a more quotidian purpose as well: They are vents to disperse car exhaust fumes from the underground garage. A bronze statue of George Washington on the square's west side was sculpted in 1909 by Lorado Taft and unveiled for the AYP Expo.

Henry Art Gallery This **Carl Gould**–designed museum boasts classical lines: Tudor Gothic architecture, striking decorative brickwork, and handsome skylit exhibition galleries. Opened in 1927, its construction was funded by Horace C. Henry, a local real estate and railroad magnate, who also donated an art collection worth more than $400,000 to it. The gallery blends past and present, so you might stumble upon a video exhibition just as easily as you would a display of historical Western landscapes or modern Chinese painting. The permanent collection contains the 19th- and early 20th-century American and European paintings from Henry's original contribution. ◆ Donation requested. Tu-Su; Th until 9PM. Central Plaza. 543.2280

Denny Hall Built circa 1895, this turreted French Renaissance structure was the first—and for some time the only—building on campus. Given the hall's original importance, its very ordinary location (with no expansive view over Lake Union) seems curious. But campus legend has it that officials argued for so long over the building's proper site that one exasperated regent finally stuck his umbrella into a fallen fir tree and said, "You fellows can put the building where you want it; I'm going to put it here." And there it's been ever since. ◆ Off Memorial Way

Thomas Burke Memorial Washington State Museum Exhibits in natural history, anthropology, and geology from Pacific Rim cultures span many epochs in this museum. High on the list of must-sees is the collection of Northwest Coast Indian artifacts. An Alaskan Arctic collection of basketry, ivory, beadwork, and masks (like the three pictured above) wins accolades. Children will enjoy the dinosaur skeletons, fossils, and totem poles. Take a look at the stained-glass window portraying a peacock in the **Burke Room**: It's by master Louis Comfort Tiffany himself. The museum was designed in 1962 by **James J. Chiarelli** in honor of Judge Thomas Burke, an attorney who negotiated early Seattle land acquisitions for **Great Northern Railroad** builder James J. Hill. ◆ Donation requested. Daily; Th until 10PM. NE 45th St (between Memorial Way and 15th Ave NE). 543.5590

Within the Thomas Burke Memorial Washington State Museum:

The Boiserie ★★$ The museum's basement contains the toniest and one of the most pleasant coffeehouses in Seattle. The high-ceilinged room features 18th-century French pine panels and artwork, antique wooden tables, classical music, and very tasty pastries. It's a favorite spot for students between classes, and a rest stop for campus cops. Desserts are plentiful and delicious; the carrot cake comes from the Broadway Baking Company. The tree-shaded patio is ideal for lounging on warm days. ◆ Coffeehouse ◆ Daily; M-F until 8PM. 543.5884 ⊛

Penthouse Theater Built in about 1940 as the nation's first theater-in-the-round (the frescoes and seats have been restored to their original state), this is the stage for the **School of Drama**'s productions. Tickets are available here at the box office or at the **UW Ticket Office** (4001 University Way NE, at NE 40th St, 543.4880), which is open Monday through Friday from 10:30AM to 6PM. ◆ Box office opens one hour before show time. NE 45th St (opposite 20th Ave NE). 543.4880

Architecture Hall This is the only major structure built for the Alaska-Yukon-Pacific Expo that is left standing. San Francisco's **John Galen Howard,** who in 1909 was campus architect for the University of California, Berkeley, created the eclectic classical style design. Today, the building houses the **Department of Urban Planning.** ◆ Stevens Way

 Frosh Pond, Rainier Vista During the AYP Exposition this body of water was a geyser basin. Afterward it became a spot where first-year students received honorary dunkings from sophomores (hence the name). And today it's a decorative pool with a fountain—officially called the *Drumheller Fountain*—that's especially appealing when the surrounding roses are in bloom. Proud moms and dads snap Polaroids of students here. The walkway down to the Montlake Bridge was designed by the Olmsted Brothers in 1909 as a culminating viewpoint from which fairgoers could eyeball Mount Rainier. ◆ South of Central Plaza

Sylvan Theater The grassy glade, site of an annual summer Shakespeare series, is easily missed. Tucked away within a grove of trees, it contains a cool, shady amphitheater and four white columns standing by themselves with nothing to support. These columns, shaped of cedar poles, were transported—at the insistence of Professor Edmond Meany—from their positions at the entrance to the original downtown **Territorial University** building, when that old edifice was finally being torn down in 1908. Each of the four columns has a name—Loyalty, Industry, Faith, and Efficiency—the first letters of each spelling LIFE. ◆ Stevens Way

The University of Washington was founded in 1861 by the Reverend Daniel Bagley. Bagley had originally wanted to build a church in what is now the University District, but the city government refused to give him permission, so he built the university instead.

Restaurants/Clubs: Red   **Hotels:** Blue

Shops/ ☂ Outdoors: Green   **Sights/Culture:** Black

There's Something Fishy Here

Turn over a rock at **Golden Gardens** park on **Shilshole Bay** and you have a good chance of encountering *Pachygrapsus crassipes* (the lined shore crab). You may only have a moment or two before this inch-long green creature scurries off sideways in search of a new hideout. Don't bother giving chase. Plenty of other charming, if equally reclusive, animals can be found along this sandy stretch of land.

Puget Sound is inhabited by several thousand marine species. Most are small-bodied invertebrates (oysters, clams, urchins, crabs, anemones, and squids), but some are certifiable giants, thriving on this briny soup's ample food supply and fairly mild oceanic climate. Less than a hundred feet off the **Golden Gardens** shore, for instance, lurks *Octopus dofleini,* the world's largest octopus, a mottled red Schwarzenegger of a cephalopod with an arm span extending 25 feet. A bit farther out, on the Sound's silty bottom, rests the 10-pound geoduck (pronounced *goo*-ee-duck), a mega-mollusk that qualifies as the world's largest burrowing clam.

Like the secretive shore crab *Pachygrapsus,* many local invertebrates are beach dwellers, occupying cozy niches in the intertidal zone—that thin strip of earth bathed by ocean waves as the tides move in and out. To survive under such transitional conditions, many animals have changed their looks and behaviors. For example, the small colonial sea anemone, *Anthopleura,* resembles a plant more than an animal, while the limpet (a tiny, rock-hugging cousin of the snail) could pass for a smooth stone.

On the rocky beaches (such as in **Mukilteo,** 20 miles north of Seattle), fish and invertebrates hide in the cracks and crevices between boulders or among the kelp and other seaweeds that grow abundantly at the water's edge. Sandy shores (like those at **Golden Gardens** or the city of **Edmonds,** another short excursion 10 miles north of Seattle) are usually featureless plains that merge into eelgrass beds—underwater meadows that offer food and shelter to anything that lives on or near the bottom. Both beach types make fine destinations for intertidal explorers.

To get better acquainted with this curious, often colorful, community of the sea, visit the **Seattle Aquarium** (Pier 59 on the Waterfront, 386.4320), where you'll meet all local beach dwellers face-to-face. Afterward pick up a good field guide to intertidal life, either Gloria Snively's revised edition of *Exploring the Seashore in British Columbia, Washington, and Oregon* (1991, The Writing Works) or *Seashore Life of the Northern Pacific Coast* by Eugene Kozloff (1983, University of Washington Press). And finally, procure a local tide table, available from larger bookstores in the city. Tidepooling requires taking advantage of two brief windows of opportunity, periods of approximately four to six hours each day, when the tides ebb and the intertidal zone is most accessible to exploration. Exactly how long and how wide these windows swing varies daily. But in the summer the lowest tides generally occur around midday. As winter approaches they fall between 9PM and midnight, making tidepooling a more difficult enterprise but no less rewarding as long as you have a flashlight in hand.

Don't presume, however, that only cold-blooded creatures will be joining you at the beach. A vast array of waterfowl and shorebirds also visit Seattle's coastline. Several of these, including the diminutive Bonaparte's gull, travel thousands of miles from central Alaska to winter in the Emerald City. Others, such as the western and glaucous-winged gull, prefer the year-round comfort of urban beaches, piers, and marinas over life on the road. Regardless of their summer plans, all arrive at these seashores with one thing in mind: the seafood smorgasbord that's uncovered with every outgoing tide.

Binoculars might help you espy some warm-blooded mammals—particularly harbor seals and California sea lions. Still farther from shore swim the area's sleek black-and-white killer whales, highly intelligent and surprisingly swift hunters of salmon, cod, halibut, and hake. Killer whales (or orcas) are actually more closely related to dolphins than to whales, and they spend their entire lives in extended family groupings called pods. For an excellent background on these mammals, read *Field Guide to the Orca* by David G. Gordon and Chuck Flaherty (1990, Sasquatch Books).

Husky Stadium Football-crazed fans watch the **Huskies** (often called "The Dawgs" but never "Dogs") here in the Northwest's largest stadium, which seats 72,500 people. It's said that the Wave cheer was invented here in 1981 by the marching band director and cheerleader, Robb Weller. The south section of the cantilevered steel balcony and roof was finally erected in 1987, after a calamitous construction accident in which steel support beams weakened and the entire section crumbled into a massive pile of twisted metal. No one was hurt, but the scene was immortalized when a photographer, John Stamets, riding by on his bicycle, snapped a frame-by-frame account of the collapse and published it in a local newspaper. ♦ Montlake Blvd NE. 543.2200

 Waterfront Activities Center Rent canoes or rowboats to cross Union Bay and then wander through the soft, lily-padded backwaters near the **Washington Park Arboretum** (see the "Capitol Hill to Seward Park" chapter on page 90) for a Monet-like experience. Bird-watchers might want to go north from the center, creeping along the shore to see blue herons, eagles, and other wild creatures in a protected reserve.

◆ M-F Feb-Oct. Walla Walla Rd (on Union Bay). 543.9433

3 College Inn Guest House $ Popular with visiting professors and other university types on a budget, this bed-and-breakfast was built as a hotel for the 1909 AYP, and is on the National Register of Historic Places. The 25 rooms are very plain and spare (no TV, no telephones, no private baths), but they are clean and generally pleasant. ◆ 4000 University Way NE (at NE 40th St). 633.4441

4 Burke-Gilman Trail This beloved, 12.5-mile recreational route runs along an abandoned **Burlington Northern** railbed. More than a million people bike, jog, or walk here each year. The scenic trail hugs Lake Union and then crawls east and north, virtually through the backyards of lakefront homes, until it reaches Kenmore's **Tracy Owen Station Park** at the northern tip of Lake Washington. One caveat: 70 percent of trail users are bicyclists, so walkers should take extra care. ◆ From Gas Works Park, Fremont, to Tracy Owen Station Park, Kenmore

4 Northlake Tavern & Pizza House ★★$ The principal wall decorations here are cartoons from the *Seattle Post-Intelligencer*'s David Horsey, but there's nothing comic about the pizza here. Crusts (including a respectable whole-wheat variety) are chewy without threatening to yank out your wisdom teeth, and the cooks have nothing against piling on the toppings. Build your own pie from a 14-ingredient list, or just order the Italian Special (salami, Italian beef sausage, mushrooms, onions, and tomatoes). You can even buy an uncooked pizza to pop in the oven later on. ◆ Pizza/Takeout ◆ Daily lunch and dinner. 660 NE Northlake Way (at I-5). 633.5317 &

5 University Inn $ A $2.5-million wing (erected in 1992) has added a sleek touch to this small, friendly, modern hotel (pictured above). There are 102 comfortable rooms—none with a view worth mentioning, however—a small heated outdoor pool, a coffee shop, and complimentary continental breakfast. ◆ 4140 Roosevelt Way NE (between NE 41st and NE 42nd Sts). 632.5055, 800/733.3855; fax 547.4937 &

6 European Restaurant & Pastry Shop ★$ German-style food (Hungarian goulash, stuffed cabbage rolls, sausage sandwiches) is served in an Old World atmosphere. Most people, though, come here for the pastries,

especially the Black Forest cake. ◆ German ◆ M-Sa breakfast, lunch, and dinner; Su lunch. 4108 University Way NE (between NE 41st and NE 42nd Sts). 632.7893 &

7 Folk Art Gallery—La Tienda Begun in the early 1960s by an anthropology aficionado who brought back a carload of trinkets from Tijuana, this small shop has flowered into a folk art treasure trove. Gift-hunters can choose items from 80 countries: Chilean rain sticks, Guatemalan ceremonial *huipils* (woven ponchos), Balinese masks, and Indonesian shadow puppets. ◆ M-Sa; Th until 9PM. 4138 University Way NE (between NE 41st and NE 42nd Sts). 632.1796

7 Shultzy's Sausage ★$ The homemade sausages served at this hole-in-the-wall are ground and stuffed with Uncle Norm's recipe. Lines form out the door for the spicy-hot Ragin' Cajun and milder andouille choices. ◆ Deli ◆ Daily lunch and dinner. 4142 University Way NE (between NE 41st and NE 42nd Sts). 548.9461

8 Big Time Brewery and Alehouse This tavern-turned-brewpub offers six kinds of beer made on the premises, all flavorful, unpasteurized, and heavier than your standard-issue Bud. An 80-year-old back bar, hardwood floors, vintage signs, and a jukebox create a traditional American alehouse atmosphere. Large front windows allow for a maximum of people watching. The small kitchen produces hefty sandwiches, pizza, and very acceptable nachos. ◆ M-Th, Su until 12:30AM; F-Sa until 1AM. 4133 University Way NE (between NE 41st and NE 42nd Sts). 545.4509

9 Magus Bookstore Unswept floors, books stacked precariously high, and an erudite, helpful staff—this is your quintessential college used-book seller. Don't expect to find Judith Krantz among the piles of literature, philosophy, history, and art books. ◆ Daily; F-Sa until 10PM. 1408 NE 42nd St (at University Way NE). 633.1800

9 Cafe Allegro ★$ Reputed to have introduced Seattle to espresso during the 1960s and still a funkier, more traditional coffeehouse than most in the city, this small, smoky, brick-lined cafe enjoys a remarkably loyal clientele. There's great coffee, ordinary pastries, and a staff that will let you curl up in a corner to read *War and Peace* in its entirety, if you so desire. ◆ Coffeehouse ◆ Daily until

169

11PM. 4214 University Way NE (in the alley around the corner from Magus Bookstore). 633.3030

10 Bulldog News The largest, most eclectic newsstand in the Northwest carries everything from the *New Yorker* and *National Review* to *Spin, Story,* British *Esquire, The Hockey News,* and *British Columbia Report.* Hundreds of alternative weeklies, out-of-town papers, and foreign periodicals are also on hand. Service can sometimes be indifferent to your requests. An espresso counter dispenses drinks to sidewalk patrons; watch out, the lines here can get long. ♦ Daily 8AM-9PM. 4208 University Way NE (between NE 42nd and NE 43rd Sts). 632.6397. Also at: Broadway Market (401 Broadway E at E Harrison St). 322.6397 &

11 University Book Store Banished from campus in 1925 when its location was deemed a fire hazard, the business landed here, the former site of a pool hall that was closed by state authorities to protect students from "distractions." The present store, now the largest bookstore in Seattle and one of the largest college bookstores in the nation, offers an extensive selection of general fiction, mysteries, science fiction, and travel books. The children's department is estimable, and textbooks and academic press offerings can be found in almost overwhelming proportions. There's free gift wrapping on the second floor and frequent sales on general-interest books. ♦ Daily; Th until 9PM. 4326 University Way NE (between NE 43rd and NE 44th Sts). 634.3400. Also at: 990 102nd Ave NE (at NE 10th St), Bellevue. 632.9500

12 Toscana ★★$$ Sit down to a candlelit dinner with white tablecloths and imagine yourself in an intimate, no-name *ristorante* off the Via Veneto. The homemade pastas are light and zesty (especially the ravioli stuffed with either cheese or venison), the stuffed chicken and sautéed squid are expertly prepared, and the desserts are wonderful. ♦ Italian ♦ M, W-Su dinner. 1312½ NE 43rd St (between University Way NE and Brooklyn Ave NE). 547.7679

13 Safeco Building At 23 stories in height, the tallest—and some would say the ugliest—building in the district is corporate head-quarters for an insurance company. More interesting, the company has assembled a $1-million, 600-piece collection of modern Northwest art and makes some of it accessible to the public. Go into the lobby or up to the mezzanine to see rotating exhibitions of Pilchuck School glass and abstract paintings. The bronze fountain outside was created by famed local sculptor George Tsutakawa. **Naramore, Bain, Brady & Johanson** (precursors of today's **NBBJ Group**) designed the tower. ♦ M-F. 4333 Brooklyn Ave NE (at NE 45th St)

14 Neptune Theater One of Seattle's first-run movie houses, this elaborate palace was built in 1921 to showcase silent movies. It was renovated in 1993, when plastic "stained glass" was covered up and the original plasterwork featuring renditions of Neptune's head was restored. Grillwork over the organ pipes features tridents and starfish. ♦ 1303 NE 45th St (between University Way NE and Brooklyn Ave NE). 633.5545 &

15 Meany Tower Hotel $$ The district's first luxury hostelry, this 14-story building opened to great fanfare in 1931. The architect was **Robert C. Reamer,** who also designed those oversize mountain cabins known as the Old Faithful Inn and the Canyon Hotel in Yellowstone National Park (a far cry from the Art Deco column here). Today, it's one of the neighborhood's nicer hotels—not as luxurious as some of the downtown spots, but much more economical. **Reamer** (whose other credits include the **Skinner Building** and the **1411 Fourth Avenue Building** downtown) shaped the hotel so that each of the 155 guest rooms provides a broad corner view. (Ask for a room facing either south to the city or east across Lake Washington.) On the first floor, the **Meany Grill** serves prime rib, steaks, and seafood in an undistinguished setting. The lounge has a big-screen TV and an oyster bar. ♦ 4507 Brooklyn Ave NE (at NE 45th St). 634.2000, 800/648.6440

16 New Seattle Massage A longtime district fave for relaxing, hands-on treatments, this salon offers a variety of techniques, including Swedish, shiatsu, and sports styles by 39 licensed massage therapists. ♦ Daily until 9PM. Call for an appointment. 4519 ½ University Way NE (between NE 45th and NE 47th Sts). 632.5074

The term "flying saucer" was first used after Civil Air Pilot Kenneth Arnold, who was searching on 24 June 1947 for a military plane that had gone down near Mount Rainier and spotted instead a formation of nine brilliant, boomerang-shaped objects flying from Rainier toward Mount Adams. Asked to describe his odd encounter, Arnold compared the flight of his bogeys to an undulating kite tail or a "saucer skipping across the water." Thus was born one of the most popular unsolved mysteries of the 20th century.

Restaurants/Clubs: Red   **Hotels:** Blue

Shops/ ♥ Outdoors: Green   **Sights/Culture:** Black

17 **The Continental Restaurant** ★$ Old-timers play backgammon, the post-grad crowd sips retsina in an unhurried atmosphere, and parents of young children return time and again because owner Demetre Lagos works magic with unruly tots. The souvlaki sandwiches, Greek fries, and feta cheese omelettes are all good. ♦ Greek♦ Daily breakfast, lunch, and dinner. 4549 University Way NE (between NE 45th and NE 47th Sts). 632.4700

17 **University Seafood & Poultry** Very fresh, high-quality gifts from the sea—Dungeness crabs, local oysters, salmon, halibut, caviar—are sold at this third-generation, family-owned business. The shop will pack and ship your fish by overnight courier or put it in an airline-approved, odorless, leakproof carton good for 48 hours. ♦ M-Sa. 1317 NE 47th St (at University Way NE). 632.3900

18 **Greek Row** Six blocks of stately, traditional, brick-faced fraternity and sorority houses set amid a long archway of tall trees will make you want to get out your college letter sweater and yell, "Sis boom bah!" Of the 31 frat houses and 18 sororities, the most interesting include the **Sigma Nu House** (1616 NE 47th St), built in 1926 and designed by architect **Ellsworth Storey**) with Wrightian overtones; the **Alpha Tau Omega House** (1800 NE 47th St), completed in 1929 and designed by **Lionel Pries**, a former professor at **UW**'s **Department of Architecture**; and the **Phi Gamma Delta House** (5404 17th Ave NE), a Tudor Revival edifice built in 1927 and designed by **Mellor, Meigs & Howe** with **J. Lister Holmes.**

Sadly, this Ivy League atmosphere was also the setting for the 1975 disappearance of Georgann Hawkins, an 18-year-old coed living at a nearby sorority house. She was among the victims of serial killer Ted Bundy, a good-looking, smooth-talking former **UW** psychology student who terrorized Seattle during the 1970s before he was caught and finally executed in Florida in 1989. Bundy confessed to more than a dozen murders in Washington, Oregon, and Utah, but detectives suspect he actually committed somewhere between three dozen and a hundred. ♦ Between NE 45th and 50th Sts, and 22nd and 17th Aves NE

19 **The Chambered Nautilus** $$ Innkeepers Bill and Bunny Hagemeyer opened this charming bed and breakfast in the mid-1980s, naming it after a type of seashell. Built in 1915, the historic Georgian Colonial was originally the home of Dr. Herbert Gowan, a British missionary who founded the Asian Studies department at the university. It

features six antique-filled guest rooms (four with private baths), a living room with a fireplace, a formal dining room with a spectacular view of the Cascades to the east, and a large enclosed sun porch overlooking the garden. It's conveniently located close to the university, **Ravenna Park,** Green Lake, and downtown Seattle. A full breakfast is included in the room rate, and complimentary tea and cookies are served each afternoon. ♦ 5005 22nd Ave NE (between 21st Pl NE and NE 54th St). 522.2536

20 **University Village** Several large chain stores (including **Eddie Bauer** and **Barnes and Noble**) anchor this shopping center, and more than 60 independent shops sell clothes, gift items, and home furnishings. Brick walkways, a fountain, and a casual pace suited to browsing help reduce the frenzy and stress that so often accompanies mall shopping. **Caldwell's** (522.7531) carries ethnic and decorative home accessories such as New England crafts, Mexican folk art, African pots, as well as wicker tables, chairs, baskets, and boxes; **VIVA** (525.8482) and **Marlee** (522.6526) are popular for their exclusive women's apparel; **Paint the Town** (527.8554) sells plain ceramics for you to paint and decorate as you wish; **Teri's Toybox** (729.0750) sells kids' playthings and games; and **Pasta and Co.** (523.8594) offers tempting appetizers and salads (try the marinated chicken breasts, tortellini, or Chinese vermicelli). The most recent addition is **Sundance** (729.0750), the first retail outlet of Robert Redford's catalog company offering Western- and Southwestern-inspired clothing, jewelry, and home accessories. ♦ 25th Ave NE and NE 45th St. 523.0622

21 **Grand Illusion** This independently owned theater regularly books experimental or political films. The screen is small and the viewing room is claustrophobic, but a blue velvet couch in the back row gets a thumbs-up for romance. ♦ Box office opens a half-hour before show time. 1493 NE 50th St (at University Way NE). 523.3935

22 **University Heights Elementary School** Established in 1902, the district's first primary school grew in the 1920s to become the largest in Seattle. Contending that major repairs were needed, the school district closed the school down several years ago, despite widespread community protest. The wooden-framed structure, designed by **Bebb & Mendel** (who would later create the **Ballard Firehouse**), is now used by nonprofit organizations and community groups. ♦ 5031 University Way NE (between NE 50th and NE 52nd Sts). 527.4278

23 **Giggles Comedy Nite Club** Stand-up comics with national reputations (including Jerry Seinfeld and Ellen DeGeneres) have appeared here. Music acts are sometimes featured as well. ♦ Cover. Shows: Th-Sa 8PM and 10PM. Reservations recommended. 5220 Roosevelt Way NE (between NE 52nd and NE 55th St). 526.5653

24 University Branch Library Architects **W. Marbury Somervell** and **Joseph C. Cote** were busy in the year 1910. Not only were they putting the final touches on this building, but they were also working on two other Seattle libraries that opened that same year: the **Green Lake Public Library** and the **West Seattle Public Library.** All three structures look eerily similar, all showing Mediterranean touches, as perhaps was the architects' intention. In any case, this building, like its brethren, is a handsome legacy of an ambitious project. It is one of eight libraries still standing in the Seattle area that were built thanks to the largess of iron-and-steel-magnate Andrew Carnegie. ♦ M, W-Sa. 5009 Roosevelt Way NE (at NE 50th St). 684.4063

25 Mamma Melina Ristorante ★★★$$ Excellent Neapolitan cuisine is served in an open, elegant room decorated with bright frescoes. The sounds of Puccini (sometimes too loud) flow through the air and Mamma herself may be in the kitchen. Reviewers rave over the lasagna, which is strewn with tiny meatballs, but you can't really go wrong with any of the dishes. The appetizers, the spinach cannelloni, and the veal dishes all deserve stars. Singers perform arias from Italian operas on Friday and Saturday evenings. ♦ Italian ♦ Tu-Su dinner. 4759 Roosevelt Way NE (at NE 50th St). 632.2271 &

25 Cinema Books A major find for film buffs, this specialty shop sells movie picture books, celebrity bios, screenplays, guidebooks to shows, technical and analytical treatises, and some film memorabilia (posters, stills, a hundred different Marilyn Monroe postcards). ♦ M-Sa. 4753 Roosevelt Way NE (between NE 47th and NE 50th Sts). 547.7667

25 Seven Gables Theater Once upon a time there was a single theater in Seattle that showed high-quality films. Called **Seven Gables**, it grew into a chain and then sold out to a California operator. Now with nine theaters and 28 screens in town, it operates on the premise that if given the chance, people will support literary and/or noncommercial movies. Often used as a test market for independent productions, this chain has "saved" several small, noteworthy films (among them *The Black Stallion, The Stunt Man,* and *Never Cry Wolf*) that Hollywood had written off. This theater is the chain's flagship and specializes in fine foreign films. Its viewing room is small, but the antique-decorated lobby is beautiful. ♦ 911 NE 50th St (between Roosevelt Way NE and Ninth Ave NE). 632.8820

26 Metro Cinemas With 10 screens, Dolby sound, and a mix of good-quality, first-run commercial and independent films, this theater

is a sanctuary on a rainy afternoon. There's even a soundproof room for infants. ♦ 4500 Ninth Ave NE (at NE 45th St). 633.0055 &

26 Stella's Trattoria ★$$ This lively, bistrolike establishment is ideal for grabbing a quick bite before or after a movie at the adjacent **Metro Cinemas.** Nighthawks, rejoice: one of Seattle's rare all-night eating spots, this joint is still jumping at 3AM. Pastas, fish, and breakfast are served after 11PM when the full menu isn't available. This is one of a small chain of restaurants that also includes **Trattoria Mitchelli** in Pioneer Square and **Angelina's** in West Seattle. ♦ Italian ♦ Daily 24 hours. 4500 Ninth Ave NE (at NE 45th St). 633.1100

27 Blue Moon Tavern Poet Carolyn Kizer once described this tavern as "a grubby oasis just outside the university's one-mile-limit Sahara. Here, the jukebox roars, Audrey the waitress slaps down schooners of beer, and poets, pedants, painters, and other assorted wildlife make overtures to each other." She wrote that in 1956, but not much has changed. This fabled bar, supposedly frequented by Ginsberg, Kerouac, Roethke, and Tom Robbins, still attracts free spirits and loosely wrapped crazies. In 1990 it was scheduled to be razed, but an 11th-hour campaign to save the bar prevailed. Sunday night the tape deck plays only **Grateful Dead** music; Monday is Opera Night. ♦ Daily noon-2AM. 712 NE 45th St (between Eighth and Seventh Aves NE). No phone

Ravenna

28 Salvatore Ristorante Italiano ★★★$$ Specializing in Southern Italian cuisine, including veal so tender you could cut it with a plastic fork, this dining spot serves a varied selection of delicious pastas and features an extensive wine list with gentle prices to complement your meal. ♦ Italian ♦ M-Sa dinner. 6100 Roosevelt Way NE (at NE 61st St). 527.9301

29 Sunlight Cafe ★$ This vegetarian restaurant serves a full menu, including soyburgers, tofu scrambles, and various stir-fry concoctions. Whole-wheat waffles, blueberry pancakes, and nutritious muffins draw healthy crowds on weekends. ♦ Vegetarian ♦ M-F breakfast, lunch, and dinner; Sa-Su breakfast and dinner. 6403 Roosevelt Way NE (at NE 64th St). 522.9060 &

30 Cowen Park Donated in 1907 by Charles Cowen, an Englishman reared in South Africa, this area was undeveloped until the city filled and flattened it with dirt from freeway construction in 1961. The result is an eight-acre patch of picnic grounds with a playfield used for softball. The park is used heavily by the neighborhood despite periodic incursions by transients. ♦ University Way NE and Ravenna Blvd NE

31 Bagel Oasis ★★$ Some of the best bagels in town are available here: big, soft, chewy, and often sold hot right out of the oven. Nosh on any of these with cream-cheese spreads and Port Chatham lox, or order them as part of a sandwich. Also served are soups, salads, and filling breakfast omelettes. ♦ Deli ♦ Daily breakfast and lunch. 2112 NE 65th St (between Ravenna and 21st Aves NE). 526.0525

32 Santa Fe Cafe ★★★$$ Enjoy New Mexican cooking at its best. Blue-corn tortillas are used in many of the zingy, flavorful dishes. One longtime favorite is the artichoke ramekin appetizer, baked with green chilies and kasseri cheese. The *chiles rellenos* tart is also outstanding. Try any of the dishes that come with the house green sauce. And the margaritas have won newspaper polls as the best in the city. ♦ Southwestern ♦ M-F lunch and dinner. 2255 NE 65th St (between Ravenna and 22nd Aves NE). 524.7736 ♿. Also at: 5910 Phinney Ave N (between N 59th and N 60th Sts). 783.9755 ♿

33 Ravenna Park Clarence Bagley, a Seattle pioneer and local historian, complained in the early 20th century that this 52-acre park was "a dark, damp, dismal hole in the ground for which the city paid an outrageous price." Bagley must have been quite a sourpuss, because in our opinion this is an urban gem.

A creek bed once ran from Green Lake through this heavily wooded ravine and drained into Lake Washington. History buffs say the area was home to an invigorating mineral springs and a magnificent stand of trees—giant evergreens 30 to 60 feet in diameter. It so impressed a realtor named William W. Beck, who bought it as part of a 300-acre tract, that he named it after the parklike Italian town of Ravenna. Beck also named the largest trees after famous people—Teddy Roosevelt and Robert E. Lee among them—and charged visitors 25¢ a head to enter his sanctuary. The city coveted his land and eventually acquired it through condemnation in 1911. But it promptly destroyed much of the park's grandeur by lowering Green Lake and cutting off the creek, then constructing an underground drainage system and toppling the great trees Beck had so admired, to be sold as cordwood.

Today, the park is minus its virgin timber, but it still feels like a small piece of wilderness within city limits. It boasts two large playgrounds on either end (in **Lower Ravenna Park** and in **Cowen Park**), joined together by a natural ravine and small creek. Quiet and unsculpted, this ravine sometimes seems imbued with magic (one writer called it a hobbit's realm) as it follows Ravenna Creek through steeply sloped brush- and fern-covered forestland. A wide trail here provides a 20-minute walk for strollers and a shorter but still soothing escape for runners during the daytime. Come night, however, transients sometimes hang out in the park, so be cautious. ♦ Bounded by NE 55th and NE 62nd Sts, and 25th and 15th Aves NE

34 Lower Ravenna Park Walking east of the main park, the ravine empties into a broad field and baseball diamond. Above it, you'll come across a small playfield, playground, and tennis courts with full sun exposure. Keep walking up the hill and wind through a series of small, serene meadows where you can picnic at tables, read in solitude, or just listen to the many songbirds. Go farther, and you'll dead-end at a larger meadow that has a covered barbecue pit area. ♦ 20th Ave NE and NE 58th St

35 Ravenna Boulevard Designed by the Olmsted Brothers to be part of their chain of Seattle parks linked by boulevards, this once marked the Ravenna neighborhood's northern boundary. Now, the wide, grassy, tree-lined strip is a favorite for runners. ♦ Between Ravenna Park and Green Lake

36 Killing Time What else would this place be but a mystery bookstore? It stocks new hardcovers, paperbacks, books-on-tape, even mysteries for children. The knowledgeable staff members are happy to discuss and recommend works, and there are frequent author readings and signings. ♦ Tu-Su. 2821 NE 55th St (between 30th and 27th Aves NE). 525.2266

37 Queen Mary ★★$$$ This could very well be the site of the Mad Hatter's Tea Party—from the shards of lovely crockery imbedded in the sidewalk outside to the flowered chintz curtains inside. Owner Mary Greengo has created a perfect spot for a leisurely afternoon tea of tomato-and-basil sandwiches and lemon curd tart. And, if you're late for a very important date, pick up a sweet morsel from the pastry case. ♦ American ♦ M-W, Su breakfast, lunch, and tea; Th-Sa breakfast, lunch, tea, and dinner. 2912 NE 55th St (between 30th and 29th Aves NE). 527.2770

Eastside

Places separated from others by water—Venice, Valhalla, the New World—have traditionally held a certain allure. So it's not surprising that the suburban communities nestled on the near-east side of **Lake Washington**—principally **Mercer Island, Bellevue,** and **Kirkland**—always have been and probably always will be a dreamland for somebody.

Pioneer Peter Kirk set out in the 1880s to build the "Pittsburgh of the West" on the forested slopes above **Moss Bay.** But this industrial capital of belching steel- and ironworks never materialized. And in 1928, before the first bridge was built across the lake, real estate baron James Ditty laid out a plan for an Eastside utopia that included blimps traveling to and from downtown Seattle and huge observation towers in the midst of Mercer Island; this dream also was unrealized. An advertisement from the 1940s solicited interest from Seattleites with the slogan "15 Minutes to Your Home in the Country." It seems a cruel joke now, when even a slug might outpace the heavy rush-hour traffic across the lake.

But thousands of new residents continue to be drawn here by the quality of life (including the fairly safe schools) and by booming high-tech industries (computer giant Microsoft and cellular phone purveyor McCaw Communications among them). Neighborhood strip malls and well-groomed suburban lawns characterize the Eastside of today. It's the fourth-largest urban area in Washington state, and very much ruled by the automobile. Only a few enclaves, such as **Beaux Arts Village,** southwest of downtown Bellevue, have escaped the rule of the road. Founded in 1908 as a rustic artists' commune (and for a while it was a nudists' colony), this lovely residential hideaway is still woven with streets barely wide enough for two cars to pass.

The look and attitude of the Eastside varies greatly from one district to the next. Mercer Island is primarily residential, bisected at its north end by Interstate 90. It boasts only a small commercial zone and is a leisurely ride for bicyclists. Kirkland has several art galleries, antiques shops, and good restaurants. Bellevue, the most urban of the three areas, is characterized by businesses set back from the street in retail and office valleys—the legacy of one of the Eastside's most successful dreamers, Kemper Freeman Sr., who believed businesses that provided parking in front of their buildings would flourish. A rare Bellevue exception is **Main Street** in "Old Bellevue," an area just off the downtown core that resembles compact Kirkland.

Aside from some obvious sites in Kirkland, historic buildings are in short supply throughout the Eastside, partly because of the area's relatively recent settlement, and partly because the value of its first structures was not recognized in the furor of slapdash post-World War II development. Much of the architecture of the past 45 years has failed to consider the Eastside's potential; many of the structures raised were clearly second-class. But that's changing. Several award-winning multiuse projects, such as **Carillon Point** and **Bellevue Place,** have taken great steps in making huge complexes accessible to the public and compatible with the environment. As everywhere else, developers are, for better or worse, changing the face of the area in an effort to accommodate growth, while preservation-minded citizens strive to save what they can for future generations.

Mercer Island

1 Calkins's Landing Charles Cicero Calkins was a lawyer from Illinois who abandoned the bar to become an entrepreneur, real estate gambler, and Mercer Island's best-remembered dreamer. He arrived in Seattle in 1887 and soon determined that Lake Washington's only island should shed its pioneer image. He raised a three-story hotel just up the hill from the present-day landing, which must have been a magical sight—it was an architectural amalgam of an American railroad station and a Swiss chalet, with dormers, turrets, and chimneys punctuating its tile roof, and broad elegant porches skirting its lower levels. The grounds boasted mazes, promenades, a huge greenhouse with 635 varieties of roses, and 25 fountains, one with a 60-foot-wide bowl. A bathhouse held 100 boats and 28 dressing rooms, as well as a complete system of Turkish baths. The **Hotel Calkins** was designed to be the centerpiece of a new, nonindustrial community called **East Seattle**—Puget Sound's version of Newport, Rhode Island. Hoping to start a trend, the developer built a lavish home for himself on the north tip of what is now **Luther Burbank Park.**

But an evil turn of fate put an end to Calkins's schemes. Within the span of a few years, his daughter died, his wife divorced him, and the depression of 1893 depleted his fortune. Calkins's mansion and later his hotel burned to their foundations. He set out in despair for southern California, where he again tried (and failed) to make his fortune in gold mining before he died in 1948 at the age of 98. It's sad that the only thing remaining of the elegance Calkins brought to Mercer Island is a mispunctuated sign on this tiny wedge of lawn and sand, where his hotel once had a dock.
♦ 60th Ave SE and SE 28th St

2 Roanoke Inn Bartenders here are generally versed in the colorful history of Mercer Island's longest-operating business. They'll explain how this place was a general store when it opened in 1916; how there was once a pinball machine here that would pay off in quarters; and how it used to be a popular drinking spot for city swells. Those were the good old days, back when a ferry still connected the north end of Mercer Island with Seattle, before I-90 took all the **Roanoke**'s drive-by business away and left it baby-sitting a dead-end route to a dark pier. Late owner Hal Reeck's stepfather was known to pack pistols into this place and fire them at inconvenient times, blowing holes in various walls and pieces of furniture.

Today most of the action takes place on the TV screen, but much of the tavern's classic atmosphere endures. A giant fireplace sits opposite the front door, gold trophies elbowing each other for room upon its mantel. Beer paraphernalia crowds the walls, and there's a dingy pool room in the back, although it's too cramped for anyone to properly wield a cue. During warm months the place to be is on the long front porch, swapping tall tales and watching Lake Washington capture moonbeams.

The bar stocks a few craft beers like Henry Weinhard and Rainier. Seltzers and wine coolers are available, too. Food selections run to burgers, oyster stew, and taco salads. Spaghetti dinners are served on Thursday nights. ♦ M-Sa until 2AM; Su until 10PM. 1825 72nd Ave SE (just north of I-90). 232.0800 ♿

3 Oh Chocolate! Tempting confections (including more than a dozen varieties of truffles) are handmade on the premises. ♦ M-Sa. 2703 76th Ave SE (at SE 27th St). 232.4974

4 Finders & Doodles A small store, chockablock with gift ideas: toys, handmade crafts, quilts, children's books, journals, stationery, and a wide selection of cards. ♦ Daily. 7607 SE 27th St (between 77th and 76th Aves SE). 236.1110

4 Nature's Pantry Based on the evidence here, Mercer Island has gone full circle—from a bucolic rural island to asphalted suburbia and now back to nature. Shoppers will find a good selection of organic produce, bulk foods, vitamins, cosmetics, and books. ♦ M-Sa. 7611 SE 27th St (between 77th and 76th Aves SE). 232-7900

5 Mercer Island Ski and Cycle Those touring the island by bike can get competent repairs or buy cycling equipment here. ♦ Daily. 7656 SE 27th St (between 77th and 76th Aves SE). 232.3443

6 Thai on Mercer ★★$$ Roast lamb and halibut with tamarind sauce are two of the favorites at this consistently excellent restaurant. Sit back and enjoy the restful, inviting ambience and the well-prepared, well-presented food. ♦ Thai ♦ M-F lunch and dinner; Sa-Su dinner. 7691 SE 27th St (at 77th Ave SE). 236.9990 ♿

6 Alpenland Delicatessen ★$ First look for **Island Video,** then you can spot this tiny place next door. Behind a small storefront is a well-stocked deli offering sandwiches and other treats for eat-in or take-out lunches and picnics. ♦ Deli/Takeout ♦ M-Sa. 2707 78th Ave SE (between SE 29th and SE 27th Sts). 232.4780 ♿

Sam Spade may be San Francisco's most famous fictional private eye, but he got his start elsewhere. In Dashiell Hammett's renowned novel *The Maltese Falcon*, Spade explains that in 1927 "I was with one of the big detective agencies in Seattle."

7 Island Books This excellent general bookstore has a large stock and a friendly staff made up of genuine bibliophiles. The spacious back room is devoted to kid's lit; there's also a huge playhouse and enough toys to keep any number of small-sized nonreaders occupied. ♦ Daily; Th until 8PM. 3014 78th Ave SE (between SE 32nd and SE 30th Sts). 232.6920

7 Island Beads and More In the same shopping center as **Island Books,** this shop sells more beads than you'll ever be able to twirl around your neck, wrists, *and* ankles. Classes and restringing services are also available. ♦ 3024 78th Ave SE (between SE 32nd and SE 30th Sts). 232.8121

8 Pon Proem Restaurant ★$ Colorful, cool decor and well-prepared Thai food are the offerings here. Try the chicken with cashews or fresh ginger. ♦ Thai ♦ M-F lunch; daily dinner. 3039 78th Ave SE (between SE 32nd and SE 29th Sts). 236.8424

Bellevue

9 Red Lion Hotel $$ Some say the addition of this mammoth first-class hotel to Bellevue's hospitality trade marked the city's coming of age as a business destination. Indeed, its 353 rooms and meeting space for 1,400 people are usually occupied. All rooms have balconies, and executive suites come with complimentary continental breakfast, hors d'oeuvres, and a newspaper delivered to your room. ♦ 300 112th Ave SE (between SE Sixth and Main Sts). 455.1300, 800/547.8010; fax 455.0466

Within the Red Lion Hotel:

Velato's ★$$ Color and spaciousness are the signatures here. One wall features a mural of a Venetian canal scene, while another—full of large windows—overlooks a garden, fountain and, in the distance, freeway traffic. The seafood pasta and the lasagna are both good choices. ♦ Italian ♦ M-Sa breakfast, lunch, and dinner; Su brunch. 455.1300

10 Bellevue Hilton $$ The 180 comfortable rooms here are all decorated in soft color tones, with cable TV and movies available. But it's the other amenities that win this place most of its plaudits. Hotel vans take guests around at no charge within a five-mile radius, which easily encompasses Bellevue's main attractions. Indoor activities include an indoor pool, sauna, and Jacuzzi. And security is great; upon request, solo guests are walked to their cars. ♦ 100 112th Ave NE (between Main and NE Fourth Sts). 455.3330, 800/235.4458; fax 451.2473

Within the Bellevue Hilton:

Sam's Bar and Grill $$ Northwestern and continental cuisine are served in a low-key stucco and tile-roofed setting just across the breezeway from the hotel's main entrance. The chicken Dijon sautéed with onions and shallots is a good choice, as are the clam and salmon chowders. ♦ Northwestern/Continental ♦ Daily breakfast, lunch, and dinner. 455.3330

11 Bellevue Botanical Gardens In 1947 Calhoun and Harriet Shorts bought a seven-acre cherry orchard on Wilburton Hill where they built a home and created a rhododendron glen. Today, that property is the center of a 36-acre public botanical garden (see the map below). Some of the rhododendrons are 20 feet tall, and the garden contains a special collection of native and exotic trees, as well as rare shrubs and groundcovers. Near the entrance of the **Shorts Visitors' Center** (which includes a botanical library, gift shop and meeting rooms) a miniature waterfall cascades from a granite boulder through the courtyard; bricks appear to "float" in the small stream of water on its way to a small pond that contains water plants. Beyond the visitors' center are trails to the 17,000-square-foot botanical border on a hill high above downtown Bellevue. There's also a wheelchair-accessible garden loop trail about a half-mile long, as well as individual gardens devoted to groundcovers, dahlias, herbs, fuschias, the **Yao Garden** (a sister-cities project with Yao, Japan), and a rock garden. ♦ Daily. Main St (between 124th Ave NE and 118th Ave SE). 462.2749.

12 Spazzo ★★★$$ *Spazzo* is Italian slang for "a good time," and that's exactly what you'll have in this bright restaurant atop the Key Bank Building. Diners are surrounded by murals on one side and views of the skyline and Lake Washington on the other. The food is from the cuisines of Italy, Greece, Turkey, and North Africa: lamb with vegetables, olives, and artichokes over saffron couscous, for example. There's also a fun tapas bar, where the chefs whip up tasty appetizers; and a childrens' menu. ♦ Mediterranean ♦ Daily lunch and dinner. Reservations recommended for lunch. 10655 NE Fourth St (between 108th and 106th Aves NE). 454.8255

13 Pogacha ★★$ Named for the distinctive Yugoslavian bread crust that makes pizzas served here so unusual, this affordable restaurant is an Eastside favorite. The crunchy-yet-soft bread is made fresh daily and served in three forms: dinner rolls, sandwich bread, and the hefty pizza disks. The best pizza is topped with goat cheese, sun-dried tomatoes, and spinach. Owner Helen Kranjcevich Brocard also serves chicken and lamb dishes, and has a wine list containing about 30 selections. ♦ Pizza ♦ M lunch; Tu-Sa lunch and dinner. 119 106th Ave NE (between Main and NE Second Sts). 455.5670

14 Rubato Records Bellevue's best-loved platter pawnshop carries 10,000 used compact discs, an extensive collection of old 45s, and thousands of vinyl albums. ♦ Daily; M-Sa until 9PM. 136 105th Ave NE (between Main and NE Second Sts). 455.9417

14 Giuseppe's ★$$ Like a rare plant that grows without sunlight, this Italian restaurant and lounge thrives despite its basement strip-mall location in the shadow of a colossal hardware store. Try the veal cognac. ♦ Italian ♦ M-Sa dinner; lounge M-Sa until 2AM. 144 105th Ave NE (between Main and NE Second Sts). 454.6868

15 Chace's Pancake Corral ★$ If you like a hearty stack o' cakes served with a smile at the crack of dawn, this friendly flapjack and coffee stop is for you. It's the only place of its kind left in Bellevue. Owner Bill Chace quit counting birthdays at age 82 and still takes time to sit down with the customers, whether he knows them or not. A favorite is banana pancakes with coconut syrup, but if you want to play the field, try the Joe Adams assortment: Joe was a customer who could never make up his mind whether to have buttermilk, buckwheat, potato, or strawberry pancakes, so Chace came up with this satisfying sampler. ♦ American ♦ Daily breakfast and lunch; Th dinner. 1606 Bellevue Way SE (between SE 16th St and 108th Ave SE). 454.8888

16 Stamp Gallery Proprietor John Kardos's philatelic shop specializes in European issues, but also has one of Seattle's largest collections of international stamps. ♦ Tu-Sa. 10335 Main St (between Bellevue Way SE and 103rd Ave SE). 455.3781

17 Toy's Cafe ★$ Good Chinese food at irresistible prices has made this a neighborhood institution for decades. It's not fancy, but the service is quick and courteous. Combos are the way to go; sample three or four foods for less than each would cost separately. ♦ Chinese/Takeout ♦ Tu-F lunch and dinner; Sa-Su dinner. 10311 Main St (between Bellevue Way SE and 103rd Ave SE). 454.8815

18 Azalea's Fountain Court ★★$$$$ Coming to this restaurant is like visiting your favorite auntie at her light-green farmhouse tucked away under the trees. Inside this somewhat preciously overdone space, you'll find a gracious staff and excellent chef preparing Northwestern cuisine with French overtones. Seafood is the specialty, especially the crab cakes, local mussels, and the baked salmon. The atmosphere is romantic and the service is good. ♦ Northwestern ♦ W-F lunch and dinner; M, Sa dinner. No smoking allowed. 22 103rd Ave NE (between Main and NE First Sts). 451.0426

19 Bellevue Barber Shop Nothing has changed since the days when your dad was a kid and your grandfather brought him into a place just like this to get his ears lowered. The Russel family has been giving no-frills haircuts here for almost 50 years. Their collection of Bellevue High School yearbooks, which you're welcome to peruse, predates the shop's 1926 building by two years. Opinions are plentiful and free, and haircuts are $10, which includes being finished up with a straight razor. ♦ Tu-Sa. 10251 Main St (at 103rd Ave SE). 455.0980

20 La Cocina del Puerco $ In this cafeteria-style restaurant you pay for the food—handmade tortillas and generous helpings—not for the overhead of fancy furnishings. Decor is upscale functional, but there are enough piñatas, posters, and other paraphernalia on the walls and ceiling to make you feel you've gotten tangled up in a *Cinco de Mayo* parade. Try the *chiles rellenos*. ♦ Mexican ♦ Daily lunch and dinner. 10246 Main St (between 103rd and 102nd Aves NE). 455.1151

21 Cuttysark There's a blinding assortment of brass goods salvaged from old ships for the nautically inclined: coat hooks, portholes, soap dishes, lanterns, binnacles, telegraphs, telescopes, and more. There are also thousands of nonbrass items, including flags, books, paintings, charts, and ship models. ◆ M-Sa. 10235 Main St (between 103rd and 102nd Aves SE). 453.1265

22 Christmas House This year-round ornament and gift shop comprises three buildings (two are in the back alley) carrying a large selection of knickknacks, bric-a-brac, baubles, bangles, and gewgaws to stuff every stocking. Don't miss the traditional linden-wood carvings from the German Erzgebirge and several sizes of the hand-painted Fontanini nativity figures. ◆ Daily Nov-Dec; Tu-Sa Jan-Oct. 10230 Main St (between 103rd and 102nd Aves NE). 455.4225

23 Ross and Co. Ross Bendixen has been bending metal in this neighborhood for more than 25 years, specializing in custom-designed iron-and-steel furniture. His dynamic wall sculptures have become a hallmark of Old Bellevue. ◆ M-Sa. 10220 Main St (between 103rd and 102nd Aves NE). 455.4111

24 Main Street Kids Book Company The very best thing you can do for your children is turn them loose in this marvelously stocked bookstore and let their curiosity go to work. And for adults, there are books on parenting in the back. ◆ M-Sa. 10217 Main St (between 103rd and 102nd Aves SE). 455.8814

24 Fortnum's European Cafe ★$ The name underscores the continental theme here. You will find the regular round of soups and sandwiches, a zucchini frittata, and a wonderful artichoke tart. Floral-print tablecloths add a touch of elegance. ◆ Continental ◆ Daily breakfast and lunch. 10213 Main St (between 103rd and 102nd Aves SE). 455.2033

25 Oriental Interiors This shop specializes in rosewood furniture from China, but the building in which it's housed is equally interesting. Ostentatiously named the **City of Paris,** it was Bellevue's first bank, but became a casualty of the Depression as soon as it opened. The structure once housed Bellevue's first library as well as the first offices of the *Bellevue American* newspaper, now the daily *Journal American*. ◆ Daily. 10203 Main St (between 103rd and 102nd Aves SE). 637.0860

If visitors from San Francisco feel a bit more at home in Seattle than the rest of us, it may be because part of their city is here. A good portion of the land used to regrade the waterfront area came from Telegraph Hill. The dirt had been brought over on ships from San Francisco as ballast, then dumped here.

26 Dilly Dally The wooden cow that hangs out on the sidewalk during business hours was ticketed for being an illegal sign, but owner Nadine Lukoff took her case to court and won. Look closely; the baskets, cards, boxes of cookies, and most of the items carried here can't be found anywhere else in the Northwest. ◆ M-Sa. 10202 Main St (between 103rd and 102nd Aves NE). 454.1518

27 The Collection This shop carries lines from about eight different contemporary women's sportswear collections. ◆ Daily. 10149 Main St (between 102nd Ave SE and Meydenbauer Way SE). 453.5791. Also at: Rainier Square. 622.4147; University Village. 524.6954

28 Bloomingals "Sportswear for fun" is the slogan intended to draw women who shun trends and want distinctive designs from New York and San Francisco. ◆ Daily. 10133 Main St (between 102nd Ave SE and Meydenbauer Way SE). 451.2880

29 Wildwood Park This little lawn surrounded by trees is all that's left of a park that once reached west to what is now the **Meydenbauer Yacht Club.** In the first years of the 20th century Seattleites crossed Lake Washington on a ferry to picnic on the grass here, dance in a pavilion, and mess about in canoes. ◆ 260 101st Ave SE (just south of Main St)

30 Bellevue Downtown Park At a total cost of $20 million, the City of Bellevue purchased nearly four blocks of prime downtown real estate in the early 1980s and set it aside (ostensibly forever) as sacred, idle space, dedicated to daydreams and dawdling. From the park, a proper study can be made of downtown Bellevue's skyscraper growth during the late 20th century. The two blue ones most in evidence to the east, **Security Pacific Plaza** (10620 NE Eighth St) and **One Bellevue Center** (411 108th Ave NE), were built during the 1980s as bookends to anticipated heavy development along 108th Avenue NE (alas, the "books" never materialized). Depending on the sky, they can become beacons of fire or disappear altogether. The copper-toned **Koll Center** (500 108th Ave NE), at 27 stories Bellevue's tallest building, incorporates multiple angles and sides on a common center to suggest one building exploding out of another. All three reflective glass structures were designed by Seattle architect **Gerald Geron.** The most active area is the west side of the park, where kids play on a colorful, turreted jungle gym and swings. Elsewhere, workers and shoppers can enjoy a low waterfall and a hypnotic canal crossed by charming little bridges. Perhaps the leveling of two of Bellevue's oldest grade schools for this park will prove forgivable (the foundation of one remains as a topographic attraction), as people take refuge not far from the madding crowd. A stone marker and four elms planted in 1926 in memory of three World War I soldiers were left undisturbed. ♦ 10201 NE Fourth St (at 102nd Ave NE)

31 Games and Gizmos The back half of this store is dedicated to role-playing games of the Dungeons and Dragons sort, but up front you'll find all the old favorites—tiddledywinks, chess, Twister. There are some interesting cribbage and backgammon boards, and plenty of brainteasing puzzles for those who've mastered the Rubik's cube. The floor is checkered black and white, of course. ♦ Daily; M-F until 9PM. 211 Bellevue Way NE (between NE First and NE Fourth Sts). 462.1569

PSYCHO 5

31 Psycho 5 Die-hard superheroes Thor and Spiderman rub elbows with Spawn, Ren and Stimpy, and such Japanese animated creations as Youngblood in this comics, video, and card shop. The owner knows his stuff and relates to kids on their own level, enthusing about soon-to-be-released issues or a rare Steve Largent football card. ♦ Daily. 221 Bellevue Way NE (between NE First and NE Fourth Sts). 462.2869

32 DeLaurenti's Specialty Foods A familiar name from **Pike Place Market,** this international food market (emphasis on the Italian) is also one of the relative oldies in downtown Bellevue. There's a sandwich and espresso bar, so you can try the pâtés, salads, cheeses, meats, and fresh breads on the spot. Walk it off among the shelves of imported olives, olive oils, pastas, beans, ground semolina, basmati rice, teas, jams, and cookies. ♦ M-Sa. 317 Bellevue Way NE (between NE First and NE Fourth Sts). 454.7155. Also at: Economy Market, Pike Place Market. 622.0141

33 Bellevue Square Mall About one-third of Bellevue's retail business is conducted under this roof, which has skylights along its entire length to lend the mall below an ambience that architects **Cober-Slater** hoped would suggest a narrow European street. Real ficus trees planted here support this effect, as do the indoor clock tower (with a late 19th-century bell and movement salvaged from Mississippi's Winona County Courthouse)

and the bow window storefronts and blade signs protruding into the mall. The usual heavyweights can be found here: **Nordstrom, J.C. Penney,** and **The Bon Marché.** ♦ NE Eighth St (between Bellevue Way NE and 100th Ave NE). 454.8096

Within Bellevue Square Mall:

The Nature Company It's like stepping into an expensive rain forest, with its very green gallery of pricey gadgets, learning devices, and offbeat entertainments. There are globe puzzles, fish ties and bird shirts, telescopes, polished geodes, birdhouses, posters, children's science kits, CDs of ocean sounds, tea, Saturn holographs, and life-size inflatable Emperor penguins. In a bind for some quartz? This store stocks it in four colors. M-Sa 9:30AM-9:30PM; Su 11AM-6PM. First floor. 450.0448

Kenneth Behm Art Gallery Dalí and Matisse prints vie for wall space with limited editions by Michel Delacroix and Jiang. The leaning is toward big, busy, and bright, but the gallery has presented a collection of small monochrome sketches and engravings by Rembrandt, two of which are part of the inventory. ♦ M-Sa 9:30AM-9:30PM; Su 11AM-6PM. First floor. 454.0222

The Body Shop This international chain of soap and lotion shops is known for its politically active business policies. In the "Trade, Not Aid" program, founder Anita Roddick buys nature-friendly products from Third World countries. Items include paper from Nepal, acacia footsie rollers from southern India, and Brazil-nut oil from the Kayapo Indians of South America. High prices separate the dedicated from the curious. ♦ M-Sa 9:30AM-9:30PM; Su 11AM-6PM. First floor. 637.9535

Cellophane Square Anyone who knows the funky used records, tapes, and CDs store in Seattle's University District will be happy to know that this posh mall location hasn't altered its bottom line. The selection of new and used music is as good as ever. ♦ M-Sa 9:30AM-9:30PM; Su 11AM-6PM. First floor. 454.5059. Also at: 1315 NE 42nd St (between University Way NE and Brooklyn Ave NE). 634.2280

Northwest Discovery About 70 percent of the jewelry and decorations sold here are by Northwest artists, including vases by Bremerton glassblowers Scott and Linda Curry and wall designs by Seattle tilemaker Paul Lewing. ♦ M-Sa 9:30AM-9:30PM; Su 11AM-6PM. First floor. 454.1676

Monterey Pasta Bar $ An anomaly among mall dining choices, this small cafe (formerly **Lucca's Pasta Bar**) radiates cheerfulness. It's bright, clean, judiciously decorated with tinted photographs of Venice and Rome, and staffed by a youthful crew. Focaccia with a Caesar salad is a good quick lunch. Of course, they serve espresso. ♦ Italian ♦ M-Sa breakfast, lunch, and dinner; Su lunch and dinner. First floor. 451.2278 &

The Bombay Company The home of a retired English colonel could not be more stuffed with fox-hunt paintings, cricket tables, Italian leather decanters, and solid-brass lamps. Queen Anne and other reproductions are mostly of cherry or birch with mahogany finish, many adapted to the modern function of housing files, VCRs, or tapes. ♦ M-Sa 9:30AM-9:30PM; Su 11AM-6PM. Second floor. 455.8544

Pendleton In the 1800s the Bishop family of Pendleton, Oregon, began making wool blankets based on Native American designs. The wool is still cleaned, dyed, spun, and woven at Washougal on the Columbia River, and all garments are made in the US. The Chief Joseph blanket is the same pattern that has been made and sold since the 1920s. ♦ M-Sa 9:30AM-9:30PM; Su 11AM-6PM. Second floor. 453.9040. Also at: 1313 Fourth Ave (between University and Union Sts). 682.4430

Port Chatham Smoked Seafood A handwritten note from Julia Child on the wall calls the salmon here the best she's ever had. Whether cold-smoked or kippered, the Alaskan king salmon and other seafoods prepared in Ballard and sold in this shop can be packed to travel. There's also wild capers and caviar for sale. ♦ M-Sa 9:30AM-9:30PM; Su 11AM-6PM. Second floor. 453.2441

Excalibur The quantity of sharp edges alone makes this shop an intrigue: kitchen cutlery by such household names as Henckel, Mundial, and Forschner; reproduction Viking and Samurai swords by Marta of Spain; Buck and Victorinox pocket and hunting knives. There are even battle-axes, just in case you've been looking for one. ♦ M-Sa 9:30AM-9:30PM; Su 11AM-6PM. Second floor. 451.2514

Mrs. Field's Cookies Treat yourself after an afternoon's mall walking. Pick any semi-sweet chocolate variety. ♦ M-Sa 9:30AM-

9:30PM; Su 11AM-6PM. Second floor. 454.1790

The Wallflower With an inventory of largely Victorian items—antiques, cards, some clothing, lace items, and linens—this shop is a good place to find unusual gifts. ♦ M-Sa 9:30AM-9:30PM; Su 11AM-6PM. Second floor. 827.5337

Bellevue Art Museum Not your typical mall resident, this small museum does not display a permanent collection but offers rotating exhibits, primarily of Northwest crafts. Strengths are jewelry and all manner of wearable art. ♦ Admission; free Tuesday. Daily. Third floor. 454.3322

34 La Residence Suite Hotel $ This 24-unit inn caters to the corporate traveler, but is also a good choice for families on a budget: all apartments have full kitchens. The views, unfortunately, are mostly of a parking garage, but elegant rosewood and leather furnishings, a friendly and hard-working staff, and complimentary fax service make it an attractive choice right on the edge of the Bellevue business district. There is no restaurant. ♦ 475 100th Ave NE (between NE Fourth and NE Fifth Sts). 455.1475, 800/800.1993; fax 455.4692

35 Veneto's Grab a paper from the newsstand across the hall and indulge in a good espresso. ♦ Daily from 6:30AM. 10116 NE Eighth St (between 102nd and 100th Aves NE). 451.8323

35 Mr. "J" Kitchen Gourmet Everything you need to operate your professional-level kitchen is available here. Hanging baskets, skillets, and giant utensils form a junglelike upper canopy. Bins full of citrus peelers, honey dippers, butter spreaders, and poultry lifters are constantly restocked so that no peg or shelf space is empty. An electric pepper grinder with a light (for poorly lit romantic dinners?), a crumb box with a removable trivet, a tripod-mounted solid-brass cork extractor, and a marble rolling pin can be found nea Waterford crystal and Henckel's cutlery. ♦ Daily. 10116 NE Eighth St (between 102nd and 100th NE). 455.2270

Seattle's first public ordinance—passed in 1869—was a law against drunkenness.

Pocket-Size Parks

Most people know about Seattle's major parks, including **Discovery, Volunteer, Seward,** and the **Washington Park Arboretum.** Their large size and abundant greenery ensure that they'll be noticed and appreciated. But scattered here and there throughout the city are several small, out-of-the-way green spaces that also feature lovely scenery and panoramic views—and you'll be more likely to have them to yourself. A number of these parks are named after prominent local people, giving you a taste of history along with the scenery. Though easy to overlook, the following spots are worth taking time to visit.

On **Queen Anne Hill,** there's a steep, multilevel layout called **Bhy Kracke Park** (Bigelow Ave N and Comstock Pl N). It was named after its owner, Werner H. "Bhy" Kracke (1902-71), a bank auditor, world traveler, and gardener. A winding path passes through the park, and terrific views can be had from almost everywhere; the vantage point at the top shows off downtown Seattle, **Lake Union,** the **Space Needle,** and **Capitol Hill** to fine advantage. There are also several landscaped flower gardens with ivies, azaleas, and rhododendrons.

The **Schmitz Memorial Overlook** (4503 Beach Dr SW) in West Seattle was a gift to the city in 1945 from the wealthy Schmitz family. The panoramic view here includes **Bainbridge Island, Kitsap Peninsula,** and **Vashon Island.**

Another spot with a historical background is **Jose Rizal Park** (12th Ave S and S Judkins St), a patch of land which was named for a 19th-century Filipino patriot who was active in political and social reform in his home country (the city paid this tribute to him at the urging of its sizeable Filipino population). It boasts a sweeping view that encompasses the **Kingdome, Elliott Bay,** the **Olympic Mountains,** and the city skyline. Then there's **Louisa Boren View Park** (15th Ave E and E Garfield St), named after the last surviving member of the party that founded Seattle in 1851. High above **Interlaken Park,** it faces northeast with views of **Montlake,** the **University of Washington, Lake Washington,** and the **Cascades.**

The formal **Parson's Gardens** (Seventh Ave W and W Highland Dr) are the perfect setting for a quiet stroll or a secluded picnic. Located across the street from **Betty Bowen Viewpoint,** the tiny space affords a vista that takes in Elliott Bay, downtown Seattle, and even **Mount Rainier** in the distance. It's especially stunning at sunset. Attractive sunset views can also be had from **Magnolia Park** (W Garfield St and Magnolia Blvd W), a 16-acre area that sits on a high bluff overlooking the Olympic Mountains; and **Sunset Hill Park** (NW 77th St and 34th Ave NW), from which you can see **Puget Sound, Shilshole Bay,** and the Olympics.

Kobe, Japan, one of Seattle's sister cities, donated the Mount Fuji cherry trees and the antique, four-ton stone lantern that decorate **Danny Woo International District Community Garden** (bounded by I-5 and Sixth Ave S, and S Main and S Washington Sts). The lantern is named *Yukimidoro,* which means "view of the snow" in Japanese. You get to see much more than just snow from here, though: There's a fine panorama of the **Duwamish Valley** to the south and **Harbor Island,** Elliott Bay, and **West Seattle** to the southwest.

For a different perspective on the city, head for **South Passage Point** (Fuhrman Ave E and Fairview Ave E), located just below the south side of the **University Bridge.** This tiny park is tucked between the pillars of the **Freeway Bridge,** looking onto the many boats traveling the watery passage between **Portage Bay** and Lake Union. Peaceful and quiet, it's the ideal spot for relaxation and introspection.

36 University Book Store The University District original is so successful that branching out seemed inevitable, but the selections of specialty literature, such as mysteries or science fiction, pale against those at the older main store. This outlet, however, contains two aisles of volumes about cooking, nutrition, and international cuisines. Browse to your heart's content. ◆ M-F 9AM-9PM; Sa 9AM-6PM; Su 11AM-5PM. 990 102nd Ave NE (at NE 10th St). 632.9500. Also at: 4326 University Way NE (between NE 43rd and NE 45th Sts). 634.3400

37 Starbucks ★$ Along with some of the best espresso made in the Seattle area, this coffeeteria sells everything for the home *latte* junkie. ◆ Coffeehouse ◆ Daily; M-F from 5:30AM.

10214 NE Eighth St (between Bellevue Way NE and 102nd Ave NE). 454.0191. Also at: Numerous locations throughout the Seattle area

37 Silberman/Brown Stationers Owner Sue Silberman sums up the selection of new and antique pens, inkwells, and letter openers with a quip: "There's nothing in here you *need.*" But there may be things you *want*—like a Lorenzo de' Medici sterling-silver fountain pen ($1,500)—making this a gift shop for the executive that has almost everything. ◆ M-Sa. 10220 NE Eighth St (between Bellevue Way NE and 102nd Ave NE). 455.3665

Restaurants/Clubs: Red   Hotels: Blue
Shops/ 🍴 Outdoors: Green   **Sights/Culture: Black**

38 Bellevue Place This high-rise complex was the first multiuse project of such magnitude in the Northwest, but as architecture it is only mediocre. The complex includes the **Seafirst Building,** the **MGM Building,** and the glass-domed **Wintergarten,** linking the towers. ◆ 10500 NE Eighth Ave (between 106th Ave NE and Bellevue Way NE). 453.5634

Within Bellevue Place:

St. Michael's Alley Named after the famous London back street where the 17th-century intelligentsia and literati hung out, this espresso shop and bookseller, wedged into an awkward space on the first floor of the **Seafirst Building,** has captured the work force's coffee-break and last-minute-gift market. The two or three shelves of new and old books (perhaps 1,300 of them, total) are there mainly to whet the appetite; the owners are happy to order and gift wrap. ◆ M-Sa. Seafirst Bldg, First floor. 453.9456

Daniel's Broiler ★★$$$$ Simultaneously chic in appearance (dark woods, onyx table-tops) and simple in its meal preparations, this is an ideal spot for entertaining. Its 21st-floor setting in the **Seafirst Building** provides Bellevue's best dining views. A specialty is the veal Daniel's—tenderloin sautéed with wild mushrooms, olives, garlic, herbs, and stock. And in both the 1987 and 1990 Puget Sound Chowder Off competitions, this eatery has served up the prize-winning bowl. There's live piano music Tuesday through Saturday nights, a jazz trio plays on Sunday, and a jazz guitarist riffs on the deck Monday nights. The **Oyster Bar Lounge** is frequented by designer-suited people. ◆ American ◆ M-F lunch and dinner; Sa-Su dinner. Seafirst Bldg, 21st floor. 462.4662. Also at: 200 Lake Washington Blvd S (at the Leschi Marina). 329.4191 &

Cucina! Cucina! ★★$$ Bicycles hanging from the ceiling reflect the offbeat spirit of the after-work crowd that keeps this hot spot going. Try the focaccia as an appetizer. Dinner choices range from pizzas and pastas to seafood, soups, salads, and more. The veal scallopini sautéed with fresh sage, prosciutto, pine nuts, and garlic is a specialty. ◆ Italian ◆ Daily lunch and dinner; bar until 1AM. MGM Bldg, First floor. 637.1177 &. Also at: 901 Fairview Ave N (at Lake Union), Belltown. 447.2782 &

38 Hyatt Regency at Bellevue Place $$$ The 382 rooms here are the most centrally located in Bellevue. Appointments are classy, without being ostentatious, decorated in neutral and pastel hues with cherry trim. Best choices are those rooms located high up on the south side, which feature views of Mount Rainier and Lake Washington. The **Regency Club** on the 23rd and 24th floors is a luxury hotel within a hotel, offering complimentary concierge and executive business services. All the usual Hyatt amenities apply. ◆ 900 Bellevue Way NE (at NE Eighth St). 462.1234, 800/233.1234; fax 451.3017

Within the Hyatt Regency at Bellevue Place:

Eques ★★$$$ Northwestern cuisine—especially seafood—is served in an elegant venue among paintings and stone sculptures of horses. Natural-wood floors and private alcoves make this a great place to relax. One of the most popular entrées is the salmon fillet with roasted–red-pepper sauce, but the grilled ahi with pineapple cilantro relish is also a winner. ◆ Northwestern ◆ Daily breakfast, lunch, and dinner. 451.3012

39 Tower Books The fire marshal must make special dispensation for this book-jammed store that's an even better resource for bibliophiles than its other location in Belltown. Especially generous are the mystery and science fiction sections. ◆ Daily until midnight. 10635 NE Eighth St (between 108th and 106th Aves NE). 451.1110. Also at: 20 Mercer St (at First Ave N), Belltown. 283.6333

39 Barnes & Noble Bookstore The green arches of a former bowling alley shoulder this chain's superstore. Largest departments are general fiction, business, and computer books. ◆ Daily until 11PM. 626 106th Ave NE (at NE Eighth St). 451.8463.

Thinker TOYS

40 Thinker Toys A large, imaginatively decorated shop full of toys, games, and puzzles designed to entertain and challenge. Besides the popular construction sets by Lego, Brio, Erector, and Playmobile, you'll find fingerprint kits, chemistry sets, and other intriguing toys from around the world. ◆ Daily; M-F until 9PM. 10680 NE Eighth St (at 108th Ave NE). 453.0051

The lowest recorded temperature at Seattle-Tacoma International Airport was 0 degrees Fahrenheit, on 31 January 1950. That's a far cry from the usual winter temperatures here (in the mid-40s on average).

Rosalie Whyel MUSEUM of DOLL ART

41 Rosalie Whyel Museum of Doll Art
This Victorian-style museum was built slightly oversize to make visitors feel a little … well, doll-like. The exhibits showcase antiques and collectibles—not reproductions—from ivory Eskimo dolls to Barbie gift sets. ♦ Free for children four and under. Daily; Th until 8PM. 1116 108th Ave NE (at NE 12th St). 455.1116

42 The Pumphouse ★$ In such a car-oriented place, "neighborhood joint" has more to do with camaraderie than location. Aggressively nonglitzy, this tavern is Bellevue's version of "Cheers." Burgers are large and juicy (order the bacon-and-cheese version), and potato skins are stuffed with green onions, melted cheese, and sour cream. ♦ American ♦ M-Sa lunch and dinner; bar until midnight. 11802 NE Eighth St (between Bellevue-Redmond Rd and 116th Ave NE). 455.4110

42 I Love Sushi ★★$ Chef Tadaski Sato creates delectable raw-fish delicacies at this very popular restaurant. Specialties include tuna sashimi in the shape of a rose, an excellent *futumaki* roll of pink fish cake and mushrooms, and even Dungeness crab sushi. ♦ Sushi ♦ M-Sa lunch and dinner; Su dinner. 11818 NE Eighth St (between Bellevue-Redmond Rd and 116th Ave NE). 454.5706. Also at: 1001 Fairview Ave N (at Lake Union). 625.9604

Kirkland

43 Carillon Point The six bells or carillons in the center of this office and hotel complex were forged in France and chime every half hour, giving it the atmosphere of a small European plaza. The public dock, ample parking, and waterfront paths make the place accessible by boat, car, and foot, and the low-rise buildings don't jar against the wooded hillside to the east. This bulge in the shoreline started out as the **Lake Washington Shipyards** and later became the training grounds for the **Seattle Seahawks** football team for a time; the new buildings are the world headquarters of such firms as McCaw Cellular Communications and Univar, and the street level offers a healthy handful of retail shops and restaurants, including the inevitable **Starbucks.** Lots of parking is available, mostly underground. ♦ Off Lake Washington Blvd NE (at 102nd Ave NE). 822.1700

At Carillon Point:

Toppers This florist specializes in English floral design, using Northwest natives such as salal and huckleberry as a base and flowers from all over the world as accompaniments. The shop doubles as an art gallery, presenting glassworks ranging from a $12 vase to a $500 Dab Bergsma glass sculpture. ♦ M-Sa; irregularly extended summer hours. No. 1260. 889.9311

Hannigan/Adams Goldsmith Frank Hannigan is an avowed constructivist, but he will make whatever you can dream up. Partner Beth Adams's more organic, sculpted pieces complement Hannigan's Bauhaus designs, and if you like the classic Tiffany look, they can do that in their tiny workshop, too. The prices are realistic for hand-crafted gold jewelry. ♦ M-Sa 11AM-6PM. No. 1230. 889.9450

Yarrow Bay Grill and Beach Cafe ★$$$ One small kitchen creates sophisticated dishes for both the restaurant upstairs and the **Beach Cafe,** a lower outdoor deck where yuppies chill after work. There are at least three fresh seafood entrées daily, but if you're not fond of fish, you can sink your teeth into an 11-ounce New York steak topped with a green peppercorn–and-brandy sauce. But that's not all; for a further change of pace, venison and rack of lamb are also available. In the **Beach Cafe,** order a gin-and-tonic and one of the appetizers (like the zesty New Mexico artichoke dip served with bread, veggies, or crackers) and sit back comfortably on the deck to watch the sun set upon Seattle. ♦ Northwestern ♦ M-F lunch and dinner; Sa-Su dinner. Reservations recommended for the Grill. No. 1270. Grill 889.9052, Beach Cafe 889.0303 ♿

Woodmark Hotel $$$ A bright atrium flanked by a curved staircase and filled with piano music welcomes you to the only hotel on the shores of Lake Washington. All 100 rooms and suites have TVs and VCRs, and most boast balconies with views westward. For the insomniac with an appetite, a "Raid the Pantry" program offers complimentary late-night snacks. If you really live it up, stay in the **Woodmark Suite,** a 1,456-square-foot apartment with two balconies and a fireplace enjoyed by the likes of Paul McCartney, Arnold Palmer, and Harry Connick Jr. Expensive but satisfying meals are available at the **Carillon Room,** where the salmon fillet comes with some of the best crab cakes to be found in these parts. ♦ No. 1200. 822.3700, 800/822.3700

Seattle's location in the Pacific Northwest puts it closer to the Orient than any other port in the continental United States. It's nearly 300 nautical miles closer to Japan than San Francisco, and 600 miles closer than Los Angeles.

44 Marsh Estate In the exclusive residential park called **Marsh Commons** sits an elegant 1929 Tudor-style home (illustrated on page 187) that is anything but common. It was erected by Louis Schuster Marsh, born in Wisconsin in 1892, who moved his family to the Seattle area in 1904. Marsh studied engineering at the **University of Washington**; in 1916 he went to work for William Boeing's airplane company, becoming that outfit's chief metallurgist.

Marsh was the engineer who invented all-metal fuselages, and Boeing stock made a small fortune for him. Just over 10 years after joining the company, Marsh commissioned the architectural firm of **Edwin J. Ivey** to build a home reflecting his success. It's been said that much if not most of the design work was

Marsh Estate

COURTESY OF THE KIRKLAND HERITAGE SOCIETY

done by **Ivey**'s partner at the time, **Elizabeth Ayer,** the first woman graduate of **UW**'s architecture program and the first female architect licensed in Washington state. The finished estate included a series of waterfalls, tremendous hand-carved beams in the living and dining rooms, a darkroom in the basement, a pistol range, and an extensive wine cellar. A weather vane on the rooftop features the likeness of Marsh, an avid golfer, dressed in his sporting knickers. It remains a private residence. ♦ 6604 Lake Washington Blvd NE (across from Marsh Park)

45 Shamiana ★★★$$ The kitchen at this popular eatery (it's best to come on week-nights, when the crowds are smaller) prepares a westernized derivation of traditional Indian fare, mixing in Northwest ingredients and toning down spices some-what for tender American palates; the results are pleasing and provide a slightly exotic gustatory experience. A lunchtime buffet offers the opportunity to sample many dishes, including cardamom-flavored lamb curry; cumin-scented chicken in a tomato and cream sauce; potatoes studded with crushed peanuts; and a smooth *dal* of pureed lentils. At dinner, try the intensely flavored beef vindaloo, marinated in vinegar, ginger, and chili. The restaurant's moniker is taken from the name used for the colorful tents that hang bannerlike from the dining room ceiling. ♦ Indian ♦ M-F lunch; Sa-Su dinner. 10724 NE 68th Pl (at Sixth St S). 827.4902 ♿

46 Anthony's Homeport ★★$$ Some people come here for the sunset view over Lake Washington, but even if this first of many branches were located in an underground parking garage people would visit for the sautéed scallops, grilled salmon, and oysters. For views, the next best **Anthony's** choice is on Shilshole Bay, in Ballard. ♦ Seafood ♦ M-Sa dinner; Su brunch and dinner. Reservations recommended. Moss Bay Marina, 135 Lake St S (at Second Ave S).

822.0225 ♿. Also at: 6135 Seaview Ave NW (on Shilshole Bay). 783.0780 ♿; Des Moines Marina (Dock St between S 227th and S 222nd Sts), Des Moines. 824.1947; Edmonds Marina (Dayton St and Admiral Way), Edmonds. 771.4400; Everett Marina, Everett. 252.3333

46 Third Floor Fish Cafe ★★$$ Just yards from the famous **Anthony's** is this classy upbeat upstart. The views are as good as any on Moss Bay, and such thoughtful entrées as grilled sea scallops with orange-curry couscous and tomato chutney are complemented by some of the best appetizers and desserts around. Service here is con-sistently efficient. Kathy Casey, the wunder-kind who made her reputation originally at **Fuller's** restaurant downtown, created this cafe's concept. ♦ Seafood ♦ M-F lunch and dinner; Sa dinner. Reservations recom-mended. 205 Lake St S (at Second Ave S). 822.3553; fax 827.1364 ♿

47 Gunnar Nordstrom Gallery Contemporary original prints and paintings by international and local abstract expressionists are found at this gallery. Featured are Robert Motherwell's works, James Rizzi's 3-D paper constructions, and prints by Toko Shinoda, the grande dame of Japanese abstract expressionism. ♦ Tu-Su. 127 Lake St S (south of Kirkland Ave). 827.2822

48 Danish-Swedish Antiques The country furniture carried here is mostly unpainted, old country pine and turn-of-the-century antiques imported from Sweden and Denmark by Scandinavian owners Ib and Alaina Knoblauch. Here and there among the armoires are china cabinets, washstands with marble tops, porcelain accessories, and Mora clocks with hand-painted faces. ♦ Daily. 207 Kirkland Ave (between State St and Lake St S). 822.7899

49 Davinci's Flying Pizza and Pasta ★$ By day the bar is a quiet sports pub and the restaurant's garage-door front is opened to create a relaxing sidewalk cafe. But at night, the dance floor becomes a quasar of Kirkland nightlife. Mannequin parts spin from the ceiling among neon planets. Inventive poultry and seafood pizzas are available in the bar, but if you're really hungry, try the restaurant where the pasta is a savory alternative. The Cajun chicken fettuccine is a favorite. ◆ Italian ◆ Daily lunch and dinner; bar until 2AM. 89 Kirkland Ave (at Lake St S). 889.9000 ఉ

49 Kirkland Clock Captain John Anderson, who ran ferries and steamboats on Lake Washington for more than 40 years, gave this handsome pedestaled timepiece to the City of Kirkland in 1935. ◆ Lake St S and Kirkland Ave

50 Avoir Gallery One of Kirkland's first art galleries (and certainly its narrowest) is squeezed into a sliver of an old downtown building (shown at right). Owner Scott Fitzgerald exhibits traditional, contem- porary, and three-dimensional works by such established local artists as Take Hama and Marilyn Schultzky. There's also a museum-quality framing service offered. ◆ Tu-Su. 216 Kirkland Ave (between Third and Main Sts). 827.8349

51 Kirkland Antique Gallery More than 90 dealers are represented under this one roof (formerly **Old Heritage Place**), each occupying a small space jammed with relics from yesteryear. The rub is that the dealers are not present, so there's no one to answer your questions about the old banjo or bookshelf or set of fine china that catches your eye. You're on your own—great if you know just what you're looking for and don't like being pressured by commission-hungry salespeople. ◆ Daily. 151 Third St (at Commercial Ave). 828.4993 ఉ

52 Coyote Coffee Company Technically, this is a retail store, not a restaurant, but there are six tables inside. The shop sells Michaelo's coffee, a full-flavored espresso, as well as sandwiches, salads, and fresh-baked bread and desserts. Try the *zufolo*—ambitiously seasoned Italian bread with provolone cheese, salami, tomato, green pepper, onion, and sweet basil—served, if you're lucky enough to come on the right day, with a delicious tabbouleh. Pottery, masks, paintings, prints,

and basketry by local artists are also for sale. On Friday and Saturday nights, there's live folk music, as well as storytelling and poetry readings. ◆ M-Th 6AM-4PM; F-Sa 6AM-10PM. 111 Main St (between Kirkland Ave and Park La). 827.2507 ఉ

53 The Norsemen This Scandinavian gift shop is loaded with such things as wooden plaques declaring "It's a Blessing To Be Finnish," but what it lacks in class is perhaps made up for in variety. Sweatshirts, books, crackers, shelves of dolls and Swedish crystal, and even open-faced sandwiches are all for sale. It's the ultimate in niche marketing. ◆ M-Sa. 140 Park La (at Main St). 822.8715

54 Parklane Gallery A cooperative effort, this gallery is owned and operated by the artists represented. Among the regular painting selections are Loreita Richards's depictions of Native Americans and some powerful Vietnam images by Norm Bergsma. ◆ Tu-Su; F-Sa until 8PM. 130 Park La (between Main St and Lake St). 827.1462

55 Moss Bay Gallery Original Northwest paintings by a variety of artists are featured, including some by Alaskan artist Rie Muñoz. ◆ Daily. 128-A Park La (between Main St and Lake St). 822.3630

56 Ristorante Paradiso ★★$$ Sardinian Fabrizio Loi's Mediterranean cafe has a terrific location on Kirkland's most charming street, and in good weather several tables materialize on the sidewalk outside. Inside or out, the cioppino—mussels, scallops, shrimp, clams, and the fish of the day served in a marinara sauce with homemade croutons—is a house specialty, as is the *vitello scampi* (veal pounded thin and wrapped around tender sage shrimp with butter, garlic, and a white-wine-and-lemon sauce). The wonderful, soft bread is made fresh at least twice daily. ◆ Mediterranean ◆ M-Sa lunch and dinner; Su dinner. 120 Park La (between Main St and Lake St). 889.8601 ఉ

57 Wood 'n' You This gallery carries originals and limited edition prints by national and local artists. Ken Ledbetter's elegant hand-crafted picture frames of teak, koa, purple heart, and other exotic hardwoods are equally original. ◆ Daily; F until 9PM. 107 Park La (between Main St and Lake St). 827.6835

58 The Corner Shop One of the best newstands on the Eastside, this shop still carries a wide variety of periodicals, from local to international in scope. ◆ Daily; M-Th until

9PM; F-Sa until 10PM; Su until 8PM. 113 Lake St (at Central Way). 827.6486

59 Ballard Furniture Twice as deep as it looks from the sidewalk, this successful Seattle furniture store is packed with reproductions and antique-looking originals. You'll see the distinctive hand-painted corners of the venerable Hitchcock line, as well as some of Lexington's hard-to-find solid cherry pieces. The earth-friendly accessories are by Robert Beauchamp, who uses only fallen trees for his ducks and other woodcrafts. Ask to sit in the Amish rocker made of steamed hickory boughs. ♦ M-W, Sa 10AM-6PM; Th-F 10AM-8PM; Su noon-5PM. 108 Central Way (between Second St and First St). 827.3331

60 Kirkland Roaster & Ale House ★$$ This dazzling place has lots of glass and brass and a nine-foot-high vertical spit. Roasted meats, including lamb and ham, are the specialty, though they also serve a hearty bowl of clam chowder. And there are 19 draught beers on tap. It's generally crowded and noisy on Friday and Saturday nights. ♦ American ♦ Daily lunch and dinner. 111 Central Way (between Lake St and Market St). 827.4400; fax 827.4580 &

60 Yuppie Pawn Shop This business is based on the concept that while young urban professionals may have it all, they may also be willing to hock it all (or at least some of it) for ready cash. The result is a store full of such high-end used goods as computers, keyboards, espresso machines, radar equipment, sailboards, and riding lawn mowers, as well as the usual watches and cameras. ♦ M-Sa. 107 Central Way (between Lake St and Market St). 827.9438

60 Triple J Cafe $ You'll have trouble getting your mouth around one of the huge sandwiches at this tiny lunch joint owned by brothers Jim, Jeff, and Jason Harnasch. Split the meat loaf, the veggie, or the turkey and cranberry with a friend. Or enjoy an espresso and homemade muffins while you ponder the local artists' paintings featured on the walls. ♦ American ♦ Daily lunch. 101 Central Way (between Lake St and Market St). 822.7319 &

61 Parkplace Unlike a typical mall, this blissfully uncovered shopping center seems more like a collection of creative and accessible shops. The complex also includes a five-story office tower with a clock on the top. Nestled among the 45 shops and restaurants are the **Parkplace Theater** (with six screens), a health club, and, needless to say, a **Starbucks.** ♦ 401 Park Pl (between Kirkland Way and Central Way)

Within Parkplace:

City Thai ★$ Visit this small, quiet, and surprisingly elegant restaurant where owner Joe Suwanvichit takes much care with the presentation of food. For beginners, the *pad thai* noodles (with shrimp, egg, vegetables, and tofu in a peanut sauce) make a great introduction to an often daunting cuisine. Also tasty is the house special beef dish, cooked with carrots, potatoes, and roasted peanuts and served in a spicy curry with coconut milk. They'll be happy to turn down the temperature in any dish. ♦ Thai ♦ M-Sa lunch and dinner; Su dinner. 827.2875 &

62 Dr. Trueblood/Creger Home In 1907 this slender wood-frame house (pictured below) was bought by Kirkland's first physician, Dr. Barclay Trueblood. The now-quiet street in front of the house was once the busiest avenue in town. It's a private residence. ♦ 127 Seventh Ave (between Second and First Sts)

Dr. Trueblood/Creger Home

COURTESY OF THE KIRKLAND HERITAGE SOCIETY

Selling Seafood by the Seashore

When it comes to supplying savory salmon and other seafood delectables, Seattle is not only Washington's largest seaport, but Alaska's as well. The salmon, halibut, and sablefish caught in Alaskan waters generally pass through this city to be processed or shipped to international markets. Seattle also has easy access to seafood from all around Washington State: mussels from **Penn Cove** on **Whidbey Island**, pink swimming scallops from the **San Juan Islands**, octopus from **Puget Sound**, Pacific oysters from the **Hood Canal** and **Willapa Bay**, Olympia and Kumamoto oysters from southern Puget Sound, and Dungeness crab from offshore waters. Oysters and salmon are the big favorites here, and there are so many species of each of these available—all with different flavors and textures—that it can easily boggle the mind of the average landlubber. Here's a reference guide to the local catch.

Oysters

Four varieties of oysters are commonly found in Seattle-area restaurants and seafood markets, from the native Olympia to the often pricey European Flat. In general, these oysters are in season from late October through May or June—as long as the Puget Sound waters remain cold. Oysters prepare to spawn and turn milky and soft during warm weather, which is why they are usually not at their best during the summer months (but that's all right, since summertime is when salmon is most abundant in local waters). Each kind is best served raw on the half-shell.

European Flat Oyster Often erroneously called "belon," after the most famous French beds of this delectable mollusk, they have a delicate yet satisfying flavor. Primarily raised in the pristine waters off San Juan Island (especially in **Westcott Bay**), supplies are limited (and the prices for these oysters often are higher than for the other varieties raised hereabouts), so feast on them whenever they are available. (Some Seattle restaurants serve a related oyster, the Chiloë, in midsummer when local oysters are out of season.)

Olympia Oyster The tiny Olympia oyster's superb taste—which makes it much in demand—more than compensates for its drab exterior. This is the Northwest's only native oyster; all other species were first raised from spawn shipped in from Asia or Europe.

Kumamoto Oyster Deeply cupped, thus better preserving their tasty juices, the Kumamotos have a complex and subtle flavor. At their best they surpass the renowned Olympia.

Pacific Oyster Seattle's primary commercial variety is a plump, lusciously flavored bivalve, originally imported from Japan but now ubiquitous in Washington's inland waters. Fatter than other shellfish, they have a rich, satisfying flavor that's excellent raw or cooked. Pacific oysters are often named after the areas they're grown in, such as **Samish Bay,** Hood Canal, **Shoalwater Bay,** and **Skookum Inlet.**

Salmon

There are five species of salmon caught in Seattle's local waters. The earliest to migrate are the spring salmon, which are also the last to spawn. Sockeyes run in August, silver salmon in August and September, pinks in summer, and chums in fall. These dates are important to know, because most local salmon are caught just before they enter the rivers to spawn.

When buying salmon, look for fish with red gills, a complete coat of scales, and bright, unclouded eyes. To avoid buying fish that has turned sour, smell the stomach cavity. The flesh should be firm, glossy, brightly colored, and resilient to the touch (meaning your finger shouldn't leave an impression when you poke it). Atlantic and silver salmon can be farmed, but try to buy wild fish whenever possible for their superior texture and flavor. **University Seafood & Poultry** (1317 NE 47th St at University Way NE, 632.3900) and **Mutual Fish Company** (2335 Rainier Ave S at S College St, 322.4368) sell the best seafood in town.

Since it's often difficult to tell salmon apart in the markets, a few identification tips may prove helpful:

Spring Salmon These fish, also called "chinook" or "king," have gray or brown spots on the upper body, tailfin, and head (other salmon don't have spotted heads). The flesh is rich in oil and often deep red in color, but it may be white or even streaked with white, red, and pink (particularly in the rainbow king variety). Whatever the color, spring salmon make for great eating.

Silver Salmon Also known as "coho," they have dark spots on the back and upper tail, and are smaller and more slender than spring salmon. Silvers are commonly featured on local menus, since they are farmed in Washington and caught in the wild. Farmed silver salmon are smaller than others but are still very flavorful, and they're especially good served with sauces made from fresh, tart berries.

Chum Salmon They're similar in shape to silver salmon but have a more deeply forked tail with a rounded slender base. Sometimes sold as "silverbrite," chum is low in oil and should be grilled or smoked.

Steelhead Large oval spots on the tail and back and small scales are the predominant features of these fish. Steelhead flesh is low in oil (it's delicious when smoked).

Sockeye Salmon These are the oiliest and most richly flavored of salmon. Their flesh is deep red and the bodies are slender, with a few tiny specks on the back but none of the spots found on other salmon. Consider yourself lucky if you see Fraser River sockeyes in a Seattle seafood market; they're brought in from British Columbia.

If you prefer to have your oysters shucked by a professional or want to have the catch of the day cleaned and cooked for you, Seattle offers a wide assortment of first-rate seafood restaurants. For example, **Elliott's Oyster House & Seafood Restaurant** (Pier 56 off Alaskan Way, 623.4340) on the **Waterfront** is renowned for its oysters on the half-shell. **Ray's Boathouse** (6049 Seaview Ave NW on Shilshole Bay, 789.3770 ♿) specializes in salmon dishes, while its neighbor, **Anthony's Homeport** (6135 Seaview Ave NW on Shilshole Bay, 783.0780 ♿), features a superbly rich Yukon River king salmon in the spring. And for salmon and pasta entrées, don't miss **Saleh al Lago** (6804 E Green Lake Way N between Second and First Aves NE, 522.7943 ♿) at **Green Lake.**

COURTESY OF THE KIRKLAND HERITAGE SOCIETY

63 Peter Kirk Building Kirk's urban dream began to materialize with the construction of this handsome 1891 brick edifice (illustrated above). Refurbished by the Creative Arts League, it now houses the **Kirkland Arts Center,** which holds classes and presents shows in all media. ♦ Arts Center Tu-Sa. 620 Market St (at Seventh Ave). 822.7161

64 Joshua Sears Building In 1891 Boston millionaire Joshua M. Sears built this two-story brick triangle in what was then the center of town to be the official bank of the Great Western Iron and Steel Works. The steel mill never produced so much as an ingot, and the bank failed without ever opening. The beautiful brick arches inside were covered up when the building's interior was divided into apartments in the 1940s. They were rediscovered by developer Lloyd Powell and his wife when they bought the place in 1982 and went at it with $800,000 and a trowel. The restoration won the Powells numerous awards, including *Metropolitan Home* magazine's "Home of the Year," and was featured on the "This Old House" TV show. ♦ 701 Market St (at Seventh Ave W)

65 The Bucklin Home The Kirkland Land and Improvement Company built this wood-frame house (pictured at right) in 1889, and in 1904 it was bought by Harry Thompkins, who started a successful shipyard at what is now **Carillon Point.** This house was nearly condemned after a fire in 1975, but the Bucklin family was allowed to buy it with the promise that they would restore it. Renovations began with beams and other lumber salvaged from—of all places—the old shipyard. It is now a private residence. 202 Fifth Ave W (between Second and Third Sts W)

66 Cafe Juanita ★★★$$ Back in the 1970s you couldn't get into this restaurant without either a reservation months in advance or a personal letter from the pope. But as the trendoids moved on, room opened up again for local guests, and owner Peter Dow could sit back a little and keep closer watch on his kitchen. Dow is a cautious steward of his menu, rotating in some of his favorite specials without forgetting any tried-and-true successes. That means the *spiedini misti* (two skewers of lamb and Italian sausages, roasted with onions and green peppers) you order this week will probably always be on the menu. Dow also offers about 250 Italian wines, as well as three varieties produced under his own Cavatappi label: a Sauvignon blanc, a small amount of Cabernet Sauvignon, and a dark red, potent, and dry Maddalena which he makes himself from Nebbiolo grapes. ♦ Italian ♦ Daily dinner. Reservations recommended. 9702 NE 120th Pl (between NE 120th St and 98th Ave NE). 823.1505 ♿

The Bucklin Home

COURTESY OF THE KIRKLAND HERITAGE SOCIETY

Day Trips

After four or five days in Seattle, travelers may start to feel somewhat edgy, a little trapped, worried that there isn't anything more to do than revisit **Pike Place Market, Pioneer Square,** or the **Space Needle.** But nearby are volcanoes, vineyards, and villages ... and that's just the beginning.

Within three hours from the city are the rustic **San Juan Islands,** the majestic **Mount Rainier National Park,** ceremonial wine-grape crushings on the east side of **Lake Washington,** ski slopes, exotic summer gardens, and bird refuges. Architecture aficionados might want to head south for a look at Washington state's impressive capital complex at **Olympia,** while true urbanites who want a taste of international travel could venture north into two of Canada's most interesting cities: **Victoria** is the modest but growing island-bound capital of **British Columbia,** providing a wealth of history in a cozy, shop-laden English atmosphere; and **Vancouver,** just across the **Strait of Georgia** from Victoria, is Canada's third-largest metropolis (after Montreal and Toronto). Rudyard Kipling, seduced by the Vancouver area's beauty, proclaimed in his *Letters of Travel* that "such a land is good for an energetic man . . . it is also not bad for the loafer."

And then there's **Mount St. Helens,** to the south of Seattle, which caught the world's attention when it violently blew its stack back in 1980. Although the state of Oregon tries to claim St. Helens as its own (it is physically closer to the city of Portland than to Seattle), the now-decimated peak remains one of Washington's prime attractions.

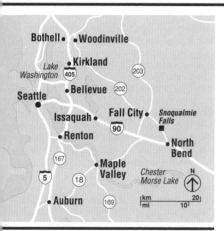

Eastside Wine Country

Washington State's oldest producer of premium wines is the **Columbia Winery** (14030 NE 145th St between the Sammamish River and Woodinville-Redmond Rd, Woodinville, 488.2776), located northeast of Seattle, across Lake Washington. There are daily wine tastings, and tours are given on weekends. Visitors can enjoy the patio, picnic grounds, and lawns, and purchase cheese and crackers in a small gift shop. Phone ahead to check on occasional concerts held on the premises. Just across the street is the state's largest winery, **Chateau Ste. Michelle** (14111 NE 145th St between the Sammamish River and 140th Pl NE, Woodinville, 488.1133). The extensive grounds here are open to picnickers, and classical concerts are held in an amphitheater during the warm months. If you have time, take a tour of the two-acre garden behind the grounds' historic **Stimson Mansion.** Timber magnate Frederick S. Stimson arrived in Seattle in 1889, bought 206 acres of prime agricultural land on the **Sammamish River,** and built **Hollywood Farm,** a state-of-the-art dairy and poultry ranch, anchored by the manse. Around 1910 he hired the famed Olmsted brothers to plan a garden, bordered by trees and shrubs, that would be filled with exotic plants. The formal results are still maintained today.

For a guide to Washington's wine-touring opportunities, check out *Northwest Wines* (1994, Sasquatch Press) co-authored by Paul Gregutt, wine columnist for the *Seattle Weekly,* and Jeff Prather, wine manager at **Ray's Boathouse** in Ballard.

Heading back to Seattle after a full day of tapping the grape, plan to take a detour from the Lake Washington floating bridges in favor of Highway 522 or Bothell Way, and stop for a sumptuous French dinner at **Gerard's Relais de Lyon** (17121 Bothell Way NE, Bothell, just inside the city limits, 485.7600). Owner/chef Gerard Parrat, a student and follower of famous French foodmeister Paul Bocuse, has been running this restaurant for more than 20 years. Parrat's cuisine remains firmly rooted in his Lyonnaise heritage. Presentation is exceedingly fancy (imagine a terrine with slivers of artichoke heart, squab breast, and rare foie gras embedded in aspic). Some offerings should not be missed (the lobster bisque, for instance). And the tangy Grand Marnier soufflé, from a Bocuse recipe, is especially popular. Reservations are essential.

Another excellent dining choice is **The Herbfarm** (32804 Issaquah–Fall City Rd, Fall City, 784.2222), about 30 minutes east of Seattle. Chefs Ron Zimmerman and Jerry Traunfeld have created a restaurant that provides an exceptional experience as well as excellent food. Meals begin with a lively tour of the grounds, with Zimmerman nipping off leaves for you to rub and smell. After that sensual experience, you'll be far more aware of the flowers and herbs in what you taste; the legendary salads are a good example. All the produce (except for lemons) and herbs used in the food preparation are grown here. Prix-fixe meals (six courses at lunch, nine at dinner) are composed from fresh seasonal bounty and span the globe with their culinary influences—everything from Italian to Native American.

Unfortunately, getting a reservation here is no easy task. First, only 32 people can be accommodated at one time. Second, there is just one seating per day (either lunch or dinner), and only on Friday, Saturday, and Sunday. Third, the restaurant takes six months of advance bookings on two days each year (a Wednesday in early April and a Wednesday in mid-August; dates vary, so call ahead). About 25 percent of the seating, however, is kept open until a week before serving. So if you call at 1PM on a Friday to check the following week's availability, you might hit the jackpot. If not, you can stop by the farm store (open daily April through February) for herbs and other gourmet items to bring home.

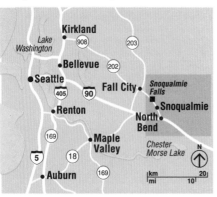

Snoqualmie and Snoqualmie Falls

King County's eastern cantons won international fame when Washington native David Lynch chose to shoot his unsettlingly kinky TV series "Twin Peaks" in the small towns of **North Bend** and **Snoqualmie.** Begin your exploration of this area by taking Interstate 90 from Bellevue to Exit 27. Follow the signs to Snoqualmie, then through the north end of town to **Snoqualmie Falls;** or take **Highways 908** and **202** from Kirkland to reach the falls by a more scenic route. This 270-foot cascade is *the* place to bring out-of-town guests. City folks and other tourists have been coming here to gawk since the late 19th century. A lookout point on a bluff to one side of the falls was improved and expanded not long ago, but crowds mount quickly on weekends, everybody equipped with cameras; arrive early if you hope to beat the stampede.

The Snoqualmie Indians have traditionally viewed this as a sacred site, and they've been struggling in recent years to maintain its natural appearance. The tribe has not had a happy relationship with Puget Power, the hydroelectric company that owns the land surrounding the falls and regulates how much water passes over its lip. Information panels at the overlook outline these additions and renovations, which include consideration for fisheries, wetlands, and even flood prevention; the Snoqualmie are mentioned only in relation to the discovery of the falls by whites. Ironically, Puget Power's buildings at the falls are historic landmarks, while the Snoqualmie have no legal means to protect the falls.

The world's first underground electric generator, built in 1898, lies 270 feet deep in a chamber excavated from solid basaltic rock behind the falls. From the lookout point, you can see the opening of the tailrace, a 450-foot-long tunnel where water diverted through the turbines rejoins the river at the base of the falls. A one-mile round-trip trail will take you down for a closer look and a faceful of spray.

Perched at the very edge of the gorge is the **Salish Lodge** (Hwy 202, 888.2556). Formerly the **Snoqualmie Falls Lodge,** the landmark was remodeled in the late 1980s. Although a country feel was retained, the place has lost its authentic weathered look. The **Salish Lodge Dining Room** is famous for its front-row view of the falls and its six-course country breakfast: a platter of fruit accompanied by the Eye Opener (fresh-squeezed orange juice blended with lime juice, honey, and egg, and topped with grated nutmeg), an assortment of bran and fruit muffins baked every half hour and served with honey butter, old-fashioned rolled oats with cream and brown sugar, and the main course of apple-pork sausage, smoked bacon, and a grilled ham steak with your choice of egg preparations, plus hash browns, and sourdough biscuits—buttressed by a stack of whole-wheat buttermilk flapjacks. (Be prepared to loosen your belt a notch—or two.) The wine list is also legendary. Sommelier Randy Austin says that at last count there were 725 labels available on the roster, including an 1882 Madeira Verdeljo ($250). Don't worry if you're not an expert oenophile; Austin has always been very helpful in educating the patrons about novel or arcane vintages to complement their meals.

Leaving the falls, backtrack through the town of Snoqualmie. Train buffs shouldn't miss a steam-train ride on the **Puget Sound and Snoqualmie Valley Railway** (746.4025), a 90-minute round-trip excursion between Snoqualmie and **North Bend** offered on weekends from April through October. The town of North Bend is sprinkled with Swiss chalet-style shops and restaurants and loomed over by **Mount Si.** With a sweeping view of the **Snoqualmie Valley** and a trailhead that starts just outside of town, Si is a popular hike; on weekends the 4.5-mile trail, though strenuous, is crowded with nature lovers. To get there, drive south on **North Bend Way,** turn left on **Mount Si Road** and continue for about 2.5 miles, watching for the trail sign. Just one caution: Keep track of the time—many people have spent miserable nights lost in these woods because they didn't allow enough time to hike back before dark. And the Haystack, a knob of bare rock at Si's top, is officially off limits. Views from there may be panoramic, but sudden sidewinds and updrafts can pick off even the most macho sight-seers like ripe fruit.

Bainbridge Island

Bainbridge has enjoyed some interesting history. In the late 19th century the island's southern end sported a couple of saloons, a giant mill that could cut 500,000 board feet a day over two 10-hour shifts, and the 75-room **Bainbridge Hotel.** (All have since disappeared.) In the early 20th century the island figured briefly into the well-publicized and often comic escape of Butch Cassidy cohort Harry Tracy from a maximum-security prison in Oregon. Most of that colorful heritage is gone, leaving a fairly peaceful, still heavily wooded retreat.

For years, Bainbridge—about 35 minutes west of Seattle by ferry—was a haven for hippies and others whose supreme desire was to drop out of the public eye. But things change. Although threats to build a bridge across **Puget Sound** have come to naught, as Seattle grew, well-to-do residents who didn't fancy moving to the Eastside suburbs looked west instead.

The Bainbridge-bound ferry (464.6400) leaves from the **Colman Dock/Pier 52** on Seattle's **Waterfront.** Ferries depart every 40 to 60 minutes from just after 6AM until slightly after 2AM; the last return trip leaves Bainbridge at about 1:15AM. Ferries dock at the **City of Bainbridge Island,** home to a small Saturday farmer's market (held mid-spring through fall at **Winslow Green,** on the corner of Madison Avenue and Winslow Way), plus a couple of cafes and the small but interesting **Eagle Harbor Books** (157 Winslow Way at Madison Ave, 842.5332).

Stop in at the **Streamliner Diner** (397 Winslow Way at Bjune St, 842.8595; no credit cards accepted), an island institution, and get in line. Breakfasts are legendary (just ask any of the people waiting for a table) and they're served all day. Try the omelettes, buttermilk waffles, or potatoes deluxe—a stir-fry of diced spuds, lots of onions, and fresh veggies, all beneath a generous layer of melted cheese.

Head north along **Highway 305** and, in less than a mile, you'll come to the **Bainbridge Island Winery** (682 Hwy 305, 842.9463), the only estate winery in the Seattle area. Founded in 1981, it's only seven acres in size but has a growing reputation. Owners Gerard and Jo Ann Bentryn style the vintages in the German fashion—low in alcohol with some residual sweetness. The flagship wine is Müller-Thurgau, but Corbet Clark, in his book *American Wines of the Northwest,* also gives raves to the "surprising" Siegerrebe, "a cross of Gewürztraminer with Madeleine Angevine, itself an old French cross." The Bentryns also produce a popular strawberry wine. There's a picnic area, a wine-oriented antiques shop, and a wine museum on the premises.

The 150 acres of **Bloedel Reserve** (7521 NE Dolphin Dr off Hwy 305, 842.7631), about four miles farther north along Highway 305, were once the estate of a Canadian lumbering family. But since the 1980s, these woodlands and gardens have been open to the public from Wednesday through Sunday, with trails that give visitors a good look at exotic plant life imported from around the globe. Rhododendrons and azaleas are the most plentiful plantings, so spring is the prime viewing season. Bring binoculars; birds enjoy a refuge here. Only 150 guests are allowed in each day; make reservations early; admission charge.

Finally, cross the bridge onto the **Kitsap Peninsula** at **Agate Pass** and turn right onto **Sandy Pass Road** and follow the signs to the **Suquamish Museum** (15383 Sandy Hook Rd, 360/598.3311). This small museum recounts local history in a manner sensitive to the perspective of Puget Sound's Salish tribe. The life of Chief Sealth is illuminated through both displays and photographs. The museum is open daily; admission is charged.

Chief Sealth's burial site is nearby, next to **St. Peter's Catholic Mission Church** in the Kitsap village of **Suquamish.** It's hard to miss the leader's tomb, which is marked with a pair of long canoes mounted atop poles.

Anacortes

Dewey (20)

Deception Pass
State Park

La Conner

(20)

Whidbey
Island

Oak Harbor

Skagit
Bay

(20)

San de Fuca

Utsalady

Fort Ebey
State Park   Coupeville

(532)

Camano
Island   Port
Susan

Fort Casey
State Park   Keystone   Camano

Port
Townsend

(20)

Camano Island
State Park

Whidbey
State Park   Greenbank

Saratoga   Mabana

Nordland

Saratoga Passage

Langley

Freeland

(525)

Austin

Puget
Sound

Useless
Bay   Clinton

Port
Ludlow

Maxwelton   Columbia
Beach

Hansville

Possession

N

km   10
mi   5

Whidbey Island

Thanks to the US Supreme Court, Whidbey Island—a 50-mile snake of soil northwest of Seattle—is the longest island in the United States. (The court declared that challenger Long Island is a mere peninsula.) Unfortunately, the island's natural beauty and easygoing charm may soon be overrun in the rush to attract tourists. More and more amenities are being planned for Whidbey, causing a local backlash from Seattleites who liked the island before it became popular. The time to see this place is now, before it's too late.

Whidbey is reached via a 20-minute ferry ride from the town of **Mukilteo,** 20 miles north of Seattle. Ferries leave every half-hour on Saturday and Sunday, from about 6AM until 1AM; the last return ferry leaves Whidbey at about 12:30AM on Sunday. Weekday service is more limited; call 464.6400 for schedules and information. The boat docks in the town of **Clinton,** where motorists can pick up **Highway 525.**

Once on Whidbey, follow the highway for three miles, then take the marked turn-off east to **Langley.** This

tiny town maintains a distinctly quaint air; it may be rivaled only by La Conner, Washington, in the number of new curio shops that sprout here annually. Yet Langley seems especially susceptible t the encroaching tourist industry: The town already has a glut in its number of high-priced but small-occupancy "boutique hotels," which sell themselves on expansive views of **Saratoga Passage** and the **Cascade Mountains.** One of the most quietly luxurious establishments is **Galittoire** (5444 S Coles Rd off Hwy 525, 360/221.0548), a woodland escape surrounded by gardens and tall trees. Architect and innkeeper **Mahesh Massand** offers two sumptuous suites—one with a hot tub and private gym—and loves to surprise guests with gourmet canapes and drinks in the afternoon.

Several fine restaurants draw day-trippers from the mainland. Try the Middle Eastern **Cafe Langley** (113 First St at the south end of town, 360/221.3090), renowned for its crab cakes and hummus. Or sample innkeeper/chef Stephen Nogal's delectable five-course, prix-fixe weekend dinners at the **Inn at Langley** (400 First St at the south end of town, 360/221.3033), which concentrate on Northwest ingredients from vegetables to seafood. There's one seating a night, two nights a week, expanding to three nights weekly in the summer; reservations are taken three months in advance.

A visit to the **Meerkeek Rhododendron Gardens** (360/678.1912), 15.5 miles north of the ferry landing on Highway 525 to Resort Road, is a must for spring visitors. There are 53 acres covered with some 2,000 varieties of Washington's official state flower in peak bloom from mid-April to mid-May. The gardens also feature wild flowers and summer perennials. Energetic types might want to head up-island for a walk around the gorge at **Deception Pass** (near **Oak Harbor**), with its 2,300 acres of forests and beaches. The gardens are open Wednesday through Sunday; admission charge.

Midway between those two attractions, three miles south of **Coupeville** on **Admiralty Inlet,** is **Fort Casey** (360/678.4519), decommissioned but still boasting its old gun mounts and some dramatic outlooks. It's open daily and is free.

Get a sense of history and stay a night or two at the **Fort Casey Inn** (1124 S Engle Rd, two miles west of Coupeville, 360/678.8792). Children are welcome at this restored two-story, two-bedroom, Georgian Revival officers' quarters decorated with rag rugs, stenciling, and plenty of eagle motifs. Bikes are available free to guests. While in Coupeville visit the free **Island County Historical Museum** (Alexander and Front Sts, 360/678.3310), which is full of old photographs and Native American artifacts. The museum is open daily May through October; Saturday-Sunday in April.

As the sun finally fades from the sky, stop by the **Captain Whidbey Inn** (2072 W Captain Whidbey Inn Rd off Madrona Way, Coupeville, 360/678.4097, 800/366.4097). This 1907 madrona log lodge (pictured on page 197) was once most reachable by

steamship from Seattle. Now you can wheel up here
n just a few hours for dinner or drinks on a terrific
deck overlooking **Penn Cove,** where some of this
region's finest mussels are harvested.

There is a plethora of bed-and-breakfast establishments on the island, as well as a number of cottages
for rent; contact the **Langley Chamber of Commerce**
(360/221.6765) for more information.

San Juan Islands

There are 743 islands in the San Juan archipelago,
but during high tide only about 170 of them are
visible. Sixty of these are populated, most are
privately owned (a few by hermits), and the vast
majority are unreachable except by private craft.

Kenmore Air (486.8400) offers scenic scheduled
floatplane service from Seattle to the San Juans. But

certainly the most relaxing means of travel to the four
largest islands—**Lopez, Shaw, Orcas,** and **San Juan**
(with an international spur on to **Sidney, British
Columbia**)—is by ferry.

Washington State Ferries (464.6400) bound for the
islands leave from the town of **Anacortes,** 78 miles
north of Seattle (take Exit 230 from Interstate 5 and
head 20 miles west to the terminal). During summer
months there are 17 daily departures scheduled from
Anacortes; fewer between Labor Day and Memorial
Day. Return schedules vary per island. The wait for
space on ferry car decks can be long, so bring
reading material; folks have spent two or more hours
in line during the summer tourist crush. But if you
begin early (the first sailing of the day varies slightly
each quarter, but is sometime around 6AM), you'll
improve your chances of getting on when you want.

While at sea, the boats provide huge picture windows
for ample viewing of madrona-forested hills and
narrow beaches. Eagles, gulls, and other able
aviators are frequently seen, as are small fishing
craft. Weather here tends to be milder than in Seattle,
as the islands snuggle into the "rain shadow" of the
Olympic Mountains to the southwest. It takes
approximately 1.5 hours to sail from Anacortes
directly to **Friday Harbor,** on San Juan, the farthest
you can go by ferry among these islands. But some
visitors slow the journey's pace by getting off and on
the boat periodically to tour the four principal isles.

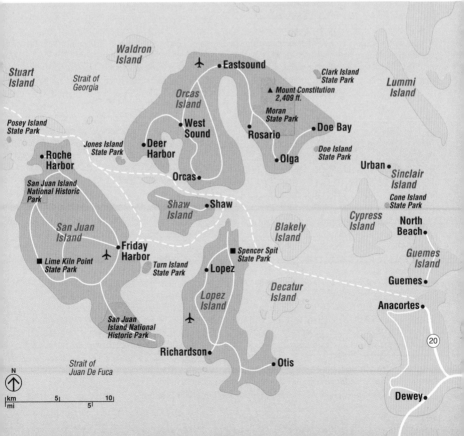

The islands can be very crowded in the summer, so book accommodations early—preferrably *weeks* before your planned excursion. **Visitor Information Service** (360/468.3663) provides accommodations listings, and the **Washington Bed and Breakfast Guild** (800/647.2918) lists inns, farmhouses, and cottages run by charming and friendly innkeepers.

Flat, pastoral Lopez (about 45 minutes by ferry from Anacortes) provides the easiest bicycling on the islands, a 30-mile jaunt past sheep and cattle pastures that can be handled even by younger family members. One of the best ways to enjoy the island is to stay at the **Inn at Swifts Bay** (Port Stanley Rd, one mile south of the ferry landing, 360/468.3636). Robert Herrman and Christopher Brandmeir offer whatever amount of pampering or seclusion you might desire in their tasteful, comfortable mock Tudor home surrounded by perennial gardens. (They'll even pick you up at the ferry landing.) Five guest rooms are available in the inn, and there's also a romantic waterfront cabin for two. All guests have access to the hot tub down the garden path, and are provided with robes, flashlights, and flip-flops.

Ride down to the island's southwest corner and visit **Shark Reef Preserve** to observe seals barking and flopping about. Lopez village (known for its grapevine of information and liberal politics) barely makes it on the map. It boasts the small but interesting **Lopez Island Historical Museum** (Lopez Plaza, 360/468.2049) that is open Friday through Sunday May through September (donation requested) and a bakery, **Holly B's** (Lopez Plaza, 360/468.2133).

All four islands can claim parks, but underpopulated Shaw Island—dominated by three orders of Catholic nuns (one member of which always comes down to meet the ferry)—offers very little else in the way of traveler amenities.

At 57 square miles, horseshoe-shaped Orcas (an hour and 20 minutes by ferry from Anacortes) is the largest of the islands. Generally hilly (okay for bike riding if you're in good shape), it's dominated by 2,409-foot **Mount Constitution,** on top of which is an old stone lookout that offers views of everything between **Mount Rainier** and Vancouver, BC. Drive up this peak or get a better feel for the island by huffing to it on foot through 4,934-acre **Moran State Park,** overlooking the island's eastern end.

The town of **Eastsound,** about 10 miles north of the ferry landing, is slowly being transformed into a mini-Carmel, with bookstores, art galleries, and restaurants. On Saturday, April through October, local artisans and growers gather at a farmer's market on the grounds of the modest **Orcas Island Historical Museum** (N Beach Rd, 360/376.4849). Also in Eastsound is **Bilbo's Festivo** (N Beach Rd and A St, 360/376.4728), a restaurant that serves food influenced by New Mexican, Mexican, and Spanish cooking styles in a setting of adobe walls and Navajo weavings. Mesquite-grilled dinners of sirloin tips and of local fish are excellent, but so are the burritos. The best seating is in the courtyard, where you can enjoy the quiet of early evening, and where it's not unheard

of for patrons to begin sing-alongs. **Christina's** (N Beach Rd and Horseshoe Way, 360/376.4904) is a more romantic restaurant, a collection of small rooms with a dining porch that overlooks the water. Offerings consist mostly of satisfying preparations of local seafood (including halibut and oysters).

Take a little time to stroll the grounds of **Rosario Resort** (Horseshoe Way, on the east side of Orcas, 360/376.2222), about 15 minutes from the ferry landing and three miles beyond Eastsound. A glistening white mansion on the waterfront, it was built in the early part of this century by former Seattle mayor and zillionaire boat-builder Robert Moran, who left the city in 1904 after his doctor told him he had only six months to live. (As it turns out, Moran avoided the Reaper for another 37 years.) With 179 charmingly decorated guest rooms, this resort is a wonderful place to hang out when the weather is good, drinking buckets of margaritas by the pool and finishing off lunch with a soothing afternoon massage. Meals in the dining room (including an almost-overwhelming Sunday brunch) are acceptable but not outstanding. Phone ahead for information on historical programs, including organ concerts and a history of the estate.

The most populated of the islands is San Juan. This was the site of a bizarre border dispute, the comic Pig War of 1859, at a time when the British and the Americans shared an uneasy joint occupation of this island. The war was set off by an American farmer who shot and killed a pig that had been rooting in his garden. Turns out the porker belonged to the British Hudson's Bay Company. When the Brits sought to arrest the offending farmer, American infantry soldiers stepped in. Tempers and armaments escalated, until President James Buchanan dispatched General Winfield Scott to negotiate a temporary truce. Joint occupation of the island continued until 1871, when none other than Kaiser Wilhelm I of Germany was asked to settle the border dispute. He drew the Canadian-US border to the west of the island, through **Haro Strait,** thereby ceding San Juan to the Americans. You can visit the national historic sites of **American Camp** and **British Camp.** To reach the former, follow **Cattle Point Road** about six miles from the town of **Friday Harbor** toward the island's southeast tip. The nattier British Camp is about 12 miles from the American Camp, located off West Valley Road.

Before or after taking in the old British installation, stop at **Lime Kiln Point State Park** (6158 Lighthouse Rd on the west side of the island, 360/378.2044), which provides some of the best whale-watching opportunities in Washington state; posted signs will help you distinguish one species from another. (Premier viewing season is from late spring through early fall.) The **Friday Harbor Whale Museum** (62 First St, 360/378.4710) in town is a warehouse-like structure stuffed with gray whale baleen, cetacean skeletons, and information about orcas and dolphins. The museum can also provide information about whale watching excursions. It's open daily; admission charge.

An unusual aspect of the San Juan Islands' beauty is that much of it is fairly new, reclaimed from previous devastation. As the 19th century became the 20th, the air here was muddied with noxious fumes from lime kilns operating on San Juan Island. **Roche Harbor,** on the north end of San Juan, once hosted some of the busiest kilns—not to mention a steam-belching railroad and lumberyards. Today the harbor's focal point is the **Hotel de Haro and Roche Harbor Resort** (Tirte Memorial Dr at Roche Harbor, 360/378.2155) built in 1886 by John Stafford McMillin, a Tacoma lawyer and owner of the old Roche Harbor Lime and Cement Company here. McMillin built the hotel so his business clients (as well as a few other distinguished guests, including Teddy Roosevelt) might have a proper place to stay nearby. Accommodations include the 20-room hotel, 20 condos, and nine cottages. Worth visiting—if only for its Stephen Kingish oddity—is a mausoleum, tucked amid a stand of Douglas firs about a half-mile from the inn. The seven-pillared monument contains a round table and six chairs in its middle, each representing a member of McMillin's family. After a roam in the woods, stop on the hotel's deck, overlooking the harbor, for a cold beer and to watch great blue herons coast forlornly over the evergreens.

Victoria, British Columbia

Author Rudyard Kipling may have gone a bit overboard when he described this city on the southern tip of **Vancouver Island** in the early 20th century. "To realize Victoria," he wrote, "you must take all that the eye admires in Bournemouth, Torquay, the Isle of Wight, the Happy Valley at Hong Kong, the Doon, Sorrento, and Camp's Bay—add reminiscences of the Thousand Islands and arrange the whole around the Bay of Naples with some Himalayas for the background." But things are changing here—rapidly. Finally shedding its reputation as a retirement camp to the world, Victoria has attracted some innovative shops and restaurants, and downtown sidewalks no longer roll up after 10PM.

To get there, you can extend your meandering journey through the San Juans via the **Washington State Ferries** (464.6400) to the town of **Sidney** on Vancouver Island, and then drive 20 miles south to Victoria. Direct service to Victoria from Seattle is available via seaplane from **Kenmore Air** (486.8400), which offers four scheduled flights daily; and by the **Victoria Clipper**'s (448.5000) passenger-only catamarans, which leave from **Pier 69** on the

Waterfront. There are two to four daily catamaran departures, with tour frequency highest from June through September. The trip lasts 2.5 hours. Board early for the best seats on the upper deck. Fares vary according to the time of year. **Victoria Line Limited,** a Canadian enterprise, operates the 190-car, 900-passenger *Royal Victorian* ferry from Seattle's **Pier 48** mid-May through mid-October. The crossing time is 4.5 hours; there is one trip in each direction daily. For recorded information, call 800/668.1167; for reservations, call 625.1880 in Seattle, 250/480.5555 in Victoria.

A good starting point for your explorations is the wonderfully innovative **Royal British Columbia Museum** (675 Belleville St between Douglas and Government Sts, 250/387.3701). Here dioramas record the extinction of woolly mammoths and the rise of Victorian storefronts; the area's Native American heritage is also well represented. The museum is open daily; there's an admission charge. Just across **Government Street** is the imposing Neo-Gothic **Parliament Building.** Free 25-30–minute tours are offered daily May through Labor Day, and Monday through Friday the rest of the year; call 250/387.3046 for reservations.

One block north is the 487-room **Empress Hotel** (721 Government St between Belleville and Humboldt Sts, 250/384.8111, 800/441.1414), opened in 1908 by the **Canadian Pacific Railway,** and host to such luminaries as Winston Churchill, John Wayne, and Richard Nixon (he and Pat honeymooned here). Several luxury attic guest rooms offer magnificent perspectives over **Inner Harbour.** There was talk in the mid-1960s of razing this grand dowager; instead, **Canadian Pacific** spent $45 million on her restoration. The investment paid off, as the hotel is now an elegant center of Victoria life. While you're here, try to experience high tea; it's held in the lobby every afternoon (reservations required).

Continue still farther north on Government Street to downtown's central shopping district. Here you will find the Dickensian treasure box of **Roger's Chocolates and English Sweet Shop** (913 Government St between Courtney and Broughton Sts, 250/384.7021), replete with chocolate creams, almond brittle, and marzipan bars; **Munro's Books** (1108 Government St between Fort and View Sts, 250/382.2464), a 1909 bank transformed into the city's best and classiest bookstore; **Murchie's Tea and Coffee** (1110 Government St between Fort and View Sts, 250/383.3112), redolent with the scents of buttery pastries and hot drinks; **Old Morris Tobacconist, Ltd.** (1116 Government St between Fort and View Sts, 250/382.4811), with a floor-to-ceiling humidor, along with pipes and related products; and **Sasquatch Trading** (1233 Government St between View and Yates Sts, 250/386.9033), which offers handmade sweaters. **Bastion Square,** on **Wharf Street** between **Fort** and **Yates Streets,** is home to many sidewalk restaurants, a maritime museum, and what is reportedly the location of Victoria's old gallows.

East of downtown is **Craigdarroch Castle** (1050 Joan Crescent off Fort St, 250/592.5323), a spooky climb of stone mounted above the city by coal tycoon Robert Dunsmuir, who built this estate in the late 19th century after the discovery of coal deposits made him the province's first millionaire. West of downtown, cross the **Johnson Street Bridge,** turn left on **Catherine Street,** and head down to the water and **Spinnaker's Brew Pub** (308 Catherine St, 250/386.2739) in the nearby **Esquimalt** community, for a giant burger, a cold beer, and a soothing view back toward Victoria.

For a relaxed, pampered stay along the ocean, drive out to **Sooke Harbour House** (1528 Whiffen Spit Rd at the end, 250/642.3421), about 45 minutes west of Victoria in the town of **Sooke.** All 13 guest rooms overlook the ocean, and most have a balcony or terrace. The meals served in the restaurant are outstanding: Dinner may include fresh seafood caught by one of the owners, Sinclair Philip—an expert diver—and will definitely include vegetables, herbs, and edible flowers from the inn's extensive gardens.

When the weather is good, Victoria dresses up in nature's splendor with jewel-colored blossoms in its many gardens—from pocket-size to large estates—and in hanging baskets on nearly every street downtown. Contact the **Travel Infocentre** (812 Wharf St near Humboldt and Government Sts, 250/382.2127) for information on gardens at **Royal Roads,** the **Royal BC Museum, Beacon Hill Park, Government House, University Finnerty Gardens,** and the **Gorge Waterway.**

The most famous spot is **Butchart Gardens,** 13 miles north of Victoria in **Brentwood** (off Hwy 17, 250/652.5256). The 50-acre manicured property is suffused with lavish displays of flowers and foliage, as well as fountains, gurgling brooks, a water-driven wooden chime, and deep rock bays. If you do nothing else, be sure to pay a visit to this beautiful and serene place. The scents are splendid and photo ops abound. Light meals, including a decadent high tea, are available at a restaurant with views of the garden, and concerts are held here during the summer months. There are special nighttime lighting displays around Christmas. The gardens are open daily; there's an admission charge.

The deepest snowfall—a whopping 93 feet—ever recorded in the US was in Paradise, located at the 5,400-foot level on Mount Rainier, during the winter of 1972-73.

The 1991-1992 opening of The Outback, Keystone Resort's third peak, was the largest expansion in Colorado ski country of the last decade. The addition of this 256-acre area, with a high-speed quad accessing 17 trails and bowls, increased the resort's ski terrain by more than 40 percent.

Vancouver, British Columbia

A little more than 200 years ago Captain George Vancouver sailed into nearby **Burrard Inlet** in 1792 to proclaim the area's beauty and claim it for England. Today Vancouver is a big city, with all the civic, cultural, and mercantile amenities (as well as the traffic). It's a cosmopolitan city too. Residents of Hong Kong, wanting to escape the city before the 1997 takeover by the Chinese, are migrating here in huge numbers. Meanwhile, Seattle has extended its tourist-oriented grasp 150 miles north to Vancouver, opening more than 50 **Starbucks** outlets in the area. Daily **Amtrak** service between Seattle and Vancouver has recently been restored; call 382.4120 or 800/872.7245 for reservations. Make your plans well in advance, as the four-hour trip is very popular.

Begin your explorations at **Stanley Park,** a great peninsular greensward northwest of downtown (reached via Georgia Street), where there are swimming beaches, totem poles, and a zoo. Head downtown where all the establishments along **Robson Street** will attempt to drain away in an afternoon every dollar you've reserved for a week's worth of sightseeing. On a sunny summer afternoon shoppers flock to the stretch between **Jervis** and **Granville Streets** to browse for linens and modernist lamps, or to circle

vulturelike around the shoe stores. The culturally inclined will want to visit the **Vancouver Art Gallery** (750 Hornby St at Georgia St, 604/682.4668), a former courthouse designed by Canadian architect **Francis Rattenbury,** who is also responsible for the **Empress Hotel** and **Parliament Building** in Victoria. Then it's on to big-ticket department stores, such as **Eaton's,** within the **Pacific Centre** mall (701 Granville St at Georgia St, 604/685.7112), where the background music is of plastic slapping confidently against countertops.

If you have a car, take a scenic drive along the water to the **University of British Columbia,** stopping at the **Museum of Anthropology** (6393 Northwest Marine Dr, 604/228.5087), an architectural marvel that contains an extensive collection of artifacts from native cultures of coastal BC, including cedar war canoes, jewelry, sculpture, dishes, and a spectacular display of totem poles. It is open daily; there's an admission charge (except for Tuesdays 5-9PM June through August and all day Tuesdays the rest of the year).

Granville Island Public Market (604/666.6477), an island and former warehouse district on the south shore of **False Creek,** is thick with shops selling fresh produce, Southwestern art, and the makings for beaded bracelets. Stop by the market area's **Granville Island Brewing Company** (604/687.2739)

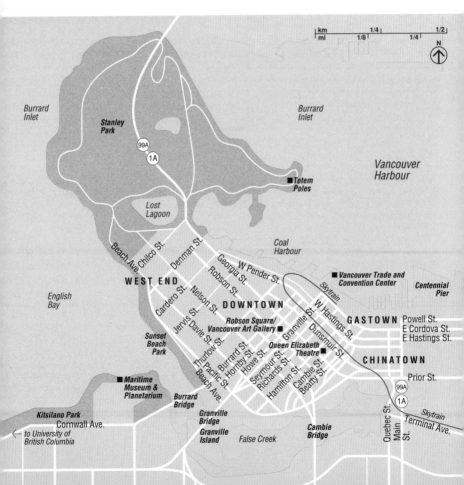

for excellent local craft beers, especially the Lord Granville Natural Pale Ale. If you visit on a Saturday or Sunday, arrive early or count on being engulfed by the masses who descend upon this place at any hint of sunshine.

More endearing—for its eclecticism and richness of architectural fenestration—is **Gastown,** located on the opposite side of town. This area was once the center of Vancouver; then it was known as **Granville** (or "Luck-Lucky" to the local Indians) before an 1886 fire leveled much of it. Vancouver residents have preserved much of their heritage in this historic district.

The huge brick-and–terra-cotta **Canadian Pacific Railway Station** (601 W Cordova St, between Seymour and Granville Sts) has been refurbished as a terminus for the **Sky Train** system that links downtown Vancouver with the community of New Westminster. Several turn-of-the-century edifices have been connected with a skylight to become **Sinclair Centre** (757 W Hastings St between Granville and Howe Sts, 604/666.4438), a vast hive

of card shops and art outlets. Others have been divided with ethnic restaurants and furniture outlets, leading some to say that Gastown has become too commercial.

Its opposite is **Chinatown,** just to the east, where gentrification has not shown its face. The area along **Pender** and **Hastings Streets** is thronged with humanity, particularly on weekend grocery shopping days. And, of course, there are plenty of restaurants to choose from.

Vancouver's restaurants (especially the Asian ones) offer a range of excellent dining choices that serve a wide variety of cuisines. One of the best in town is the **Imperial** (355 Burrard St at W Hastings St, 604/688.8191), which serves wonderful Cantonese food in a beautiful, well-maintained Art Deco building with a fabulous harbor view. If continental food is more your style, try **Le Crocodile** (100-909 Burrard St off Smythe St, 604/669.4298), where chef/owner Michel Jacob prepares such succulent dishes as salmon tartare, duck in a light orange sauce, and sautéed scallops; there's also an excellent wine list.

Olympia Capitol

In 1928 Governor Roland E. Hartley fumed over $7 million that had been spent to create a magnificent capitol complex for Washington state. Even on the day before state executives were to move into their new **Legislative Building** (off Capitol Way, between 16th and 11th Aves, 360/586.8687), Hartley couldn't resist launching a few last darts at Washington's profligate lawmakers. "Today is an epochal day," he told reporters, "but it brings no joy to the heart of the taxpayer." Hartley worked himself into a bluster as the newspaper reporters scribbled wildly. "May the new building be a deterrent, rather than an incentive, to future extravagance on the part of those in whose hands the business affairs of the state are entrusted." And he didn't stop there. After the complex's dedication, Hartley loaded some of the new capitol's "sumptuous furnishings"—including a few $47.50 spittoons—into an automobile and paraded them about the state to prove that his opponents in Olympia wouldn't hesitate to spend the taxpayers' hard-earned money. Of course, the governor neglected to mention that he had made sure his own office would be the most sumptuous in the building. Perched over **Budd Inlet,** at the southern tip of Puget Sound, Olympia shares the mediocrity of other small state capitols. But it is still worth visiting, if only for the legislative campus and a couple of other sights.

Washingtonians first started talking about raising a permanent statehouse in 1892. The following year, a nationwide competition was launched to select an architect for the project. From 186 submissions, the commission chose **Ernest Flagg** of New York City, a young relative of Cornelius Vanderbilt and a graduate of the Ecole des Beaux Arts in Paris. **Flagg** planned a compact, heavily ornamented structure with a short dome and Corinthian columns running the length of its entry facade. Unfortunately, income from government land grants fell short and construction on the building had to be halted soon after its foundations were laid. In 1901 the state made do with downtown Olympia's lordly old **Thurston County Courthouse** (now the **Board of Education Building**) as the temporary residence for Washington state government.

Forces didn't gear up to launch another capitol design competition until 1911. More money was available this go-around, but the organizers of the competition insisted that **Flagg**'s foundation should be integrated into any new conception, probably as the base for one of several buildings on a government campus. **Flagg** naturally assumed that his original commission was still in effect; in the ensuing years, he had enhanced his reputation by developing Manhattan's Singer Building and the Corcoran Art Gallery in Washington, DC. But the committee chose a couple of virtual unknowns: architects **Walter Wilder** and **Harry White.** Both had labored for a time with the famous New York firm of **McKim, Mead & White,** and in fact their plan for Washington's capitol owed an obvious debt to the work of that firm's late principal, **Stanford White,** who had created the Rhode Island capitol building in the early 1890s.

Wilder and **White**'s initial Roman Classical Revival design called for a **Legislative Building** surrounded by five office structures (one of which would replace the 1908 brick **Governor's Mansion**), as well as an arrangement of stairs and landings descending to **Capitol Lake** and a grand promenade stretching into downtown, with a new railroad station at its terminus. Budget limitations doomed some embellishments, but results were still impressive. Of Olympia, architecture historians Henry-Russell Hitchcock and William Seale wrote in their seminal work *Temples of Democracy: The State Capitols of the U.S.A.,* "the American renaissance in state capitol building reached its climax." At the time of its raising, the building's dome was the fourth tallest in the world—287 feet from the base—sliding into order behind those of St. Peter's of Rome (408 feet), St. Paul's Cathedral in London (319 feet), and the US Capitol (307 feet). A massive Tiffany chandelier was hung inside the Alaskan marble rotunda. Other components are less ostentatious. Stairs leading to the north-side main entrance offer an imposing approach but pass beneath a largely unadorned pediment. The building presents colonnades on all four elevations, but most are fairly plain-looking.

Wilder and **White** concentrated much of their decoration along the roofline, giving it an anthemion cresting, and at the east and west ends of the building, where gables are fringed with dentilled cornices. A 1986 face-lift, directed by **Barnett Schorr Architects** of Seattle, scrubbed Mount St. Helens' ash from the dome's exterior. Polish and color—including 48 rosettes and false-gold flourishes on column capitals—now brighten the rotunda's interior. Architecture and history enthusiasts should not miss an opportunity to visit. Free guided tours are offered daily.

A number of other structures on the eight-acre campus are also worth seeing: the **State Library Building** (16th and Sylvester Sts, 360/753.5590), a more contemporary colonnaded edifice designed in 1959 by noted architect **Paul Thiry,** contains Northwest art by Mark Tobey and Kenneth Callahan, as well as a collection of published works by Northwest authors; the **Governor's Mansion** (Capitol Way and 15th Ave, 360/753.1488), a Georgian Revival–style relic, was designed in 1908 by **Ambrose J. Russell** and **Everett P. Babcock,** who created other manses and some churches around Puget Sound; and the Spanish-style **State Capitol Museum** (211 W 21st Ave, off Capitol Way, 360/753.2580), formerly the home of banker Clarence J. Lord, which now houses old logging photos, Native American baskets, and more. The museum is open Tuesday through Sunday; donation requested.

Not far away is the **Board of Education Building** (Legion Way, between Franklin and Washington Sts, 360/753.6715), the former **Thurston County**

Courthouse that was once home to Washington state's government. Architect **W.A. Ritchie,** armed with only a correspondent's education in architecture from the US Treasury Department, created this and other grand county courthouses in Spokane and Port Townsend. This imposing building blends massive stone archways nicely with rounded tower bases in a Romanesque Revival whole. There was originally a polygonal central tower on this structure, adding to its authoritative image, but that was destroyed by fire in 1928. A compatible west wing dates from 1905, when the courthouse began doubling as Olympia's City Hall. Restoration has made this a most inviting structure.

Mount Rainier National Park

About 98 miles southeast of Seattle, Mount Rainier soars to a commanding height of 14,410 feet above sea level. The towering mountain and the surrounding Cascades afford splendid views, including fascinating flora and fauna. Each year, more than two million visitors come to the 378-square-mile **Mount Rainier National Park** to picnic, climb, hike, cross-country ski, or just gaze in awe at the peak and its many glaciers.

Mount Rainier is the largest volcano in the coastal range, and though it is dormant, steam emissions form caves in the summit's ice cap and often melt the snow around the rim of the twin cones. The mountain supports the largest glacier system in the continental US, with 27 different glaciers covering 35 square miles. **Carbon Glacier** is the longest, at 6 miles; **Emmons Glacier,** at almost 4.5 miles long and a mile wide, is the largest. The **Nisqually Glacier** may shift as much as 50 to 400 feet a year.

Because of its height and its proximity to the Pacific Ocean, Mount Rainier gets an average of 15 feet of snow each winter. Summer weather is warm and clear, and beginning in June, snowmelt fills the streams and creates thundering waterfalls, and flowers pop up in the alpine meadows.

You'll need to leave early in the morning if you plan to visit the park in a day trip; the drive from Seattle takes about two and a half hours. The most popular destination is the **Paradise Visitors' Center,** 5,400 feet above sea level; get there by taking **I-5** south to **Highway 7** to **Highway 706.** When you get to the park, pass through the Nisqually entrance on the southwest side.

Another option is to approach Rainier from the northeast, off **Highway 410;** the distance and driving time are about the same. The attraction here is the **Sunrise Visitors' Center,** which at 6,400 feet is the highest point of the mountain that can be reached by car. Other visitors' centers in the park include **Ohanapecosh** and **Longmire.** All of them feature spectacular views, modern visitor facilities, plenty of brochures and information, and miles of easy-to-moderate-level hiking trails. Guides conduct interpretive walks throughout the park in summer, and in winter the **Paradise** section of the mountain is headquarters for snowshoe walks and cross-country skiing.

From **Paradise, Longmire,** or **Sunrise,** you can pick up the **Wonderland Hiking Trail,** a 90-mile route that circles the base of the mountain. The trail takes you past **Box Canyon,** waterfalls, fields of wildflowers, **Golden Lakes, Carbon River,** Carbon Glacier, and the **Mowich Glaciers.** The **Northern Loop Trail** extends 17.5 miles from **Wonderland Trail** through backcountry meadows to **Crescent Mountain,** at an elevation of 6,400 feet.

The park gets most of its visitors between June and October; the Nisqually entrance is open year-round, but in winter some of the other entrances, roads, and facilities close, and access to some areas is limited. If you plan to visit off-season, check current road and weather conditions and the status of park services by calling the 24-hour information line (360/569.2211). If you decide to stay overnight, campsites are available on a first-come, first-served basis (get the required permits at a visitors' center); or you can lodge at the 25-room **National Park Inn** or the 125-room **Paradise Inn,** both on the park grounds. For accommodations information and reservations, contact the **Mount Rainer Guest Services** (PO Box 108, Ashford, WA 98304, 360/569.2275; fax: 360/569.2770).

In 1907 moralist William Hickman Moore was elected mayor of Seattle and began a campaign to eliminate saloons and other vices from the city's borders. But Moore was out of office and his reform efforts were out of favor by 1910, when city councilman Hiram C. Gill was elected mayor. Gill favored a wide-open town. In fact, *McClure's* magazine reported that 30 to 40 gambling places opened during Gill's term. Seattle's police chief himself was taking kickbacks from prostitution—$10 per person per month.

Mount St. Helens

Many mountains are taller than Mount St. Helens, with its summit 8,365 feet above sea level (it was 1,300 feet higher before its 1980 eruption), but the thrill of poking about what was very recently an active volcano can hardly be beat. Over the decade and a half since the volcano last exploded, plants and wildlife have been returning to these slopes, and so have people—Mount St. Helens is now a national volcanic monument, attracting more than 600,000 people every year.

Begin your explorations with a stop at one or both of the two visitors' centers west of the mountain. Take Exit 49 off **Interstate 5** and head about five miles east on **Highway 504** to the **Silverdale Visitors' Center.** This center focuses on the area's history and geology, Native American legends, and events leading up to the eruption; there's also an interesting 22-minute video of the blast. A few miles farther along Highway 504 is the **Coldwater Visitors' Center,** which offers panoramic views of the crater and dome, as well as interactive exhibits that concentrate on the returning flora and fauna; there's also a bookstore, cafeteria, and gift shop.

For a good view of the blast's results (a crater two miles across and a half-mile deep), head to the northeast side of the mountain. You can pick up maps and get directions at the two visitors' centers (there are two additional information centers along the way) to guide you through the park. **Windy Ridge** (accessed via Forest Road 99) is about four miles north of Mount St. Helens and offers an unforgettable perspective. Park the car and climb a log-and-gravel

path from there for still-better views of the mountain and what has become of **Spirit Lake,** once a popular vacation spot. It's so quiet up here it's hard to imagine that in 1980 this place echoed with a sound equivalent to 400 million tons of exploding TNT.

The mountain reopened to climbers in 1987; all must be registered, and steep fines are levied against hotdoggers. The peak season is mid-May through October, when 110 climbers per day are allowed up to the crater's lip. Permits may be obtained in advance from the **Forest Service** (Mount St. Helens National Volcanic Monument, 42218 Northeast Yale Bridge Rd, Amboy, Washington 98601, 360/750.3900). Seventy spaces per day are filled in advance, but 40 additional spaces are available on a first-come, first-served basis. Interested parties must put their names on a list at **Jack's Restaurant and Sporting Goods** (Rte 503, 23 miles east of Woodland and six miles from Cougar, 360/231.4276) the day before they hope to scale the mountain. At 6PM, the names for the next day are called until all 40 spaces are filled. (Unfortunately, each person can carry 12 people on a permit, so spaces go quickly.) During the off-season (mid-November through mid-May), climbers must still register at **Jack's,** but no advance permits are offered. Most climbers head up **Monitor Ridge** on the south face, a steep trek that may take seven to 10 hours round-trip. (Other routes are also available; ask the Forest Service for maps.) It's a dusty climb during most of the summer, after the snow has melted, so wear high boots to keep the ash out of your socks. Also, don't wear contact lenses—as the ash can get between them and your eyeballs—and bring plenty of water and energy food.

If you want to spend the night here (it's a four-hour round-trip drive from Seattle on Interstate 5), consider staying at the **Flying L Ranch** (25 Flying L La, Glenwood, 509/364.3488), a guest ranch popular with hikers.

Bests

Jeremy Hardy
Co-owner/Jitterbug, The 5 Spot, and Coastal Kitchen

The **Elliott Bay Book Company** and **Barnes & Noble Bookstore** are two huge bookstores you can lose yourself in (the nod goes to **Elliott Bay**).

If secondhand items are your thing, go to **Deluxe Junk** in Fremont.

Young, up-and-coming bands and fringe productions are what you'll find at **The Velvet Elvis Arts Lounge Theatre,** a small, intimate, funky theater in Pioneer Square.

Take in a movie at the **Egyptian Theatre,** the headquarters of the Seattle International Film Festival.

For Mexican food that will make you sweat, check out **El Puerco Lloron** at the **Pike Place Market.**

Magic Mouse in Pioneer Square is truly an authentic toystore. It features thinking toys for thinking kids, an "imaginarium" if you will.

History

Archaeological evidence points to the existence of humans in western Washington as far back as 12,000 years ago. Native Americans living in this area were part of the Northwest Coast culture, which thrived from Oregon to southern Alaska. These clans were different than the great tribes found elsewhere in North America. In fact, they weren't organized as tribes at all, but instead gathered in small villages of family-size clans. Like the pioneers who would later invade the Pacific Northwest, the Native Americans who lived here were fiercely independent. Men became leaders not through any inheritance, but by dint of their abilities. They governed their fishing and gathering societies by example rather than might. Warfare was rare among these villages, and the land was bountiful, with plenty for all. What raids were made on other native groups may have had more to do with procuring slaves than territorial or clan rivalries.

Today's **King County** was populated by natives of the Coast Salish group. They averaged just under five-and-a-half feet in height, and the men had more facial hair than was common among North American Indians. Pressure boards were often applied in infancy to flatten their foreheads. They were fine woodworkers, if somewhat less given to ceremonial carving than their counterparts in what is now **British Columbia,** using mostly red cedar in their canoes, often-conical hats, and long, narrow houses. Their culture grew up around rivers, and each enclave had a slightly different subdialect (which would later frustrate whites trying to negotiate treaties). Storytelling was a rich tradition and provided an important historical record.

Bustling downtown Seattle occupies land that once belonged to the Duwamish people. (The Suquamish, another significant native group in the area, lived on the west side of **Puget Sound** and claimed all the islands between.) After King County's Indian War of 1855-56, which wasn't precipitated by the Duwamish but tainted them nonetheless, the Duwamish were forced onto reservation lands on the western shore of Puget Sound. But over the next decade they drifted back to their old village sites near Seattle and were employed as laborers. Government promises to award them their own reservation were not kept. Once one of the largest Native American groups on Puget Sound, numbering in the thousands, today there are only several hundred Duwamish still inhabiting King County.

1775 Spanish explorer Bruno Heceta sends a boat ashore south of today's **Cape Flattery,** a headland at the entrance to the **Strait of Juan de Fuca.** The crew is captured and killed by Native Americans.

1778 British Captain James Cook, on his third round-the-globe tour, discovers Cape Flattery; however, he plies north rather than east, so he misses Puget Sound completely.

1786 Sealth, son of Schweabe, chief of the Suquamish and Scholitza Indians, and a future chief himself, is born on **Blake Island,** in western Puget Sound.

1790 The Spanish establish the first white settlement at **Neah Bay,** on the northwest Washington coast.

Spanish explorer Manuel Quimper sails deep into the Strait of Juan de Fuca, encountering and naming some of the **San Juan Islands.**

1792 After circumnavigating **Vancouver Island** in southwestern British Columbia, English Captain George Vancouver and his second

M. BLUM

lieutenant, Peter Puget, launch two separate explorations of the "inland sea," which Vancouver names Puget Sound.

1803 President Thomas Jefferson dispatches Meriwether Lewis and William Clark west to the mouth of the **Columbia River,** which they reach in 1805. Other Yankees followed.

1821 The Florida Treaty transfers all rights to territory north of the 42nd parallel to the United States. Britain's Hudson's Bay Company (HBC), however, still claims sole rights to the **Oregon Territory,** especially property north of the Columbia River, including present-day Washington state.

1845 In defiance of HBC hegemony, Yankees begin spilling north across the Columbia River.

1846 Finally yielding to US pressure, Great Britain agrees to cede lands south of the 49th parallel (today's US-Canada border) to the Yankees.

1850 The Donation Land Law encourages settlement of America's western territories by awarding 320 acres to every white or "half-breed" who will occupy and farm the land for at least four consecutive years. Another 320 acres are given to any couple married by 1 December 1851.

1851 On 13 November, seven months after leaving Illinois, Seattle founder Arthur Denny and his party of 23 arrive at **Alki Point** aboard the ship *Exact.* Soon after, the families begin relocating to the east side of **Elliott Bay** for its thicker forests and deeper harbor.

1852 Pioneer Dr. David Swinton ("Doc") Maynard from Ohio arrives at Elliott Bay and befriends Sealth, who was then the chief of the Suquamish and Duwamish. When he and other city founders decide that their settlement's informal moniker, **Duwamps,** is too inelegant, Maynard suggests "Seattle," a spin on the good chief's name that's easier to pronounce than the guttural Salish original.

Henry Yesler builds Seattle's first steam sawmill. Yesler's initial location is in **West Seattle,** but other pioneers convince him to build instead on Elliott Bay. The strip of land over which he drags his felled trees becomes known as "Skid Road."

1853 President Millard Fillmore signs the act creating the **Washington Territory.**

1855 Tensions between whites and Native Americans precipitate King County's so-called Indian War. The American battle sloop *Decatur,* sailing from Honolulu to protect Seattle settlers, rains cannonballs and grapeshot into forests beyond Third Avenue where invaders might be hiding. Natives retaliate by burning nearly every building in the county. After a final skirmish in March 1856, first Territorial Governor Isaac Stevens encourages punishment of warring Indians and the banishment of others to reservations.

1861 Washington's **Territorial University** (which is later named the **University of Washington**) is built where downtown's **Four Seasons Olympic Hotel** now stands.

1863 Seattle's first newspaper, the *Gazette,* rolls off its homemade presses. It will publish irregularly for the next three years.

1866 Chief Sealth, who had persuaded his people to stay out of the Indian War, dies at the Port Madison Reservation in Kitsap County.

1867 Former San Franciscan Samuel Maxwell founds the *Weekly Intelligencer,* which becomes a daily in 1876 and merges with the failing *Post* five years later to form what is known today as the *Seattle Post-Intelligencer.*

1869 The territorial legislature grants Seattle a city charter. City population: 1,107.

1870 Seattle's first grade school is erected.

1872 Representatives of the Northern Pacific Railroad visit Puget Sound to discuss the location of the railway's western terminus. To the shock of Seattleites, Tacoma is selected.

1878 German immigrant Andrew Hemrich founds a small brewery in south Seattle. He calls his beer Rainier.

1879 The city's first big fire destroys a number of wooden structures bordering the Waterfront, including **Yesler's Mill.**

1885 Violence erupts when Seattleites hold an anti-Chinese congress and demand that local Asians leave western Washington. A similar declaration is made in Tacoma, which quickly puts its Chinese on trains headed for Portland. Seattle's Chinese don't depart so easily. After 197 of them are shipped to San Francisco, martial law is declared and US troops halt the forced exodus.

1889 In mid-summer the Great Seattle Fire destroys 30 city blocks in what is now the historical **Pioneer Square** area.

Washington becomes the 42nd state of the Union on 11 November.

1892 Reginald H. Thomson is appointed city engineer and begins a 20-year regrading program that will drastically change Seattle's topography.

1893 The first train traveling James J. Hill's new **Great Northern Railroad** line reaches Seattle from St. Paul, Minnesota. Hill goes on to create the country's first trade and passenger services, between Puget Sound and the Orient.

1896 Bombastic former Midwestern publisher Alden J. Blethen buys the ailing *Press-Times* newspaper and re-creates it as the *Seattle Daily Times.*

1897 The steamship *Portland* arrives in Seattle with a ton of gold from Alaska, beginning a well-publicized and profitable rush through this city of men bound for the Klondike.

1898 Hundreds of thousands of men are processed through a new 640-acre US Army base on **Magnolia Bluff,** bound for the Spanish-American War. The outpost is later named **Fort Lawton,** honoring a general killed in a Philippines skirmish.

1900 Illinois lumberman Frederick Weyerhaeuser, escaping diminishing timber reserves in the Midwest to land at Puget Sound, assembles a partnership to buy 900,000 forested acres in Washington and Oregon from the Northern Pacific Railroad. The Weyerhaeuser Company will dominate Northwest lumbering throughout the century.

The population of Seattle is 80,761—double what it had been just 10 years earlier.

1907 **Pike Place Market** opens.

1908 William Boeing, the son of a wealthy Michigan timber baron, moves to Seattle after several years of running an independent timber operation in Grays Harbor in south Puget Sound.

1909 Seattle holds its first world's fair: the Alaska-Yukon-Pacific Exposition. After its close, the Olmsted Brothers, famed landscapers from Massachusetts, replan the fairgrounds as today's **University of Washington** campus.

1910 Washington's constitution is amended to give women the vote, about 10 years before most other states do so.

The US Congress authorizes construction of a ship canal linking **Lake Washington** with Puget Sound, and ground is broken within a year for the first lock.

Bill Boeing attends an air meet in California, where he becomes fascinated with the art of flying.

1914 As Europe comes to a boil with World War I, a barge loaded with dynamite for shipping to Russia explodes in Elliott Bay. Sabotage is suspected but never confirmed.

1916 Bill Boeing, along with navy officer G. Conrad Westervelt, founds an airplane enterprise on the **Duwamish River**—the beginnings of the Boeing Company.

In **Everett,** just north of Seattle, labor conflicts between members of the Industrial Workers of the World ("Wobblies") and lumber companies lead to the so-called Everett Massacre, during which at least seven men are killed and 31 others are wounded by rifle fire.

Washingtonians vote to make the sale and consumption of alcoholic beverages unlawful—four years before national Prohibition begins.

1917 In April, President Woodrow Wilson engages the United States in World War I. A month later, the **Lake Washington Ship Canal** opens and US Navy training craft begin docking off the **University of Washington** campus.

1918 The nation's influenza epidemic hits Seattle hard, killing 252 people out of every 100,000. Public assemblages are prohibited, and the local health department orders citizens to wear flu masks. The ban on congregation is lifted on 11 November, the day after the war's armistice is signed and a national holiday, so Seattleites can celebrate with each other.

1919 Three years after the Everett Massacre, Seattle hosts the nation's first general strike. A total of 60,000 organized workers walk off their jobs in protest of the growing power of capitalists. The city lies tense and quiet for several days, until strikers agree to return to work. Unlike the protest in Everett, no blood is shed here.

1926 Bertha Landes is elected mayor of Seattle. She is the first woman to hold such an exalted post in a major US city.

1929 New York stock markets crash in late October. As with so many other trends since, it takes several months for the Great Depression to affect Seattle.

1931 Huge shantytowns spring up near the Waterfront to house Seattle's many unemployed, mostly men. Officials try to burn out these "Hoovervilles," but they always sprout anew.

1934 Longshoremen in Seattle, San Francisco, and elsewhere are idled for 98 days by the Pacific Coast waterfront strike. Strikebreakers are tossed into Elliott Bay or killed. Mayor Charles Smith fires his police chief for being too lenient with protesters, and orders a crowd of 2,000 strikers clubbed before the strike is settled.

1940 The **Lacey V. Murrow Floating Bridge** opens on what is now I-90, connecting Seattle with its eastern suburbs.

1941 After the bombing of Hawaii's Pearl Harbor, the United States enters World War II. Boeing Company, the **Puget Sound Naval Shipyard** in nearby Bremerton, and other area manufacturers kick into high gear to feed the war machine. The US Navy assumes control of Puget Sound shipping, and Seattle becomes a major Army transport center.

1942 Fearful of spies and saboteurs, the Western Defense Command orders that Japanese people living in Seattle and elsewhere on the coast be interned. Asians from **Bainbridge Island** are the first ones sent to detainment camps in Idaho.

1945 The atom-bombing of Hiroshima and Nagasaki ends the war with Japan. Victory celebrations are cooled, however, by news of peacetime economic declines, especially at Boeing, where annual sales drop from $600 million to $14 million.

1949 The worst earthquake recorded in Seattle history (measuring 7.2 on the Richter scale) strikes in mid-April.

1962 Seattle's second world's fair, the Century 21 Exposition, opens to six months of tremendous success.

1963 Proposals to level **Pike Place Market** in favor of high-rise rookeries prompt an aggressive preservation campaign.

1965 Efforts begin to revitalize **Pioneer Square,** the city's original—but deteriorating—downtown.

1967 National unrest reaches Seattle when the **University of Washington**'s Black Student Union takes control of the university administration building.

Protests against the Vietnam War begin citywide.

Seattle advertising exec David Stern creates the now-ubiquitous Happy Face symbol.

1968 The city launches its "Forward Thrust Program" for improvements that include a new domed stadium and parks, and street repairs. However, a plan to reduce traffic congestion by constructing light-rail train lines radiating from downtown into the suburbs fails at the voting booth.

Seattle's population has grown to 587,000—seven times what it was at the turn of the century.

1970 Boeing, suffering after demand for its jets fails to measure up to estimates, lays off 65,000 workers over the next two years—two-thirds of its work force. Unemployment in the city leaps 12 percent as a result. Despair grows and a billboard proclaims "Will the Last Person in Seattle Please Turn Out the Lights?"

1971 The Starbucks coffee company is founded. Its name comes from the java-dependent first mate in Herman Melville's novel, *Moby-Dick.*

1974 A seven-acre historic district is created to save **Pike Place Market.**

1975 *Harper's* magazine names Seattle the country's most livable city.

1980 **Mount St. Helens** explodes a hundred miles south of Seattle, sprinkling King County with ash.

IBM execs meet with Bill Gates, a 25-year-old techie and co-inventor (with Paul Allen) of the computer language BASIC, who IBM hopes will help create the software needed for a first generation of personal computers.

1983 Citing financial woes, the *Seattle Post-Intelligencer* wins a joint-operating agreement with its rival, the *Seattle Times.*

The Washington Public Power Supply System (not-so-fondly nicknamed "Whoops") defaults on its $7-billion debt, ending hopes for cheap nuclear power in Washington and causing a tremendous ripple effect through Seattle financial circles.

1985 Aldus Corporation, an all-but-unknown Seattle computer software company, ships its first product, PageMaker, and creates a catchphrase to describe its operation: desktop publishing.

1986 Microsoft, Bill Gates's growing computer software company, offers its stock to the public. The value will go up 1,200 percent in just six years.

1989 Voters who are upset by a plague of new skyscrapers and construction-clogged streets in Seattle approve a cap on the height and bulk of downtown buildings.

Well-off Oregonians and Californians move to Seattle in hordes, creating a bizarre seller's market for real estate that drives local home shoppers out of town.

Norm Rice, first African-American mayor of Seattle, is elected.

Seattle is named the most livable US city by *Money* magazine and the *Places Rated Almanac.*

1990 The Lacey V. Murrow Floating Bridge sinks into Lake Washington; it is later completely rebuilt.

1992 Race rioting in Los Angeles (a reaction to four LAPD officers being acquitted of beating Rodney King) spills over into laid-back Seattle, where vandals and arsonists control city streets for most of a week.

After 60 years, **Longacres** horse track is shut down; Boeing plans to raze it in favor of a flight-training center.

1993 Boeing announces production cutbacks and massive layoffs, causing a tidal wave of doubt over Seattle's fiscal future.

1994 Nirvana rocker Kurt Cobain commits suicide by shooting himself at his home in Seattle.

1995 *Time* magazine puts Microsoft owner Bill Gates on its cover, proclaiming him "the world's richest man."

1996 Seattle is featured in a *Newsweek* magazine cover story that focuses on the city's growth as a cultural and business center.

Ken Griffey Jr. signs a contract with the **Seattle Mariners** for $8.5 million a year, making him the highest-paid baseball player in history.

Index

A

A&J Meats **127**
Accessibility, wheelchair **4**
Accommodations **8**
Ace Hardware/Tweedy & Popp **149**
Ace Loan **56**
Adams/Freedman Building **29**
Admiral Benbow Inn $ **113**
Admiral Theater **113**
Adriatica Cucina Mediterranea ★★★★$$$ **120**
A.E. Doyle Building **44**
Airlines **5**
Airport services **5**
A La Francaise **24**
Alaska Building **32**
Albertson, Wilson & Richardson **98**
Al Boccalino ★★★$$ **21**
Alexander Pantages House **91**
Alexis Hotel $$$ **64**
Alfi News **148**
Alki Bathhouse Art Studio **110**
Alki Beach Park **110**
Alki Bicycle Company **113**
Alki Cafe ★$ **111**
Alki Community Center **110**
Alki Homestead ★$$ **112**
Alki Playground **110**
Alki Point Light Station **112**
All the Best **104**
Alpenland Delicatessen ★$ **176**
American Camp **198**
American Eagles Inc. **137**
Anderson, Ralph **128**
Angelina's Trattoria ★$ **113**
Anhalt Apartments **97**
Anhalt, Fred **97, 98**
Annex Theatre **47**
Ann Taylor **40**
Anthony's Homeport (Ballard) ★★$$ **139**
Anthony's Homeport (Kirkland) ★★$$ **187**
Archie McPhee's **147**
Architecture Hall **167**
Arctic Building **32**
Arita Japanese Restaurant ★★$ **158**
Art around the Plaza **166**
Art by the Foot **20**
Arthur, Pat **67** (bests)
Art/Not Terminal **77**
ArtsWest **116**
Athenian Inn ★★$ **52**
Aurora Bridge **145**
Austin A. Bell Building/

Odd Fellows Hall **71**
Avoir Gallery **188**
Ayer, Elizabeth **187**
Azalea's Fountain Court ★★$$$$ **179**
Azalea Way **90**

B

Babcock, Everett P. **203**
Bacchus Restaurant ★★$ **98**
Backstage, The **137**
Bagel Oasis ★★$ **173**
Bahn Thai ★★$ **84**
Bailey/Coy Books **100**
Bainbridge Island **195** (map)
Bainbridge Island Winery **195**
Bakeman's Restaurant ★$ **32**
Bakery The Original **117**
Bakewell and Brown **93**
Ballard **132** (chapter and map)
Ballard Avenue **136**
Ballard Building **137**
Ballard Centennial Bell Tower **137**
Ballard Computer **137**
Ballard Firehouse **135**
Ballard Furniture **189**
Ballard-Howe Mansion **124**
Ballard Smoke Shop $ **137**
Bamboo Garden ★$$ **84**
Banana Republic **41**
B&O Espresso ★$ **100**
Bardahl Manufacturing Corp. **134**
Barnes & Noble Bookstore **184**
Barnett Schorr Architects **203**
Bartholick, George **50**
Bassetti, Fred **57, 65**
Bassetti/Norton/Metler **56**
Bastion Square **200**
Bathhouse Theatre **156**
Bay Cafe $ **134**
Bebb & Mendel **97, 124, 135, 171**
Bebb, Charles **24, 33, 38, 64, 91**
Be Bop-A-Latte ★$ **125**
Bellevue **177, 178** (map)
Bellevue Art Museum **182**
Bellevue Barber Shop **179**
Bellevue Botanical Gardens **177** (map)
Bellevue Downtown Park **180**
Bellevue Hilton $$ **177**
Bellevue Place **184**
Bellevue Square Mall **181**
Bell Street Pier **66**
Belltown/Seattle Center **68** (chapter and map)
Belvedere Viewpoint **115**
Bethel Temple **76**

Beth's Cafe $ **156**
Betty Bowen Viewpoint **125**
B.F. Day Elementary School **147**
Bhy Kracke Park **121**
Biagio **38**
Bicycles **6**
Big Time Brewery and Alehouse **169**
Bilbo's Festivo **198**
Bittman, Henry **32, 39, 44**
Bizango **158**
Bizzarro Italian Cafe ★★★$ **147**
Black House **125**
Blacksmith Shop, The **22**
Black Sun **95**
Bloedel Reserve **195**
Bloomingals **180**
Blue Moon Tavern **172**
Board of Education Building (Thurston County Courthouse) **203**
Bodley, J. Alfred **93**
Body Shop, The **181**
Boehm's on Ravenna **154**
Boiserie, The ★★$ **167**
Bombay Company, The **182**
Bon Marché, The **44**
Bookstore Bar, The **64**
Boston Sox **44**
Boulangerie **149**
Bowie & Company, Inc., Booksellers **23**
Boxer Bay **40**
Bread of Life Mission **22**
Breitung, C. Alfred **24, 97, 150**
Brentano's **44**
Bright Lights, Small City: Seattle's Theater Scene **34**
British Camp **198**
Broadway Clock Shop **127**
Broadway Market **100**
Brooklyn Cafe and Oyster Bar Lounge ★$$$ **37**
Brooks Brothers **41**
Brown, Denise Scott **64**
Brownell-Bloedel House **93**
Buckaroo Tavern **147**
Bucklin Home, The **191**
Bud's Jazz Records **23**
Bulldog News (Broadway Market) **100**
Bulldog News (University District) **170**
Bumgardner Architects **64, 67, 121**
Burke-Gilman Trail **169**
Burk's Cafe ★★$$ **137**
Buses **6**
Bushell's Auctions **76**

Business District **30** (chapter), **31** (map)
Butchart Gardens **200**
Butch Blum **40**
Bystrom, Arne **59**
Byzantion ★$ **99**

C

Cactus ★★$$ **91**
Cadiz Espresso ★$ **128**
Cafe Allegro ★$ **169**
Cafe Counter Intelligence ★$ **55**
Cafe Flora ★★★$$ **104**
Cafe Huê ★★$ **27**
Cafe Illiterati ★$ **136**
Cafe Juanita ★★★$$ **191**
Café Lago ★★$$ **90**
Cafe Langley **196**
Cafe Lôc ★$ **78**
Cafe Los Gatos ★★$ **154**
Cafe Sabika ★★$$ **103**
Cafe Sophie $$ **61**
Café Vizcaya ★★$$ **150**
Caffè Appassionato ★$ **130**
Caffè D'Arte ★$ **76**
Caffè Minnie's ★$$ **81**
California and Alaska Street Brewery **116**
Calkins's Landing **175**
Calvin/Gorasht and Sanders **54**
Cameron, Mindy **29** (bests)
Campagne ★★★$$$ **57**
Camp Long **116**
Canadian Pacific Railway Station **202**
Canlis ★★★★$$$$ **128**
Capers ★$ **115**
Capitol Hill **86** (map), **88** (map), **92**
Capitol Hill Addition **95**
Capitol Hill to Seward Park **86** (chapter and map)
Capons Rotisserie Chicken ★$ **148**
Captain Whidbey Inn **196**
Carefree (and Car-Free) Sightseeing: Seattle by Bus **62**
Carillon Point **185**
Carkeek Park **159**
Carl S. English Jr. Ornamental Gardens **138**
Carnegie Library **135**
Carrot Cafe ★$ **92**
Cars, rental **6**
Casa-U-Betcha ★★$ **71**
Catfish Corner ★★$ **105**
Catherine Blaine Elementary School **130**

Cat's Eye Cafe $ **117**
C.D. Stimson Company **136**
Cellophane Square **181**
Center for Wooden Boats **84**
Center House **81**
Center on Contemporary Art (COCA) **72**
Central District and Madrona **104**
Central Plaza **166**
Central Tavern and Cafe **21**
Chace's Pancake Corral ★$ **179**
Chambered Nautilus, The $$ **171**
Chamber of Commerce Building **32**
Champion Wine Cellars **82**
Chandler's Crabhouse and Fresh Fish Market ★$$$ **84**
Charity Begins Away from Home: Helping Seattle's Homeless **85**
Charlie Mac's Sports Club **161**
Charlie's Bar & Grill $ **139**
Charlotte Martin Theater **81**
Chateau Ste. Michelle **193**
Chau's Chinese Restaurant ★$ **27**
Cherry Blossom Teriyaki $ **110**
Cherry Street Parking Garage **32**
Chester L. Lindsey Architects **33, 76**
Chez Shea ★★★$$$$ **55**
Chiarelli, James J. **81, 167**
Chicken and Egg **54**
Chief Sealth **96**
Chief Seattle Fountain **78**
Children's Park **29**
Child's Play **71**
Chinatown **202**
Chinook's ★★$$ **134**
Choe, Martha, Councilmember **47** (bests)
Choy Herbs **29**
Christina's **198**
Christmas House **180**
Chutney's ★★★$$ **82**
Cinema Books **172**
Cinema Espresso ★$ **83**
Cinnamon Works **57**
City Cafe ★$ **147**
City Fish **52**
City Hall Park **30**
City of Bainbridge Island **195**
City Peoples' Mercantile **99**
City Thai ★$ **189**
C.J. Smith House **93**
Climate **8**
Clinton **196**
Cloud Room, The ★$$ **43**
Cobb Building **37**
Cobb House **97**

Cober-Slater **181**
COCA (Center on Contemporary Art) **72**
Coldwater Visitors' Center **205**
Collection, The **180**
College Inn Guest House $ **169**
Colman Building **65**
Colman Dock **67**
Colman Pool **117**
Colour Box **20**
Columbia Seafirst Center **33**
Columbia Winery **193**
Comedy Underground **27**
Comet Tavern **102**
Commodore Park **138**
Conor Byrne's Soccer Stadium **135**
Conservatory **94**
Continental Restaurant, The ★$ **171**
Cooper's Northwest Alehouse **160**
Copacabana Cafe ★$ **57**
Corner House, The $ **101**
Corner Market Building **55**
Corner Shop, The **188**
Cornish College of the Arts **98**
Cors and Wegener Building **135**
Cote, Joseph C. **115, 155, 172**
Couth Buzzard, The **157**
Cow Chip Cookies **19**
Cowen Park **173**
Coyote Coffee Company **188**
Crabtree & Evelyn **43**
Craigdarroch Castle **200**
Crepe De Paris **38**
Crocodile Cafe **73**
Crumpet Shop, The ★$ **55**
Cucina! Cucina! (Bellevue) ★★$$ **184**
Cucina! Cucina! (Belltown) ★$$ **85**
Cucina Fresca **59**
Current **66**
Cutter, Kirtland K. **33, 93, 102, 136**
Cutter's Bayhouse ★$$$ **60**
Cuttysark **179**
Cyclops ★★$$ **72**

D

Dahlia Lounge ★★★$$$ **46**
Daily Dozen Doughnuts **50**
Daily Grind, The ★$ **90**
Daily Planet, The **143**
Dancer's Series: Steps **99**
Daniel's Broiler (Bellevue) ★★$$$$ **184**

Index

Daniel's Broiler (Leschi) ★★$$$$ **106**
Danish-Swedish Antiques **187**
Danny Woo International District Community Garden **28**
Dashasa Studio **41**
David Ishii Bookseller **22**
Davidson Galleries **26**
Davinci's Flying Pizza and Pasta ★$ **187**
Daybreak Star Indian Cultural Center **131**
Day Trips **192** (chapter and map)
DeGraff Books **58**
DeLaurenti's Specialty Foods (Bellevue) **181**
DeLaurenti's Specialty Foods (Pike Place Market) **50**
Delmar Building (State Hotel) **19**
Deluxe Junk **144**
Deluxe 1 Bar and Grill ★$ **98**
Denny-Blaine Park **104**
Denny Hall **167**
Denny Park **78**
Design Concern **40**
Dethlefs, Gary **129**
Dick's Drive-In $ **151**
Dietz, Robert **130**
Dilettante Chocolates **58**
Dilettante Patisserie & Cafe ★$ **100**
Dilly Dally **180**
Dimitriou's Jazz Alley **77**
Dingo Gallery **73**
Discovery Park **130**
Disney Store, The **44**
Ditto Tavern **77**
Doc Maynard's Public House ★$ **17**
Dr. Trueblood/Creger Home **189**
Don Armeni Park Boat Ramp **109**
Doong Kong Lau ★★$ **159**
Drinking **8**
Driving **6, 7**
du jour ★★$ **61**
Duke's Chowderhouse and Outrageous Canoe Club ★$ **84**
Duwamish Head **109**

E

Eagle Harbor Books **195**
Eagles Auditorium/Kreilsheimer Place **39**
Eames & Young **32**
Earl D. Layman Street Clock **23**
Eastlake **92**
Eastside **175**
Eastside Wine Country **193** (map)

Eastsound **198**
Easy Streets Records **116**
Eaton's **201**
Economy Market **50**
Eddie Bauer, Inc. **39**
Edgewater Inn $$$ **72**
E.F. Kirsten Tobacconist **134**
Egan House **93**
Egyptian Theater **102**
Eleganza Ltd. **130**
Elephant Car Wash Sign **77**
Elliott Bay Book Company **23**
Elliott Bay Cafe ★★$ **23**
Elliott Bay Marina **128**
Elliott Bay Yachting Center **129**
Elliott's Oyster House & Seafood Restaurant ★$$$ **67**
El Palacio ★★$ **107**
El Puerco Lloron ★$ **54**
El Tapatio ★$ **159**
Emerald Suite $$$$ **80**
Emergencies **10**
Emmett Watson's Oyster Bar ★★$ **59**
Empress Hotel **200**
Enersen, Jean **107** (bests)
Engine House No. 2 **78**
Eques ★★$$$ **184**
Erotic Bakery **150**
Espresso Roma ★$ **101**
Esquimalt **200**
European Restaurant & Pastry Shop ★$ **169**
Evans House **106**
Excalibur **182**
Exotique Records **78**
Ezell's Fried Chicken ★★$ **105**

F

Fast Forward **61**
Fauntleroy Ferry Dock **117**
Ferries **7**
Ferry Tales **65**
Fifth Avenue Theater **39**
Financial Center **36**
Finders & Doodles **176**
Firehouse No. 11 **148**
FireWorks Gallery (Business District) **43**
FireWorks Gallery (Pioneer Square) **21**
First Hill **102**
First United Methodist Church **33**
Fisher, Elmer **17, 20, 65, 71**
Fishermen's Terminal **133**
Fish Ladder **138**
5-Spot, The ★★$ **126**
521 Cafe ★$ **32**

Flagg, Ernest **203**
Flora & Fauna Books **19**
Flying Fish ★★★$$ **71**
Flying L Ranch **205**
Flying Shuttle **20**
Folk Art Gallery—La Tienda **169**
Foreign Accents **115**
Fort Casey **196**
Fort Casey Inn **196**
Fortnum's European Cafe ★$ **180**
Foster Island Walk **89**
Foster/White Gallery **26**
Four Seasons Olympic Hotel $$$$ **38**
Fourth and Blanchard Building **76**
Fourth and Pike Building **41**
1411 Fourth Avenue Building **41**
1001 Fourth Avenue Plaza **35**
Fowl Play **135**
Fox's Gem Shop **39**
Frank and Dunya **143**
Fred Bassetti and Company **66**
Freeway Park **36**
Fremont **143**
Fremont Antiques Mall **144**
Fremont Place Book Company **144**
Fremont Public Library **145**
Fremont Sunday Market **144**
Fremont Troll **145**
Fremont/Wallingford **142** (chapter and map)
Friday Harbor **197**
Friday Harbor Whale Museum **198**
Fritzi Ritz **144**
Frosh Pond, Rainier Vista **167**
Frye Art Museum **105**
Fuller's ★★★★$$$ **40**
Fun Forest Amusement Park **80**
F.X. McRory's Steak, Chop and Oyster House ★★$$ **25**

G

Gable House **124**
Gaggin & Gaggin **18**
Galittoire **196**
Games and Gizmos **181**
G&G Cigar Store **18**
Garden Center **58**
Garden Spot **148**
Gaslight Inn $ **102**
Gastown **202**
Gas Works Park **151**
George's Corner **158**

Georgian Room, The ★★★★ $$$$ 38
Georgie Cafe ★$$ 117
Gerard Relais de Lyon 193
Geron, Gerald 180
Getting Around Seattle 6
Getting to and from SEA 6
Getting to Seattle 5
Giggles Comedy Nite Club 171
Giuseppe's ★$$ 179
Glass Eye Gallery 58
Globe Cafe & Bakery ★$ 102
Godden, Jean 151 (bests)
Golden Age Collectables 53
Golden Gardens 140
Good Shepherd Center 150
Goodwin, Frank 50, 52
Gould, A. Warren 32
Gould, Carl 33, 38, 46, 64, 89, 93, 95, 138, 166
Governor's Mansion 203
Graham, John, Jr. 80
Graham, John, Sr. 28, 42, 61, 90, 103, 124, 160
Graham, Thom 137
Grand Central Arcade 22
Grand Central Baking Co 22
Grand Central Mercantile 23
Grand Illusion 171
Grandma's Attic 53
Grand Pacific Hotel 64
Granville Island Brewing Company 201
Granville Island Public Market 201
Gravity Bar (Belltown) ★$ 70
Gravity Bar (Broadway Market) ★$ 100
Great Winds Kite Shop 25
Great Wind-Up, The 50
Greek Row 171
Green Lake Boat Rentals 155
Green Lake/Greenwood 154
Green Lake/Greenwood/North Seattle 152 (chapter and map)
Green Lake Public Library 155
Green Lake Small Craft Center 154
Greenwood 152 (chapter and map), 154
Greenwood Bakery 158
Greetings Trend Shop 19
Gregg's Greenlake Cycle 155
Greg Kucera Gallery 32
Group Health Building (P-I Building) 77
Group Health Cooperative of Puget Sound 101

Guadalajara ★$ 148
Guess Where 144
Guido's Pizzeria ★$ 156
Guitar Emporium 136
Gunnar Nordstrom Gallery 187

H

Haag, Richard 59
Hainsworth House $ 115
Hamilton Viewpoint 110
Hannigan/Adams 185
Han II ★★$ 28
Hardy, Jeremy 205 (bests)
Harvard-Belmont Historic District 98
Harvard Exit 98
Heide, August 17, 124
Heins & LaFarge 103
Henry Art Gallery 166
Henry M. Jackson Federal Office Building 65
Herbfarm, The 193
Highland Drive 124
High Point 117
Hillclimb Corridor 54
Hill House $ 101
Hing Hay Park 28
Hiram M. Chittenden Locks 138
Hi-Spot Cafe ★$ 104
History 206
Hoge Building 32
Holiday Inn Crowne Plaza $$$ 36
Holly B's 198
Holmes, J. Lister 171
Holy Names Academy 97
Honey Bear Bakery ★$ 154
Honey Court Seafood Restaurant ★$$ 29
Hopscotch ★★$ 100
Horizon Books 100
Hornblower & Marshall 93
Hot Cha Cha 130
Hotel de Haro and Roche Harbor Resort 199
Hotels, rating 4
Hotel Vintage Park $$$ 35
Houghton, E.W. 47, 124
Hours 8
Howard, John Galen 167
Howells & Stokes 37
Hunt Club ★★★$$$ 103
Huntington, Daniel R. 33, 56, 67, 78, 98, 145, 148
Husky Delicatessen 116
Husky Stadium 168
Hyatt Regency at Bellevue Place $$$ 184

I

Ibsen Nelsen & Associates 58
Iida, Juki 90
Il Bistro ★★$$$ 51
I Love Sushi (Bellevue) ★★$ 185
I Love Sushi (Belltown) ★★$ 85
Il Terrazo Carmine ★★★$$$ 24
Imperial 202
Inn at Langley 196
Inn at Queen Anne $ 82
Inn at Swifts Bay 198
Inn at the Market $$ 57
Interlaken Park 92
International District 14 (chapter and map), 27
International Fountain 81
Interurban Building (Smith Tower Annex) 18
In the Market for a Good Time? 54
Isaac Stevens School 97
Island Beads and More 177
Island Books 177
Island County Historical Museum 196
It's About Time 145
Ivar's Acres of Clams and Fish Bar ★$ 67

J

Jack's Fish Spot $ 56
Jackson, Arai 131
Jack's Restaurant and Sporting Goods 205
Jalisco ★$ 99
J&M Cafe ★$ 21
Japanese Tea Garden 90
Jay White Law Offices 136
Jessica McClintock Boutique 43
Jet City Vintage 70
Jillian's Billiard Club 84
J. Lister Holmes and Associates 130
JoAnn's Cookies 41
John, Esther "Little Dove" 47 (bests)
John Graham & Company 65
John Leary House 93
Jones Brothers Meats 136
Joshua Sears Building 191
Junction Block, The 136

K

Kabul ★★$$ 150
Kaleenka, The ★$$ 61
Kasala 54
Kaspar's ★★★$$ 82

Index

Kell's Restaurant & Pub ★$$ 58
Kenneth Behm Art Gallery 181
Ken's Market 158
Kerry Park 124
Key Bank Tower (Olympic Tower) 44
Keystone Corner Cards 83
Kidd Valley ★$ 101
Killing Time 173
Kimball, W.D. 97
King County Courthouse 30
Kingdome 24
King Street Station 27
Kinnear Park 120
Kirkland 185, 186 (map)
Kirkland Antique Gallery 188
Kirkland Clock 188
Kirkland Roaster & Ale House ★$$ 189
Kirk, Paul 130
Kismet ★$ 158
Klondike Gold Rush National Historical Park 26
Kohn Pederson Fox 36
Kreilsheimer Place/Eagles Auditorium 39
Kubota Gardens 107
Kyllo's Lakeside Deli ★$ 155

L

La Buca ★★$$ 66
Labuznik ★★$$$ 61
La Cocina del Puerco $ 179
Lake View Cemetery 93
Lake Washington Boulevard 91
Lampreia ★★★$$$ 72
Landes House $ 97
Langley 196
La Residence Suite Hotel $ 182
Larry's Greenfront 21
Larry's Market (Belltown) 84
Larry's Market (North Seattle) 160
LaSalle Hotel 51
Latitude 47 121
Latona Elementary School 151
Latona Pub 154
Lava Lounge 73
Lawton and Moldenhour 41
Le Crocodile 202
Left Bank Books 55
Legacy, The 65
Legislative Building 203
Le Gourmand ★★★$$$ 134
Le Panier 59
Leschi Lakecafe ★★$$ 106
Leschi Park 106

Leschi to Seward Park 106
Liberty Deli ★★$ 111
Liberty Malt Supply Company/Pike Place Brewery 51
Life on the Cutting Edge—Music in the Emerald City 25
Lights, Camera, Action: Seattle on Film 140
Lime Kiln Point State Park 198
Limousines 6
Lincoln Park 117
Lincoln Towing "Toe Truck" 85
Linde, Carl J. 42
Linyen ★★$$ 28
Local Brilliance 62
LockSpot Cafe & Tavern ★$ 138
Lockwood-Greene 77
Lombardi's Cucina ★$$ 138
Lopez Island 198
Lopez Island Historical Museum 198
Louie's on the Pike 59
Louisa Boren View Park 92
Loveless, Arthur B. 65, 98
Loveless Building 98
Lowell's Restaurant $ 52
Lower Post Alley 51
Lower Ravenna Park 173
Lowman Beach 117
Lowman Building 17
Luna Park Cafe ★$ 115

M

MacDonald, Charles 130
Madame & Co. 18
Made in Washington 56
Madison Park 87
Madison Park and Beach 91
Madison Park Hardware 91
Madison Renaissance Hotel $$$ 35
Madison Street 104
Madrona 104
Madrona Park Bathing Beach 104
Mae's Phinney Ridge Cafe ★★$ 157
Maggie Bluffs $ 129
Magic Mouse 20
Magnolia 118 (chapter and map), 128
Magnolia Boulevard 129
Magnolia Library 130
Magnolia Park 129
Magnolia's Bookstore 129
Magus Bookstore 169
Mahlum & Nordfors McKinley

Gordon 81
Main Arcade 52
Main Events, The 11
Main Street Kids Book Company 180
Malmgren, Karl 93, 102
Mama's Mexican Kitchen ★$ 73
Mamma Melina Ristorante ★★★$$ 172
Maneki Restaurant ★★$$ 28
Map Key 4
Maple Leaf Grill ★★$ 160
Mario's Pizza ★★$ 17
Market Clock 52
Market Information Booth 50
Market Magic Shop 53
Market Spice 52
Market Tobacco Patch 59
Marsh Estate 186
Maximilien-in-the-Market ★★$$$ 53
Mayflower Park Hotel $$ 46
Maynard Building 19
McCarthy & Schiering Wine Merchants 127
McCauley, John L. 32
McCormick & Schmick's ★★$$ 64
McCormick's Fish House and Bar ★★$$ 33
McGraw Street Bakery 127
M. Coy Books 44
Meany Hall 166
Meany, Stephen 65
Meany Tower Hotel $$ 170
Mecca Cafe ★$ 83
Mediterranean Kitchen ★$ 83
Meerkeek Rhododendron Gardens 196
Mee Sum Pastries 57
Megan Mary Olander Florist 22
Mellor, Meigs & Howe 171
Mendel, Leonard L. 24, 91
Mercer Island 174 (map), 175
Mercer Island Ski and Cycle 176
Merchant's Cafe ★$ 19
Meridien West and Meridien East 42
Metro Bus Tunnel 44
Metro Cinemas 172
Metropolitan Grill ★★★$$$ 33
Metsker Maps 52
Mike's Chili Parlor ★$ 134
Millionaires' Row 97
Millstream 19
Mini-Guide to Seattle, A 122
Mrs. Field's Cookies 182
Mr. D's Greek Deli ★$ 57

MisterE Books **53**
Mr. "J" Kitchen Gourmet **182**
MOHAI (Museum of History and Industry) **87**
Money **8**
Monorail **7, 43, 76, 80**
Montana, Ruby Z. **47** (bests)
Monterey Pasta Bar $ **181**
Montlake Bridge **89**
Monument to the Birthplace of Seattle **112**
Monument to William H. Seward **95**
Moore Theater and Hotel **47**
Moran State Park **198**
Moss Bay Gallery **188**
Mount Constitution **198**
Mount Rainier National Park **204** (map)
Mount St. Helens **205** (map)
Mount Zion Baptist Church **104**
Munro's Books **200**
Murchie's Tea and Coffee **200**
Murphy's Pub **149**
Musashi's ★$ **148**
Museum of Anthropology **201**
Museum of Flight **107**
Museum of History and Industry (MOHAI) **87**
Mutual Fish Company **106**
Mutual Life Building **20**
My Friends Cafe ★$ **155**
Myrtle Edwards Park **82**

N

Nancy's Sewing Basket **127**
Naramore, Bain, Brady & Johanson **77, 170**
Nature Company, The **181**
Nature's Pantry **176**
NBBJ Group **35, 38**
Neighbours **102**
Nellie Cornish Memorial Sculptures **87**
Nelly Stallion **126**
Neptune Theater **170**
New Hong Kong Seafood Restaurant and B.B.Q. ★★$ **105**
New Orleans Creole Restaurant ★$ **19**
New Seattle Massage **170**
Nikko ★★★$$$ **46**
Nippon Kan Theater **27**
Nordic Heritage Museum **140**
Nordstrom **41**
Norsemen, The **188**
North Arcade **55**

North Bend **194**
Northgate Shopping Center **160**
Northlake Tavern & Pizza House ★★$ **169**
North Seattle **152** (chapter and map), **159, 160** (map)
Northwest Art & Frame **116**
Northwest Discovery **181**
Northwest Gallery of Fine Woodworking **23**
Northwest School/Summit Grade School **102**

O

Occidental Avenue **25**
Odd Fellows Hall/Austin A. Bell Building **71**
Oh Chocolate! **176**
OK Hotel Cafe/Gallery **21**
Old Federal Office Building **65**
Old Morris Tobacconist, Ltd. **200**
Old Pequliar Ale House, The **135**
Old Public Safety Building **30**
Old Seattle Paperworks **53**
Old Timer's Cafe $ **17**
Olsen's Scandinavian Foods **137**
Olson/Walker **57, 63**
Olympia Capitol **203**
Olympia Pizza & Spaghetti House ★$$ **126**
Olympia Pizza and Spaghetti House III ★$ **99**
Olympic Tower (Key Bank Tower) **44**
1411 Fourth Avenue Building **41**
1001 Fourth Avenue Plaza **35**
Opera House **81**
Orcas Island **198**
Orcas Island Historical Museum **198**
Oriental Interiors **180**
Orientation **2** (chapter and map)
Orpheum **99**
Oven, The ★$ **101**
Ozzie's ★$ **83**

P

Pacific Dessert Company, The ★★★$ **84**
Pacific Galleries **76**
Pacific Inn **147**
Pacific Marine Schwabacher Building **23**
Pacific Northwest Brewing Company ★$$ **26**
Pacific Plaza Hotel $ **36**
Pacific Science Center **80**
Pagliacci ★$ **100**

Pailin Thai Cuisine ★★$ **115**
Painted Table, The ★★★$$ **64**
Painting the Town **114**
Palisade ★★$$$ **129**
Palmov, Ivan **85**
Palomino ★★★$$ **40**
Pandasia (Magnolia) ★★$ **128**
Pandasia (North Seattle) ★$ **161**
Panos ★★$$ **72**
Paper Cat, The **22**
Paragon ★★★$$ **126**
Paramount Theater **42**
Parker House **95**
Parking **8**
Parkinson, John **18, 147**
Parklane Gallery **188**
Parkplace **189**
Parkside News Cafe ★$ **113**
Parliament Building **200**
Pasta Bella ★$$ **126**
Patterson, D.J. **27**
Peace Cafe ★$$ **113**
Pegasus Book Exchange **116**
Pegasus Pizza & Pasta on Alki ★$ **111**
Pelayo's Antiques **158**
Pendleton **182**
Pensione Nichols $ **61**
Penthouse Theater **167**
Perennial Tea Room, The **58**
Personal safety **8**
Peter Kirk Building **191**
Peter Miller Books **61**
Pete's Eggnest ★$ **158**
Phad Thai ★$ **159**
Phnom Penh Noodle House ★$ **28**
Phoenicia at Alki ★★★$$ **110**
Phoenix Rising Gallery **60**
Pho Hòa ★★$ **107**
P-I Building (Group Health Building) **77**
Pier 70 **72**
P-I Globe **82**
Pike & Western Wine Merchants **59**
Pike Place Bar & Grill ★$ **55**
Pike Place Brewery/Liberty Malt Supply Company **51**
Pike Place Fish **53**
Pike Place Market **50**
Pike Place Market/Waterfront **48** (chapter and map)
Pillars of the Community **45**
Pining for Nature: Seattle's Lush Evergreens **131**
Pink Door, The ★★$$ **58**
Pinto Pony II **32**
Pioneer Building **17**

Pioneer Place Park **16**
Pioneer Square **16**
Pioneer Square Hotel $$ **21**
Pioneer Square/International
    District **14** (chapter and map)
Pirosmani ★★★$$$ **127**
Place Pigalle ★★$$ **53**
Platt, Charles A. **94**
Pocket-Size Parks **183**
Pogacha ★★$ **179**
Point Grill ★$$ **111**
Pon Proem Restaurant ★$ **177**
Ponti Seafood Grill ★★$$ **143**
Poor Italian Cafe, The ★★$ **76**
Port Chatham Smoked Seafood
    182
Portland Building **137**
Post Alley Market **56**
Post, George B. **38**
Pottery Northwest **82**
Prego ★★★$$$ **35**
Pries, Lionel **171**
Prince of Wales $ **101**
Priteca, B. Marcus **41, 42, 81,
    103, 113**
Procopio **54**
Psycho 5 **181**
Publications **8**
Puget Sound and Snoqualmie
    Valley Railway **194**
Pumphouse, The ★$ **185**

Q

Queen Anne **120**
Queen Anne Avenue Books **126**
Queen Anne Branch Library **125**
Queen Anne Counterbalance
    120
Queen Anne High School
    Apartments **121**
Queen Anne Hill **121** (map)
Queen Anne Hill Bed & Breakfast
    $ **127**
Queen Anne/Magnolia **118**
    (chapter and map)
Queen Anne Thriftway **126**
Queen City Grill ★★$$ **70**
Queen Mary ★★$$$ **173**
Quite a Road Show: The Campy
    Flair of Aurora Avenue North
    159

R

Rachel, the Market Pig **52**
Radio stations **9**
Ragazzi **22**
Ragin' Cajun ★★$$ **62**
Rainier Chapter House of the
    DAR **98**

Rainier Club **33**
Rainier Tower **37**
R&L Home of Good Barbeque
    ★★$ **105**
Rasa Malaysia (Broadway
    Market) ★$ **100**
Rasa Malaysia (Green Lake)
    ★★$ **155**
Rasa Malaysia (Pike Place
    Market) ★$ **56**
Rattenbury, Francis **201**
Ravenna **162** (chapter and map),
    172
Ravenna Boulevard **173**
Ravenna Park **173**
Ray's Boathouse ★★★$$$ **139**
R.D. Merrill House **94**
Read All About It **50**
Reamer, Robert C. **38, 41, 78,
    170**
Re-bar **103**
Red Door Ale House **143**
Redhook Ale Brewery **144**
Red Lion Hotel $$ **177**
Red Onion Tavern **91**
Reflections **115**
REI **103**
Reichert, Robert **93**
Reiner's ★★★$$$ **103**
Remo Borracchini's **106**
Rendezvous **73**
Rental cars **6**
Restaurants **9**
Restaurants, rating **4**
Retro Viva **63**
Reyes, Lawney **131**
Riddle House **124**
Ristorante Buongusto ★★$$
    127
Ristorante di Ragazzi ★$ **113**
Ristorante Paradiso ★★$$ **188**
Ritchie, W.A. **204**
Roanoke Inn **176**
Roanoke Park Place Tavern **92**
Roberta's Bed & Breakfast $ **95**
Robertson and Blackwell **20**
Roche Harbor **199**
Roger's Chocolates and English
    Sweet Shop **200**
Romio's Pizza (Eastlake) ★★$
    92
Romio's Pizza (Magnolia) ★$$
    128
Romper Room **82**
Rosalie Whyel Museum of Doll
    Art **185**
Rosario Resort **198**
Rosita's ★$ **155**
Ross and Co. **180**

Rouse Company **43**
Rover's ★★★★$$$$ **104**
Royal British Columbia Museum
    200
Rubato Records **179**
Ruby Montana's Pinto Pony **32**
Runions House **128**
Russell, Ambrose J. **203**
Ryan, Henderson **135**

S

Safeco Building **170**
Safety, personal **8**
St. Charles Hotel **135**
St. James Cathedral **103**
St. Joseph's Catholic Church **97**
St. Mark's Episcopal Cathedral
    93
St. Michael's Alley **184**
St. Spiridon Orthodox Church **85**
Saleh al Lago ★★★$$ **155**
Salisbury House $ **97**
Salish Lodge **194**
Salmon Bay Bridge **139**
Salmon Bay Cafe ★$ **136**
Salty's on Alki ★$$ **109**
Salute in Città ★$$ **46**
Salvatore Ristorante Italiano
    ★★★$$ **172**
Sam Hill House **93**
Sam's Bar and Grill $$ **177**
SAM (Seattle Art Museum) **63**
Sam's Super Burgers ★$ **104**
Sanitary Market Building **56**
San Juan Island **198**
San Juan Islands **197** (map)
Santa Fe Cafe (Greenwood)
    ★★★$$ **156**
Santa Fe Cafe (Ravenna)
    ★★★$$ **173**
Sasquatch **50**
Sasquatch Trading **200**
Satterwhite, Skip **144**
SBC ★$ **56**
Scandie's at Ballard $$ **137**
Schack, James **33**
Schack, Young & Myers **32**
Schmitz Park **113**
Seacrest Park and Boathouse
    109
Sea Garden ★★★$ **28**
SEA (Seattle-Tacoma
    International Airport) **5** (map)
Seattle *See inside front cover*
    (map), **2** (map)
Seattle Aquarium **66**
Seattle Art Museum (SAM) **63**
Seattle Asian Art Museum **95**
Seattle Bagel Bakery **66**

Seattle Center **68** (chapter and map), **79** (map)
Seattle Club **60**
Seattle Fishermen's Memorial **134**
Seattle Garden Center **58**
Seattle Hilton $$$ **39**
Seattle Mystery Bookshop **17**
Seattle Pen **41**
Seattle Pendleton **37**
Seattle Public Library **35**
Seattle Sheraton Hotel and Towers $$$$ **40**
Seattle Ship Clothing **134**
Seattle-Tacoma International Airport, ground transportation **6**
Seattle-Tacoma International Airport (SEA) **5** (map)
Seattle Times Building **78**
Seattle Tower **36**
Seattle Transit System *See inside back cover* (map)
Seattle Yacht Club **90**
Second & James Parking Garage **17**
2nd Hand Hube **157**
Second Story Bookstore **149**
Secret Garden Bookshop **135**
Selling Seafood by the Seashore **190**
Serafina ★★$$ **92**
Seven Gables Theater **172**
Seventh Church of Christ, Scientist **128**
74th Street Ale House ★★$ **158**
Seward Park **106**
Seward Park, Capitol Hill to **86** (chapter and map)
Seward Park, Leschi to **106**
Shamiana ★★★$$ **187**
Shark Reef Preserve **198**
Sharky's Beach Bar **140**
Sharper Image **41**
Shaw Island **198**
Shilshole Bay Marina **139**
Shiro ★★★$$ **73**
Shopping **9**
Shultzy's Sausage ★$ **169**
Shuttles **6**
Siam on Broadway ★★$ **99**
Sidney **199**
Signature Bound **73**
Silberman/Brown Stationers **183**
Silverdale Visitors' Center **205**
Simpatico ★$ **149**
Simply Desserts **144**
Sinclair Centre **202**
Singer, Jack W. **107** (bests)
Sisters ★$ **57**

Sit 'n' Spin ★$ **78**
Sixth Avenue Inn $ **77**
Skillings and Corner **125**
Skinner Building **38**
Smith Cove Park **129**
Smith Hall **166**
Smith Tower **18**
Smith Tower Annex (Interurban Building) **18**
Smoking **9**
Snoqualmie and Snoqualmie Falls **194** (map)
Soames-Dunn Building **59**
Soap Box, The **59**
Somervell, W. Marbury **115, 125, 155, 172**
Sooke **200**
Sooke Harbour House **200**
Sorel's ★$ **148**
Sorrento Hotel $$$ **103**
Sorry Charlie's $ **83**
Souk, The **59**
Sound Winds/Air Arts **21**
South Arcade **63**
Space Needle **80**
Space Needle Restaurant $$$ **80**
Spazzo ★★★$$ **179**
Speakeasy Cafe $ **73**
Spinnaker's Brew Pub **200**
Spud Fish and Chips (Green Lake) ★$ **155**
Spud Fish and Chips (West Seattle) ★$ **110**
Stamp Gallery **179**
Stamp Happy **50**
Stanley Park **201**
Stan Sayres Memorial Park **106**
Starbucks (Bellevue) ★$ **183**
Starbucks (Magnolia) ★$ **130**
Starbucks (Pike Place Market) ★$ **59**
Starbucks (Queen Anne) ★$ **126**
Starbucks (Wallingford) ★$ **149**
Starbucks (West Seattle) ★$ **113**
State Capitol Museum **203**
State Hotel (Delmar Building) **19**
State Library Building **203**
Statue of Liberty **111**
Steinbrueck, Victor **59, 80, 92, 125**
Stella's Trattoria ★$$ **172**
Stephen, James **97, 102, 121, 148, 151**
Steve's Broadway News **101**
Stewart House **58**
Still Life in Fremont ★$ **144**
Stimson-Green Mansion **102**
Stone Way Cafe ★$ **147**
Store Next Door, The **148**
Storey, Ellsworth **106, 171**

Streamliner Diner **195**
Street plan **9**
Sub-Pop Mega Mart **76**
Summit Grade School/Northwest School **102**
Sunday Funnies, The **26**
Sunfish Seafood ★$ **112**
Sunlight Cafe ★$ **172**
Sunset Building **136**
Sunset Hill Park **140**
Suquamish **195**
Suquamish Museum **195**
Sur La Table **58**
Suzzallo/Allen Library **166**
Swingside Cafe ★★$ **147**
Sylvan Theater **167**
Szmania's ★★★★$$$ **130**

T

Tabernacle Missionary Baptist Church **105**
Taki's ★$ **78**
Tan Duc ★$ **159**
Taxes **9**
Taxis **6, 7**
Teacup **127**
Teahouse Kuan Yin ★$ **149**
Telephone numbers, essential **10**
Telephones **9**
Temple de Hirsch Sinai **103**
Tenzing Momo **51**
Terra-cotta Town **74**
Terra Mar **157**
TestaRossa ★★$ **101**
Thai on Mercer ★★$$ **176**
There's Something Fishy Here **168**
Thinker Toys **184**
1201 Third Ave **36**
Third Floor Fish Cafe ★★$$ **187**
13 Coins ★$$ **78**
Thiry, Paul **105, 203**
Thomas Bordeaux House **97**
Thomas Burke Memorial Washington State Museum **167**
Thomas, Grainger & Thomas **128**
Thomas, Harlan **32, 55, 103, 125**
Thomas, Val **125**
Three Girls Bakery ★$ **56**
Thurston County Courthouse (Board of Education Building) **203**
Tickets **9**
Ticket/Ticket **101**
Tidemand, August **65**
Times Square Building **46**
Time zone **10**
Tio's Bakery & Cafe ★$ **92**
Tipping **10**

Index

Titlewave **83**
Toppers **185**
Torrefazione Italia ★$ **26**
Toscana ★★$$ **170**
Totem House $ **139**
Tours **10**
Tower Books (Belltown) **83**
Tower Books (Eastside) **184**
Toy's Cafe ★$ **179**
TRA **32**
Trains **7**
Transportation **5**
Trattoria Mitchelli ★★$$ **20**
Travel Infocentre **200**
Triangle Building **57**
Triangle Hotel Building **24**
Triangle Tavern ★★$ **144**
Trinity Parish Episcopal Church **103**
Triple J Cafe $ **189**
Trolleyman Pub **144**
Trolleys **7**
T.S. McHugh's Restaurant & Pub ★$$ **83**
Tulio Ristorante ★★★$$ **35**
Turret House **128**
Tweedy & Popp/Ace Hardware **149**
12-Step Bookstore and Gift Shop **157**
Twice Sold Tales **150**
Twin Teepees Restaurant ★$ **156**
Two Bells Tavern ★★$ **77**
2-11 Billiard Club **73**

U

Umbrecht, Max **64**
Undercover Quilts **63**
Un Deux Trois ★★★$$$ **63**
Union Station **27**
University Book Store (Bellevue) **183**
University Book Store (University District) **170**
University Branch Library **172**
University District **165**
University District/Ravenna **162** (chapter and map)
University Heights Elementary School **171**
University Inn $ **169**
University of British Columbia **201**
University of Washington **164** (map), **165**
University Seafood & Poultry **171**
University Village **171**

Uno-Duo **71**
Upper Post Alley **58**
Uptown Espresso ★$ **83**
Urban Outfitters **101**
US Bank Centre **40**
Uwajimaya **28**

V

Vancouver Art Gallery **201**
Vancouver, British Columbia **201** (map)
Vancouver Island **199**
Velato's ★$$ **177**
Veneto's **182**
Venturi, Robert **63**
Vertical World **143**
Victoria Apartments **124**
Victoria, British Columbia **199** (map)
Victoria's Secret **44**
Victor Steinbrueck Park **59**
Village Pub ★$ **130**
Villa Heidelberg $ **116**
Virginia Inn **60**
Visitors' information **10**
Visitors' Information Center (University District) **165**
Vogue **70**
Volunteer Park **94**
Von's Grand City Cafe ★★$ **42**

W

Waiting for the Interurban **143**
Walker-Ames House **91**
Walker Rock Garden **117**
Walking **7**
Wallflower, The **182**
Wallingford **142** (chapter and map), **147**
Wallingford Center **148**
Warshal's Sporting Goods **65**
Warwick Hotel $$$ **76**
Washington *See inside front cover* (map)
Washington Court Building **26**
Washington Park Arboretum **90**
Washington State Convention & Trade Center **40**
Washington Street Public Boat Landing **67**
Waterfall Garden **26**
Waterfront **48** (chapter and map), **60** (map), **66**
Waterfront Activities Center **168**
Waterfront Park **67**
Waterfront Streetcar **66, 72**
Watermark Tower **64**
Wawona **84**
Weather Watch Park **112**

Weber, P.J. **35**
WE Hats **20**
WestCoast Camlin Hotel $ **42**
WestCoast Roosevelt Hotel $$ **42**
WestCoast Vance Hotel $ **46**
Westin Hotel $$$ **46**
Westlake Center **43**
West Queen Anne Elementary School **125**
West Seattle **108** (chapter and map), **111** (map)
West Seattle Golf Club **116**
West Seattle Library **115**
West Seattle Nursery **116**
West Seattle Speedway and Hobby **115**
Westside Stories **125**
Wetmore, James A. **65**
Wheelchair accessibility **4**
Whidbey Island **196** (map)
White, Harry **203**
Wickersham, Albert **19**
Wide World Books **149**
Wilder, Walter **203**
Wild Ginger ★★★$$ **66**
Wild Salmon **134**
Wildwood Park **180**
Willatsen, Andrew **125**
Williams House $ **121**
Williams-Sonoma **44**
Wilson & Loveless **91**
Wilson, Clayton **30**
Wilson, Joseph **36, 97**
Wind Works **140**
Wing Luke Museum **28**
Winkelmann, Don **35, 36**
Winter Garden **90**
Woodland Park Zoo **156, 157** (map)
Woodmark Hotel $$$ **185**
Wood 'n' You **188**
Wood Shop, The **23**
Word Out West, The **146**
World Class Chili ★$ **63**
Wurdemann Mansion **161**

Y

Yamasaki, Minoru **37**
Yankee Diner ★$$ **138**
Yanni's Lakeside Cafe ★★$ **158**
Yarrow Bay Grill and Beach Cafe ★$$$ **185**
Ye Olde Curiosity Shop **67**
Yesler Building **20**
Yesler Way **20**
Yesterdaze **53**
YMCA **115**
Young, Bud **29** (bests)

You Wanna Bet? **105**
Yuppie Pawn Shop **189**

Z

Zanadia **149**
Zebra Club **62**

Restaurants

Only restaurants with star ratings are listed below. All restaurants are listed alphabetically in the main (preceding) index. Always call in advance to ensure a restaurant has not closed, changed its hours, or booked its tables for a private party. The restaurant price ratings are based on the average cost of an entrée for one person, excluding tax and tip.

★★★★ An Extraordinary Experience
★★★ Excellent
★★ Very Good
★ Good

$$$$ Big Bucks ($30 and up)
$$$ Expensive ($20-$30)
$$ Reasonable ($10-$20)
$ The Price Is Right (less than $10)

★★★★

Adriatica Cucina Mediterranea $$$ **120**
Canlis $$$$ **128**
Fuller's $$$ **40**
Georgian Room, The $$$$ **38**
Rover's $$$$ **104**
Szmania's $$$ **130**

★★★

Al Boccalino $$ **21**
Bizzarro Italian Cafe $ **147**
Cafe Flora $$ **104**
Cafe Juanita $$ **191**
Campagne $$$ **57**
Chez Shea $$$$ **55**
Chutney's $$ **82**
Dahlia Lounge $$$ **46**
Flying Fish $$ **71**
Hunt Club $$$ **103**
Il Terrazo Carmine $$$ **24**
Kaspar's $$ **82**
Lampreia $$$ **72**
Le Gourmand $$$ **134**
Mamma Melina Ristorante $$ **172**

Metropolitan Grill $$$ **33**
Nikko $$$ **46**
Pacific Dessert Company, The $ **84**
Painted Table, The $$ **64**
Palomino $$ **40**
Paragon $$ **126**
Phoenicia at Alki $$ **110**
Pirosmani $$$ **127**
Prego $$$ **35**
Ray's Boathouse $$$ **139**
Reiner's $$$ **103**
Saleh al Lago $$ **155**
Salvatore Ristorante Italiano $$ **172**
Santa Fe Cafe (Greenwood) $$ **156**
Santa Fe Cafe (Ravenna) $$ **173**
Sea Garden $ **28**
Shamiana $$ **187**
Shiro $$ **73**
Spazzo $$ **179**
Tulio Ristorante $$ **35**
Un Deux Trois $$$ **63**
Wild Ginger $$ **66**

★★

Anthony's Homeport (Ballard) $$ **139**
Anthony's Homeport (Kirkland) $$ **187**
Arita Japanese Restaurant $ **158**
Athenian Inn $ **52**
Azalea's Fountain Court $$$$ **179**
Bacchus Restaurant $ **98**
Bagel Oasis $ **173**
Bahn Thai $ **84**
Boiserie, The $ **167**
Burk's Cafe $$ **137**
Cactus $$ **91**
Cafe Huê $ **27**
Café Lago $$ **90**
Cafe Los Gatos $ **154**
Cafe Sabika $$ **103**
Café Vizcaya $$ **150**
Casa-U-Betcha $ **71**
Catfish Corner $ **105**
Chinook's $$ **134**
Cucina! Cucina! (Bellevue) $$ **184**
Cyclops $$ **72**
Daniel's Broiler (Bellevue) $$$$ **184**
Daniel's Broiler (Leschi) $$$$ **106**
Doong Kong Lau $ **159**

du jour $ **61**
Elliott Bay Cafe $ **23**
El Palacio $ **107**
Emmett Watson's Oyster Bar $ **59**
Eques $$$ **184**
Ezell's Fried Chicken $ **105**
5-Spot, The $ **126**
F.X. McRory's Steak, Chop and Oyster House $$ **25**
Han II $ **28**
Hopscotch $ **100**
Il Bistro $$$ **51**
I Love Sushi (Bellevue) $ **185**
I Love Sushi (Belltown) $ **85**
Kabul $$ **150**
La Buca $$ **66**
Labuznik $$$ **61**
Leschi Lakecafe $$ **106**
Liberty Deli $ **111**
Linyen $$ **28**
Mae's Phinney Ridge Cafe $ **157**
Maneki Restaurant $$ **28**
Maple Leaf Grill $ **160**
Mario's Pizza $ **17**
Maximilien-in-the-Market $$$ **53**
McCormick & Schmick's $$ **64**
McCormick's Fish House and Bar $$ **33**
New Hong Kong Seafood Restaurant and B.B.Q. $ **105**
Northlake Tavern & Pizza House $ **169**
Pailin Thai Cuisine $ **115**
Palisade $$$ **129**
Pandasia (Magnolia) $ **128**
Panos $$ **72**
Pho Hòa $ **107**
Pink Door, The $$ **58**
Place Pigalle $$ **53**
Pogacha $ **179**
Ponti Seafood Grill $$ **143**
Poor Italian Cafe, The $ **76**
Queen City Grill $$ **70**
Queen Mary $$$ **173**
Ragin' Cajun $$ **62**
R&L Home of Good Barbeque $ **105**
Rasa Malaysia (Green Lake) $ **155**
Ristorante Buongusto $$ **127**
Ristorante Paradiso $$ **188**
Romio's Pizza (Eastlake) $ **92**
Serafina $$ **92**
74th Street Ale House $ **158**
Siam on Broadway $ **99**
Swingside Cafe $ **147**
TestaRossa $ **101**
Thai on Mercer $$ **176**

Third Floor Fish Cafe $$ **187**
Toscana $$ **170**
Trattoria Mitchelli $$ **20**
Triangle Tavern $ **144**
Two Bells Tavern $ **77**
Von's Grand City Cafe $ **42**
Yanni's Lakeside Cafe $ **158**

★

Alki Cafe $ **111**
Alki Homestead $$ **112**
Alpenland Delicatessen $ **176**
Angelina's Trattoria $ **113**
Bakeman's Restaurant $ **32**
Bamboo Garden $$ **84**
B&O Espresso $ **100**
Be Bop-A-Latte $ **125**
Brooklyn Cafe and Oyster Bar
  Lounge $$$ **37**
Byzantion $ **99**
Cadiz Espresso $ **128**
Cafe Allegro $ **169**
Cafe Counter Intelligence $ **55**
Cafe Illiterati $ **136**
Cafe Lôc $ **78**
Caffè Appassionato $ **130**
Caffè D'Arte $ **76**
Caffè Minnie's $$ **81**
Capers $ **115**
Capons Rotisserie Chicken $ **148**
Carrot Cafe $ **92**
Chace's Pancake Corral $ **179**
Chandler's Crabhouse and Fresh
  Fish Market $$$ **84**
Chau's Chinese Restaurant $ **27**
Cinema Espresso $ **83**
City Cafe $ **147**
City Thai $ **189**
Cloud Room, The $$ **43**
Continental Restaurant, The $
  171
Copacabana Cafe $ **57**
Crumpet Shop, The $ **55**
Cucina! Cucina! (Belltown) $$ **85**
Cutter's Bayhouse $$$ **60**
Daily Grind, The $ **90**
Davinci's Flying Pizza and Pasta
  $ **187**
Deluxe 1 Bar and Grill $ **98**
Dilettante Patisserie & Cafe $ **100**
Doc Maynard's Public House $
  17
Duke's Chowderhouse and
  Outrageous Canoe Club $ **84**
Elliott's Oyster House & Seafood
  Restaurant $$$ **67**
El Puerco Lloron $ **54**
El Tapatio $ **159**
Espresso Roma $ **101**
European Restaurant & Pastry

Shop $ **169**
521 Cafe $ **32**
Fortnum's European Cafe $ **180**
Georgie Cafe $$ **117**
Giuseppe's $$ **179**
Globe Cafe & Bakery $ **102**
Gravity Bar (Belltown) $ **70**
Gravity Bar (Broadway Market) $
  100
Guadalajara $ **148**
Guido's Pizzeria $ **156**
Hi-Spot Cafe $ **104**
Honey Bear Bakery $ **154**
Honey Court Seafood Restaurant
  $$ **29**
Ivar's Acres of Clams and Fish
  Bar $ **67**
Jalisco $ **99**
J&M Cafe $ **21**
Kaleenka, The $$ **61**
Kell's Restaurant & Pub $$ **58**
Kidd Valley $ **101**
Kirkland Roaster & Ale House $$
  189
Kismet $ **158**
Kyllo's Lakeside Deli $ **155**
LockSpot Cafe & Tavern $ **138**
Lombardi's Cucina $$ **138**
Luna Park Cafe $ **115**
Mama's Mexican Kitchen $ **73**
Mecca Cafe $ **83**
Mediterranean Kitchen $ **83**
Merchant's Cafe $ **19**
Mike's Chili Parlor $ **134**
Mr. D's Greek Deli $ **57**
Musashi's $ **148**
My Friends Cafe $ **155**
New Orleans Creole Restaurant $
  19
Olympia Pizza & Spaghetti House
  $$ **126**
Olympia Pizza and Spaghetti
  House III $ **99**
Oven, The $ **101**
Ozzie's $ **83**
Pacific Northwest Brewing
  Company $$ **26**
Pagliacci $ **100**
Pandasia (North Seattle) $ **161**
Parkside News Cafe $ **113**
Pasta Bella $$ **126**
Peace Cafe $$ **113**
Pegasus Pizza & Pasta on Alki $
  111
Pete's Eggnest $ **158**
Phad Thai $ **159**
Phnom Penh Noodle House $ **28**
Pike Place Bar & Grill $ **55**
Point Grill $$ **111**
Pon Proem Restaurant $ **177**

Pumphouse, The $ **185**
Rasa Malaysia (Broadway
  Market) $ **100**
Rasa Malaysia (Pike Place
  Market) $ **56**
Ristorante di Ragazzi $ **113**
Romio's Pizza (Magnolia) $$ **128**
Rosita's $ **155**
Salmon Bay Cafe $ **136**
Salty's on Alki $$ **109**
Salute in Città $$ **46**
Sam's Super Burgers $ **104**
SBC $ **56**
Shultzy's Sausage $ **169**
Simpatico $ **149**
Sisters $ **57**
Sit 'n' Spin $ **78**
Sorel's $ **148**
Spud Fish and Chips (Green
  Lake) $ **155**
Spud Fish and Chips (West
  Seattle) $ **110**
Starbucks (Bellevue) $ **183**
Starbucks (Magnolia) $ **130**
Starbucks (Pike Place Market) $
  59
Starbucks (Queen Anne) $ **126**
Starbucks (Wallingford) $ **149**
Starbucks (West Seattle) $ **113**
Stella's Trattoria $$ **172**
Still Life in Fremont $ **144**
Stone Way Cafe $ **147**
Sunfish Seafood $ **112**
Sunlight Cafe $ **172**
Taki's $ **78**
Tan Duc $ **159**
Teahouse Kuan Yin $ **149**
13 Coins $$ **78**
Three Girls Bakery $ **56**
Tio's Bakery & Cafe $ **92**
Torrefazione Italia $ **26**
Toy's Cafe $ **179**
T.S. McHugh's Restaurant & Pub
  $$ **83**
Twin Teepees Restaurant $ **156**
Uptown Espresso $ **83**
Velato's $$ **177**
Village Pub $ **130**
World Class Chili $ **63**
Yankee Diner $$ **138**
Yarrow Bay Grill and Beach Cafe
  $$$ **185**

Hotels

The hotels listed below are
grouped according to their price
ratings; they are also listed in the
main index. The hotel price
ratings reflect the base price of a

standard room for two people for one night during the peak season.

$$$$ Big Bucks ($200 and up)
$$$ Expensive ($140-$200)
$$ Reasonable ($100-$140)
$ The Price Is Right (less than $100)

$$$$

Four Seasons Olympic Hotel **38**
Seattle Sheraton Hotel and Towers **40**

$$$

Alexis Hotel **64**
Edgewater Inn **72**
Holiday Inn Crowne Plaza **36**
Hotel Vintage Park **35**
Hyatt Regency at Bellevue Place **184**
Madison Renaissance Hotel **35**
Seattle Hilton **39**
Sorrento Hotel **103**
Warwick Hotel **76**
Westin Hotel **46**
Woodmark Hotel **185**

$$

Bellevue Hilton **177**
Chambered Nautilus, The **171**
Inn at the Market **57**
Mayflower Park Hotel **46**
Meany Tower Hotel **170**
Pioneer Square Hotel **21**
Red Lion Hotel **177**
WestCoast Roosevelt Hotel **42**

$

College Inn Guest House **169**
Corner House, The **101**
Gaslight Inn **102**
Hainsworth House **115**
Hill House **101**
Inn at Queen Anne **82**
Landes House **97**
La Residence Suite Hotel **182**
Pacific Plaza Hotel **36**
Pensione Nichols **61**
Prince of Wales **101**
Queen Anne Hill Bed & Breakfast **127**
Roberta's Bed & Breakfast **95**
Salisbury House **97**
Sixth Avenue Inn **77**
University Inn **169**
Villa Heidelberg **116**
WestCoast Camlin Hotel **42**

WestCoast Vance Hotel **46**
Williams House **121**

Features

Art by the Foot **20**
Bright Lights, Small City: Seattle's Theater Scene **34**
Carefree (and Car-Free) Sightseeing: Seattle by Bus **62**
Charity Begins Away from Home: Helping Seattle's Homeless **85**
Chief Sealth **96**
Child's Play **71**
Ferry Tales **65**
Fowl Play **135**
In the Market for a Good Time? **54**
It's About Time **145**
Life on the Cutting Edge—Music in the Emerald City **25**
Lights, Camera, Action: Seattle on Film **140**
Main Events, The **11**
Mini-Guide to Seattle, A **122**
Painting the Town **114**
Pillars of the Community **45**
Pining for Nature: Seattle's Lush Evergreens **131**
Pocket-Size Parks **183**
Quite a Road Show: The Campy Flair of Aurora Avenue North **159**
Selling Seafood by the Seashore **190**
Terra-cotta Town **74**
There's Something Fishy Here **168**
You Wanna Bet? **105**

Bests

Arthur, Pat (Project Director, Institutions Project/Columbia Legal Services) **67**
Cameron, Mindy (Editorial Page Editor, *Seattle Times*) **29**
Choe, Martha, Councilmember (Seattle City Council) **47**
Enersen, Jean (TV News Anchor, KING-TV) **107**
Godden, Jean (City Columnist, *Seattle Times*) **151**
Hardy, Jeremy (Co-owner/ Jitterbug, The 5 Spot, and Coastal Kitchen) **205**
John, Esther "Little Dove" (Flutist, composer, record label owner/Dove-Paloma Music **47**
Montana, Ruby Z. (President/Ruby Montana's Pinto Pony, Ltd.) **47**

Singer, Jack W. (Research Chairman, Executive VP and Founder, Cell Therapeutics, Inc.) **107**
Young, Bud (Owner, Bud's Jazz Records) **29**

Maps

Bainbridge Island **195**
Ballard **132**
Bellevue **178**
Bellevue Botanical Gardens **177**
Belltown **68**
Business District **31**
Capitol Hill detail **88**
Capitol Hill to Seward Park **86**
Day Trips **192**
Eastside Wine Country **193**
Fremont **142**
Green Lake **152**
Greenwood **152**
International District **14**
Kirkland **186**
Madison Park **86, 88**
Magnolia **118**
Map Key **4**
Mercer Island **174**
Mount Rainier National Park **204**
Mount St. Helens **205**
North Seattle **152, 160**
Orientation **2**
Pike Place Market **48**
Pioneer Square **14**
Queen Anne **118**
Queen Anne Hill **121**
Ravena **162**
San Juan Islands **197**
Seattle *See inside front cover*, **2**
Seattle Center **68, 79**
Seattle-Tacoma International Airport (SEA) **5**
Seattle Transit System *See inside back cover*
Seward Park, Capital Hill to **86**
Snoqualmie and Snoqualmie Falls **194**
University District **162**
University of Washington **164**
Vancouver, British Columbia **201**
Victoria, British Columbia **199**
Wallingford **142**
Washington *See inside front cover*
Waterfront **48, 60**
West Seattle **108**
West Seattle detail **111**
Whidbey Island **196**
Woodland Park Zoo **157**

Credits

Writers/Researchers
Dena Dawson
David Dawson
Constantine J. Singer

Writer and Researcher
(Previous Edition)
Loralee Wenger

ACCESS®PRESS

Editorial Director
Lois Spritzer

Managing Editor
Laura L. Brengelman

Senior Editors
Mary Callahan
Beth Schlau

Associate Editors
Patricia Canole
Gene Gold
Susan McClung

Map Coordinator
Jonathan Goodnough

Editorial Assistant
Susan Cutter Snyder

Senior Art Director
C. Linda Dingler

Design Supervisor
Joy O'Meara

Designers
Elizabeth Paige Streit
George Baez

Map Designer
Patricia Keelin

Associate Director
of Production
Dianne Pinkowitz

Director, Electronic
Publishing
John R. Day

Special Thanks
Jeanne Anderson
Gale Barre
Nancy Bergquist
Russ Hanbey
Arlene O. Lev
Mary V. McGuire
Janet Vail
Stan Vail

Elliott Bay

PRINTED IN HONG KONG